THE MILLENNIAL AND GEN Z'S GUIDE TO BECOMING A RENTAL PROPERTY MILLIONAIRE

Detailed, Actionable, Information and Experiences on How to Get Started, Survive, and Make Millions in the Rental Real Estate Business!

JACOB KOCH

The Millennial and Gen Z's Guide to Becoming a Rental Property Millionaire

MINDSTIR MEDIA

Published by MindStir Media, LLC
45 Lafayette Rd | Suite 181 | North Hampton, NH 03862 | USA
1.800.767.0531 | www.mindstirmedia.com

Printed in the United States of America.
ISBN-13: 978-1-965340-38-7

DISCLAIMER

The contents of this book, the Author's website, and the Author's social media accounts are intended only to provide information about the activities and experiences of the Author/Creator and should not be understood as a guarantee or assurance of future success in any matter. The results portrayed were dependent on a variety of facts and circumstances involved. Neither the Author nor the Publisher make any guarantee, promise, or other assurance that the same or similar results can be obtained. Your experiences and results may vary! While the Author and Publisher have made their best attempts at preparing and providing the information found in this book, the Author's website, and the Author's social media content, NEITHER THE AUTHOR NOR THE PUBLISHER ASSUMES ANY RESPONSIBILITY FOR ERRORS, INACCURACIES, OR OMISSIONS, AND THEY MAKE NO REPRESENTATIONS OR WARRANTIES WITH RESPECT TO THE ACCURACY AND COMPLETENESS OF THE CONTENT. FURTHERMORE, THE AUTHOR AND THE PUBLISHER, SPECIFICALLY DISCLAIM ANY IMPLIED WARRANTIES OF MERCHANTABILITY OR FITNESS FOR A PARTICULAR PURPOSE. THE INFORMATION IN THIS BOOK, THE AUTHOR'S WEBSITE, AND THE AUTHOR'S SOCIAL MEDIA CONTENT, SHALL NOT BE CONSTRUED AS AN OFFER TO REPRESENT YOU IN ANY FASHION, NOR IS IT INTENDED TO CREATE, NOR SHALL THE RECEIPT OF SUCH INFORMATION CONSTITUTE, ANY TYPE OF AGENCY RELATIONSHIP.

FOREWORD

If you're reading this you were most likely born between 1981 and 2012. Most of your life has been spent rolling from one crisis to the next. AIDS, The Gulf war, the Enron scandal, 9/11, the war in Iraq and Afghanistan, Hurricane Katrina, The Great Financial Crisis, climate change, the Pandemic, civil unrest, political uncertainty, the highest inflation in 40 years, crazy fuel prices, supply shortages, the war in Ukraine, did I miss anything?

You're blessed, or cursed, depending on how you look at it, by having tremendous access to information via the internet which has enlightened you to just how much bullshit is out there. Go to school, get good grades, get a college degree which will all but guarantee you a great paying job that allows you to get the house and car of your dreams and start a family. Put away 10% of your earnings in the stock market and you'll be able to retire comfortably and travel the Caribbean. Just follow these instructions, give us your money, and you'll be fine!

As you've probably come to find out, a college degree usually only guarantees you a student loan payment, and those well paid gents on Wall Street get paid whether your stocks increase in value or not. I mean, in all their great wisdom, they didn't see the Great Depression coming, the 1987 crash coming, the 2008 crash coming, high inflation, the 30% decline in the NASDAQ in 2022, and the Crypto crash. If they did, they sure didn't warn you about it! How about those cool new gamified investing apps that make it fun and easy for you to invest? How'd you end up doing on Gamestop? I'm sure they meant to have your best interests in mind. I guess they didn't feel it was important to teach you all of this in school. Well, as you can see, all is not as it seems, and being financially successful in this life is not as easy as they make it out to be. If you want success and stability for yourself and your family, you're going to have to do it yourself!

On a national level, real estate has only declined in price more than a few percent, two times in the last 57 years!

Compare that to a historical chart of stock market prices.

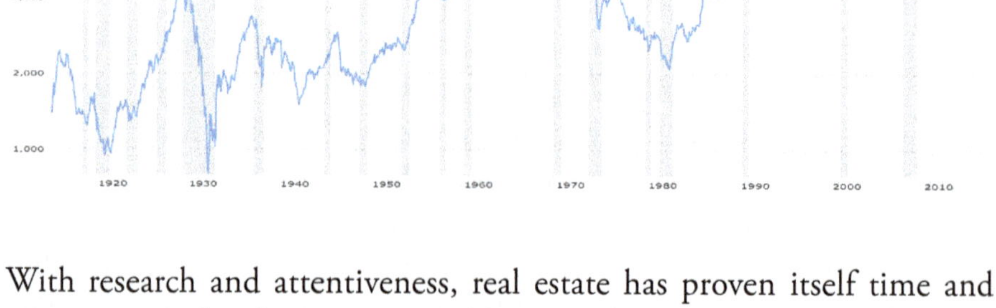

With research and attentiveness, real estate has proven itself time and time again to be the way to steadily get rich over time. There's a good reason rich people own multiple houses, apartment buildings, industrial land, or commercial real estate, it works! At some point, everyone is going to need a place to live, set up their business, or store their stuff! If you own the real estate they need, they're going to go to work all week, every week, so they can pay you at the end of the month!

As good as real estate is however, if not done carefully, it can bankrupt you and ruin any relationship you might be in during the process. In this book I've gone to a great deal of trouble to share everything I've learned about real estate including, saving for your first down payment, locating a good property in a good area, mortgages and the mortgage process, different types of financing, insurance, building construction pitfalls, deeds, calculating your return on investment, how to buy on value and not price, leases, tenant screening Red Flags, how to find and keep good tenants, renovating for increased profits, forced appreciation through rent increases, cash out refinancing to buy your next property, and some of my personal struggles with tenants so you can get a true idea of what it's like to own a rental property and whether it's right for you or not.

If you're tired of the broken promises and the stock market casino and you're ready to take control of your financial future and build generational wealth with real assets you can touch, read on! The longer you wait, the harder it gets and the clock is ticking!

CONTENTS

CHAPTER 1

GETTING STARTED

Quick takeaways from this chapter.

- **Get your perspective on money right**
- **Cut down on your expenses**
- **It's hard to buy something when you're broke!**
- **An example of how I saved for my first duplex**
- **A little history on one of your biggest partners**
- **If you want to be like everyone else, do like everyone else**
- **Practice isn't just for athletes**

Step 1: Play lottery. **Step 2:** Win lottery, end of book! Just kidding! I guess it could be that easy. The task ahead is by no means simple and I'd be wary of anyone who tries to tell you it is. I have found that when I'm presented with complex tasks or situations, I perform best when I break down said task or situation into smaller more manageable chunks. That said, I'd like to start by talking about money and your perspective on it. Buying a piece of real estate is cash intensive to say the least and if you're like I was, making just about median income ($43,000 a year at the time, 2008), coming up with the down payment is a significant challenge, that, at first glance, seems to be something you'll struggle many, many years to attain and if you live like most of us live, you'd be correct! I can tell you, it doesn't have to be that way, but there are no free lunches, and to that I ask you, HOW BAD DO YOU WANT IT? The fact that you're reading or listening to this book gives me an idea. So let's get started!

PERSPECTIVE ON MONEY

I'm going to assume, like me, that you don't have the down payment money required to buy a property. So first we'll need to make a budget. When you first start thinking about a budget, you should think about your perspective on money. What I mean by that is, look at your money as a precious and limited resource. I'm by no means saying that you should treat money like an Idol or a God, rather, a powerful tool that if used correctly can do tremendous things for you, your family and your community. If used incorrectly however, it can fast track you into a life of servitude, anguish and strife.

An example of perspective would be cruising over to your local coffee shop to buy your morning coffee. In my area, conservatively speaking, you're going to spend around $2.00 for a cup of coffee at your local fancy coffee shop. Now we need to look at this singular purchase in the perspective of value. A 12 ounce cup of coffee sells for $1.85. A $1.85 divided by 12 ounces equals 15.4 cents per ounce. Now a 48 ounce plastic can of Folgers medium roast purchased at one of the big box stores will cost you $10.42. Per the 48 ounce can, you can make 384, 6 ounce cups. We want to compare apples to apples, so we need to divide the 384 cups by 2, to make it equivalent to our 12 ounce cup from the fancy coffee store, which gives us 192, 12 ounce cups. When we divide $10.42 by 192 cups we get a cost per cup of 5.4 cents vs. the $1.85 per cup from our fancy coffee store.

Now I know what some of you may be saying, Folgers is a putrid liquid, undeserving of the moniker coffee. I am not saying you have to trade your fancy coffee for Folgers, it's mostly to give you an idea on perspective. If you do the math, you could have 34 cups of Folgers for the price of one cup of the fancy stuff. A lot of people blow me off when I give this example, saying it's just $1.85! To which I respond," If you were in the market for a new Honda Accord, would you pay $801,380 for it?". The response I get is usually an absurd look. To which I respond by saying, "Why not?, You will happily pay that absurd markup for something that is just a liquid and has no complex moving parts!" How about an average, 1500 sq. ft., three bedroom, two bath home for $6.4 million? Hopefully you get my point. You should be insulted that they ask you to pay that much money for a cup of coffee, or lunch, or to have the lawn mowed, or to have your oil changed etc. It is all in how you look at it.

Now I'm fully aware that a business has overhead and they are in business to make a profit. I'm also not saying businesses are bad for making a profit, just don't make a profit off of me! I'm kidding, sort of. The financial hurdle that stood before my first property was significant and I wanted to achieve my goal as quickly as possible. That little mind trick of, "There's no way I'm paying that absurd markup!", helped me psych myself up and dig in for the times when the sacrificing got tough. If you want to achieve your goal quickly, you'll be going against the grain of society and it's going to be a mental challenge. So, do what you need to do (morally and legally of course) to psych yourself up. And if you absolutely can't drink Folgers, try to find something in between or at the very least buy your fancy coffee in bulk at a discount store and make it yourself.

CUTTING DOWN ON EXPENSES

If you really want to accelerate your savings, try taking this perspective on all the goods and services in your life. Cable T.V., how many channels do you actually watch? How much are you paying to watch those 4-6 channels? $30 a month per channel? Say you spend 3hrs. per channel, per week watching T.V., 3hrs. x 4 weeks = 12hrs. a month. Now we divide $30 by 12hrs. to get our cost per hour of viewing pleasure, which comes out to be $2.50 per hr.. For a typical movie we're going to pay $5.00 to watch it. Let me repeat that, for a movie that's most likely many years old, we're going to pay $5.00 to watch it! At the time I was saving for my first duplex a movie ticket for a brand new movie was around $7.00. Cable didn't seem like that great of deal.

Now let's take a look at our electricity usage. Electronic devices in standby mode tend to use almost as much energy as when they are in use. It's like parking your car at work and just leaving it running the entire time you're on the job. Hard to believe but you can test this for yourself by using one of the commercially available meters like the "Kill-A-Watt" which goes between the device you want to test and the outlet. Another good one is air conditioning an entire house all day while no one is there or keeping water hot for 23 hours even though you only use it for one hour a day. When I was in extreme saving mode to buy my first duplex, I would run my water heater until it cycled off and then turn off the breaker. For a single guy, showering 1-2 times a day, I could leave the water heater off for 5 days before the water was uncomfortable. When I realized how much it saved me every month, I uh, took it a few steps further.

A LITTLE ABOUT ME

I guess now would be a good time to tell you a little about me. I like a good challenge. I'm a competitive person. Anything I chose to try and be good at, I usually took to an extreme. Basically, I wanted to see how far I could go. What could I accomplish and how fast? One thing I definitely want to try and get across to you is, everything is mental! You can have the skill and power of an elite MMA fighter but without spirit, drive, focus, and belief that "you can", you're nothing! Bad things are going to happen, mistakes will be made, at some point you'll become uncomfortable, nervous or scared. It's OK, this too shall pass! Keep your nose to the grind stone and never stop believing! Henry Ford said, "If you think you can, or you think you can't, YOU'RE RIGHT!" How bad do you want it?

HOW I SAVED MONEY

When I saw the reduction in my power bill I wanted to see just how far I could go. I was living in Florida at the time and most of the houses that were built before 1965 had no air conditioning. I thought, if they could do it, so could I. So, off went the air conditioning, then off went the water heater, PERMANENTLY! To eliminate any power vampires, I shut off the breakers to all the other items except my clock and the fridge until I needed to use them. Cold showers, no air conditioning, microwaved food, I was going to do this! I'd make a pot of coffee, let it cool on the counter and then store it in the fridge and microwave a cup when I wanted one. The coffee would last for 4-5 days. By this time we were a couple years into the financial crisis and empty foreclosures were everywhere. My power company would send out letters encouraging you to reduce your power consumption while ranking your usage against your neighbor. I went from being number 11 out of the 40 homes near me to number 6, to number 1. I had the least power usage out of the 40 homes in my area and 7 of those homes were vacant! The lowest electric usage I was able to achieve was $8.00, for a whole month!

I went on to apply this to every aspect of my life. I only shopped at discount stores and only bought food on sale, in bulk. My mother told me once, "Mind the pennies and the dollars will watch after themselves.". She was definitely right! No unnecessary spending. I went to work, ate a lunch I made at home, went home after work and sat in the dark. No going out, no wasting gas. You do a lot of push ups and sit ups when there's nothing else to do by the way. All that sacrifice allowed me to pay off $16,800 in STUPID credit card debt that I previously ran up and save $25,000 for a property in 18 months, all while earning $43,000 a year! Now, you need not go to the extremes I went to, but it illustrates what one can do if they choose to! If you want it bad enough, you can do it!

Start to pay attention to what you use and how you use it. Do you blow through paper towels instead of using a cloth towel that you wash? Do you do your laundry during the day or on the weekend? Most power companies have different rates that they charge during "peak" hours, 6 am -10 pm. Wash and dry your clothes at night. Squeeze every bit of toothpaste out of the tube! Cut your shampoo with 50% water. Buy the cheap toilet paper. You won't have to sacrifice forever! Experiment with what you can reduce or eliminate. When you've figured that out, make a budget. See how much you can save every month then calculate how long it will take to reach your goal of a down payment. If you're happy with the timeframe, great! If not, make more cuts or get a second job. Having "extra" cash is really the difference between the haves and the have not's. You may be fully capable of making a house payment right now, but….. you don't have any extra cash!

I wrote this book because I was constantly getting asked, "How'd you do it?". After I explain how I did it, what I hear most often is, I can't do that! I have to have my yearly cruise. I'm going to have to spend how many hours of research on the computer and all that driving around! I'm going to have to wait how long before the big payoff? I'm not mowing lawns for free every week. I need my relaxing time! Hmmm. How bad do you want it?

Now, at this point my Uncle would say, "start your own business!" In one respect, he is 100% right. Unless you work in sales or have a high paying job like a surgeon, you'll never make as much money working for someone else as you would for yourself, assuming you're successful of course. Owning your own business is kind of like an all or nothing affair. If you want to make a substantial amount of money, you're going to have to devote a significant amount of time to it. What we are trying to do here is build quasi passive income to give us the extra cash flow we want every month and build equity for use later down the road or as retirement money without having the 70 hour work weeks for 10-20 years. That said, owning rental property, especially when you buy properties at a discount because they need work, is a lot of work up front but then eases back to what most people think of, with of course, the occasional emergency.

A LITTLE HISTORY ON MONEY AND BANKING

If you're like most of my peers and I, you'll probably have a good bit of idle time on your hands while you're saving for your down payment and emergency cash. Other than push-ups and sit-ups, there are a few things you should consider doing during this time. In the previous chapter we talked a little bit about the value of things in relation to money. Now would be a good time to dip our toes into the banking world. Suffice to say, the banks are smart. They've really studied this money thing for quite some time now. It is believed by many that the Knights Templar were the worlds' first bankers. After Jerusalem was captured during the first crusade in 1099, Christian pilgrims began to travel thousands of miles across Europe to visit the city. This trip would require months of supplies and food along with transport and accommodation costs. During this time in history it would appear to be very dangerous to carry a large amount currency on a long trip like this. The Knights Templar set out to defend the traveling Christians and their money by allowing them to deposit their money before their trip and take with them instead a letter of credit that they could cash in at another Templar "bank". Others believe it was the Tang Dynasty in China some 200 years earlier that had a similar system. Either way the powers that be have had a mighty long time to think about their business of money.

Since money "makes the world go 'round", you'd think they'd spend quite a bit of time in school teaching about it. Not so much. Maybe this is by design or by happenstance, who knows. What they do teach is very general in nature, buy low-sell high, supply vs. demand, we pay taxes for services and save money for a rainy day, now get out there! We graduate and get into the real world and start to learn a little more about how things actually work. It seems like as soon as one makes a dollar, there's a credit card offer in their mailbox. I'm sure the credit card companies and the banks have our best interests in mind, although it is hard to tell from the fine print.

OUR GOOD FRIENDS AT THE BANK

Side story- I'll never forget the time when I received a phone call from a representative at the bank I had used for the last 25 years (I was 16 years old when I started my first savings account). "Good afternoon Mr. Koch! We were just reviewing your account and noticed you had some money sitting idle. Did you know that you could be earning much more interest on that money?" I replied, "As a matter of fact I am aware, thank you." Representative-"Well Mr. Koch it appears you have over $150,000.00 just sitting in a savings account, I would like to suggest some financial products that could earn you a better return than your savings account rate." I guess he didn't hear my initial reply. I said, "Sir, do you have any idea how long I've had an account with your bank?" Representative- "Well yes sir I see that, your account number is starts with zeros." I replied," I guess it's been about 25 years now. You know I came into your branch back in 2006 and asked to learn about the mortgage process and also asked your mortgage originator if it seemed weird that the median income was around $40,000.00 but the average price for a starter home was around $230,000.00 since it seems like banks will only loan around 3 times a person salary for a starter home." Her reply- "Now is a great time to buy before prices go higher!" Hmmm. Sage advice from an expert in the industry! Glad I didn't listen to her! There was a deep inhale as if to give a quick response but nothing came out. Before I let him spew another line of crap at me I told him that no one from the bank had cared one ounce about me for the past 25 years until $150,000.00 popped into my account and now everyone from the bank wants to be my best friend. Oh, and as far as that money sitting idle, it's been in there for 5 days (it was right after I sold a foreclosed farm I bought). So, write it in the notes, do what you gotta do and let everyone there know that I know you guys are only out to help yourselves so NEVER call me again! I will say this, he must have done a good job with the notes because no one from that national bank has called since. That bank took a huge payout after the financial crisis by the way.

Now, not all people have ill intent, but I'd bet many are on autopilot and just don't know what's going on. They'll regurgitate things they've heard from wherever and sell them to you like they've been burning the midnight oil for the last 3 months doing research. When they're done be sure to politely ask, "oh wow, where'd you hear that?" Whether it's a credit card, student loan, auto loan, or mortgage, remember at the end of the day YOU agreed to all of those terms! Do the best you can to know what you're doing because there are a lot of sharks out there just waiting for you!

JOE BLOW WANTS IT NOW – AND SO DO I

Before we get too carried away hating the evil banks and lending institutions, we need to remember, that with great freedom, comes great responsibility! America truly is, comparatively speaking, the land of opportunity! Just keep in mind that there is just as much opportunity to fail as there is to succeed and with hard work, perseverance, and smart decisions, you will better your situation! I have a saying, "Just because you can, doesn't mean you should!" We have to be smart and disciplined! Joe Blow told me the bank said they'd give him a $50,000 HELOC (Home Equity Line of Credit)!! Sweet! Said Joe, I'm going to use that to buy a boat, I deserve it!! Well....depending on Joe's situation, that may or may not be good idea. Does that put Joe and his family in a vulnerable position? Does the net effect make more money than doing nothing at all? What's Joe's exit strategy? Does Joe have a plan or is he just excited about getting that boat he's always wanted? Would having the boat for a few years be worth losing the boat and his house? You have to have a plan!

I can tell you for a fact that the banks have a plan! The banks calculate the movement of money down to the minute and maybe the second. They use arbitrage (arbitrage is the practice of taking advantage of a difference in prices in two or more markets; striking a combination of matching deals to capitalize on the difference, the profit being the difference between the market prices at which the asset is traded) to make money on the money you have in your savings account. They pay you say 1% and then lend that money for say 3% and make 2% on your hard earned money!

In the mid 2000's, some smart, regular folks like us were using arbitrage to pay their mortgages using their HELOCs'. Their mortgages were around 6.5% and their HELOCs' were around 4%. At the beginning of the month they'd use their HELOCs' to pay their mortgage reducing the calculated balance of the loan for that month. They'd then pay off their HELOC as they got paid during the month. The savings is small but over 10-15 years make a big difference. At the end of the year they'd also get to reduce their taxable income by the amount of interest the bank charged them on the first mortgage and the HELOC. Pretty cool. Mind the pennies and the dollars will watch out for themselves!

That said, there are a tremendous number of financial vehicles which allow the product user **much** more opportunity to advance, **much** faster, than if you had to buy everything cash. It would take multiple generations to realize the wealth gains that the average person can obtain today in only 10-20 years. So don't hate the banks, make patient, smart money decisions! You have to have discipline. Now, I'm just as guilty as Joe for wanting it easy, wanting it cheap and wanting it now, just look at the credit card debt I had. So don't think I'm pointing the finger at anyone in judgement. I'm only trying to help by giving some knowledge, some experience and some encouragement.

MENTAL PRACTICE

If there's one thing I've learned in this life, it's, everything takes practice! When I say this, people are usually thinking about physical things like a basketball shot or a golf swing, but the most important thing to practice is controlling your mind. Controlling your thoughts, perspectives and attitudes will allow your body to accomplish just about anything! About 20 years ago I watched a documentary, I believe it was on the National Geographic channel, on the Himalayan Monks and how they could do super natural things through the power of meditation. The final big exhibition was when 2 or 3 monks and a camera crew went up high on the mountain to spend the night. The camera crew was fully equipped and dressed to the spend the night in the sub-zero temperatures, sleeping in a tent and checking their camera from time to time to wipe the snow off of it. The monks on the other hand only had a thin cotton shawl to protect them from the freezing temperatures. They got into their meditative positions and remained there throughout the night with light snow occasionally building up on their shoulders and then melting away. Their faces and ears were not covered. They sat there, perfectly still, the only movement was there breath.

In the morning as the sun crept over the mountain, they slowly emerged from their meditative states with smiles on their faces, none the worse for wear, no frostbite, nothing! They walked down the mountain back to their monastery. Amazing! If that doesn't prove to you the power of the computer that God has so graciously blessed us with I don't know what else to tell you! Think about that the next time you say you can't do something! What you really mean is, I won't or I don't want to, do whatever it is. It's OK, it's your life, do as you wish, just be honest with yourself and definitely don't hate on other people who have had success, you don't know what sacrifices they had to or are still going through to achieve that success. Remember, what you say is what you think. What comes out of your mouth goes right into your ears and your mind listens. I can't this, I can't that. Say it enough times and your mind believes it. I don't know if Stéphane Mifsud knew when he began his journey to winning a world record for an unassisted breath hold, that he'd be able to do it for 11 minutes and 35 seconds, but I can guarantee you he never said he couldn't! So, if you find yourself constantly saying "I can't", then you're right, you've already made up your mind! Remember, you can't do anything without first believing you can!

Remember what it was like to be a child? My friends and I thought we could do anything. Watch a movie where a 16 year old jumps into an F-16 and flies to the middle east for a rescue mission, that could happen! I can totally jump my bike over that fence! I can take a few lessons from Mr. Miagi and I'll be a badass! Children will attempt to do crazy things because they haven't been conditioned to question their abilities or fear the consequences. Thank God we have our parents to pull back on the reins! Unfortunately but understandably, we over compensate to the cautious side. As time goes by we get conditioned to think that we can't or we shouldn't. Somehow, whoever is doing what we're admiring, is so super special that we shouldn't even attempt it! How do you know you're not that special too? Maybe you won't be able to make it to their level but you might make it 90% of the way and that's still awesome! Not everything will be quickly and easily attained but that doesn't mean it's impossible for you. Things in your life have conditioned you both positively and negatively. Try to understand these things and get rid of the ones that have no basis. So, am I saying to run out there and try things with the fervor and ignorance of a 10 year old, no! I'm saying, have a good perspective on your challenge, educate yourself, form a good plan, run it by a few people smarter and more experienced than you, believe you can, then see it through! Break out of your chains and believe in yourself! Remember, the only failure is the failure to try!

Well, you have your personal homework to do. Believe in yourself, practice good thoughts, say positive things, educate yourself and make a plan. Cut down on those expenses and save that money! Make adjustments to your plan along the way but see it through! Don't quit! If you ever need a little motivation, check out Admiral McRavens' 16 minute video on making your bed!

CHAPTER 2

WHAT'S IT TAKE TO BUY AN INCOME PROPERTY?

****I originally had the building construction and building systems section after Chapter 1, "Getting started", because I feel that it is crucial to begin, as soon as one can, to study the areas, neighborhoods, and properties themselves. It's very hard to understand value when you don't know what you're looking at. I did the best I could to make that portion of the book as interesting as I could, but at the end of the day, it's about wood, concrete, wires, pipes, and things of that nature. After hearing feedback from my mini focus group, my family, it was suggested that I put that section at the end of the book. So, the majority rules, it's now at the end of the book. As dry as it may be, I highly suggest that you read and understand it during your idle time while you're saving for your first property. That said, if you don't want to do it that way, it will always be there for your review as you come across different properties during your real estate journey.****

Quick takeaways from this chapter.

- **There's no replacement for the drive by**
- **Screaming deals can leave you crying**
- **Get rich quick, sorry, not here**
- **There's many different ways to purchase a property**

- **You need to fit in the banks financial boxes**
- **The 30 year mortgage is a big tool for building wealth**
- **Not all debt is bad**
- **Be conservative**
- **PMI, MIP, DTI, LTV, PITI, what the heck?**

After getting yourself on a good savings plan, you'll need to get an idea of the price range of the properties you'll be purchasing in the near future. This will also dictate the general areas you will be able to purchase in. There is **ZERO** replacement for leg work here. Technology has made it much easier to do this, for example, "driving" down the street on Google street view, but there is no replacement for being there, and being there multiple times at different times, over a period of time. Get it?

If you drive by it two times over the course of two to three weeks, you won't know that those two rundown properties which are a blight on the street are causing other people to list their property for sale in the spring. On the contrary, maybe one of the properties is owned by an older person who's tired of dealing with the deferred maintenance and is going to move in with family soon. The son or daughter that they're moving in with is busy with their family and has no idea which is the working end of hammer anyway so they don't want to deal with the clean up and renovation that it'll take to get the property sold for top dollar. They end up convincing mom or dad to sell for less just to get rid of it. Maybe the house on the corner has a bad tenant who's about to get evicted. Maybe you research this property and find out the owner bought the property fifteen years ago and has rented it the entire time. Maybe that owner has made their money on the property and is ready to get out of the game. Studying what's going on in the area over a period of time will give you a lot of information!

DIFFERENT WAYS TO PURCHASE A PROPERTY

There are a few basic ways with which you'll be able to purchase an income property. There are other "fancier" ways to go about it, but for the beginner you're most likely going to be stuck with the basics. The first and easiest is, if for whatever reason, you're able to buy the property all cash. This is a no brainer so I won't spend much time on it. With cash, you bring a higher probability of closing (actually buying the property) for the seller because you don't need to convince a bank or lender that you AND the property are a worthy of them lending to you. You also bring a certain level of prowess and maturity (whether earned or not) to the deal if you have that much "extra" cash. You can also close (buy) the property in about two weeks, depending on where you are, instead of the usual four to six weeks. The property also doesn't need to have or pass any inspections or appraisals.

Basically, it's your money and you can buy a jewel or a pile of crap if you want. If nobody will insure the property because it's a disaster waiting to happen, no problem, you bought it cash and it's alllll yours! The appraisal came in $30,000 under contract price, no problem, you're buying with cash! You can and should use this financial brawn to negotiate a better deal. The market conditions will determine just how much better of a deal you will get, if any.

So, whatever the amount is that you have set aside for your property purchase, minus about two percent for closing costs, is your budget. In the excitement of being able to purchase a property cash, there are a few things that people tend to overlook. A few things to keep in mind are, once you decide to rent your property, you will definitely need insurance, and even though you won't have a mortgage to pay, you will still have to pay property taxes and maintenance costs. I often hear people relate that they can't wait to pay off their home so they can live (have their housing) for free. Unfortunately, you're still going to have homeowners insurance and property taxes to pay for. To give you a rough idea of this, on a $300,000 property, you're still going to have the equivalent of a $500 to $600 a month payment. Now, this is definitely better than a $1500 to $1600 a month payment with a mortgage, but you're not going to be hanging out with Elon Musk on the weekends.

YOU HAVE CASH? BUY ONE PROPERTY OR FOUR?

You'll definitely want to consider whether it's the best use of your money to purchase one property using all cash. This can get a little complex as far as where each individual is in their financial journey and what their risk appetite is but I'll give you a quick example. We'll say you're looking at a $400,000 property. You can either spend all of your cash on that one property and get an average appreciation of 3.5% plus whatever it cash flows, say $1000 a month from rent, which equates to an annual return of 6.4%, or use that $400,000 to buy four properties, each of which you'll have 25% equity in, each of which will give you a 3.5% rate of appreciation and each of which will cash flow ZERO but give you a 13.5% rate of return. For rough numbers, that's double the return on your hard earned money! I'll go into this in more detail later in this book.

BORROWING FROM FRIENDS, FAMILY, OR YOUR 401K

The second option you'll have, which is what most of us are forced to do, is get some kind of a loan, be it from a bank, a family member, or your 401k. Depending on the situation, 80% of the time, I'd advise most people to NOT use their 401k to purchase a property. Diversification is definitely a good thing and I do regularly use my IRA as a store of "emergency cash" when getting loans, (More on that later) but most of us when starting out are on financial thin ice. That said, leave that money where it is, and save new money to acquire a property. As far as borrowing money from family and friends, 99% of the time I would advise AGAINST taking a loan, especially for your first property. Most people have a highly sensitive nerve that runs from their limbic system, deep in the brain where emotions originate, directly to their wallet! There can be a lot of fallout if you don't come through on your part of the deal, either partially or wholly. Plus, what you're saying to them is, I haven't sacrificed like you to save the money that you have, and I want to risk a sizeable chunk of your money on something I have zero experience with. Done mostly right, real estate is a great investment. Done mostly wrong, you can lose your ass!

BE CAREFUL OF THE SCREAMING DEALS

As a real estate investor friend of mine once said in regards to one of his properties, "I'm hemorrhaging cash!" He said this while sarcastically laughing and shaking his head about a property that looked to be like a screaming deal which needed to be scooped up quickly! An extra $38,000 in cash later, that he didn't budget for, and he's OK, but keep in mind, he paid a lot of dues over a lot of years and saved up a lot of cash, so he had enough extra cash to take care of this gamble that didn't go so well. If you are like I was, and most small investors starting out, you don't have an extra $38,000 laying around, so this would crush you, and the family member you borrowed money from. Two lessons to be learned here; 1. Even a seasoned investor can make a mistake. 2. You can and will make mistakes, so take your time, be smart, and leave a cushion so that your mistakes are recoverable and not catastrophic.

GETTING A TRADITIONAL BANK LOAN

All that said, I hope you've decided to give up some of the returns on your investment to let a huge financial institution, the bank, take 70% to 80% of the risk! What I mean by that is, you will most likely be risking, or putting down, 20% to 30% of your own money to acquire a rental property and the bank will provide the rest. This is called Loan to Value, or LTV in the biz. If a property is valued at $100,000, the bank will loan a certain percentage of its value, in our case, 70% to 80%, being $70,000 or $80,000. You would provide the $20,000 or $30,000 for the down payment. These loans would be referred to as 70% LTV or 80% LTV.

So the bank wants, let's say, a 4% or 5% return on their money which will come out of your pocket (your tenants pocket really). Let's say your total mortgage, Principle, Interest, Taxes (property), and Insurance (homeowners) or commonly referred to as PITI, is $2000 a month. Your tenant pays you $2100 a month in rent. The principle portion of your mortgage is say, $300 a month and you cash flow, money left over after you pay your total mortgage, $100 a month. Your $400,000 property appreciates in value over the next year by 3%.

In total your income property has generated $16,800 for you during the course of that year, $12,000 in appreciation, $3600 in principle pay-down or equity, and $1200 in cash flow. Let's say you had to put 25% down and you had to pay 1% of the loan in closing costs, for a total of 26% cash out of pocket or in this case, $104,000. Your $104,000 investment just paid you $16,800 in dividends or a 16.15% return! Think about that for a second, the bank had to give $300,000 out of its pocket and it's only getting a 4% or 5% return, you put up $104,000 to get a 16% return (3% return on the $400,000 property, you got to keep $300 of each mortgage payment and almost all of the cash flow!). When the rental real estate game is working well, it's awesome! Let the bank take most of the risk and give up most of the money! More on this in detail, later.

YOUR INCOME

So what is the bank going to want from you? They are typically big and they're in the business of loaning money. That said, they typically process a lot of loans so they need to be efficient at it so they have neat little boxes they're going to want you to fit into. Do you own your own business and make $100,000 a year? Guess what, that's not one of those boxes! Do you feel offended? You probably should. I've always understood that small business is what makes America run and building a successful business isn't easy. Someone who's built a successful business and earns $100,000 a year should be respected as a calculated risk taker who, for the most part, knows what they're doing. Yeah, the bank looks at you, and your business, like an unsupervised liability with unproven, unguaranteed income and possible financial disruptions, like a machine that breaks and will cost $20,000 to replace. Ask me how I know. That said, If you've owned and operated your successful business for the past fifteen years and have always earned your $100,000, have plenty of cash reserves for you and your business, and have solid bookkeeping, you probably won't have too much of a hassle.

The bank would rather you make $75,000 a year and work for AT&T. They want plain vanilla stability that is common and easy to assess or model, nothing outside the box that they have to "think" about. They want stable income, two years or longer, a high credit score, plenty of emergency cash, a low debt to income ratio, low revolving credit balances, almost no movement of cash other than the pay you receive going into your bank account and the bills you pay going out of your bank account. Take $300 out of the ATM for your kids birthday party and you're going to have to write a letter to the underwriter explaining that!

Ask me how I know. Oh, there's one more thing they'll need from you, drumroll please......... A BIG DOWN PAYMENT! You didn't think this would be that easy, did you?

I'M JUST GONNA KEEP GOING TO SCHOOL AND GET A GOOD PAYING JOB

I don't want to discourage you with that last sentence, it's all about perspective. Think about anything that has an easy or cheap entry point. A $500 car is easy to get and a lot of people can get one, if they want one, but what do you have? A mostly worn out car that will most likely be much less reliable and in turn cost more money down the road. Similarly, if we look at employment, getting a starter job at a fast food restaurant or the local grocery store isn't that hard, the education requirements are almost non-existent, but then again, it doesn't pay that much. On the flip side, if you want to be a doctor, engineer, or architect, you're going to need expend a significant effort before, during, and after you get that job and you will need a significant amount of money to acquire the education required for such a job. These jobs however, will give a high return on your investment. Typical annual salaries for these jobs are $150,000 to $350,000. So, in that perspective, let's look at investments. Say you want to buy a share of Coca-Cola. It's super easy to set up a trading account and will only cost you around $62 to grab a share. This share of Coke may return you 7% or 8% (before subtracting for inflation) over time, not bad, but nothing earth shattering. How about something rock solid and guaranteed like a treasury bond that will return you a whopping 2% to 3%, awesome. Cheap and or easy entry points, both in education, skill, labor, and money, usually offer low returns. Remember, no free lunches here.

I'LL JUST START MY OWN BUSINESS

Say that you're going to start your own business. You're going to work at a lower paying job and save a bunch of money, make a detailed business plan, sell that idea to a bank who's going to loan you money on that business with your house as collateral, if you have one. Then you're going to have to grind out 70 hour work weeks doing EVERY job from planning, sales, accounting, labor, purchasing, inventory, human resources, etc. etc. for "X" number of years until you build enough revenue and profits to hire more people and stabilize your business. If you did it right, at some point you'll be able to work 30 or 40 hour work weeks, go out on your boat on a Wednesday with the family, live in a nice house in a nice area and make $200,000 a year. If you're in the top 1%, you'll make millions. Just like the doctor, you'll have a high effort and high priced entry point, but if done right, you'll get a high return on your investment.

I'M SORRY TO REPORT, THERE IS NO GET RICH QUICK FOR 99% OF US

Real estate has historically had a high return on investment for the amount of ongoing effort required. Unlike showing up for work every day like an engineer or a small business owner, once stabilized, real estate requires very little maintenance. The initial cost to get in the game is very high for most of us and because most of us start this journey making around the median income (basically average salary), getting in the game will also require a significant effort in labor. What I mean by that is, because we only have so much down payment money and only so much income, we will only be able to get so nice of a property. The aforementioned doctor will have the resources to get a very nice property, in a very nice area, that is turn key and needs no updating or maintenance. You and I however, not so much. Small down payment, small cash reserves, small income, means that we'll most likely have to get a so-so property, in a so-so area, that needs a lot of work. No free lunches! But fear not my friends, hard work pays off and once you get the property stabilized it will richly pay you back for decades to come!

CREDIT SCORE

OK, back to what the banks want. The income part is fairly easy to understand from the banks point of view. The more stable the job, (ie; you've worked for 10 years as an engineer for Ford vs. 1 year as an engineer for a new tech start up) the better. Obviously, the more money you make, the better. One caveat to this is, it doesn't matter how much money you make if you spend it all every month. You have to have money left over at the end of the month to pay the mortgage and have a safety cushion. There's a metric that banks look at called Debt to Income ratio or as commonly referred to, DTI. I'll go more in depth on this later.

The next thing banks look for is a good credit score. This is also logical, they're going to loan money to you and they want to see if you're going to pay it back. If you had two brothers, one who was very responsible and always lived up to his commitments and the other who lived for today and was always making up excuses why he couldn't fulfill his commitments, who would you lend $300,000 to? Your credit score is your report card on how financially responsible you are. The higher the score (grade), the better. Remember this concept, especially when first starting out, it's just like a resume for a job, it's all about how you look on paper! Are you an A-B student who graduated from Harvard or a C- student from the local community college? No offense to C students because I was one, it just comes with consequences.

So you're going to want your credit score to be as high as possible. Achieving this can get a little complicated and there plenty of websites with good advice so I'll go over the basics. From my experience, the credit agencies want to see a history (as long as possible) of your practice at using credit. They want to see a progression from small loans for small durations to larger loans for longer durations. They want to see your ability to do what you promised, make payments, on time, every time.

The credit that you get early on wont' let you borrow too much because they don't trust you yet. If you don't pay them back, they won't lose much. They also charge you a very high interest rate so they recoup as much money as they can before you default (not pay them back). Banks are similar to insurance agencies in that they assess and assign risk. The insurance company looks at the odds of your house being destroyed by a hurricane and decides whether they want to take that risk. If the risk is low, your insurance premium is low, if you live in the Florida keys and the risk is high, guess what, your premium is going to be astronomical.

Banks assess and assign credit risk. If you are a low risk of not paying them back, you'll get a low interest rate. If you're like the aforementioned excuse laden brother, you may not get a loan at all due to your high risk of default. If you do get a loan, the terms (down payment, interest rate, time period) will be very unfavorable. You are risky! Banks and insurance companies don't like "Risky" they like "Boring"! As such, a big part of your score is your ability to make POOR DECISIONS and get into FINANCIAL TROUBLE (yes, you read that right), but NOT DOING IT! It's like working your way up to a credit card that gives you a $20,000 line of credit. The banks gave you a bunch of freedom to spend money, $20,000 worth, but you only have a $2500 balance and a high balance of $5000. In other words, at one time you only borrowed 25% of the total amount that you could and you currently only have 12.5% of the $20,000 that you could borrow, out. You've made all of your payments on time and have paid more than the minimum payment each time. Credit agencies typically don't want you to have more than 50% of your credit limit borrowed otherwise they ding you.

In the above example, you showed financial discipline by being able to easily run up your credit card to the maximum of $20,000, but not doing it. You made your payments on time and have paid down your high debt of $5000 to $2500. You're doing great. Now, some people, and I used to be one of them, would say, "I don't want to use a credit card, I just use cash, having no debt should be better!" Well, that's not how they see it. Having "no credit history" is almost as bad as having bad as having a negative credit history. Remember, they want to see you go through the process of borrowing and paying back a bunch of times before they're willing to lend to you. It's like building trust or paying your dues. The cynical side of me is a little bitter because you have to play their game and pay high borrowing costs along your credit building journey but, as I'll show you later, it's well worth it!

So they've been watching you and you've done well with your $20,000 limit credit card, but what's to stop you from getting four $20,000 limit credit cards and only using $5000 of credit on each? Well, if you're income would allow that, you could, but your credit score would take a big hit! You see, they also want someone who's not dying to spend money every chance they get and every time you apply for new credit (with the exception of shopping for a real estate loan), be it a credit card, car loan, furniture store credit, tire store, jewelry store, whatever, they drop your score. Depending on how fast you run around looking for new institutions to loan to you, will depend on how much they drop your score. If, in the last 3 months, you've applied for five credit cards, a car loan, and furniture store credit, you scream that your lifestyle requires these numbers of purchases and oh, yeah, you don't have the money for them or the discipline to wait until you do. Remember, slow, steady, and boring!

NOT ALL DEBT IS BAD

In my humble opinion, debt is a tool that can allow an individual to accelerate their wealth building and ultimately, lifestyle, by orders of magnitude, IF used carefully and correctly! As much as people can and do, hate the big banks, they provide tremendous opportunity! Take the average person in 2008 and a hypothetical $300,000 property. Average Joe makes $48,000 a year gross (before taxes), after taxes he takes home $41,000 a year. If we divide $41,000 by 12 months of the year, we find he brings home $3416 each month. Average Joes apartment costs him $900 each month, cable and internet - $150, cell phone - $100, the electric bill - $150, water/sewer/garbage - $30, food and fuel - $28 a day or $840, health insurance -$250, vehicle insurance - $125, rainy day fund -$150, fun/entertainment - $400, for a grand total of $3095 a month and that's with no car payment.

So, with a monthly net (after taxes) income of $3416 minus his bills of $3095, he has $321 a month left over to improve his life. If he wants to buy a house, or even better, an income property that costs $300,000 and there are no banks to make mortgages, he'd have to save up $300,000. Hmmm, how long would that take? Well, $300,000 divided by his $321 a month in savings equals 934 months. 934 months divided by 12 months in a year equals 77 years. Joe better settle in for the long haul because just about the time he dies, he'll be able to afford a house. Kind of puts things into perspective doesn't it.

Well, I have some good news and some bad news for Joe. Good news is, hopefully he's going to make more money over time by promoting or making himself more valuable somehow. The bad news for old Joe is inflation. The price of that $300,000 property over the next 77 years is going to go up just a tad. The fifty year national average price appreciation for real estate in the U.S. is 3.1% per annum (year). If we only use 2% per year and compound that for 77 years Joe's dream of home ownership is going to cost him $1,378,270.00! Even if Joe's income and saving rate keeps up with inflation it will still take him 77 years to buy his property with cash. Talk about taking the wind out of someone's sails!

So, hate the banks if you want, but damn, 77 years! Even if you increased Joe's savings by 10 fold per year it would still take him almost 8 years to buy that house. Suffice to say, it's crucial to be a good credit risk! Make sure you have a good credit score!

MORTGAGE MARKET LIQUIDITY BASICS

Freddie Mac and Fannie Mae basically allow banks to originate or issue loans, knowing that the principle and interest payment of those loans will be guaranteed by the U.S. government (read – taxpayer). Neither institution originates or services these loans. They basically buy home mortgages, primarily from smaller banks and savings and loans. By doing this, they keep their lender networks liquid so they can keep making loans. This has been a vital aspect in keeping the mortgage industry in continuous operation over the years.

> ***Note:*** *In financial terms, liquidity means one can easily convert assets into cash without a big disruption to it's price. Basically, one can easily sell something without having to drop the price to entice a buyer. For example, you may have a rare coin that's worth $30,000, but how many people, A. want that coin and B. have $30,000 in cash to buy it from you? So as you can see, it may take you a few years to find the right buyer who both wants the coin and has the cash to trade you for the coin. If you needed to convert that rare coin into actual cash quickly, you'd have to drop the price or give a discount to entice someone to "tie up" their liquid cash. If you offered that $30,000 coin for sale at say, $10,000, it would sell much quicker, but you will have paid a significant cost for that "liquidity". That coin would be considered as NOT liquid.*

> *On the other hand, say I have a an extra, new generator that cost me $800 sitting in my garage and a hurricane just knocked out power for the next week. Say I want to convert that generator into cash for no discount, a great many people would trade me $800 for that generator immediately, that's liquidity!*

Think about this scenario for a second, 2.7 million people have moved to Florida over the past ten years or about 270,000 per year. Let's say only 25% or 67,500 of them need and buy a home. Let's say the average price of these homes is $350,000 and for this exercise is also the mortgage amount. So the banks of Florida would end up lending out $23.625 Billion dollars that year alone (The 2019-2020 fiscal year budget for Florida was $90.8 Billion). I don't know exactly how many lending institutions there are in Florida but that is a decent chunk of change, almost 27% of Florida's yearly budget. Now imagine your family moves to Florida on January 1 of 2021 and wants to buy a house. You cruise over to the bank and ask for a mortgage. The bank goes, Uhhh, sorry, we don't have any money to lend to you because we lent it all out last year, come back in a few years when we've built up some capital.

Boy, that'd be a bummer! So we need to keep the money flowing from as many sources as we can. Let's say a few states in the midwest have a bunch of money laying around and don't currently have much demand for loans. They could take that extra money and put it to work by buying Mortgage Backed Securities (MBS) from Fannie Mae and Freddie Mac. These institutions "buy" mortgages that are originated by smaller banks then pool the mortgages they buy into securities (MBS), which they then sell to investors (those midwest banks with low loan demand) on the secondary mortgage market. This creates a secondary demand for mortgages, to satisfy investor demands, which in turn provides stability to the overall mortgage market.

I don't want to get too deep into this for now but understand that the flow of money from an area of low use to an area of high demand, is vitally important and it is what makes America a financial powerhouse. America has made it very easy for money to flow from all over the world, to every part of the U.S., even down to the average Joe on the street. An investor in Europe may be partly financing your mortgage.

BRIEF HISTORY REVIEW

If we remember the great financial crisis of 2008, it wasn't the fact that a bunch of bad mortgages were made and a bunch of money would be lost on those bad mortgages, that destroyed the economy, it was the lack of movement of money. Basically, because everyone was lying and or unsure about the value of the assets they had, no one was sure of how to value the other entities assets. This caused people to pull money out of these institutions by selling their assets or stocks before anyone else realized that those assets weren't valued correctly. This was basically, the same as a run on the banks except it was happening everywhere.

That said, no one was sure of the financial condition of the other institutions and it got so bad for example, that big banks wouldn't loan money to other big banks because they didn't know if that bank would be able to pay them back. Money stopped moving. I watched this unfold on CNBC and during testimony on CSPAN where I saw the fear in Hank Paulson's eyes, (former CEO of Goldman Sachs and Secretary of the United States Treasury at the time) as Congress mulled over for days, the basically blank check of $787 Billion dollars, he was asking for. Congress was leery of his request because they basically invented the saying in politics, never let a good crisis go to waste. As the window of action was closing, Treasury Secretary Paulson basically told them, (my interpretation) if you wait any longer the entire world financial system is going to collapse. As a result of the very fast thinking of the Treasury Department led by Hank Paulson, Ben Bernanke and Tim Geithner of the Federal Reserve, $787 Billion dollars was injected into the economy to take the place of the money that wasn't moving anymore under the T.A.R.P. program. This, in my opinion, saved the global economy from an unbelievably *bad shock that would have been far, far worse and lasted probably twice as long as the 2008 crisis did.*

After this measure was passed, things began to settle down a bit. People and institutions were of the understanding that if they had an asset that nobody else wanted to buy and they needed to sell it, the government would buy it from them. Basically making an illiquid asset, liquid again. This is how, in my opinion, the Federal Reserve is known as the lender, or in this case, the buyer of last resort. Money started moving again, albeit at a much, much slower and cautious rate. The United States started to stabilize and people around the world saw that the U.S. government was willing to do anything necessary to make sure the U.S. economy didn't collapse.

This caused a huge influx of money from around the world into the United States. Scared money from around the world was looking for a safe home, that home was the U.S. Treasury market. A U.S. Treasury security, bill, note, or bond is guaranteed by the full faith and credit of the government of the United States. That amount of demand chasing supply, along with the spooky financial environment would drive 10 yr. Treasury yields at 4.63% in 2007, down to 1.8% in 2012. That means people and institutions were willing to loan the U.S. government money and only get a 1.8% annual return. In many other cases around the world, people were willing to actually lose money as long as their loses were guaranteed to be only so much. Yes, you read that correctly, other governments were issuing bonds that had a NEGATIVE annual rate of return, and there was tremendous demand for them! If you didn't know, this is how bad things looked AFTER the T.A.R.P. program was enacted! The world economy was truly on the edge!

As time went on and the Federal Reserve began to buy all kinds of assets with its Quantitative Easing program, many would raise concerns to the Federal Reserves Chairman, Ben

Bernanke about the ballooning Federal budget deficit in relation to the countries ability to borrow money via Treasury Securities. Because the U.S. Government ALWAYS pays its bills (has a good credit score), in times of crisis, the world is ready and willing to loan the U.S. money at almost any rate of return. Bernanke would relate this by telling congress that the world is willing to lend us money at a rate of 1.5% for ten years and we have the deepest, most liquid capital markets in the world! BOOM! As Warren Buffet says, "Don't bet against the United States."

There are some lessons to be learned from this. Liquidity is King! Given the right conditions, an unbelievably bad economic event can happen to any economy, so don't just float along, not paying attention, hoping everything will be OK. The track record of a country fulfilling its obligations along with very smart, savvy, people at the helm will determine that countries economic outcome. Given the right conditions, you have to cut your losses and move on, if that entails bailing out big banks or General Motors because they made stupid decisions, so be it, they got lucky, I wouldn't sink the ship to prove a point. How does your personal liquidity look? How well would you withstand a financial shock? Are you on the edge or do you have financial reserves? How liquid are those financial reserves in times of panic? Maybe you don't have the level of reserves that you think you do.

DEBT TO INCOME RATIO OR DTI

Debt to income ratio or DTI as it is commonly referred to in the mortgage industry is calculated by taking the sum of the minimum monthly payments of **ALL** your debts and dividing that by your gross income. Now you can break this down however you please be it monthly or yearly but it doesn't change anything. Each lenders requirements are different and of course can change whenever they feel like it (in general, private banks are more strict and federally backed lenders have looser requirements) but most private banks will want to see your DTI between 36% to 39%. On the other hand, Freddie Mac and Fannie Mae will go as far as a 45% DTI. Freddie Mac and Fannie Mae are government institutions that basically guarantee mortgages that fulfill a specific set of standards or requirements.

So your DTI is the ratio between your gross income and your total combined debt service (payments). When doing your DTI calculations to see if you qualify for a house, remember that the mortgage is going to be included in whatever maximum percentage that your lender has set. If your lender sets a maximum DTI of 36% and you're at 36% right now, you won't qualify. What if you're at 26%? You most likely still won't qualify. Why? Lenders like to see no more than 28% to 33% of your gross income going towards your TOTAL mortgage costs.

Some rough math tells us that for Average Joes income of say $52,000 a year, no more than 33% can be towards a mortgage or $17,160 a year. If we divide that by 12 we get $1,430 a month as the maximum towards his mortgage. Sounds reasonable right? Remember, this is his total mortgage payment which will include property taxes and insurance. On a $350,000 property, the yearly taxes will typically be around 1.5 to 2%, say $6000 and Property insurance will be around $1500 a year. So we add them together to get $7500 a year. If we divide by 12, we get $625 a month. If Average Joe selects an FHA mortgage which allows only 3.5% down he'll have to come up with $12,250 for a down payment and about 2% of the loan as closing costs, or another $7000, for a total of $19,250 to close on the loan.

Let's say Average Joe has this $19,250 to close on the loan and the required emergency cash which I'll go over next. So Average Joe is going to finance 96.5% of $350,000, or $337,750, for 30 years at a fixed rate of 4%. This comes out to a Principle and Interest (P&I) payment of $1,612 per month. Already we can see that old Joe can't afford this house with this loan set up. To finish the example though, we still need to add in the $625 a month in Taxes and Insurance (T&I) remember PITI, for a total mortgage payment of $2,237 a month, yikes! I know, it's a punch in the gut.

If we go back to reality, Joe would have to start looking at houses in the $200,000 range. If we take a home listed for sale at $220,000 and using the same down payment and loan we'll find that, not surprisingly, his P&I drop to around $1000 a month and his T&I drop to around $400 a month which puts him right were he needs to be, as far as the maximum amount lenders allow to go towards a mortgage. But where does that put him overall? He makes $52,000 a year and his lender says he can a maximum DTI of 36% or $18,720. If we divide by 12 we get a total monthly debt service of $1,560. If his mortgage payment is going to be around $1,400 a month, that means ALL of his other monthly payments, car, phone, car insurance, credit card etc. can only add up to $160! Ouch!

If you're in Average Joes income range, let's say from $50,000 to $70,000 a year, your total monthly debt service (payments) should be around 10% or lower. So this really ends up being about how much you try to finance but as the above example shows, you'd have to put an extra $130,000 dollars down to qualify for that $350,000 house. Kudos to you if you have that kind of flexibility! As you're probably starting to see, you need to be very careful with your finances and start planning early, and in some cases, years in advance. Real estate is a great gig and has made me a lot of money, but it's not easy to get in the game, especially the rental game! Fear not, and keep reading, YOU CAN DO THIS!

EMERGENCY CASH

As stated previously, each lenders requirements are different, but in my experience, most lenders will require anywhere from two to six months worth of emergency cash. Emergency cash is the cash or cash equivalent (remember liquid vs. illiquid) assets that you have saved up in case for example, you lose your job and are no longer receiving income. If you were to unfortunately lose your source of income, how long could you continue to make payments on your mortgage? Remember that the bank assesses credit risk and they want you to prove that if you have an unforeseen event you can still make payments long enough for you to get through that event. I'm sure that somewhere in the bank there's a group of people that look at the average number of months that it takes someone to change jobs, for whatever reason that they must, and have come up with six months.

So, do you need emergency cash for all of your debts? In my experience, no, the bank only really cares about the total mortgage payment. I guess the bank assumes you'll stop paying everything else before you stop paying on your house. So the emergency cash includes the Principle, Interest, Taxes and Insurance, PITI, remember? If the principle of your loan is $850 a month, the interest is $250 a month, the taxes are $300 a month, and the insurance is $100 a month, your total PITI would be $850 + $250 + $300 + $100 = $1,500 a month. Take that $1,500 a month and multiply it by six months and you get an extra $9,000 that you need to have laying around. Everybody has that, right?

So if we use the previous example of a $350,000 property, you're going to need $19,250 to close on the loan AND another $9,000 sitting somewhere, just in case. I know, the banks throw around thousands like it's no big deal. You can do this! If you have an IRA, it's acceptable as a form of emergency cash. The bank may want to see the terms of withdrawal for your IRA and most likely won't give you full credit for the money you have in it, but it qualifies.

Now, I know what some of you are thinking, I'll just ask Mom and Dad to borrow $9000 while I'm going through the loan process and as soon as it closes I'll pay them back. That's cute, but, number one, it's mortgage fraud and number two, banks have been around for a long time and just like a seasoned teacher, they're not going to believe that your dog ate your homework. Lenders will want to look at your past bank statements and see how and where that money came from. If two months ago your parents transferred $9000 into your bank account, the lender will see that. If your parents made three, $3000 transfers, again, the lender will see it and you're busted. The lender will treat your "emergency cash" as a gift, which they don't allow for this requirement and will disqualify you. They want to see that you're able save and hang onto this money on your own.

Think carefully about this because in the end, you'll be in the middle of your loan process, will have spent money on inspections and all the time that is involved with all of that, along with wasting the realtors, and mortgage originators time, just to get your loan denied and lose the property. Thinking in total terms, and in an environment like there was in Florida during the sharp recovery in 2015, 2016, and 2017, when one had to put a contract on a property within hours of it being listed, piss poor planning could have literally cost you $100,000 in missed opportunity!

DOWN PAYMENT

That was a good segue to down payment and a theme you should know by now is each lender has its own requirements during different economic and political times. As of the writing of this book, private lenders will generally require a 20% down payment on a Single Family Residential (SFR) income/rental property, a 10% down payment on a "second home" or "vacation home" (specific rules apply), and a 25% down payment on a two to four family income property. I can't tell you how many times well intentioned friends have told me that lender "X" will do a two to four family loan for only 10% or 20% down only to call them and find out it's, you guessed it, 25%. If you can find a lender that will go that low great, but keep in mind, you want to stay conservative and safe!

Federal agencies like Fannie Mae and Freddie Mac are similar in their requirements and will buy loans with down payments as follows, SFR primary residence (meaning you're going to live there) 5% down, a two family property like a duplex where you live in one side (primary residence) 15% down, three to four family property where you live in one unit 20% down. So they're a little more lenient but you must live in the property or, you guessed it, it's 25% down.

FHA loans are by far the most lenient as far as down payment goes. If you want to buy a duplex, live in one side and rent the other side (which is how I got my start!), you'll only need to put down 3.5%! So, on a $350,000 duplex, I only need to have $12,250 as a down payment if I'm going to live in one side. Now, if I want to buy that same duplex as an investor and rent both units, I'll have to put 25% or a whopping $87,500 down, combine that with around $7000 in closing costs and six months worth of emergency cash, around $11,000, I have to come to the closing table with $105,500! It hurts, I know, but it's worth it!

All things being equal, total cash required to close on the FHA, owner occupied duplex, you'll need $30,250. That's over $75,000 less than an investor will have to pay! At that rate I could buy three duplexes and still have enough money left over to buy a good used truck. Unfortunately, I haven't found a way to live in three duplexes at once! All kidding aside, an FHA loan is great way to get in the game. That said, and as is usually the case, there are no free lunches, you're going to pay for it, you just don't have to pay for it up front.

From my experience and understanding, banks don't want to own, maintain or manage anything other than money. They really don't want to take back that property if you default on it. Unless of course, the taxpayers and mortgage insurers pay them for that asset and then pay them to maintain that asset until it sells much later for more than they have in it (2008)....weird, huh? In normal times however, they're not set up to manage thousands of properties so they don't want the hassle.

That being the case, they've come up with a model which they believe greatly lowers their risk of becoming property managers. So, property "X" fair market value at the time of purchase in 2018, determined by a professional appraiser, is say, $250,000. It's a single family residence (SFR) and will have an owner occupant or be a primary residence of its buyer. The bank knows that you'll be late or stop paying altogether on your Netflix account and gym membership long before you'll be willing to lose your one and only place to live. They also know there is much higher demand for single family residence than there is for a four family quadplex. They're also pretty sure that as time goes by, the house will go up in value slightly over the rate of inflation or in the worst case only depreciate slightly.

During this time you will have paid them back, to some degree, what you originally borrowed from them. On top of this, they're getting a substantial amount of interest payments by you each month. So, in this hypothetical situation, their risk is lower so they're willing to take a lower down payment. Let's take a look at this in more detail. We have a SFR with an appraised value of $250,000. We have a buyer who is going to live in the house as his or her primary residence and is going to use an FHA loan and put 3.5% down.

FHA requires that the house appraises for what the sales price is, which it did, and requires it to pass a four point inspection, known in the biz as simply "a 4 point." A 4 point inspection is designed to make sure that the properties main and high cost items are in good working order. By the nature of the loan, they know you probably don't have a bunch of money laying around and if you need a new $15,000 roof, you most likely won't be able to pay for it. Whether they are looking out for you or looking out for themselves by looking out for you, can be debated, but in either case, they increase the odds of success of the property, the borrower and themselves.

A four point inspection (4 point) looks at the properties roof, electrical components, plumbing components, and the HVAC system. The 4 point inspector will look at all of these items, as much that can be seen anyway, and determine the safety and efficacy of them. This insures that you buy a house that's in good working condition. This protects the novice buyer that may not know what to look out for, makes it easier and cheaper for you to own the home, and if you happen to default, makes it easier, cheaper, and faster for them to sell the home.

So, our buyer has given 3.5% of $250,000 or $8750 as a down payment to the bank, and as such, only borrows $241,250 from the bank. Our buyer borrows this money using a fixed rate loan of 4% over a repayment period of 30 years. If we run that through a mortgage calculator that shows the amortization table, we find that our buyers P&I payment each month will be $1,151.76. The principle portion of this payment, (the portion that goes to paying back what was borrowed, or the principle), is $347.60. The interest portion, (the price you pay the bank for loaning you money) of the buyers payment is $804.17.

AMORTIZATION

If you just noticed that you're sending the bank $347 to pay down what you owe them and $804 in interest that you'll never see again, congratulations, now you know what "amortization" is! Gee, I wonder who came up with this amortization thing anyway? Fun isn't it? In brief, amortization makes the interest that you pay the bank for their risk in lending to you, front loaded, meaning, they get a major portion paid to them early in the loan. A quick and sloppy example would be, say your P&I payment is $1,500 a month. The first months payment has $500 going towards what you borrowed (the principle) and $1,000 going towards interest. The second months payment has $501 going towards your principle and $999 going towards interest. The third months payment has $502 going towards principle and $998 going towards interest and so on and so on. Yes, it's a bummer but remember how long it'd take you save up enough money to buy that house with cash! And let's not forget that 'ol Uncle Sam allows you to reduce (write off) your taxable income by the yearly amount of interest you pay to the bank, which can be substantial!

PMI OR MIP, EITHER WAY IT'S EXPENSIVE

Back to our original example, we're super happy and appreciative to Mommy and Daddy Government for letting us buy a property with only putting 3.5% down, BUT, they still don't really trust us. Unfortunately, we have to add PMI or MIP to our monthly mortgage payment. MIP (mortgage insurance premium) and PMI (private mortgage insurance) is basically an insurance product that you pay for (remember, no free lunches) that protects the bank if you default. I don't have any concrete evidence, but I deduce that MIP or PMI covers whatever portion of the 20% down payment that the bank wants, that you didn't pay. I came up with that because the banks require that you pay it if you put less than 20% down.

Let's look at that for a second. Basically, lending institutions are only willing to loan anyone 80% of the value of a property. Why could that be? My opinion is, in their model, if they have to take the property back (remember, they only want to hold and manage cash, not properties) they can "fire sale" it for up to a 20% discount of market value, sell it super fast because it's such a good deal, and turn that property back into cash, which of course, is what they love!

That said, it would make sense that the more you put down, the lower your PMI payment would be, because the PMI company is insuring less money that they would have to pay the bank in the event that you default. This is one of the reasons, the other being your credit score, why

PMI or MIP costs vary from around .25% up to 2% of the loan amount. If this leaves you feeling blue, FHA MIP rates are a little less, currently varying from .45% to 1.05% of loan value, with .85% being the average. With FHA, you will however, be charged 1.75% of the loan amount up front for MIP. No free lunches, so sorry!

Alas, there is some good news, if in our example, you don't have the $4,221.88 for that upfront MIP charge, you may add it or "roll it into" as they say it in the biz, your loan. This will of course, increase the amount of your loan, thereby raising your interest paid to the bank and your monthly MIP payment. I gotta say it again....no free lunches! To keep it easy, let's say you have the extra $4,221.88 for the upfront MIP payment. This allows us to keep our original loan amount of $241,250.00. So we take $241,250.00 and multiply it by the FHA MIP charge of .85% to get $2,050.63. If we then divide that by 12, we get $170.89 per month that's added to your mortgage payment, and that's if you have a great credit score!

That would look like this:

$241,250.00 x .85 = $2,050.63 (yearly MIP charge.)
$2,050.63 / 12 = $170.89 (monthly MIP charge.)

So what if your credit score isn't so bueno, like 620? No big deal, your MIP charge goes to $4,366.63 per year. If we divide that by 12 we get $363.89 a month, ADDED to your mortgage payment! Oh, one more bright spot to lift your spirits, the MIP payment NEVER GOES AWAY! Ten years from now, your outstanding principle balance may be only 60% of the property's fair market value but, too bad, PAY UP!! I can't stress having a good credit score enough!

PITI – PRINCIPLE, INTEREST, TAXES, AND INSURANCE

As you may be noticing, there are a lot of moving parts to this game and it pays to think long and hard before making a move! So back to our example. We have a P&I of $1,151.76 plus our MIP of $170.89 (for year one. MIP is recalculated each year.) which equals $1,322.65 plus our homeowners insurance premium (I) of $1,500 per year, divided by 12 gives us $125 per month plus our property taxes (T) of $4800 per year, divided by 12 gives us $400 per month for a total mortgage payment of $1,847.65!

That looks like this:

(P) = Principle
(I) = Interest
(T) = Property taxes
(I) = Insurance (I know, there's two I's, I didn't make this stuff up.)
All together, known as PITI.

HOI (homeowners insurance) $1,500 per year / 12 = $125.00 per month. (I)
Property taxes $4800 per year / 12 = $400.00 per month. (T)
P&I $1,151.76 per month. + MIP in this case, $170.89 = $1,322.65 (Total P&I)

T $400.00 per month + I $125.00 per month = $525.00 per month. (T&I)

P&I	$1,322.65	per month.
T&I	$525.00	per month.
PITI	$1,847	or your total mortgage payment.

Hmmm, quite a bit more than the mortgage calculator on that real estate website said, huh? It seems as though they want to get people excited about how much they can afford so they get in contact with a realtor, eh, who knows. Not to worry, I'll give more examples later.

Let's get back to the banks risk in all of this. Remember that the bank is taking a risk on 80% of the property's value. If you make it through the first year without defaulting on your loan, odds are, your home will increase in value, well, price actually, but we'll get into that later, by 3% which is the national annual average. At the end of that first year you will have paid down your principle balance (what you owe the bank) by $4,248.53 or 1.76% of the original loan amount.

Your property is now worth $257,500 and you owe $237,001 or 92% of its current value. In other words, you went from 3.5% equity (how much of the house YOU own) to 8% equity, pretty cool huh? The banks original risk was $200,000, original value $250,000 x .80 = $200,000, (remember, you paid 3.5% and MIP promised to pay the remaining 16.5%). So MIP promises to pay 16.5% of the original $250,000, or $250,000 x .165 = $41,250. You paid 3.5% of the original $250,000 or $250,000 x .035 = $8750. If we take MIP's portion of $41,250 and add your contribution of $8750 we get $50,000.

That looks like this:

MIP's coverage $250,000 x .165 (16.5%) = $41,250
Your contribution $250,000 x .035 (3.5%) = $8750

MIP's portion $41,250 + $8750 (your 3.5%) = $50,000.

Your contribution + MIP's $50,000 / $250,000 = .20 or 20%
Put another way $250,000 x .20 (20%) = $50,000
Put another way $250,000 / 5 = $50,000

Property value increase $250,000 x .03 (3% appreciation) = $7500

So, the bank received $4,248.53 in principle payments (on top of their nearly $9400 in interest) and the properties value went up by $7500 ($250,000 x .03 = $7500). In the first year, not counting the interest the bank earned on the loan, it reduced it's risk by 4% from 80% down to 76%, not bad! If you defaulted now, they could sell the property fast, at a 24% discount if they wanted to. Make it two years without defaulting and your properties value goes up to $265,225. Rough math tells us you will have paid down your principle another $4300, reducing your principle to around $232,700. The banks risk however has gone from $200,000 down to $191,452. The banks original risk thanks to you and MIP $200,000 - $4248 (in year one) - $4300 (in year two) = $191,452. If we take $191,452 and divide it by the new value of the house which is $265,225 we get .72 or 72%. So after year two, the bank reduced its risk by another 4% from 76% down to 72%.

The example above isn't 100% inclusive of all variables, but you can get an idea of just how rapid the risk to the bank is reduced. You should also be realizing that, One – When you want to buy something you don't have the money for, you really get whacked! Two – Loan products are set up for fairly specific or narrow customer models. Three – Depending on how long you choose to remain in or use that loan product will determine whether it helps you or hurts you. At a rough average of $100 a month over the 30 year life of an FHA mortgage, you will have paid $36,000 in MIP costs that you'll never get back!

By now, hopefully you're starting to realize how the banks view you and real estate, and how easy it is , if you're not careful and have a plan, to make a bad decision that you could be stuck in for years. You should sit down and carefully plan your path, having several options if things change, as they always do to some degree or another. I'll give more examples of what I mean by that later in this book. Sometimes it's better to wait until you get your financial house in order versus buying now and getting a bad interest rate and a ton of fees!

As a recap, the banks want long term, stable employment, making as much money as possible, high credit scores, acceptable DTI ratios, emergency cash, as big a down payment as possible plus the cash for closing costs as required. You should be armed with enough information now to get a general idea of what price range you'll be able to qualify for. I've also given you enough information to figure out how long it will take you to get there. So get started, do your math, see where you can save money and how much you'll need. Figure out how long it will take you and get out and start looking at properties so you can begin to be able to value them.

CHAPTER 3

GET OUT THERE AND START LOOKING!

Quick takeaways from what you're about to learn

- **The sooner you start looking at properties, the better**
- **Look at properties above and below your target price**
- **Don't get lazy**
- **Create good habits**
- **Location, location, location – it still matters**
- **A property can generate income in many ways**
- **Value the property right – miss a deal or set yourself back years**
- **God is good**
- **Hard work pays off – make an extra $100,000 in two years**
- **Don't buy on price, buy on value!**

For the following discussion, I'm going to use a $300,000 property as an example. Now that you have a pretty good idea of what it takes to buy an property, I would like you to start looking, today, for properties in the $200,000 to $400,000 range. You'll probably start looking online first which is fine. Once you find say, ten to twenty properties in that price range, I want you to physically go look at all of them. Why do I have to go look at them and why should I look at properties that are $100,000 above and below my price target? Well, unless you're an active realtor who has ten deals a month come across their desk, you won't have a solid idea of value unless you look at properties above and below your target price range.

There are a lot of things that go into valuing a piece of property, does it have Formica or granite counters? Is it lake front or next to a garbage dump? Is the lake that it is on just a big pond or a decent sized lake? Are motorized aquatic vehicles allowed on that lake or is it just to look at and spawn mosquitoes? Is it newer construction with a better layout or old with all the bedrooms next to each other and a tiny bathroom? The list goes on and on. Until you get a real good handle on property values in your area, you'll be putting yourself at a big disadvantage if you don't physically go look at the properties. If you don't do this kind of research you'll be buying on price and not value. Six months is a blip in time in the real estate market and that short snapshot of prices won't give you a detailed enough view of values. Always remember this, as investors, **WE DO NOT BUY ANYTHING BASED ON PRICE, WE BUY BASED ON VALUE!**

Two identical houses in different locations could have vastly different values. An 800 sq. ft. 1950's bungalow with a weird layout that is in a great section of a thriving downtown where there's limited rental supply and high demand will draw very high rents. Take that same exact bungalow and put it thirty five miles out in the suburbs and no one wants it! Why? Great question, this is why you NEED to get out and look at all kinds of properties within about an hours radius of your target area. Once you have a general idea of values and more importantly, why those properties are valued as they are, you can then hone in on your target area and become an expert there. The old adage that goes something like, real estate is all about, location, location, location, is 100% true, but there are still a ton of variables that will affect value, regardless of location. Harold Samuel coined this phrase in 1944 when he founded one of the largest property companies in the United Kingdom.

If you don't get out there and look, you'll never know! Get with a realtor and ask them to send you ALL of the active and sold listings going back at least a year, in that $200,000 to $400,000 price range. You will most definitely meet with some resistance from the realtor but stand strong and politely ask again. Assure the realtor that you'll look through all of them and let them know when you want to go see one. Depending on your area, you will most likely get a list of properties numbering in the several hundreds. Get comfy and grab your favorite beverage because you're going to need to go through each listing looking for its attributes and detriments. Don't get lazy on me now! I'm lazy too, I have to fight it constantly. I know, it's a lot of work, but I promise that you will quickly get better at it. After a few times going through the list, you'll start to recognize properties by the first picture in the listing. You'll also start to recognize patterns in certain zip codes and you'll most certainly find a couple properties that have sold multiple times. If you can only look at twenty properties at a sitting then so be it, but keep at it, you're becoming a real estate expert!

After looking at a bunch, you'll start to ask questions like, why did this property stay on the market for 130 days and sell for $60,000 less than this one? Was it the location, the age, interior finishes, schools, or some combination of all of those? Later in this book, I'll give you my opinion about what attributes you should look for in a property. If you're staring at 104 pages of listings on your computer and hoping that someone will sneak up behind you and just end it all, believe me, I understand, but don't quit! **When you get exhausted just remember, you're about to bet a lot of your hard earned money on hitting a home run, your first time at bat, in a game you've never played before!**

From 2008 to 2012, I looked at an average of forty properties a week. That's over eight thousand properties! I was aware that I was new to this game and severely lacked the ability to accurately value property. I also knew that there was a time limit on this window of opportunity so I greatly ramped up my rate of learning and my gas bill! By the end of 2012, you could ask me about a property that you saw online within an hour and a half radius of Orlando and chances were, as soon as I heard the street name, I would tell you something like, "oh yeah, the blue, concrete block duplex with the flat roof and the broken shutters on the left side that was bought and sold twice already, the original price was $85,000……." That's how well I knew what was for sale!

That was how I was able to make over $100,000 in two years, on a 15 acre farm that was sixty miles from my first duplex that I was living in at the time. I first drove by that farm in late 2009 when I noticed it was listed as a short sale. It was listed at well over $300,000 at the time, which was double my price point! I checked out the area and made a mental note that it checked all the boxes at "X" price point. I then just watched its status online for the next three years. I watched the price come down over that time, through short sale status, then pre-foreclosure. In pre-foreclosure the price had come down almost $100,000. Of course it didn't sell because they were asking too much for it. On top of that, the property was deteriorating during that time causing its value to go down even further.

It was finally foreclosed on and the bank took it back, soon after relisting it for sale as REO (which means Real Estate Owned – when the bank takes possession of a property). With the banks being very good at numbers, I mean after all, that's what they do, it came as no surprise that they relisted it for sale REO at the same $300,000 plus price point that it didn't sell for in the prior two years. A bold strategy indeed and being counterintuitive to the logic that most of us have (taxpayer bailout money must be awesome!). I guess when you don't have to sell something and it costs you no money to maintain it, you can just sit on it.

After another six months of checking the MLS (Multiple Listing Service) twice a day, once in the morning and once in the evening, I saw the first price drop. I did another drive by to check the condition of the property and to see if anything changed in the surrounding area. Three more months goes by and another big price drop. Now I'm starting to run detailed plans and exit strategies and best and worst case scenarios for the property if it reaches my price point. I'm also making sure that my financial house is in order and my financial life looks as uneventful and boring as my actual life was while I was in super saver mode. I contacted my lender and gave him a heads up as to what I was planning to do. I got a pre-approval letter for slightly more than my target price point and gathered all of my proof of funds paperwork so it'd be ready at a moments notice. I also learned what it would for and how long it would take to do a bank to bank wire transfer.

Three months later, at around 9 a.m. on a Sunday morning, what do you know, another $30,000 price drop and it hit my trigger number. I call my realtor and tell her to write a full price offer with no contingencies (remember, banks don't want to fix anything) and that I'm driving up there now and will pull the trigger on the contract once I make sure the property is still in acceptable condition. No time for breakfast or a shower, off I go! About an hour later, I arrive, the property has a new broken window and it looks like the well pump pipe froze and burst causing the well pump to run constantly until it burned out, other than that, the property is still a mess!

It had several broken windows and the A/C ducting in the attic was being used as a rat tunnel with holes chewed through it in several locations and rat droppings throughout the duct work. It's Florida, who needs A/C anyway! So I called my realtor and give her the go ahead to submit the contract with the pre-approval and proof of funds. By 11:30 a.m. I had a signed and executed contract for full asking price with no contingencies with 10% down and conventional 30 year fixed rate financing. I was only comfortable doing this because of my preparation and planning three months earlier on a property I might never get!

YOU BOUGHT A HORSE FARM?

You see, a 15 acre farm is a totally different animal than a downtown duplex on a third of an acre. Along with many other factors, there's a land value and use component along with an accessory structures component to take into consideration. I had spent the prior months researching, among many other things, active and sold vacant land sales in the area. From my research I determined a fair land value for that farm would be between $8,500 and $9,000 per acre (at appraisal it came in at $9,333 per acre). The farm was fully perimeter fenced and cross fenced with horse/cattle fencing, had a 30' x 60', 7 stall barn with a concrete center isle, hot and cold running water and full electric with 240V power. The house was a 1960's 2000 sq. foot, three bedroom, two bathroom, concrete block, ranch style with a metal roof. At the time, a 30' x 60' barn like that would cost around $50,000 to build. So, at a land value of around $9,000 per acre times 15 acres you'd have $135,000 in the land plus another $50,000 in the barn for a total of $185,000 not including the house or the fencing (by the way, fencing like that can be ridiculously expensive as a year later one of my farm neighbors got a quote to do the perimeter of 20 acres for $30,000!).

The price that the bank had finally dropped the property to was $180,000. The way I looked at it was, at $180,000 I was basically getting the house for free! Easy decision! That afternoon I was advised that there were four other offers on the property. All the other offers were for less money but two were all cash. Those cash offers made me nervous because the property looked like shit and was in disrepair. Not things a lender wants to lend on! I knew the bank would take an all cash offer in second over a financed offer so I assumed the two cash offers were substantially lower or they wouldn't have accepted mine.

It had only been four years since the big crash, the economy was still trending down even though the federal reserve was using every conventional tool they had to stimulate it and even inventing a number of new ways to flood the economy with money. This made anyone who was paying attention to this nervous and the banks were very reluctant to lend money. Anything that didn't fit neatly into their boxes spooked them. It turns out that the bank who owned the property decided to go with my offer and keep the other offers as back ups. Awesome!

Everything looked solid on my end, except, my lender/bank didn't like the fact that I would be buying a house that was about sixty miles from my job. They didn't like it so much that they made me write a letter promising that I was going to live there or be in default of the loan. So I wrote the letter. They still didn't like it. So I had to basically write a quasi-business plan about why I wanted to move sixty miles from my primary job and what I planned on doing "way out there".

They got spooked and were basically trying to find a way to disqualify me. I didn't hear anything for about a week then my loan originator called me up and said, uh sorry, the bank decided that they don't want to give you the loan anymore, even though you qualify across the board. I basically had to take a step back and think like a bank. Everything has a level of risk and a reward for taking that risk. The bank was basically not willing to take that risk for the return. I couldn't offer them a greater return so my only option was to reduce their risk to see if they'd take the deal.

My original lender really put me in a pinch, I had twelve days to go through the entire loan process again with a new lender and close before the next highest offer would get the property. I told my loan originator to write up the new loan with a twenty percent down payment. The extra, almost $20,000 that I used to reduce the banks risk was enough to seal the deal and with a lot of hard work on my loan originators end, I took possession of the property twelve days later. The next day I started cleaning up the property and fixing what I could, which wasn't much because I had no money left over after having to put twenty percent down.

My fiance at the time, God bless her soul, wanted to move in right away even though the property was still a mess. She probably saw the work and struggle that was ahead of us and wanted to get it over with. So my family and I moved in on an unusually cold January day in Florida. It was 20 degs. F. our first night there and the master bedroom had two completely broken windows that were only partially covered up by plywood. We bundled up together on an air mattress on the floor, we had no power or running water yet. The kids slept like rocks but for us it was a long night.

With the property being a prior horse farm, it was my intention to rent the facility as such. As I started to build up money again I fixed the horse related items first so the property could start generating some income. It turned out that the good Lord would have a surprise waiting for us! While introducing ourselves to our neighbors, one of them said she was a very busy horse border and trainer who had more horses than she had land. She only had ten acres, which I know seems like a lot, but in horse world you need about two acres per horse as a minimum. She asked if I would be willing to let her keep some horses on my property and that she'd be willing to pay me $200 per horse, per month. Uhhh, let me think about that for second, yes, yes I would be willing to rent to you! Thank you Lord! Our properties abutted one another which made it easy to install a gate between our properties to allow her easy access to my property.

Thanks to our blessings, in a few months we were averaging $800 a month in pasture rent and my total mortgage was $763 a month! Let me tell you, living for free is cool! The weather was starting to get toasty about now but we wanted to recoup the nearly $40,000 that we used to buy the property as fast as we could, so we held off on replacing the A/C ducting. Our son suffered from some allergies so we didn't want to attempt to clean and patch the ducting so we just went without. We ended up going two years without A/C not including the prior year that we went without A/C at the duplex to speed our savings. Three years without air conditioning in Florida, ***how bad do you want it?***

Two years and a couple of months later, we sold that farm to one of our neighbors for $280,000. Turns out she was one of the original offers that I competed with two years earlier. She put in a low ball offer of $115,000. She is a very nice lady and I don't want to cast her in a bad light but she was either too greedy or didn't value the property correctly and ended up missing that opportunity. All in all that property paid us back our original $40,000 used to buy it, the $10,000 used to renovate it and as a bonus $88,000 in appreciation. After closing on the sale of the farm, I sat outside in my $2000 ex police car, wearing my beat up, paint and pvc cement covered cargo shorts, staring at a check, to me, for $138,000. Up until that point I'd never thought I would see a check that large made out to me. In 26 months, that farm paid us $138,000. $138,000 divided by 26 months equals $5307 a month! That farm paid us $5300 a month to live there! That's pretty cool!

I wrote this story not to brag or boast but to hopefully give you some inspiration and understanding that blessings favor the prepared and when you combine that with hard work and sacrifice, it pays big dividends! For someone who at the time made around $50,000 a year, that farm more than doubled my income! So make a quick, rough budget and get out there and start looking!

CHAPTER 4

A MORE DETAILED LOOK INTO PROPERTY TAXES

A quick takeaway from this chapter.

- **Property taxes – you don't have to love them, but we need them**
- **Communism and socialism doesn't work – it's been proven**
- **Confidently and accurately calculate property taxes without surprises**
- **Tax exemptions that benefit real estate owners**
- **Don't fall victim to next years tax trap!**
- **Use next years tax trap to your advantage**

Over time I've noticed that there are basically two types of people who ask me about how to get started in the rental biz, the type who just wants the bullet points of everything and the type who really wants to understand all the nuts and bolts of it. I've also noticed that some people do better with "just the facts" and others do better with a story that allows them to picture how it's going to be for them. I've tried to write this book to appease both types. I know it may seem like a lot, but up until now I've only given you enough information to inspire you and allow you to get started down a safe path. For the nuts and bolts people I'll now dive into more detail about the loan process, taxes, insurance, understanding value, running numbers, making an offer and living with a rental property. So buckle up, grab a coffee or your favorite energy drink and lets get started.

A PERSPECTIVE ON PROPERTY TAXES

Taxes, whether you love them or hate them, or are somewhere in the middle, at some point you're going to pay them. There's an old saying that says there are only three things guaranteed in this life, change, death, and taxes. I've noticed that people on the far ends of the topic are equally and oppositely, short sighted. Read about or visit other parts of the world where they have super low taxes but subsequently have little to no services like Fire, EMS, Police, libraries, parks, garbage and recycling pick up, or infrastructure like roads, bridges, cell service, public schools, water and sewer, etc. and you'll see the benefits of higher taxes.

On the other end of the spectrum there are people who want to raise taxes to obscene levels. This they believe, will create a utopia where the haves, have much less and the have not's, will have much more and everyone will be equal and happy. Equal, guaranteed outcomes, crush the drive and will of those who wish to take a gamble in this life by sacrificing and working harder and hopefully smarter than the next person, to achieve ongoing dividends, with much less ongoing input.

COMMUNISM - BAD

Say your family lives on a farm and most if not all of your food comes from your farm. You and your family put the majority of your time and effort into this farm just to sustain yourselves. You guys have a family meeting and decide that, collectively, you'd like to work smarter and not harder. Your family starts researching ways to achieve this and after a big investment of time, your family settles on the idea of planting a pecan tree. Your research tells you that after a pecan tree is established, it takes very little care and will produce, on average, 110 pounds of nuts per year. Pecans are mostly fat, and at 9 calories per gram, and 453 grams per pound, will provide 4077 calories. If the tree averages 110 pounds of pecans per year, 110 pounds, times 4077 calories per pound, equals, 448,470 calories per year. If we divide that by 365 days in a year we find that the pecan tree provides 1228 calories per day, every day! Oh, and the pecan tree has a 300 year lifespan, talk about generational wealth!

Sounds amazing, right? You have a family of four hardworking individuals that probably expend about 3000 calories a day each. You guys figure that you should be able provide about 50% of the families caloric needs by planting a handful of pecan trees. There is one pretty big drawback though. Unfortunately, pecan trees require around six to ten years of time, effort, and nurturing before they start to produce any nuts. Your family decides that the initial investment of time and effort is worth the future payoff and so they get to work and after ten years of time and effort without any guarantees, the pecan trees start to provide nuts. Your family has worked hard for the past ten years and can finally slow down a bit and enjoy the dividends of their investments. Research, planning, sacrifice, time and effort has finally paid off!

One of your neighbors on the other hand is able bodied but isn't much of a planner. They don't like to work for things that don't give him or her instant satisfaction, or they're straight up lazy. They're always short on food and constantly asking you and your other neighbors for help. A new tax law gets passed this year which requires a government official to visit each farm in your neighborhood once a month and take 50% of everything that farm produces, compile it with everything gathered from the other farms, and equally divvy it up between you and your neighbors, after the government takes their portion for the extra work they have to do of course. You've been watching your neighbor swing in a hammock under an oak tree for the last ten years while you and your family have busted your asses. Now you have to share the fruits of your families labor with sleepy hollow next door. You'd be fine with that, right?

If you're ever curious about this "utopia" read about Stalin's first Five-Year Plan, and how the state wanted increased political control of agriculture to feed the rapidly growing urban population and obtain a cheap source of foreign money through increased grain exports. From the mid 1920's into the late 1930's the Soviet Union "collectivized" the peasant farms, mostly in southwest Russia which today is most of Ukraine. The Kulaks (a term referring to ***prosperous*** peasants and anyone else who opposed collectivizations) were forcibly resettled to Siberia, Kazakhstan, and the Russian far North, as well as sent to Gulags (russian prison camps). In 1930 around 20,000 "kulaks" were killed by the Soviet government and by 1936 the Soviet government had "collectivized" almost all of the peasant farms.

During this redistribution of wealth, the farmers destroyed what heavy agricultural machinery they had and slaughtered most of their livestock in defiance. Oddly enough, those who survived only to be sent to the Gulags, were not able to produce much agriculturally, go figure. With the "prosperous" farmers who really knew what they were doing, dead or in jail, production of the new collective farms were hampered just a tad, and widespread famine ensued with the death toll estimated at between 5 and 10 million. Goooooo communism!!

It has been proven time and time again, no matter how well intentioned, that equal or guaranteed outcomes don't work! Equal opportunity however, does work and has been proven. Unfortunately, in the conversation about equality, equality of effort often gets ignored. The fact that you're taking the time and expending the effort to read this book gives me a pretty good idea of where you stand on the subject. Reasonably levied taxes that are efficiently and intelligently spent is a good thing that provides a greater environment for success, for all, no matter what they pursue!

THE LAFFER CURVE

In the early 1980's America was solidly in the grips of stagflation, economic stagnation combined with very high inflation. Desperate for a way out of this nasty economic conundrum and looking for a better path forward for America, the people of the United States overwhelmingly voted for non- incumbent presidential candidate, Ronald Reagan, who won 51% percent of the popular vote and a whopping 489 electoral votes. Knowing how important a strong stable economy is and understanding that the federal governments role is to support the individual states, he implemented policies to limit big government and fix the economy. He accomplished this by surrounding himself with smart people, just one of them being Art Laffer, an economist who Reagan placed on his Economic Policy Advisory Board from 1981-1989.

Laffer had a unique view of tax rates and tax revenues. He came up with a bell curve where a 0% tax rate on the left side of the bell, brings in no tax revenues, which makes perfect sense, and a 100% tax rate on the right side of the bell, that also brings in no tax revenues. Basically his theory, and the bell curve, suggests that there is a sweet spot in tax rates where people are willing to be honest and pay their taxes at that rate. As you slide down towards the lower end of the curve, people are still honest and willing to pay their taxes but because the rate is lower, tax revenues decline. As you slide towards the higher tax rate side of the bell curve, people begin to feel that they are being excessively taxed and thus begin to be dishonest and not pay the taxes that they owe. The higher you raise the tax rate, the less people are willing to pay and thus tax revenues fall even further. *(If you're ever curious about this theory, just research Greece and there tax rates versus revenues!)*

MILLAGE RATES

Taxes on real property are in most cases, a big revenue driver for your local government. Real property is assessed or given a value every year by the local taxing authority. This value is then taxed at a certain percentage, often called the "millage" rate. A mill is one thousandth of a dollar. The millage rate is the multiplier used for each $1,000 of property value. For example, if a property has an assessed value of $100,000 and a millage rate of 1.7534, the tax bill would be $175.34. Now, this is probably only one entity's tax rate, say the public library. Your area will most likely have a bunch of entities that need your tax dollars and they'll all gang up on you at the end of the year and make your multiplier look more like this, 17.534.

AN IDEA OF HOW MUNICIPALITIES COME UP WITH PROPERTY TAX RATES

In simple terms, the taxing authority gathers the assessed values of all the properties in its jurisdiction and applies whatever millage rate that's required to pay its bills that year. In my early research of trying to understand property taxes, I looked at all of the millage rates in central Florida. I was amazed at some of the results. One municipality or county would have very little services but a very high (relatively speaking) millage rate. On the other hand, this famously wealthy area of central Florida which also had better services, had the lowest rate. What gives? I'm sure some of you have already guessed, but I had to dig deeper. So I picked two areas that had the biggest difference in millage rates and I looked at their budgets for that year, the number of assessed properties, and the total assessed value of those properties. It instantly made sense. Wealthy area "X" had fewer properties and businesses but the assessed value of those properties were through the roof!

The much, much less wealthy area "Y" had about 30% more properties, but had a substantially lower total assessed value. *Disclaimer* – I've never worked for a taxing authority and I'm making presumptions based on a small set of publicly available data. What I deduced was, it takes a certain amount of money to run a certain sized municipality with a given amount and level of services. Area "X" was much smaller than area "Y" but had many more services at a higher level. Area "X"'s total millage rate was only 17.00 or 1.7% of ***total*** assessed value (at the time). Area "Y" on the other hand was much larger and had more properties but had less services at a much lower level. Area "X"'s yearly budget was say, $50 million and area "Y"'s budget was say, $25 million. Area "X"'s total property value was $2.93 billion and area "Y"'s total property value was $1.12 billion. Area "Y"'s total millage rate was 20.3 or 2.3% of ***total*** assessed value (at the time).

So even though area "X"'s tax rate was around 26% lower than area "Y"'s, property owners in area "X" paid ***DOUBLE*** the amount of taxes than property "Y"'s did. Not to mention, there were physically less properties in area "X", by a wide margin, than area "Y", so they actually paid more than double!

So what does this all mean for you? Whatever your municipality's budget needs are, they're going to get by adjusting the millage rate and in some cases the assessed value or both. One year, I had several of my properties subject to a 10% increase in assessed value and an almost 8% increase in the millage rate, ***in one year***! I've had some well to do friends over the years relate that their property tax ***rates*** are absurd and that they have to pay $12,000 or $15,000 a year. From my research on the subject, I gently explain to them that they actually have a very low tax rate of around 1.5% of total assessed value compared to where I live that's 2.3%, it's the fact that their houses are assessed north of $900,000. You can't have it all!

Their $900,000 house at 1.5% makes for a $13,500 yearly tax bill versus, at the time, my primary residence which had an assessed value of "only" $330,000 at a tax rate of 2.3% which equated to a yearly tax bill of $7,590. So, even though my property value was only 37% of theirs, my tax bill was more than 56% of theirs. This usually quiets them down. Anyway, it should be obvious now that just because a property has a low millage rate doesn't mean it's going to have a low tax bill. All of a properties tax information is public record and usually available online.

HOW TO FIND PROPERTY TAX INFORMATION

This information is usually found on the local authority's "property appraisers" website. The first thing you need to do is find out the exact jurisdiction that the property is under. Most often this is easy, but occasionally can be a bit more tricky. In my area there's a municipality called The City of Winter Park. Let's say that you're looking to buy Rollins College which is addressed to 1000 Holt ave. Winter Park, FL. 32789 and you want to find the property taxes that you'll have to pay (buckle up!). If you don't know any better, you may try to find the Winter Park Property Appraisers website with no results.

After a while you'll probably ask someone about this and they'll tell you that there is no Winter Park Property Appraisers site and Rollins

College is located in Orange County and will be listed on the Orange County Property Appraisers website. So even though Rollins College is within the City Limits of Winter Park and the Winter Park Police and Fire Departments would respond to this address, it's listed under the Orange County Property Appraisers website. Ok, I get it now, Winter Park is in Orange County and if I want to find a property I need to go to the county website for that property not necessarily the city's name, cool.

Now, let's say you're looking to buy Lake Howell High School which has an address of 4200 Dike Rd. Winter Park, FL. 32792. Cool, you learned that Winter Park is in Orange County so you'll just zip on over to the Orange County Property Appraisers website and find, nothing! Maybe you didn't type it in right, nope, still nothing. After some research you'll find that Lake Howell High School is no where near the city limits of Winter Park and not in Orange County FL. Hmmm. This is the scenario where it can be a pain in the backside to find out where a property is listed. The school and the houses surrounding it all have a Winter Park address and zip code but happen to be in Seminole County FL. Why? Who knows? The Seminole County Police and Fire Departments will respond to these addresses not Winter Park or Orange County.

I run into this often when looking for properties in other states where I'm not too familiar with jurisdictional lines and names. If I'm looking for a vacation rental to buy it may be addressed to the widely known local attraction but listed under some obscure county, township, or parish that no one has ever heard of. This can happen anywhere, so be patient.

Find the correct property appraiser or taxing authority's website and search for that property by address or owners name. When it pops up there are usually multiple different tabs to choose from. Go to the values and taxes tab. This will bring up a bunch of information. It will give you the assessed value of the property, whether there are tax exemptions on the property, what last years tax bill was and possibly breakdown the millage rate. As stated before, in my experience tax rates are expressed per $1000 of value, hence the "mill" in millage rate. So, to make it easy on me, I just take the millage rate and divide it by 1000 so I can use that to multiply the total assessed value which would look like this; Millage rate = 19.537 / 1000 = .019537. Total assessed value = $421,296 x .019537 = $8,230.86

per year. This would be your tax bill for that year ***not*** including any fixed costs or Non-Ad Valorem assessments like garbage collection or street lights where everyone pays the same amount regardless of the value of their property.

Now that you know how to find a property on the appraisers sight you'll be able to access all kinds of information about that property like, its construction type, age, property lines, square footage, numbers of bedrooms and bathrooms, values, taxes, exemptions, sales dates and prices, zoning and sometimes permits and a link to mortgage information. As you can imagine all of that information is very valuable and can save you a bunch of time. Be warned however, the information listed isn't always 100% accurate so you need to confirm!

When that 1962 house you're looking at was built it was 1200 square feet and had two bedrooms and one bathroom. Somewhere along the line somebody may have changed the interior layout to a three bedroom, one bathroom but it's still listed as a 2/1. The most important things you want look at are age, zoning, last sale date and millage rate. People, whether investors or not, often get tripped up here and when next tax year rolls around, they're eating Ramen noodles and hot dogs to pay for it.

TAX EXEMPTIONS AND NEXT YEAR'S TAX TRAP

You see, in Florida we have certain tax exemptions like Homestead, and tax savings plans like Save Our Homes that was enacted in the early 1990's. Homestead basically allows you to take $50,000 off of your primary residences taxable or assessed value and Save Our Homes says the assessed value after year one cannot increase more than 3% per year or the percentage change in the CPI (Consumer Price Index), whichever is less. That's cool, but why would I care? Say you're looking at a house for you to live in or for investment. Say it's a single family residential (SFR) or a 2-4 family property where the owner lives in one of the units.

Say in 1969 a young serviceman buys a home near base to live in. He ends up living there until he passes away in 2020. You go to buy it using a mortgage and during the process the bank gives you an estimated P&I monthly payment of $1,200 and a monthly T&I payment of $200, for a total monthly payment of $1,400. Awesome, your total mortgage payment is going to be $1,400 a month. You figure that you can afford that if you're going to be living in it and if you're buying it for investment purposes, you've researched and found that you can rent it for around $1,400 to $1,500 a month. So, you've run your numbers and everything looks good! You buy it and your monthly payment comes in at almost exactly what the bank estimated, $1,402 a month.

You happily go about your business for the next ten or so months when you receive a letter in the mail from the mortgage servicing company stating your property taxes have gone up and you have an escrow shortage. Remember, escrow is where you task the mortgage servicing company with estimating, collecting, and paying your yearly property taxes and homeowners insurance. During the loan process the mortgage company looked at the most recent property taxes for the house and the insurance quote that you had provided. They add these together and then usually add a buffer of around 1/6th the total amount, presumably for inflation.

The letter states you have an escrow shortage of $5054.00 and you can conveniently send them a check for the shortage or they can simply divide the shortage by twelve and add it to your monthly payment. So, mail them a check or pay an extra $421.16 a month, no big deal, you've got that right? I don't know about you but an extra $421 a month is a punch in the gut for most people and some may not be able to do it at all. You have to be careful!

So what in the heck happened here? When the serviceman bought his house in 1969 it was valued at $21,000. The assessed value of the home increased each year by around 3% for last 51 years which, when compounded equates to an assessed value of $94,823 in 2020. On the other hand, actual home prices have gone up substantially more than this due to population and economic growth over the last 51 years. Mr. Serviceman is smart and also takes advantage of Florida's homestead exemption to reduce his property tax burden by $50,000 which brings his homes taxable value from $94,823 to only $44,823.

Let's say the millage rate is 2% of total value which would equate to a 2020 total tax bill of $896.46. Pretty awesome! When your mortgage company puts together an estimate for what your payment is going to be they look at the last tax bill that was levied and add some buffer, let's say 3%. So this would equate to $896 x .03 = $923. If we take $923 and divide it by 12 we get a monthly tax payment of $77. If we add that to our $1,500 homeowners insurance quote when divided by 12 equals $125 a month, we a get a total monthly T&I (taxes and insurance) payment of $202. Combine that with our estimated P&I payment of $1,200 equates to our total monthly mortgage payment of $1,402. Right on track so far.

So almost a year later the property appraiser sees that you bought the servicemans house for $350,000 and gets a warm fuzzy feeling inside. That arms length transaction just put a new value on the servicemans house of $350,000. The appraiser doesn't want any aggravation from you on this so he or she discounts or sets the new appraised value around 10% to 15% less than what you paid for it which in our example would be $297,500. The new assessed value is now $297,500 multiplied by the total millage rate of 2% equates to a new tax bill of $5950! Yikes!

So the difference between last years tax bill and this years tax bill is $5054.00, pay up sucka! Assuming your homeowners insurance didn't go up and not counting whatever buffer they apply to your escrow, your monthly payment just went up by $421 a month to $1,821! That's an enormous difference for anyone and if you're an investor could put your rental property solidly in the red (losing money)! This is a more extreme example, but does happen, and I use it to illustrate the fact that when buying a property YOU have to do your best to understand all aspects of the transaction and limit your trust in others. This is why YOU need to make your own PITI estimate using a mortgage calculator, your homeowners insurance (HOI) quote, and the millage rate for the property based on the expected purchase price.

USING NEXT YEAR'S PROPERTY TAX TRAP TO YOUR ADVANTAGE

As you get more experience and add more properties to your portfolio you can use this mortgage company oversight to your advantage. For example many investors buy properties that are in disrepair and thus bring in low rents. You may be on the edge of qualifying for your next property but know that in a few months your renovation of an older property is going to bring in an extra $900 a month. In this case you'll happily accept the mortgage companies oversight and subsequently lower monthly mortgage payment so that you can qualify for and buy that property. You just have to be disciplined and know that the mortgage payment is going way up next year.

HOW TO CALCULATE NEXT YEAR'S PROPERTY TAXES ON A NEW PURCHASE

Say you've purchased a new property or your thinking about it, and you want to have a fairly accurate idea of what your property taxes are going to be next year. Finding next year's property tax equation would look like this:

Expected purchase price - $450,000
Millage rate – 18.2635/1000 = .0182635

$450,000 x .90 (property appraisers discount) = $405,000
(the new assessed value)

The new assessed value is $405,000 x .0182635
(the total millage rate) = $7,396.72

The new tax bill when this assessed value takes affect will be $7,396.72

This doesn't include any Non-Ad Valorem charges that your area may have

If your area has a Non-Ad Valorem charge say for garbage and recycling, of $322.12. You would simply add this to your Yearly tax bill.

$7,396.72 (Ad-Valorem) + $322.12 (Non-Ad-Valorem) = $7718.84

If this will be your primary residence and you file for and receive $50,000 in homestead exemptions, the process would look like this:

Expected purchase price - $450,000 x .90
(appraisers discount) = $405,000

New appraised value - $405,000 - $50,000
(homestead exemption) = $355,000

New appraised value after homestead exemption -
$355,000 x .0182635 (mill. rate) = $6,483.54

$6,483,54 (new tax bill) + $322.12 (Non-Ad Valorem) = $6,805.66
(total new tax bill)

As you can see, the homestead exemption provides you with a tax savings of $913.18. Using this method has allowed me to very accurately predict what my total monthly payment will be. Try to find the appraiser discount trends, if any, in your area.

CHAPTER 5

REALTORS AND MORTGAGE ORIGINATORS

A quick takeaway from this chapter.

- **Buyer beware - salespeople want you to buy what they're selling**
- **Find good partners and build relationships**
- **Before you throw stones, take a look in the mirror**

In the previous chapter I gave an example of next year's property tax bill jacking up your mortgage payment and possibly sending you looking for a second job. Now I know what some of you are thinking, why doesn't the realtor or mortgage originator make you aware of this? I'm sure the reasons could range from ignorance to deviance but in either case, your going to be stuck with a problem for a given period of time that is easily avoidable. In my opinion, your realtor and or mortgage originator should make you aware of this little hiccup that happens in their industry. That said, it's also my opinion that some realtors leave ***MUCH*** to be desired! They're simply there to open the door, cheer you on and get you excited about the nice things in a property and divert your attention or downplay the negative aspects of a property in order to make a sale.

The house has aluminum wiring, "oh, that can easily be changed, and just look at these beautiful granite counters." I heard that I might have a hard time insuring a property with aluminum wiring, "oh, would you just look at this beautiful claw foot tub, they don't make those anymore you know." I've definitely witnessed a lot of bullshit over the years and I do have family members who are realtors. If you find a good, honest realtor that cares, stick with them and promote them to others.

All that said, if we're throwing stones, we also have to be fair and take a look in the mirror. Having realtors in the family, I've watched people run them around like crazy any time of the day and any day of the week. Calls and text messages about properties that they want answered immediately. Appointments for showings that they never show up for. Find out information on this property and that homeowners association. Showings at properties they can't qualify for. The realtor spends all of this time, effort, and money in fuel, running around all over the place just to get dumped without warning because the buyers family member just became a realtor and their going to use them.

The same goes for your mortgage originator. I've watched people have an originator do a bunch of work only to bail on them and go down the street to save some $300 fee that the originator charges. In my opinion, we need to go back to building relationships instead of simply trying to find the lowest price on everything. Remember, good investors look for value, not price. The value you'll receive over time will far exceed the money you save by jumping around. In the end, it doesn't matter who you're dealing with, a general contractor, realtor, or lawn maintenance guy, remember that they are people too and need to provide for their families. So, if you want success in any business, I suggest that you not be too greedy and you'll find that people will take care of you!

CHAPTER 6

HAZARD INSURANCE

A quick takeaway from this chapter.

- **Make sure you get the right policy – SFR, income property, owner occupied**
- **Not all properties are insurable – don't make this fatal mistake!**
- **Insurance companies don't like certain properties – read EXPENSIVE**
- **ISO ratings can help or hurt your wallet**
- **Buying a rental close to the beach – hope you have lots of spare cash**
- **Not all policies are the same, don't let this crush you – ACV vs. Replacement cost**
- **Make sure that you have Law and Ordinance**

Let's switch gears and talk about something fun, let's talk about insurance! Oh yeah! I can feel the energy! Clearly I'm kidding, but we have to talk about it anyway so here goes. Hazard insurance, commonly known as homeowners insurance, which is often abbreviated as HOI, is required on a residential property that you finance with a bank. Whatever lending institution that you use will require you to maintain hazard insurance with adequate levels of coverage as long as you have a mortgage with them. If you do not maintain this insurance with adequate levels of coverage, they will insure it for you for five times the cost of adequate insurance, for a given period of time, before they foreclose on you for a breach of contract.

That said, I personally don't know of anyone who has tested the waters on this and let there insurance lapse long enough for the lender to take any action other than sending them a warning letter and insuring their property for an exorbitant price. I can't speak for all mortgages of course, but the ones that I've had also state that they have the right to reject or pick themselves, an insurance company and policy that they deem appropriate. Also, when they insure you and send you the bill, if you don't pay it upon receipt, they add it to your mortgages outstanding balance which of course, accrues interest. Suffice to say, the lender wants their investment insured against loss at all times.

DIFFERENT TYPES OF POLICIES

There are two basic types of hazard insurance that you're most likely to deal with when first starting out, an HO3 policy and a DP3 policy. An HO3 policy is a home owners insurance policy where the owner lives in the insured property. It is usually cheaper than a DP3 policy, all other things being equal, because you live there. An HO3 policy will typically cover the structure, furnishings and other items inside the home, certain other structures outside the home along with a given amount of liability protection.

A DP3 or dwelling fire policy is for non-owner occupied properties that are being rented. A DP3 policy typically covers the structure only and has a given amount of liability protection. DP3 policies can have endorsements added to them to cover sheds and barns, loss of rental income and damage to any personal property that the landlord may have like an oven or microwave.

THE NEWBIE FATAL MISTAKE

Hazard insurance is a tricky thing that if you're not careful, can really blow up your returns on a property. You see, unless you're a cash buyer, you have to have hazard insurance. Just because a property is listed for sale, doesn't mean it has insurance on it or is itself insurable! Over time, and at the drop of a hat, insurance companies change what types of properties and in what locations that they want to insure. You've paid your insurance premiums on time for the last seven years, guess who doesn't care? We regret to inform you that we will not be renewing the insurance for the property at 123 any street...because....we don't want to! You have 30 days to find new insurance, any balance that you have with us will be returned to you within 30 days, thank you and have great day!

Annoying, but manageable, right? Hmmm....maybe. You start calling around to get new insurance only to find that your former insurance carrier is not the only one who won't insure your property! You could suddenly have BIG problems! Hopefully you find a carrier that will take on the risk that is your property, but the premium quadruples, oops, sorry! At worst, you'll have to sell, no joke! Now that I have you scared, remember, I operate in Florida where we have frequent violent thunderstorms and as you're most definitely aware, get tossed around by hurricanes. Newer, smaller, companies will try to gain a foothold in our market and unfortunately have bad timing or luck and end up not having enough reserves built up when a bad storm strikes. Some of them survive but need to take drastic measures to reduce their risk profile by not renewing policies and of course, raise their prices on the policies that they keep. Others get liquidated by the state. Others, for seemingly no obvious reason, decide to quit writing policies in Florida altogether. Maybe they insure other parts of the country and have sustained big losses somewhere else, who knows.

So, if you're in an area that is prone to unexpected environmental losses, you're probably going to have to deal with this. One concept that I want to drive home is, insurance companies want you to pay them, but they don't want to pay any claims. Sarcasm aside, Insurance companies, like lenders, like things, neat, tidy, and easy. They want prospective clients to fall into neat little boxes that they have pre-made so they can easily assess risk. If your property happens to fall outside of these neat little boxes, you may pay substantially higher premiums or not be able to get insurance at all!

WHAT INSURANCE CO'S LIKE AND DON'T LIKE

Now would be a good time to talk about what insurance companies like and don't like. Insurance companies like concrete bunkers in the middle of the desert, with no vegetation any where as far as the eye can see, with a 24 hour, fully manned, ISO 1, fire station within 100 feet and a fire hydrant in the front yard with an endless supply of high pressure water, seriously! Just about anything and everything to them is a possible hazard. No matter what it is, they're going to find something that they don't like about. Love them or hate them, we need them, most people would not be able to own a home without them. Most people barely have enough money to get into a house when they're first starting out, no less have an extra $20,000 cash to replace a roof that got destroyed in a storm.

Jokes aside, in my opinion, insurance companies like "risks" that they have experience with so there loss models are accurate and predictable. They like your typical single family, owner occupied homes, the newer the better, that are constructed with concrete block and have a hip style roof, more than 25 miles from the coast, within 1000' of a hydrant and within 5 miles of a highly insurance rated, fire station. This is a great start but there are more details that go into how much they like or dislike your property.

Is that fire station that's within 5 miles of your house fully manned 24 hours a day? How many firefighters are on shift at any one time? What type of equipment do they have? How much water is carried on each truck? How many of that equipment do they have? How much training do they do each year? How good are they – in dollars – how much property do they save each year? How good is the network that handles your 911 call? How good is the municipal water system that supplies all of the fire hydrants?

ISO RATINGS

There's a lot that goes into the Insurance Services Office (ISO) rating that is given to fire departments, but basically the best scenario is to have a property that is covered by a fire department with the lowest ISO number, ISO 1, like being number 1 in your class. The higher the number, the lower the level of service that they provide. Fire departments work extremely hard to achieve an ISO rating of 1. If your property is covered by a fire department with an ISO 1 rating, you will pay the least amount for hazard insurance. ISO has ratings from 1-10.

Other very important aspects the insurance companies consider are related to geographic location. If you happen to live in an area that has very benign wind related weather events then they probably won't care much about the shape of your roof. If you happen to live where there's a lot of high wind related weather events, Florida, tornado alley, than they'll want to see a hip style roof. See the building construction section of this book. They also don't like properties in geologically active areas, be it earthquake, settling like sinkholes or areas of possible erosion.

HOW CLOSE YOU ARE TO THE WATER CAN MAKE A HUGE DIFFERENCE

A huge factor in price in tropically active areas, say, from North Carolina to the Florida Keys, is the distance of the property as the crow flies, from the ocean. If you're on a barrier island, faggettaboutit! You're going to pay astronomical rates, NOT including flood insurance. Yes, you read that right, not including flood insurance. Expect rates in the range of 2% to 3% of the properties value, ie; that 1960's built 1200 square foot, 2/1, that you bought in the Florida Keys will cost you in the neighborhood of $7,500 a year, GET SOME!!

The next line of demarcation is within 5 miles of the ocean. If you're within 5 miles of the ocean, as the crow flies, you're still going to pay a ton but probably not as much as being on a barrier island. After that there's the 5 to 25 miles from the ocean range, sometimes referred to as Tier 1, depending on where you live. They like this range slightly better, or maybe a better way to describe it is, they don't dislike it as much. 25 miles or more from the ocean is where you'll find more normal rates.

So, you'd better do some research before buy that super deal beachside quadplex! Say you have a quadplex that's 50 miles from the beach and is for sale for $550,000. You put 25% down or $137,500, so you finance $412,500 for 30 years at a fixed rate of 4.25%, which gives you a monthly P&I payment of $2,029. Taxes on a $550,000 quadplex are $550,000 x .85 (property appraisers discount) x .02 (2% tax rate) = $9,350 a year. Hazard insurance is $1,600 a year. Taxes $9,350 + Insurance $1,600 = $10,950 a year. Your T&I monthly payment will be $10,950 / 12 = $912.50. You P&I $2,029 + T&I $912.50 = $2,941.50, so your total monthly mortgage payment will be $2,941.50.

Say this property rents for $850 a month per unit and for this scenario we'll assume a 100% occupancy rate (meaning your tenants stay for as long as you own the property – there's no turnover). So, $850 per month times four units equates to $3,400 per month in gross income. So we take our gross rents of $3,400 minus our total monthly mortgage of $2,941 and we have $459 per month net or positive cash flow which translates to $5,508 per year. Let's look at our one year return for practice. If we take our yearly positive cash flow of $5,508 and divide it by the total amount of money it cost us to buy the place, $137,500 for the down payment and $5,500 in closing costs for a total cash to close of $143,000, we get $5,508 / $143,000 = .0385 or 3.9% cash on cash return.

Now let's look at appreciation. We take the purchase price of $550,000 x the typical average inflation rate of 3%, $550,000 x .03 = $16,500 a year in appreciation. Next we'll look at our principle paydown of around $550 per month or $6,600 a year. Next we'll add them all together, cash flow $5,508 + appreciation $16,500 + principle paydown $6,600 = $28,608 a year in "capitalization". Next we take our total income of $28,608 and divide it by the total money it cost us to buy the place of $143,000, $28,608 / $143,000 = .2000 or 20%. So, this property has a total cap rate of 20%, pretty good!

Now let's say that same quadplex pops up by the beach for the same price, great deal right? Let's find out. We'll use all the same numbers except we'll change our hazard insurance from $1,600 per year to $7,500 per year. Our P&I is $2,029 and our new T&I is $9,350 + $7,500 = $16,850, so $16,850 / 12 = $1,404 per month. P&I $2,029 + T&I $1,404 = $3,433 per month total mortgage payment. Oops, looks like we're now coming out of pocket $33 a month! Let's look at how this affects our total return on this property. Appreciation $16,500 + principle paydown $6,600 = $23,100, now we're coming out of pocket $33 each month, times 12 months equals -$396 per year. Now we have to back out our negative cash flow, $23,100 - $396 = $22,704 of total capitalization or income. Now we take our yearly income of $23,100 and divide by our total cash to close of $143,000 to get .15876 or 15.9%. Still a good return but 4% lower and you're coming out of pocket $33 a month.

In regards to the last scenario there's something I think you should consider. I've noticed over the years that, at our level, most investors sentiment towards their properties turns exceptionally sour to down right resentful when they don't have anything tangible from their property at the end of every month. This investment still returns a solid 15.9% but is cash flow negative. The real big investors who need to park excess cash somewhere don't seem to mind much but the little guy who's mowing the lawn and fixing the dishwasher does. Food for thought.

Moving on. As stated later in the building construction section, insurance companies don't like any number of products for various reasons and thumb their noses at certain construction types. Regardless of whether the product is actually of poor quality or the installation stinks, they will just decide that they don't like a certain product. So one can't truly be sure that a product that is widely accepted today won't be blacklisted ten years from now. Speaking of moving the goal posts, architectural shingles usually have around a 30 year lifespan from the manufacturer. As of recently in Florida, many insurance companies will not insure a property with a 30 year architectural shingle roof, where that roof is older than 10 to 15 years! So, if your roof was installed 15 years ago and is still in great shape, they won't insure your property, awesome! This is why it's important to read the building construction portion of this book. I know it's not exactly riveting, but try to push through it!

In the policies themselves, look carefully at what is covered, and for how much. It has been my experience that some (maybe all) insurance companies, use computer models or algorithms that make assumptions about you and your property before spitting out a quote. When you call to get a quote, the insurance agent punches the address into the insurance companies computer which then tabulates local construction costs to rebuild your house if it was ever destroyed. As I'm sure you are aware, the same house can be built with multiple levels of upgrades to floors, countertops, cabinets, etc. It would be in your best interest to make sure the agent is punching in the correct level of finishings that your home has so you don't pay for coverage of granite counters when you have formica.

Another thing to watch out for are all the sub endorsements (if I'm saying that right) that make up your policy. Your policy may look something like this,

Replacement Value - $350,000
Other structures - $35,000
Personal property - $175,000
Loss of use/additional living expenses - $60,000
Personal liability - $300,000
Medical payments to others - $5,000

If you add those all together it's a lot of coverage that you're paying for. Do you really have a shed or fence that's worth $35,000? Do you really have $175,000 in furniture and personal belongings?

In my guestimation, these coverages are calculated using a multiplier of your properties value. For instance, "other structures" is 10% of your properties value, "personal property is 20-50% of your properties value. These values seem to be auto-generated, so if you don't have $175,000 worth of personal property, you're paying for coverage you don't need. So don't be afraid to ask your agent to lower these coverages to whatever you're comfortable with or their minimums (because they won't allow you to put certain coverages to zero).

REPLACEMENT COST VS. ACTUAL CASH VALUE

Now comes a few big ones that you'll want to learn, ACV or Actual Cash Value, Replacement Cost, and Law and Ordinance. You call agent "A" to get a quote, you have them adjust your coverages to suit your needs and you get a premium of $1,750 for the year, not bad. You then call agent "B" and do the same thing, but you get a quote of $1,150 for the year. Wow! I'll take it! Not so fast amigo! Are the two policies equal? They are exactly equal, except.... Agent "A"'s policy says "Replacement Cost" at the top and agent "B"'s says ACV or Actual Cash Value. There's a slight difference between the two, and yes I'm being sarcastic. A Replacement

Cost policy pays you whatever it costs to replace the structure. An ACV or Actual Cash Value policy lets the insurance company decide how much your property is worth based on how long you've been there. In the tax write off section I explain how the IRS will allow you to depreciate a building over time decreasing the amount of taxes that you pay. Well this is exactly the same except you **LOSE** on this one.

Say you started a policy with a structure value of $300,000, you keep your insurance company for the next five years and then a tree falls on your roof and destroys it. You call your insurance company and file a claim. After jumping through however many hoops you find out that it's estimated to cost you $25,000 to replace/repair your roof. Whatever, the insurance company is going to pay it so you're expecting a check for $25,000, cool. The insurance company comes back and says that their sending you a check for $16,665, thanks for shopping with ABC Insurance co., have a wonderful day!

Whoa! Hold on just a minute! I've paid my insurance on time for the last five years, I should be getting a check for $25,000! Well sir/madam, your roof has depreciated in value over the past five years. Your original roof value was $25,000, we assume that it will only last 15 years so if you take $25,000 and divide it by 15 years you get a depreciation of $1,667 per year. It's been five years since you began your policy so 5 x $1,667 = $8,335. Now we take your estimate of $25,000 and subtract the depreciated value of $8,335 to get a reimbursement of $16,665. I guess they figure that their not going to pay you for the portion of time that you used the roof.

LAW AND ORDINANCE

The next thing to ask about is "Law and Ordinance". Say your home, which was built in 1965, unfortunately suffers significant fire damage in 2015. Building codes have changed a lot since 1965 and to rebuild is going to require additional costs. Your municipality may require you to bring your structure up to new code if a certain portion of it is destroyed, say more than 51%. Even though 49% of your roof is fine, it is not tied to the exterior walls with straps and must be going forward. This is an additional cost which may be significant. Law and Ordinance is designed to mitigate a portion of this depending on how much extra it will cost to fix your property. The typical coverage I've seen is 4% over what the insurance company estimates.

In summary, if you're not buying with all cash, the insurance company will dictate what you can buy and where, and to some degree, how much you can pay for it. Call multiple companies before you buy a property and make sure that you're comparing apples to apples as far as policies go. Also, if you're scraping the bottom of the barrel for as cheap a policy as possible, make sure you take a look at what your biggest risk may be, hurricane, landslide, earthquake, etc. and of course the probability of that risk. If your probability is somewhat high, I'd be sure to check the financial health of the insurance company and it's reinsurance company, if applicable. Insurance companies can and do go bankrupt and if they paid their last dollar to your neighbor, you lose.

CHAPTER 7

THE LOAN PROCESS

A quick takeaway from this chapter.

- **Don't nickle and dime – build relationships**
- **There's a list of things the loan originator is going to want from you**
- **Be ready to scramble for things, explain financial events, and hurry up and wait**
- **The appraisal came in low – don't get excited yet**
- **Be conservative in your calculations, the bank may not give full credit for your rents**
- **Be EXTREMELY careful with wire transfers**

In previous chapters I've told you what the banks and credit agencies are looking for and how to get your financial house in order while saving as much as you can. We will now take an exhilarating look at the loan process in a little more detail, yeah! So we got our financial house in order, by reducing debt service to as low as possible, increasing our savings as much as possible and keeping our income and expenses as smooth and boring as possible. Now we need to find a lender. If you only plan to buy one income property and be done, you can go to one of the big lenders, as long as you fit neatly into all of their boxes.

You'll probably pay a little more and their lending requirements will be a bit more restrictive but you should be able to get the loan. If you plan on buying multiple properties over a period of time I suggest that you look for a smaller community bank or lender which you can build a relationship with, if you haven't already. Relatively speaking, these smaller lenders are taking a bigger risk by lending to you as they don't have the financial backing of a J.P. Morgan. This is good in two ways, at first they're going to be very strict with you, which will force you to make a safer loan, going forward as you prove yourself to them, they won't require you to fit into all the little boxes that the big banks will.

After a number of years of seeing your face and watching you prove that you're a man or women of your word, these local lenders will be much more willing to stretch and bend things a little for you. They will have a front row seat to see how well your business plan has worked. They better you do and the more disciplined you are, the more they'll be willing to consider things that are outside the box. These local lenders are also much more aware of what's happening in the local market which will aid in the process. Sometimes this will be the difference of you getting the loan or not!

It's rock solid evidence if over the last six years you've been able to save enough money for down payments and emergency cash for three income properties that you've gotten loans for through them. They've been able to watch your paychecks and rental income come in and your bills go out. They've seen how financially disciplined you are and how accurate your rental projections were. All of this will come into play when you want to step up into that 10 unit building and you miss or are outside of a couple of underwriting standards. The odds are that they'll work something out with you instead of just saying, NO!

When you sit down with your loan officer you're going to tell him or her your plans to get an income property, for this example we'll use a duplex. You're going tell them what areas you're looking in and what price range. You're gonna tell them that rents in the area are say \$1,200 per two bedroom unit, the average price of a property is say \$300,000, property taxes and homeowners insurance will come out to be \$558 a month, and with your down payment, your P&I should come out to around \$1,107 a month. If you add all of those together you'll have a total payment of around \$1,665 a month. You'll continue by saying that, to be safe, you're only going to use 70% of the average rent, even though the real occupancy rate (I'll explain this later) is 94%. When you take 70% of your expected rents or \$840 per unit times two units \$1,680 and subtract your total payment of $1,665 a month it will leave you with, conservatively, $15 a month in cash flow.

You may or may not realize it, but that little conversation just gave the loan officer a lot of insight about you. You're clearly not some, I just watched Income Property on HGTV last night, tire kicker. You're also not lazy or ignorant to the many aspects of owning a rental property. You've obviously put a lot of time and effort into researching this thing that you plan to do and are willing to put your money where your mouth is because you're putting 25% down and also have the emergency cash. You will have shown him or her that you also have a plan to make this thing work and you're being very conservative so that if a hiccup happens it won't bury you. I can guarantee you that, whoever the loan officer is, they respect you already! You're not just a dreamer, you're a do'er!

PRE-APPROVAL LETTER

The loan officer will then take a quick snapshot of your financial situation by asking you some questions and possibly getting a credit report on you (they will definitely run your credit report at some point). You make this much money per year, this is how much debt you have, you have this much money for emergency cash, and this much money for a down payment. They will then give you, if warranted, a pre-approval letter stating that you have been pre-approved for a property worth, say, $300,000 with a fixed rate loan of 30 years, at whatever the prevailing interest rate is. Now you have a much better idea of what price range you can buy. Hopefully you've already done a bunch of looking around and know how to spot a good deal!

THINGS THE LOAN ORIGINATOR WILL ASK FOR

The loan officer will then give you a list things that they need from you. Every lender can be different but it will probably look something like this:

1. Your last 2 years tax returns.
2. Your last 2 months paystubs.
3. Your last 2 months checking account statements.

4. Your last two savings account statements (these are often quarterly).
5. Your current mortgage statement (if any).
6. Current retirement account statements.
7. Your retirement account rules.
8. A copy of your driver license or I.D.
9. Any current property insurance policies
10. If you have any current rental properties, a copy of their leases.

YOUR OFFER HAS BEEN ACCEPTED

So you have your pre-approval letter for $300,000, which for now, is the maximum amount you can get a loan for, minus your down payment. Now let's say, you spot a good deal on a duplex for $275,000. In my opinion, it does you no good to let the selling realtor know that you can afford $300,000 by sending in your current pre-approval letter. Call your lender and ask them to please send you a new pre-approval letter for the asking price of $275,000. You run your numbers (you got a brief preview of this earlier in this book) and decide that you want to put in an offer.

Congratulations, your offer has been accepted! You now have to put whatever the deposit amount was, in escrow (kept in the custody of a third party and taking effect only when a specified condition has been fulfilled) and the race begins! You have to get all the requested paperwork in to your loan officer and do all of your inspections on the property in the time frames that are specified in the contract. Typically you'll have a certain number of days to begin the loan process and around 30 days to get your loan finalized.

HURRY UP AND WAIT

Be prepared to hurry up and wait. You'll turn in all of the information originally requested by the loan officer and then, wait. A week will go by and you'll feel like you're on cruise control and then the underwriter (person that looks through all your information and ultimately approves or denies your loan) will tell your loan officer that they need "XYZ" from you and they need it ASAP! Sometimes it's easy, sometimes it's obscure and you'll have no idea how to get it, the loan officer should be able to help but be prepared for the, "I need it right away."

Be prepared to explain in a signed letter(s), why you had an $1,800 withdrawal on such and such a date, or why you had an unusual deposit of "X" amount on another date. Also, as I alluded to earlier in this book, if your Aunt passed away and left you $10,000 that you put into a savings account 5 months ago and you're using it as part of your down payment, the bank is not going to allow it because it's a gift! The underwriter is absolutely going to notice an unusual deposit of $10,000 into your savings account which has quarterly statements and not monthly statements like your checking account.

THE APPRAISAL

Let's say that everything is checking out OK with your down payment money and emergency cash. The underwriter finishes looking at your records, all your debt and income lines up and is accounted for, about this time, the appraisal on the property should be coming in. This appraisal doesn't get done for free and unfortunately you will have to pay for it up front, usually within the first week of your executed contract. The loan officer will probably ask you for a credit card to put the charge on. Appraisal costs can vary greatly depending on the property type and how busy or slow the appraisers are. The farther out of town and bigger the property is (for example my 15 acre farm), the higher the price tag. A cleared quarter acre lot in a neighborhood near downtown, no big deal. A thirty acre wooded lot with a log home and a barn where there's no line of sight from one property line to the next, a lot more! As of the writing of this book it's safe to assume around $600 for the typical duplex near a city.

Hopefully, the appraisal comes in close to what the sales price of the contract is. If you've been working hard and valuing a bunch of properties, it will! The most I've ever been off on the value a property was $10,000. My primary residence, which I was blessed to get in Pre-Foreclosure, was appraised at $10,000 more than I thought it would. Some people get excited if the appraisal comes in below the contract price because they believe this will give them some bargaining power for a lower sales price.

That said, I would definitely try that approach but I can tell you that it is highly dependent on market conditions. In a cold market you'd most definitely be able to negotiate a better/lower price. However, in a hot market, you're more than likely going to be sorry that the property didn't appraise for the contract price. When this happens, typically the buyer won't budge on the price because they know the property will sell. The bank of course will not lend out more money than a property is appraised for, so, you get to make up the difference in cash, if you really want the property. An example would be if the property comes in $20,000 under the contract price. The buyer tells you to go pound sand and the bank says, hey, we'll still do the loan but we're going to need another $20,000 for your down payment. So, come up with an additional $20,000 to put down on the property or no loanski! Bottom line is the bank will only take a risk on 75% of the appraised value for an income property, this is called Loan to Value or LTV.

VACANCY / OCCUPANCY RATES

If the appraisal comes in OK, the underwriter will now take the appraisers expected rents on the property and apply a discount to them. Wait, what? A discount? That's right, before 2008 all one had to do to get a loan was fog a mirror, after 2008 they put you through the ringer. In my experience they take the expected rents and apply a vacancy rate of 30% to them or another way of saying this would be, apply a 70% occupancy rate. What this means is that they expect your rental units to be empty 30% of the year. It doesn't matter that the well established and publicized vacancy rate for your area is only 6%, they're going to apply 30% to your loan, just for fun. Sarcasm aside, if your property still qualifies under these underwriting standards, it will be a very safe investment which will give you higher odds of success.

You can look at vacancy or occupancy rates in two different ways. One is in relation to time and the other is in relation to money but realize that they are, one in the same. For example, if the expected rent from the appraiser is $1,000 a month, at a 100% occupancy rate for the year, this would equate to $12,000 for the year. Now, the bank is planning for the worst and says hey, your units will be empty 30% of the time. So, we can do this by taking 12 months of the year and multiplying by .30 or 30% to come up with 3.6 months. The bank is saying that for 3.6 months of each year, you will receive no rent because your unit will be empty. So, we can do this the hard way and take $1,000 and multiply it by 3.6 to come up with $3,600 and then subtract this from our $12,000 yearly income to come up with $8,400. We can then divide this $8,400 by 12 months to get $700 as our monthly income.

Now I prefer the easy way of doing this and just multiply our expected monthly rent by .70 or 70% and get $700. Time being money, it doesn't matter how you slice it. If you come within $100 or so of making your total monthly mortgage payment at a 70% occupancy rate, I would say that, barring any missteps in your structural and neighborhood evaluations, you have a very safe investment. If the discounted rents don't come in within a $100 or so, of your total mortgage payment, you'll have to have room in your DTI (Debt to Income ratio) to make up the difference.

Right about this time, your deadline to complete all of your due diligence and inspections (you usually have around 15 days after the contract is signed by both parties) is rapidly approaching. It's your last chance to get out of the contract and get your deposit money back. In Florida we have what's called an AS-IS contract that allows the buyer to get out of the contract for any reason as long as they do it within the inspection period. So let's say that everything is looking good, the property passes yours and the inspectors, inspection, and you get final approval for your loan. It's almost a slam dunk from here.

WIRE TRANSFERS

Next, the lender will send you a loan and closing costs estimate. It will have all of the details of your loan costs and how much money you will need to wire for closing. As it gets closer to the closing date, your lender will give you a revised loan and closing estimate. This is because they calculate the interest that they charge you down to the day. A few days before closing you should get wire transfer instructions by the closing agent.

> ***Note:*** *BE EXTREMELY CAREFUL WITH WIRE TRANSFERS AND CONFIRM BY ALL MEANS POSSIBLE THAT YOU ARE WIRING YOUR HARD EARNED MONEY TO THE CORRECT PLACE! WIRE TRANSFER FRAUD IS BIG BUSINESS AND THEY CAN GET IN YOUR EMAIL CHAIN AND GIVE YOU FALSE WIRING INSTRUCTIONS. I DON'T KNOW ABOUT YOU BUT I'D BE BEYOND MAD IF I WIRED $75,000 TO SOME CLOWN OVERSEAS!*

So, you've carefully confirmed all of the wiring instructions and made the transfer when you were supposed to. You're now going to head over to the closing with your picture I.D.. They will confirm that the wire transfer has been completed and you will proceed to sign an absurd amount of paperwork. Make sure to ask how they want you to sign your name, is it with your middle initial or your middle name spelled out? Be sure to sign it the same way on ALL of your paperwork and with the SAME COLOR PEN or you'll be back to sign again. I guess the big banks got real nit-picky on how people signed paperwork after they got busted for forging all those mortgage documents during the financial crisis. After you've signed all the paperwork and paid your closing costs, congratulations, you're the proud new owner of 25% of an income property that you're 100% responsible for managing! Sarcasm aside, it really is a great deal!

CHAPTER 8

TAX WRITE OFF'S

A quick takeaway from this chapter.

- **The tax code heavily favors real estate**
- **Take advantage of the multiple real estate tax write offs**

Disclaimer time – I am not a Certified Public Accountant and nothing in this book should be taken as tax advice! Let's move on to income taxes and how they can be affected by real estate. To say that real estate is a good tax shelter is an understatement! From the single family homeowner to the big boys, the tax code is set up to encourage real estate ownership! I believe the concept behind this is, if you own something, you'll take much better care of it and in doing so will make and keep the area that the real estate is in, much nicer. A nicer environment is conducive to better human results. Whatever way you want to look at it, real estate has very good tax benefits. Let's look at some of them.

Primary Residence – If you own a house that you live in full time, you may reduce your taxable income by the amount of interest that you paid the bank that year on your mortgage. You may also write off interest that you paid on a HELOC (Home Equity Line Of Credit), see IRS rules. There are also tax credits for energy efficient upgrades to your home like windows, HVAC systems, renewable energy like solar and water heaters.

Income Properties - Because income properties are considered a businesses, the IRS lets you write off more things than a primary residence. The number and type of things that you are allowed to write off is more similar to business. The structure of your property will degrade over time and at some point may become obsolete. Those who own a business will liken this to a piece of equipment that wears out over time and must be replaced. The IRS calls this **"depreciation"**, instead of that piece of equipment going up in value over time, or, appreciating, it goes down in value, like a car as it gets older and gains more miles. In either case, the IRS is aware of this and to encourage people to start their own businesses they allow you to reduce your taxable income by a predetermined amount of "depreciation" per year.

These predetermined amounts are referred to as depreciation schedules. The IRS along with business people, have looked at a broad range of items and come up with an acceptable average rate of depreciation. For example, computers, office equipment, vehicles, and appliances are given a depreciation schedule or rate of 5 years. Office furniture for example is given a rate of 7 years. Commercial buildings and non-residential property is given a rate of 39 years. Residential property is given a rate of 27.5 years. Basically what this means is, whatever you paid for that office computer, say $5,000, will be divided by 5 (years) which equals $1,000. You may reduce your taxable income by $1,000, every year, for the next 5 years, after which the IRS will assume that your computer is worthless and you'll have to buy another one. If your computer is still working and you don't buy a new one in year 6, you will no longer get that write off.

In our scenario it would look like this, you buy a $350,000 duplex and the property appraiser has it assessed like this, "Building value" = $250,000, "Land value" = $100,000, for a total value of $350,000. Come tax time, your accountant will take the building value of $250,000 and divide by the number of years that the IRS allows, 27.5, to come up with a yearly depreciation value of $9,090.00. This means that every year that you own and operate all units of that duplex as rental, you may reduce your taxable income by $9,090.00, for the next 27.5 years.

> ***Note:*** *Land is not considered a depreciable asset and as such you can not write it off.*

How the property is valued by the property appraiser is an important item to look at both before and after you purchase as sometimes the land will be valued much higher than the structure which can significantly reduce your write offs. Sometimes this is a mistake and sometimes it's a tax strategy that some previous owner has used in the past. Either way, you typically want the building valued as high as possible in relation to the land, when you first get started. For more reading on this look up IRS recapture!

Mortgage Interest – You may write off 100% of the interest that you pay on an income property regardless of whether you live in the property or not. This is because you can write off 100% of your mortgage interest as a normal homeowner and if you don't live in the property it means that it is being fully used as a rental business.

Property Taxes – The IRS says that you may write off 100% of your income properties taxes as long as 100% of the property is being used as a business, in other words, you don't live in one of the units. If you live in one of the units you must reduce the amount of the write off by whatever percentage of the property that you occupy. For example, if you live in one unit of a duplex, you can only write off 50% of any allowable cost incurred by the duplex. If you live in one unit of a triplex, you may write off 66% of your expenses, a quadplex, 75%. Get it?

Hazard Insurance – You may write off 100% of your property related insurance premiums as long as you don't live in any of the units. If you do, the same rules stated above apply. Are you starting to see a trend?

Operating expenses – Do you need to buy a for rent sign to stick in the yard? What about a hammer drill to make a repair in concrete? Does that online rent collection service charge you anything? Does your CPA charge you to do your taxes for the rental property? What if you need to buy a trailer so that you can take your mower and other lawn equipment over to your rental property so you can mow the lawn? Yes, I mowed all of my properties for the first 11 years… I paid myself $20 per hour in savings….how bad do you want it? After mowing the lawn at your rental for 4 months do you need new lawnmower blades? If the answer is yes to any of these, you can write it off. Basically any expenses that you incur running your rental business can be written off in some form. That said, not all write offs are categorized the same and some can reduce your taxable income that year and others are filed away for when you sell the property. Also, if you live in the property, you guessed it, the same rules above apply. For a greater understanding you should visit the IRS website and or talk to a good CPA who's familiar with real estate rules.

Repairs – You may write off 100% of any and all things related to a repair. Be careful though, you can't decide to rip out perfectly good cabinets and put fancy ones in and call it a repair. The IRS looks at that as a capital improvement and is not necessarily deductible in that year. The IRS views a capital improvement as adding value to a property for years to come and thus will not allow you to deduct the entire cost of the improvement in one tax year. Capital improvements will depreciate slowly, so the government requires you to track and deduct that cost over a period of time. Of course, if you live in it, the same aforementioned rules apply, sorry.

Travel – Your tenant calls you and tells you there's a problem. You drive to the property, find the problem, drive to your local home improvement store and back to the property. The trip from the rental property to the home improvement store and back can be written off.

SAMPLE TAX WRITE OFF SCENARIOS

Here is an example of a hypothetical property that will hopefully help you bring it all together. You have a $350,000 duplex and each side rents for $1,500 per month. The property appraiser has this property valued at $250,000 for the building and $100,000 for the land. In your operations during the year you paid: Lawn service - $150 per month, Property taxes - $5,000 for the year, Hazard insurance - $2,000 for the year, Mortgage interest - $12,643 for the year, You had to have it painted and paid - $2,500, You had to replace and oven - $900, You bought a for rent sign - $9, You paid to advertise your unit for rent - $100, You paid for background checks - $100, You paid for online rent collection service - $50 a month, at the end of the year you paid your CPA to do your taxes - $100. Your cost of doing business would look like this;

Depreciation - $250,000 building value / 27.5 years = $9,090
Lawn maint. - $150 per month x 12 = $1,800
Property Taxes - $5,000
Hazard Insurance - $2,000

Mortgage Interest - $12,643
Paint exterior - $2,500
Replace oven - $900
For rent sign - $9
Advertising - $100
Background checks - $100
Rent collection service - $50 x 12 = $600
CPA = $100
Total = $34,842

Now let's take a look at the income side. You have a typical mortgage on your duplex that consists of $1,385 per month in Principle and Interest payment and $583 per month in Taxes and Insurance for a total of $1,968 a month. If you want to check this for yourself, I used a purchase price of $350,000 and a typical income property loan that requires a 25% down payment which means that you'll need to finance 75% of the purchase price or $262,500. This example uses a 30 year fixed rate mortgage at a 4.85% interest rate. From the above example we have $5,000 in property taxes and $2,000 a year in hazard insurance for a total T&I of $7,000. If we divide $7,000 by 12 we get $583 a month. So, our rents are $1,500 per unit and we have two units so our gross monthly rent is $3,000. If we subtract our mortgage expenses from our rental income, $3,000 - $1,968, we get $1,032 a month in positive cash flow, which is fantastic for a duplex by the way. If we multiply our monthly cash flow we get, $1,032 x 12 = $12,384 per year in positive cash flow. Now putting it all together fro taxes would look like this;

Income - $3000 x 12 = $36,000
Total expenses - $34,842

Income - $36,000 - $34,842 = $1,158 (taxable income from your rental business)

So, for the year, in the IRS's eyes, you made a total of $1,158 in income from your rental property. If you happen to make $50,000 a year from your primary job, you'd have to add another $1,158 to your total taxable income. Some of you may be saying, wait a minute, I had $1,032 a month in cash, every month, that I was putting into my bank account and I had $3,995 in principle paid to the bank for me, but I'm only going to get taxed on $1,185? Welcome to the real estate rental game!

Let's take a closer look at this for a second. You have a $350,000 duplex which is gaining around 3% in value per year (assuming you didn't overpay for it) and your tenants paid $3,995 towards what you owe the bank. So your duplex gained $10,500 in value, the balance that you owe the bank got reduced by $3,995 and you put $12,384 in cash in your pocket, in one year. So the property made $10,500 in appreciation, $3,995 in principle pay down, and $12,384 in cash for a total return of $26,879, and you only got taxed on $1,158. SOLID!

SAMPLE ROI INCLUDING TAX WRITE OFFS

Let's actually analyze the return on this investment. To buy this duplex you needed to put 25% down and will have probably paid around 1.5% in closing costs for a total cash to close of $92,750. I know, that number hurts, you'll get there, keep reading. We effectively used $92,750 of our hard earned cash to buy this property and in year one it returned to us $26,879. If we divide $26,879 by $92,750 we get .28980053908 or 29%. Yes, that's right! Your duplex just gave you a 29% total return! It isn't some electronic share of some stock that can go to zero and it isn't some business that you have to put 70 hours a week into. It's a solid, tangible asset that you can see and touch, has utility – you could live in it if you wanted to, and you only had to do two transactions a month for the year!

So our total CAP rate (capitalization) was 29%, but that includes things like appreciation that I can't touch until I sell and aren't guaranteed. You're absolutely right, lets be more conservative and look at our cash on cash return, what is tangible on a month to month basis. Our net monthly income was $1,032 which gives us $12,384 in cash for the year. We have to back out our lawn service, CPA and online rent processing fees of $2,500 a year which are constant and leaves us with $9,884. If we take $9,984 in cash flow and divide it by the $92,750 in cash that we had to spend to get the duplex, we find that we have a cash on cash return in year one of 10.7%. The long term average return for the stock market is between 7% and 8% after accounting for 2% to 3% inflation.

Well wait a minute, inflation is going to take its toll on that duplex too. It sure is, the cost of your insurance, taxes, lawn service etc. is going to go up by the same 2% to 3% each year. The interest on your loan however, if you got a fixed rate, is not going up. The value of your property will also be affected by inflation by making it more valuable instead of less valuable. You're also going to raise your rents by 2% to 3% every year. So all told, this is an inflation protected investment. I'll take a 10.7% annual cash return from an investment that I can drive by everyday, monitor first hand the economic environment it's in, that has utility, over an 8% return from a digital share of a company that is who knows where, with who knows what going on with it. Even if we're super conservative and we take about 10% off of our total CAP rate, we still have an inflation protected investment that pumps out almost 20% per year! BOOM!

CHAPTER 9

UNDERSTANDING VALUE

A quick takeaway from this chapter.

- **People are willing to pay for things they don't need**
- **Upgrades really payoff – but not all of the time**
- **Landscape can really be a thorn in your side**
- **It's got a pool – think about it**
- **It helps to know your history**
- **Things are expensive now – the reason might surprise you**
- **It's all about supply vs. demand**
- **Uncle Sam is a good guy**
- **Emotions – there's no crying in real estate!**
- **Be careful about who you take advice from**
- **Know your product and your customers**
- **If they could buy a house they probably would**
- **Luck favors the prepared**
- **Don't lose sight of the big picture**

I briefly alluded to understanding value in the "What it takes" chapter, I will expand on it here. One concept I would like you to keep in mind is, it's all just money! Your car, your coffee table, the coffee you're drinking, etc. Now, that said, your money is equal to time and effort. The aforementioned coffee cost you around 8 minutes worth of your time and effort at $20 per hour. That car you drive cost you, typically, about a years worth of time and work. A single family house typically costs 3 to 5 times the average salary. The point is, try to take the emotion out of investments because, most likely, the person who is going to buy your multifamily property when you decide to sell, is going to!

Generally speaking, every asset has a certain demand for it based on any singular or combination of factors. These can include emotion – it's so beautiful, I want it, it reminds me of a great time in my life, everyone else has one and I want one too, I want to belong to a group or show that I've done better than a certain group. Utility is another factor – I need a place to stay, I need an apartment, I need to cut a tree down and I need an axe. I need to cut two trees down in the next hour, I need a chainsaw. I need an investment that pays me "X" return. I need an investment that pays me "X" return but I don't want to work that hard on it or I do want to work on that investment because I also want the satisfaction of saying, "look what I did!" I could go on and on.

WHAT MAKES US BUY THINGS

That said, it's my opinion that when you're looking to buy anything that's not a consumable like milk, toilet paper, tires, etc, and not something that is solely for enjoyment or experience, that you need to consider that one day you're going to sell it. Let's look for example at an item that most of us are familiar with and involves a number of the aforementioned factors, a car or truck. A car or truck is an object that evokes emotions and is purposely marketed that way. Super Duty 4wd trucks are always marketed as someone who drives it is hands on, a do it yourself, a trouble shooter, tough and has to deal with tough situations and needs a tough capable truck that can keep up with him or her.

The reality is, most privately owned trucks like that only see a fraction of the duty they're capable of or designed to handle. In the view of utility, for the average person, it's a dumb purchase. They're paying way too much for capabilities that they will seldom, if ever, need or use. On the other hand, if we view it as a combination of utility, emotion, and experience, maybe it's not so dumb. So, our imaginary truck shopper very much needs transportation to and from, occasionally throws a bunch of stuff in the bed to do landscaping at their house and or tows a camper or a boat, feels safe, and like a better driver, because they sit up high and can see traffic better, likes the way trucks look and a little bit of that marketed stereotype that goes along with it. Is it a dumb purchase now? If we sum up the emotional, experiential, and utilitarian factors, one has to ask, what is the price of all of those?

For me it's "X", for you it's "Y", and for someone else it's "C", it's all very personal. The stereotypical older guy that buys the Corvette or Ferrari will almost never use it any differently than a Honda Accord, but the price he paid for all of the emotion and experience that he gets is worth it to him. All that said, it's my opinion that when you're about to buy something you should think about exactly what you're buying, what purpose(s) you're buying it for and who else might want to part ways with their hard earned money for it and why.

In the context of this book, a residential property has a lot of factors to think about and many different potential buyers, which of course, will affect its value. A house has a location that can be desirable or not – utility, a look that's nice or not – emotional for the occupant and utilitarian for the investor. It may have a layout that is good, say a split plan where Mom and Dad are on the other side of the house from the kids or a bad one if the parents have very young kids and would rather be very close to them. Maybe it's built using concrete block which offers the utility of being low maintenance and strong but also has an emotional content of say, the occupant feeling safe in a storm.

IT'S GOT GRANITE COUNTERTOPS, I'LL TAKE IT!

How about Granite counter tops, for the occupant it serves the purpose of holding their food up off of the floor just like Formica counter tops would do, but to them, it also looks nice, and maybe it makes a statement of success to whoever comes over. For the investor, certain colors of granite offer durable counters that hold items up off of the floor just like Formica, but adds value to the property on an emotional level for the renter. They are however significantly more expensive than Formica and are harder to make, install, and remove when damaged. On the other hand, Formica counter tops are super durable, if you don't allow the underlying wood to get wet, cheap, and easy to install and replace. I would say that for any number of reasons, most people would find granite counter tops to be more appealing than Formica to the eye.

The big question is, how much value do the granite counter tops add? How much more money in rent are people willing to spend, to have what holds their food up off of the floor, look nicer? The other big question would be, no matter how much they like those fancy counter tops, do they have the ability to spend more rent money to have them? If the property is such that it supports an owner occupant like a duplex, one day in the future when you go to sell it, you may get a good return on your granite counter top investment because the person will be buying heavily on emotion. On the other hand, if the property is such that the odds of having an owner occupant are very slim, like a six unit building, and the economy in the area just won't support getting any higher rents from those fancy counter tops, the future buyer/investor is not going to pay you for them! That said, if you're the buyer/investor, you shouldn't pay for them! I see this happen all the time. Remember, you have to know who your renter is and who your future buyer will be!

LOVELY LANDSCAPING

Let's look at some other things that our emotions quickly tell us yes, but may not be such a good idea as an investor. Beautiful, park like trees, the occupant will love how they look and they'll provide shade and most likely reduce energy bills. To the investor, it will attract more renters because of the aforementioned which is good, but how much more are they willing to spend in rent to have them? A bunch of trees for the investor is just dollars running out of their pocket. I love trees and I live on many acres surrounded by them, but they are a pain in the ass! All that wonderful shade makes it very hard to keep grass alive and having to rake 30 bags of leaves twice a year isn't much fun either. Things constantly fall out of trees, in the yard, on your tenants cars, on the power lines to the house, on the roof, etc.

Depending on the pitch and material used for the roof, overhanging tree limbs will drop significant amounts of vegetative debris on the roof that will accumulate. This debris will obstruct the removal of rain water and in short time, support bugs and more vegetative growth. You will have to schedule regular roof visits where you blow off all of that debris, which of course you will then need to remove from the yard. Storm season is getting close and you need to have that tree trimmed, that'll be $1,000, no big deal. One of your trees got struck by lightning seven years ago and died, the tree guy says it's just a matter of time before a certain large portion just falls off and crushes your roof. OK, how much to remove it? Well, it's been dead for a while so it's a dangerous removal and of course it's overhanging your building which adds risk, that'll be $7,000 to remove it. Oh, and you have two others that are dead also, have a nice day! How do you quantify the return on investment for these beautiful trees when you don't know how much they're going to cost you over the life of the investment? There are many factors to consider, but suffice to say that trees can literally be, unbelievably expensive to deal with.

POOLS ARE COOL - MAYBE

Let's say that a property that you're looking at has a pool. For the tenant this can be viewed as a big bonus. You have your own pool in the back yard that you can use any time you want. On the other hand, maybe you have very young kids and the pool freaks you out because you're afraid one of them might drown in it. Maybe a lot of renters in your area have dogs and would rather have an open back yard. Maybe the renters love the pool idea but can't stand the thought of having to maintain it which means it's on you. Maybe they're aware enough to realize that the pool pump running 12 hours a day is going to significantly increase their electric bill. I can tell you that the insurance company is going to see that pool as a big risk and of course, charge you for it.

You will most likely not be able to trust your tenants to properly take care of the pool and will quickly get tired of the, "there's something wrong with the pool again, it's green." That said, again, it's now on you! You'll either do the maintenance your self or pay someone to do it. So add up all of the extra expenses that the pool will bring and see if your pool of renters (see what I did there) can and will pay for it? I doubt it! As humans, we all want pretty, nice things, but we rarely want to work any extra or pay any extra for them. Lastly, there's the liability issue.

Is your head spinning yet? Many of the things you may have thought were a good idea may not be. You have to ask yourself, why am I buying this or why am I doing this upgrade? Maybe it won't pay you back in dollars right away but will attract better renters that will be appreciative of these fancy things and take care of your place better. Maybe you just want the place nicer and it's worth spending the money to make it that way even if you don't get it back. As long as you're honest and don't lie to yourself about what you're doing you'll most likely be fine with whatever the results are.

THE STARTER HOME

If you're more confused now about what to look for, fear not, most large companies, thanks to Edward Bernays, the nephew of Sigmund Freud, have already done huge amounts of research into what customers want. If you start to pay closer attention to products you'll start to see trends. An example in our spectrum would be, a couple decides to get married and soon after they want to start having children. They just "formed a household". What they typically do soon after that is look for a single family home, for a number of reasons. They don't want to throw away rent money that they'll never see again or they want to get out of their parents house. They may need or want more space for their growing family. They may suddenly realize that their probably not going to be packing up and moving to Australia now that they have a kid on the way. They may simply want a place of their own that's closer to work or in a good school zone.

Typically, the people that form new households are younger, at the beginning of their careers and thus don't earn as much money and as a result, don't have much in savings. They make up what I would call, a market segment. This market segment has specific demands and a fairly narrow budget that they can spend on those demands. Thus, along comes this beautiful thing called free market capitalism, where some entity notices the demand for this product and ends up producing a product that is specifically tailored to meet those demands and within that segments budget. This entity of course doesn't work for fun and charges a percentage more for this product, in turn consuming other products and providing new work opportunities for more people. So this new household gets what they desire and the company gets money with which they can pay themselves and their workers so everyone can put food on the table. It really is beautiful.

The product that they just created is called a "starter home". It is usually as close as it can be to a business center, but far enough away to keep the price of land down. It has a simple, cheaper design without many upgrades, cheaper paint, cheaper flooring, cheaper appliances, a small yard and small layout. Typical starter homes are around 1,200 square feet, have 3 smaller bedrooms and 2 smaller bathrooms and a small 2 car garage. Over the years I've heard many people complain about this as if they're getting taken advantage of and being sold a small, cheap product. The truth is that these starter homes are specifically designed that way so a new family on a tight budget can afford to buy one and maintain it without breaking the bank.

If this complainer had the money to buy something bigger and "better", they would. So in reality this starter home allowed them to make the jump into home ownership which is a far better financial situation than renting. If this product wasn't available they would have to wait another 3 to 5 years to get into a more expensive "move up" home. If we look into the psyche of this complainer we're likely to find that they imagined that their first home would be of a certain type with a bunch of nice features but stopped well short of figuring out if that dream was anywhere near their financial reality. There's nothing wrong with dreaming but at some point you're going to need to figure out how to go get it.

SOME HISTORY ON VALUE

To get a better understanding of this we should take a somewhat quick look at history. A brand new vacuum cleaner in 1954 cost, at the time, $87.85, and the median household income was $4,200 per year or $81.00 a week. So, you were going to spend about an entire weeks pay on a vacuum cleaner! Take a second to think about that in todays terms. How much do you make for a weeks worth of work? People at the time said, look, if I'm going to pay this much money for a vacuum cleaner, it'd better work very well and last a long time. And if it does break, I'd better be able to fix it myself or go down the street and get it fixed for much less than a brand new vacuum cleaner.

So they paid a lot of money for a vacuum cleaner and when it finally did wear something out or break, they went down the street to the repair shop where experts fixed it quickly and efficiently. That economic model supported the manufacturer, the customers needs and a repair network of fellow Americans. Slowly but surely however, we began to demand things be cheaper. In a free market society, if companies want to stay in business, they had better find a way to give the customer what they want. And so, these companies raced to give us what we demanded. A little thinner here, a little cheaper there. Of course it wasn't enough because we're a demanding bunch. So the company unfortunately had to lay off some workers and in doing so had to ask those who kept their jobs to do more.

The remaining workers may have been afraid that if they didn't pick up the slack, the company may close its doors, so they accepted more work for the same pay. Well, of course it was not enough. Cheaper!! They demanded! In the race to give the customers what they wanted and save their businesses, they began to look elsewhere for cheaper raw materials. They figured that they could go to less developed areas of the world where people are used to getting paid very little in relation to the U.S. and get what they needed for significantly less. And they did!

Somewhere along the line, the price to buy a new vacuum and the price to fix an old vacuum got close enough for people to stop fixing them and just throw away the old one and buy a new one. This of course, drove the final nail in the coffin of all of those Mom and Pop repair stores. They had been struggling for years anyway, you see, as the price of a new product comes down, so must the price to fix it or it no longer makes economic sense. Parts can get cheaper but labor can only go down so much, so fast (productivity), which is why certain sectors of the economy have struggled or failed over time. At the same time, people complained that certain sectors wages have been stagnant.

CPI AND INFLATION

Here is something to consider, according to the Bureau of Labor Statistics (BLS) and the Social Security Administration, the CPI or Consumer

Price Index (The Consumer Price Index is a measure that examines the weighted average of prices of a basket of consumer goods and services), the CPI from 1973 through 2019 averaged a yearly increase of 3.84% while average wages showed an annual increase of 4.41% for the same time period. By those statistics, as a whole, workers didn't need any further raises to combat inflation and it would appear that their wages were not stagnant. It seems logical that we didn't get paid much more every year because companies continued to get more efficient at producing more things, for less money.

THE LABOR FORCE AND WOMEN

According to the U.S. Census Bureau, from 1970 to 2020, the U.S. population grew at a rate of 1.08% per year, averaging 2,564,747 new Americans per year for the time period. Not all of those additions each year were of working age so if we want to get an idea of labor supply versus labor demand we have to find out just how much the labor force grew during a similar time period. According to the BLS, between 1950 and 2000, the civilian labor force grew from 62 million workers to 141 million workers, which equates to an annual rate of growth of 1.6%. Where did all of these workers come from? According to the BLS, the factor most responsible for that very high growth rate was the rapid increase in the labor force participation of women. So, basically, women are to blame for those stagnant wages! I'm only kidding! I have to try and break up this dry economics talk!

From the same source, the labor force participation rate of women was 34% in 1950 and increased to 60% by the year 2000, or 1.2% of the previously noted total 1.6% annual gain! Numbers wise, there were 18 million women in the workforce in 1950 and that increased to 66 million in 2000. The total share of women in the labor force during the same time period grew from 30% to 47%. As you can see, the economy had to adjust to changing demands and a very rapid increase in the supply of workers, remember supply and demand! It appears to me that the U.S. economy did a pretty good job keeping up with the changes.

WE WANT MORE STUFF

During the same time period, according to the St. Louis Federal Reserve, from the early 1950's to mid 2020, personal consumption (goods that we buy – cars, washing machines, pens, books, computers, etc. and services that we spend money on – lawn care, barbers, dentists, waitresses, etc.) increased from around 58% of GDP (Gross Domestic Product - the total value of goods produced and services provided in a country during one year.) to around 68% of GDP. So, it would appear that, as a country, we decided that we wanted a lot more "stuff" that we clearly (judging from the prior 50 years) didn't need.

Considering all of this information as it relates to housing, one can see when cruising through older neighborhoods that most of the houses are small, architecturally simple and or boring, and only have a one car garage or carport. Back then, one parent stayed home to maintain a portion of the property and have an intimate relationship (not in a weird way) with their kids. Whoever stayed home was able to spend a lot of time with their kids, time to show them love, time to observe and learn their quirks and behaviors, time to help them with school and life's problems.

MEDIAN SALARIES AND THE POST WWII HOUSING BOOM

Well, for every action, there is usually a good and bad consequence. For example, I want something now, I buy it using debt, I pay "X" amount more for it because I couldn't or wouldn't wait until I had the cash, but, it made me happy, good and bad. I hear people complain that all they do is work and don't have time for their families. In the 1950's they had the time. According to the Joseph Weeks report, as part of the 1880 census, and the Aldrich Report from the Senate Committee of Finance, average weekly hours worked from 1830 to 1890 was 63.6. In the 1950's it was 38.4, pretty awesome! It seems as though we may have hit a sweet spot there.

They had more time and decent pay – median salary was $4,200 per year, housing was very affordable at around 2 years salary and the average new car price was $2,400 which is only a little more than six months salary. The typical family paid for a modest house were only one person had to have a car and only one person had to work just under 40 hours a week to get it. In the 1950's the typical house was 1,065 square feet in size, cost about $11,000 or $10.33 per square foot, had no A/C, 66% had 2 or fewer bedrooms, 96% had only one bathroom and an average of 3.4 people lived in it.

Post World War II, in 1946, saw housing starts (housing starts is an economic indicator that reflects the number of privately owned new houses on which construction has been started in a given period) jump 400% over the previous year! In 1950, there were 1.9 million housing starts, 1.7 million of those were Single Family Residential (SFR) units. The home ownership rate was around 55% and couples married in their very early 20's according to the U.S. Dept. of Commerce and the U.S. Census Bureau. It was clear that we as a country wanted a space of our own.

WANT A BIGGER HOUSE, THAT'S GONNA COST YOU!

Fast forward to 1972 and the average single family home was now 1,634 square feet in size, a 66% increase from 1950, 65% of these homes had 3 or more bedrooms, 50% had 1.5 bathrooms or more, 43% had central A/C and the average price was $30,500 or $18.67 per square foot. In 1972 the median income according to the U.S. Census Bureau was $11,120 per year and there was a staggering 2.4 million housing starts! So housing was now more expensive at around 3 years salary but it was much larger and had more stuff in it. From just ten years earlier 66% of homes now had central air conditioning, up from 45%. 64% of homes now had a dishwasher, up from 46%. 31% of homes now had a fireplace, up from 24%. 52% of homes now came with a garbage disposal, up from 32%. The end result of the extra size and all this extra stuff would equate to a new home in 1972 costing 2.77 times more than it did 22 years earlier.

Now, if one had decided to build a house that was 1,065 square feet like those built in the 1950's, it would only be about 1.8 times more expensive at $19,883, and that's with all the upgrades like A/C! That equates to an annual inflation rate of 2.73% vs. a 4.74% annual increase if you followed the Joneses! Remember, wages increased at an average annual rate of 4.41%.

In 1950 the interest rate on an FHA mortgage was 4.25%, pretty good by any standard. In 1972 it was 7%! Apparently, it wasn't that shocking or expensive to most Americans because there were 2.4 million housing starts that year. I guess we could've voted with our wallets and waited for some change, say going back to a smaller floor plan, but it looks like, if we really want something, price doesn't matter. Over time the average annual housing starts, published by the St. Louis Federal Reserve, is around 1.5 million units. In 1981, with inflation at a whopping 13.5% per year and interest rates on mortgages at a high of 17.5% (YES, you read that right), we finally decided that things were getting a little pricey. Housing starts for 1981 dropped to 1.1 million units, a 27% decline.

By 1999 the average size of a new home was 2,241 square feet, an almost 40% increase in size from 1972, and around a 110% increase from 1950. The average new home now cost $87 per square foot to build, totaling $194,967. The median income for 1999 was $42,000 per year, meaning the average new home now cost 4.64 times the average salary. These new homes had some materials that were better (more expensive), some equipment that was more efficient (more expensive), and along with environmental compliance which was now around 10% of the cost of a new home, helped explain some of the added expense. Helping to ease some of the home affordability pain in 1999, interest rates on mortgages were down to sane levels, around 7.46% versus a peak of around 18.5% in October of 1981.

By now you should be starting to see a correlation between rising home prices and home size. If we decided to build a new home that was the same size of a 1950's home, 1,065 square feet, and with all of those cool new equipment upgrades that came at the time, it would only cost $92,655 or 2.2 times the median salary! You might think that a middle aged buyer at the time, having to pay over 4.5 times their salary for a new home would reduce demand for these expensive behemoths, especially considering that their parents only had to pay 2 times their salaries. Well, think again, in 1999, housing starts were back up to 1.657 million units. As it would appear, in aggregate, we don't always make the best financial decisions, rather, we are willing to spend a lot of money for material things that make us happy, for a little while at least.

Lets take a second to think about how the average person can buy a home. We already went over the details earlier, but let's think about the concept. Houses throughout time have generally been expensive endeavors. They are fairly complex, take a lot of material and labor to build and need to last a long time in varying conditions. Everyone needs some sort of shelter from the environment and if you own that shelter, you're more apt to take care of it, which as stated before, makes for a better local environment and better human outcomes. As a byproduct, home ownership also provides financial incentives, it's a win – win. Unfortunately, it's a bit of a challenge for the average person to save up 2 to 5 times their annual salary. With all of this in mind, the government and private institutions stepped in to help.

THE 30 YEAR MORTGAGE IS BORN

Wanting to support this good concept and recognizing that it would also spur economic activity, the 30 year mortgage was born. When the 30 year mortgage first came on the scene the banks required a 20% down payment which at the time equated to about 6 months of the average persons yearly salary. If I had to guess, for the average person, saving up the required 20% down payment would've taken around 1 to 2 years. I would venture to say that if you had to work your tail off and eat Ramen noodles everyday for 2 years, you'd be really cautious about what you do with that hard earned money and you definitely wouldn't want to lose it! Whoever came up with the 20% down rule deserves a round of applause because during the 1950's, mortgage default rates were only **.08%**, which is good for the banks and the homeowners!

UNCLE SAM HELPS HOMEBUYERS AND FORECLOSURE RATES SKYROCKET

It's my opinion that we have pretty big hearts in this country, and as we do well, we want others to do well also. That said, over time we wanted to make it easier for people to own their own homes and by 1959 the required down payment for an FHA loan had dropped to 10%. By 1984 only 3% of the homes appraised value, up to $50,000, would be required as down payment. Previously, down payments were 3% of the first $25,000, plus 5% of the amount over $25,000. Oddly enough, between the early 1980's and 1998, foreclosure rates increased by 300% according to the FDIC division of research and statistics. The powers that be were trying to make it easier to attain the American dream, an unintended consequence unfortunately was a huge increase in the default rate.

An advertisement from FREDDIE MAC in 1999 would illustrate just how easy it was to buy a home in the United States, it read something like this, ...it only takes a 3% down payment to buy a home in the U.S., whereas in Germany it would take 35% to 40%, Japan 50%, and terms in the U.S. were 30 years versus 15 years in France. The U.S., as it usually does, tries to solve problems and give people as many tools and options as possible. These tools and options, if used carefully and with discipline, are tremendously helpful in building wealth, I used a 3.5% down, FHA mortgage for my first owner occupied duplex.

I want to take a minute to give you an example of what I went through when I was about to buy my first property. At some point you're going to be on that fence of whether you should take the risk or not. You're going to have a given amount of fear because it is a big financial move for the average person, if you were already well to do, it wouldn't be a big deal. I had done plenty of research about how the real estate market performed in good and bad times and obviously just witnessed the, "real estate is a guaranteed winner, anyone and everyone is doing it" time and saw how that completely failed for so many people.

FOMO AND AN AVERAGE JOE TURNS REAL ESTATE EXPERT

Although unfortunate for them, it was a blessing for me, I had just had a front row seat to how people thought about or rather, didn't think about very large financial decisions. I also got to see how they're attitudes completely changed 180 degrees on a dime when the environment changed on them. "Bro, we're closing on another house over there, you've gotta get in the game before it's too late." That emotion by the way is called fear of missing out. That came from a well intentioned guy who at the time had five houses that he was flipping. At the time he was only making around $65,000 a year at his primary job. I responded to him saying that I was glad to hear of his success and I was happy for him. I just had one question though, what if it ends up that you can't sell those houses, do you have enough money to pay all of those mortgages? "Ahhh, Bro, they'll sell!"

About 8 months later he was missing the 7th payment on all five of those houses. There had been multiple signs that something wasn't right for the last year and a half. Shortly after he'd been foreclosed on and was being actively sued by the banks he expressed anger and resentment towards the evil banks that had tricked him into getting bad loans and that if were smart I'd stay away from real estate because it's too risky. Again, he was a good guy just like most of us and was just trying to make a better life for him and his family, he just made a few mistakes, one – he didn't do enough research on the game he was about to play, two - he wasn't paying enough attention to the game while he was playing it, three – he took on too much risk, and four – he had no complete plan which includes an exit strategy if things go sideways.

PERSONAL RESPONSIBILITY

A lot of people at the time were very angry with the banks and the government about what had happened. The popular view was that the U.S. was some evil capitalist regime that wanted to crush the average citizen. Although I agree that there is and always will be corruption in any society, the United States of America is the finest republic on this earth and gives the greatest amount of opportunity relative to the rest of the world. Things that are thought to be a good idea are implemented and have unintended consequences. Most of all, I think we all need to do a better job at taking responsibility for what happens to ourselves and our country. As in my cohorts case, if you were given the same tools as everyone else, you got foreclosed on and someone else prospered, it's possible that you didn't make the best decisions. Figure it out, if it was your mistakes, own up to them, learn from them, and get back after it! In regards to our republic, we vote with ballots and our wallets. Whether you decide to pay for that $9 bottle of water at your local amusement park or decide to buy that vacuum that's $12 dollars cheaper at the big box store rather than the Mom and Pop store that will give you great service, you're sending a signal. It may take 20 to 30 years to come to fruition but make no mistake, our actions have consequences!

EMOTIONS

Emotions, if you're human, you have them. We all need to do the best that we can to recognize them, evaluate and rationalize them, and move on from them. Emotions are beautiful and can allow people to do truly amazing things. Great athletes can raise the level of their emotions to a fever pitch, but not let those emotions overcome their control. In doing so, they increase their performance and focus without letting the emotions cause them to make foolish decisions. High level armed forces personnel do the same which allows them to deal with great hardships and suffering, and overcome them! On June 11th, 1963, Thich Quang Duc, a 66 year old Buddhist monk, set himself on fire on the streets of Saigon, to protest the Vietnam war. It was both a terrible and amazing thing to witness. He was so committed to ending the war and suffering that he was willing to take his own life in such a dramatic and violent fashion. He didn't even flinch as his body was engulfed in flames, unbelievable. I can't imagine the emotions he had to deal with!

My well intentioned cohort allowed the excitement of potential big paybacks and the fear of missing out cloud his judgement. After everything went bad, he let anger cloud his judgement further. This emotional rollercoaster had a very negative effect on his life for the next 6 years. The moral of this story is, life is precious and nothing is guaranteed, do your best to understand and control your emotions when it's warranted and make calculated decisions based on the best facts that you can find, not heresay. Just because everyone is doing it, doesn't mean that you should. Just because you can do something, doesn't mean that you should. What's your plan?

MY FIRST DUPLEX

I had never much liked to be in debt. It was a quick sugar high that you had to pay for, for a very long time. It had a ninja like effect of slowly and quietly suffocating you while you went about your daily routine. Before you knew it, you just couldn't do anything because your bills had piled up so high and it'd take 5 years to dig out from them. At the time my net (take home) pay was $2,450 per month and I was renting a 1 bed/ 1bath apartment for $637 a month. All my research said that if I didn't value the property wrong and I had enough reserves to last me through a given period of bad times, that I'd be ok.

At the time I wasn't really a people person to say the least, you do you and I'll do me and everything will be cool. I was about to get into a business were at certain intervals, I'd be dealing with many people at a time in both a personal and professional aspect. I would also have to deal with the unknowns of a property. At the time I didn't know much about houses and how everything was put together. Last but definitely not least, I was about to make a HUGE financial commitment that would take me a lot longer than 5 years to pay off. If things went bad, I'd be stuck with it for a very long time. I analyzed my emotions, heeded the warnings of the rational ones and threw out the rest. I made a comprehensive plan for the best circumstances and the absolute worst circumstances.

Time had gone by and I was voraciously learning about my product. It had been about 2 years since the world almost collapsed, I now had about 5 years at my current job and put my odds at being let go at around 20%. Needless to say, nobody was handing out raises so my pay remained the same and I was just happy to have it. I had spent the last 2 years looking at every property within an hours radius of Orlando and although home prices were in steady, rapid decline, multifamily list prices were the same as before the crash. Man, it must be nice being them! What was happening with those multifamily properties? Why weren't their prices going down? I did some research and found that the ones listed had very low or no mortgages on them. Most of the ones with mortgages had a low enough estimated total payment that one unit would pay for the entire mortgage. What a great position to be in, the world collapses and it's business as usual for you.

That confirmed for me that I wanted to one day be in a similar position. It was 2010 when I found the only reasonably priced (everything else was about $30,000 over priced) duplex in downtown Orlando that was in a good location and wasn't a total disaster. It was operational, but needed EVERYTHING. It was built in the 1950's, had the no-no Federal Pacific breaker boxes, awning style windows that wouldn't shut all the way, the roof only had a couple years left on it, the yard was a disaster, and it hadn't been updated, if you can even call it that, since the mid 1970's. It was listed for about $75,000 less than the turn key (everything is up to date and fully functional) duplexes in the area. I estimated that it would cost about $7,000 or $8,000 to take care of the emergent issues like the roof and the breaker boxes IF it was required, $30,000 to get it into acceptable condition and about $60,000 to get it into pristine, high end rental condition. It appeared as though this seller knew what he had, knew the market, wanted to sell, and was willing to give a decent discount for the deferred maintenance that the property required.

The duplex was listed for sale for $152,000 and the sellers had no mortgage on it. One unit was empty and the other was underented at $550 a month which, oddly enough covered their property taxes and insurance. If you're running through my numbers you probably noticed that the discount the seller was offering had no room for my troubles. In other words, the property needed $60,000 worth of work and was discounted by about $60,000 which meant I had to get all of that done and deal with any of the hassles that came with it, for free. It wasn't exactly my idea of a great deal so I put an offer for $125,000 in and a letter explaining my reasoning. They were very receptive and came back with a counter offer of $152,000. I had been watching the market for about 4 years now and this had been my only financially viable option to come along, you see, even with a tenant in the other side, the banks were so scared at the time, that I wouldn't be able to qualify for anything more expensive! It would turn out that even at this price the banks were so unwilling to lend, even with one side bringing in $550 a month, I got denied by three lenders. The fourth ones the charm, I got the loan and took the opportunity and calculated risk that was in front of me, and ran with it.

I had to be careful though, in 2010 property values were still falling precipitously. If I wanted to be able to buy another property in the near future I would need to be "lendable" in the eyes of the bank. That said, being underwater in a few years on the duplex that I just bought was out of the question. My total mortgage (PITI) was $1,558 a month and taking a quick step back to the emotions paragraph, you'll remember that I was only bringing home $2,450 a month, so if the other side went unrented it would eat up 64% of my take home pay leaving me with only $892 a month to live on. Control those emotions.

I looked at the rate of decline and what housing prices were in 2002 before the crazy run up began. I figured that prices would probably somewhat overshoot below 2002 levels with the scared environment we were in. I calculated that in order to have enough equity to get another place in the next 2 to 3 years I'd need to pay an extra $383 a month towards principle. So my mortgage became $1,941 a month, of which my tenant paid $550 a month and I paid $1,391 a month to live in the same size place with worse appliances, and oh yeah, I got to maintain the place too! So I kept my head down and my nose to the proverbial grindstone and continued with my previously mentioned recipe of extreme savings with a side dish of two jobs. Two years later I was able to buy the 15 acre farm that netted me around $88,000 on top of my $42,000 down payment.

ADVICE FROM STRANGERS

After flying over a few different concepts I'd like to bring it all together and as my co-workers would say to me, land the plane. You're going to hear advice from EVERYONE, 1% of them have actual experience with the subject, the other 99% will fill your head with stories of extreme success or extreme failure, control your emotions. Going outside of your comfort zone is going to bring on any number of emotions, if you want to grow, you're going to have to learn to control them. One way to control them is to learn as much as you can about what you're about to do and make a plan. When you make a plan, make a detailed one, considering the best case, the base case, and the worst case scenarios. Don't miss out on a good deal waiting for a great deal, it may never come. Don't be scared or too good for old fashioned hard work. Take responsibility for your mistakes and don't blame other people or institutions or you'll never learn from them. Lastly, you can achieve nothing, without first believing that you can!

None of what I just said was meant to put anyone down or anyone who's had some success on a high horse. This life is a big gamble and I often tell people that I don't know how much of my success is my own awesomeness or God's grace! If I had to guess, he probably puts a good amount of effort into me!

WHO'S GONNA RENT THAT PROPERTY AND WHAT COULD THAT MEAN

OK, let's get back to understanding the value of a property. We know that people buy housing based on a mix of emotions and utility. To a 24 year old, a 650 sq. ft. 2/1 that's downtown, close to all the action is worth $2,000 a month because they'll get a roommate and split the costs. This is where you have to stop looking at the dollar signs and think about some of the other aspects of owning a rental. Say this is a duplex, so it's 1,300 sq. ft. total with a 2/1 and a carport on each side. Let's take a look at the tenant you're most likely to attract. They'll most likely be in their early to late 20's, partying downtown 3 or 4 nights a week, having a bunch of people in and out.

It's likely that they're not going to be gentle with your property and their visitors will most definitely not care. Visitor number 1 gets in a fight with the female visitor number 2, he says some things, she throws her drink in his face and locks herself in the bathroom. Visitor number 1 then proceeds to pound on the bathroom door while trying to shove it open while your tenant is blissfully unaware in the backyard with the music blaring while making out with her boyfriend. Not bad for a Tuesday night!

Whenever I've expressed these concerns with would be landlords there's always a few who act like it's no big deal because they'll sue the tenants for damages or keep their security deposits and or evict them. Others will say that they'll stipulate in their lease that if the tenant breaks anything, they'll have to pay to get it fixed, it's just that simple! Well, number one, suing and evicting both take time and money. Number two, if your tenant does $5,000 worth of damage, which isn't hard to do these days, do they have $5,000 plus court costs? Will the judge put them on a three year payment plan? If so, you'll need to front all of that money and will of course, have spent however much time on the event. Depending on the circumstances, your unit may be empty for a significant amount of time while you're dealing with repairs and a lawsuit. Which leads me to number three, I've been dealing with tenants for over a decade now and I can tell you that most people don't know the working end of screw-driver anymore.

WHO'S OUR CUSTOMER AND HOW MUCH MONEY DO THEY MAKE

I know the path that I take you on can seem a bit convoluted at times but I'm trying to illustrate that the value of something can be viewed at many different angles. Buying a place that makes a ton of cash but drives you crazy ends up not being a very good value for you. Just because it is in a great location or has a brand new roof and A/C system doesn't mean it's going to be a good value for YOU. Maybe your best value looks like a single family house in a quiet part of town where you're likely to have a tenant live there for 10 to 15 years and not cause you much trouble because you rarely raise the rent and it's such a good deal. Your return on investment in money terms may be lower but it's better than nothing and you get to keep your sanity. So there is intrinsic value, value from the renters point of view, the buyers point of view, and the future buyers point of view and they all have many different aspects to them. Make sure that you're looking at all of the possible aspects of value.

I have noticed, generally speaking, that the easier the returns are, the higher the price of the investment is. Conversely, the more work that you have to put into the investment, the more you need to get paid for that work, so the price is cheaper. The safer and easier the investment is, the smaller the returns are. It's kind of like investing in U.S. Government Bonds, no big returns here, but easy and safe. At the end of the day, to each their own. If you're hungry and ready to get in there and take your licks, go for the big cash flow mobile home park or the multifamily in a class D neighborhood. If you're like most of us and are doing this on the side, I'd say go for the boring Government Bond on the first one!

So, we never buy on price and we don't get sucked in by big cash flow numbers, control those emotions. We don't fall in love with nice floors or countertops, we carefully look at the area, including what businesses serve the immediate area. Are there brand name supermarkets, upscale restaurants, shops that sell absurdly priced coffee, German car dealerships and investment offices or are there convenience and liquor stores mixed with payday advance and pawn stores? Is it close to a major employment center or out in the middle of nowhere?

After we look at all of these factors we can begin to get an idea of who our customer is going to be, what opportunities and lifestyle they may or may not be able have. It's really no different than a product viability study that a business goes through, except we're not thinking about coming up with a product and wondering if it will sell and to whom, the product is already there and selling, we just want to know who our consumer is.

We're then going to look at the median income of that area and look at its distribution. What I mean by distribution is what percentage of that areas population, makes how much money. Median income is a broad indicator and tells you the split, half of the areas population makes more than the median and half of the areas population makes less. Let's say median income in the area is $52,000 per year. What percent of the lower half makes close to $52,000? Let's say 60% of the lower half makes between $40,000 and $52,000 a year. That's good if you need to get $1,250 a month in rent. Just like mortgages, the prefered percentage of your income that goes to housing costs is 33% or less. If we take the average between $40,000 and $52,000 and divide by 12 we get $3,833 a month income. If we divide $1,250 by $3,833 we get .326 or 32.6% of gross monthly income. So 60% of the lower half and all of the upper half can afford your product, perfect!

However, if only 15% of the lower half make between $40,000 and $52,000 a year and the other 85% of the lower half make less than $25,000 a year, that's not so good. If a property that you're looking at is priced such that you have to get $1,250 a month in rent, then maybe that property, in that area, is overpriced. In either case, we have to assume there is a certain percentage of the areas income earners that are not renters because they own a home or married to someone who does. We also need to consider that a certain percentage of those higher wage earners may be able to afford your rental at $1,250 a month but are looking for something more fancy that will cost them $1,700 a month because they can afford it.

Staying with the same numbers above, let's say that in the upper half, 5% of earners make between $52,000 and $65,000 a year, 85% make between $120,000 and $150,000 a year and 5% make between $200,000 and $250,000 a year. At first glance that looks great for your $1,250 a month rental. Sticking to the same theme I alluded to in the end of the last paragraph, how many of those earners will want to rent your unit? If it's in a great area, has great curb appeal and is very well updated your renter pool will be larger. If it's in a more middle class area, the number of renters from that distribution who are intersted in your rental will be far lower.

Another factor to consider with targeting higher income earners is that, at almost any time, they have the ability to stop renting and purchase a home. Recapping the numbers, we have a median salary of $52,000 per year, 15% of the lower half makes between $40,000 and $52,000 per year, 85% of the lower half makes less than $25,000 a year and in the upper half, 5% make between $52,000 and $65,000 a year and 85% make between $120,000 and $150,000 a year. I won't consider the 5% that make more than $200,000 a year because they will be home owners. So, looking at the numbers we can see that we have about 20% of the areas earners (this is not exact and just for concept) that make between $40,000 and $65,000 a year. We won't really count the $120,000 to $150,000 group because we're going to assume that your rental isn't up to their standards other wise it would have been priced much higher and you'd have to get a much higher rent.

Continuing, we need to consider that this $40,000 to $65,000 income group could buy a home if they have enough money saved up, their credit is good and there are houses available in their price range. We then have to look at what housing is available in our target area, for what price, and how many units are available or coming. Are there three new neighborhoods being built with 1,500 to 2,000 sq. ft. starter homes with prices starting in the mid $160,000 range? If so, you could be buying in a declining rental market, not a good spot to be in. On the other hand if we check the population changes, the business development, the housing permits issued for both SFR and MFR over the last 10 years and find out that net inmigration is out pacing new construction by a wide margin we could be in an inclining rental market, a very good thing.

We never want to rely on a small set of data to make such a big financial decision so we're going to look at some other data that will either corroborate our findings or give us pause for concern. We're going to check with the local buisness development board to see what's cookin'. We're also going to check with the local universities as they often have a department that puts out projections for local population growth and economic development. We're not done yet. We're going to check with the state D.O.T. as they put out forcasts for population growth as it relates to road usage and demand for new roads and bridges. Because these entities continually put out forcasts we can go back and see prior forcasts and then compare them with U.S. Census bureau statistics and our own experiences with the area to see how accurate they've been. Finally we're going to check with the local authority on Drivers License issuance to see how many of those people are actually old enough to possibly rent and corroborate the all of the other population growth forcasts.

We may find out that population growth was stagnant in the first few years of the reportable period but really took off towards the end. We may find that this lulled the construction industry to sleep in the first part of the reportable period resulting in SFR and MFR construction to lag behind the net inmigration and organic household formation growth. We confirm this growth with drivers license issuance and the forecasts that were accurate calling for more growth. We check rent price growth over the same period and it's positive. All things seem to be pointing at a rental market that will see price appreciation and solid demand for the next so many years.

Now when we look at those three new neighborhoods that will have 60 homes each it doesn't concern us much because in the last two years population in the area has grown by over 1,100 people. The rental that seemed overpriced in the first scenario now doesn't look like such a bad deal based on demand. We're not done just yet, we're going to dig a little deeper and take the typical down payment on one of those new homes and figure out what the PITI would be on the remainder based on the current mortgage rates, let's say that it's $1,600 a month. We then check to see if interest rates are stable or fluctuating up or down and make adjustments accordingly.

WHY DON'T THEY JUST BUY A HOUSE

To get one of those shiny new homes our tenants are going to need a a stable job, make around 3 times what the PITI will cost, put at least $5,800 down, have another $3,300 for closing costs and around $4,200 in emergency cash that the bank requires. In total they'll need $13,300 in mostly liquid cash. How many of those earners will have $13,300 saved up? Whoever does will still have to pay $1,600 a month. That said, you will probably have quite a bit of room to raise your rent and still be a cheaper alternative to buying a house.

Your rental may be a very attractive alternative at $1,450 per month and they don't have to worry about maintenance costs or mowing the lawn. If you needed $1,250 a month to make say a 10% ROI, that extra $200 a month may put you at a 15% ROI. The value of your rental just went up too because it can generate more income. It may have gone up in value by $40,000 because of the extra $200 a month. The next person who buys it will probably accept a 10% return just like you did.

Next you'll think about how the property compares to all of the others that have sold within the last year, you have been doing your homework, right? You compare construction type, age of the roof, A/C, wiring, plumbing, upgrades like floors, cabinets, and counters. The fact that you've been doing drive bys, looking at pictures online and checking out every rental for the last year, you know that quartz counters and tile floors command a $100 a month premium. You've been studying your prodcut and your customer for a while now and you know exactly how much something will rent for and you know what's happening in your area. Now when that deal pops up you can pull the trigger within hours of its listing and be confident that you're buying on the way up and not catching a falling knife!

THE TIME VALUE OF MONEY

As a last thought on value I'm going to share an overall experience that I had were I was faced with the time value of money conundrum. Value is inherently unique to the environment at any given time. We've all probably heard the saying, "one man's trash, is another man's treasure." Value totally depends on what's going on at the time in each of those mens lives. The guy who's rich at the time will throw out a perfectly good shirt because he's tired of it. The guy who's living out of his car and ripped his last shirt will happily take that shirt.

Take a second to think about all of the daily conveniences that we take for granted. Do we give them the value that we should? If something is super critical, do we protect it and have multiple back ups for it or do we as a society spend the bare minimum on it? Drinking water is real cheap until there's none of it around after a hurricane. Almost no one spends any thought on how valuable electricity is until it's not available and they're cast back 200 years in time. No electricity, no refrigerator. It doesn't matter how much food you have crammed in that thing if it all goes bad in a few days. No electricity, no water, unless you're running down to the local stream with a bucket. No electricity, no fuel from the gas stations. No fuel, no generators. It's a really big deal that most of us don't give a second thought.

In regards to any investment we make or are about to make, that investment should have a plan that's referenced to a time frame. Remember that you have "X" amount of money that you can use to invest in any number of ways and for just about any amount of time. You should try to look at the long and short term time horizons and try to weave those together. For those who remember the Alanis Morrissette song, "Ironic", …"that death row pardon that's two minutes too late…" isn't worth the paper it's printed on. You can hold an investment too long or too short and it ends up destroying the returns on it. Everything has a time value to it.

I've spoken earlier in this book about a farm that I purchased in the depths of the 2008 recession. I carefully selected that property (and God saw fit to give it to me) because of its location a few minutes from a major expressway to Orlando, and more importantly, its very close proximity to the fastest growing retirement communities in the country, The Villages. If all went to hell in a handbasket, I would, God willing, be able to provide food, water, and a greater level of separation and security for my family.

At the same time, if all went well, which thankfully it did, I would be positioned well to both the property to pay for itself via horse boarding and pasture rent and have the property in the path of expansion from The Villages. If you recall, a little over two years later I received an unsolicited offer to buy the farm for $100,000 more than I paid for it. When I purchased the REO, I basically got it for the value of the land, fencing and maybe the barn, I basically got the house for free.

The property was 15 acres and was big enough to conservatively build around 40 homes on it including set backs for utilities and a road. If and when the developers got to my property, all of the structures would be worthless to them. Any value in the structures that had built up over time would be lost. I figured that it would take from 7 to 10 more years for them to use up the land inbetween that community and my farm. I did some guestimation on land value appreciation with a best and worst case scenario. In the worst case, I figured that I'd sell to someone who wanted a horse farm and not some big developer in another 8 years and make somewhere around $200,000 not including the rent generated or the tax write offs.

In the best case, everything would grow like gangbusters over the next 8 years (which it has) and the developers would love my property because it's 99% cleared and level, off of a paved road with utilities, and end up offering me a little more than triple what I'd paid for , based on my rough calculations on what it would cost them to build out the neighborhood. If this happened, I would end up making around $268,000, again, not including rent and write offs during the hold period.

Over the past two years my initial investment had grossed just under a 59% annual return. In the worst case scenario, if I decided to ride it out for another 8 years, which would make 10 total years, I'd knock that rate of return down to just over 17%. That's still a very good rate of return, but is it the best use of my hard earned money? In the best case scenario, my per annum return would be just under 21%. Again, anyway you slice it, great returns, to God be the Glory! But could I do better?

If you remember, one of my neighbors had just offered me $100,000 over what I paid for it. Should I take the deal or hold on to the farm for more profits? This is where you have to balance your risks to get a greater return. On the surface, taking $100,000 now instead of waiting and getting $200,000 or more seems like not the best idea.

If we think about it, I'd only paid for 20% of that property, but I'd received a return on 100% of it, not because I'm some financial wizard, because that's how it works. So, with my continued savings, my initial capital investment, and my profit from selling to my neighbor, I'd have around $160,000, which would be enough to buy close to three properties. If I only had to pay for 20% or 25% of a property but I could get a return on 100% of the property, those bigger numbers might play to my favor. The return on the bigger numbers, being the total property value, would be lower of course, but the principle would be higher. Let's take a look at how this turned out.

Now, I could get all happy about the fact that I have enough down payment money to buy 3 properties but my income and emergency cash would of course have to also be high enough to support what the banks required for the additional properties. What this means is I couldn't just go out and buy 3 properties all at once. Doing the math and having a buyer in place I decided to forgoe the future returns and sell the farm.

I had been watching a house (among about 50 others at the time) go in and out of the short sale and foreclosure process for the last 3 years. The price finally came down to a reasonable value, I of course (given the market conditions at the time) offered about $20,000 less and it was quickly accepted. I put 20% down to keep my DTI in a lendable range for the next property. So, I basically used $50,000 to get a 3.5% return on $250,000. If we take $250,000 and multiply it by .035 or 3.5% we get a return of $8,750 for year one, which is a 17.5% return on the cash that I used to acquire the property, BOOM! I'd basically just been fortunate enough to make a similar return on 1/3 of my money as I would have if I'd kept the farm.

LUCK FAVORS THE PREPARED – AGAIN!

About a year later, someone made a mistake and underlisted a duplex near downtown Orlando. Because I lived and breathed real estate over the last 8 years, I put an offer on the duplex within hours of it being listed. I didn't want to get too risky and lose that good deal so I offered only around 3% under asking and it was accepted. One side was rented, albeit, substantially lower than the going rate and the other was vacant. I used some money to renovate and make renter proof, the vacant side. A few months later I had both sides rented, and after all expenses, the property was cash flowing $568 a month. At the purchase price of $250,000, which was about $25,000 under fair market value, and using an annual appreciation rate of 3.5%, the property was returning $8,750 a year in unrealized gains. The property was also cash flowing $6,816 a year ($568 a month x 12) and the tenants were paying down the principle by around $3,300 per year. In total, the $66,000 I'd used to purchase the property along with the $5,000 to do a light renovation on the one unit was returning $18,866 a year for a 26.6% return on $71,000, BOOM!

A year and a half later, early on a Sunday morning, I noticed a good looking duplex pop up for sale in a good area near the beach. It was well underpriced so I wasn't sure if something was wrong with it or not. The pictures looked good and I had researched the area a few years ago so I had my agent call the listing agent to try to get a look at it immediately. Both units were vacant which would allow this. As blessings would have it, the listing agent lived only a few minutes away and agreed to show it but only if I hurried because she had a family gathering to go to.

I grabbed all of my tools and my ladder and rushed over there to meet both agents. I did a quick but thorough inspection and didn't find anything of concern. I politely asked her how she came up with the list price. Exasperatedly she replied, "Well! I've been doing this for 35 years!" I said, OK, and filled out an offer on the ipad on the spot. It was docusigned and sent to seller. She was made aware of my "investor" status and my proof of funds and with that walked outside to call the sellers. After about 5 minutes on the phone she came back inside and said that the sellers agreed and were docusigning the contract now and I'd have email confirmation by the time I got home. Cool!

By this time about 2 ½ hours had gone by, I guess to make a sale she'd be late to her family gathering. As we walked out, there was a person sitting in an SUV parked out front. My agent and I got in our vehicles and started to leave. I called my agent and started to drive down the street. I watched in the rear view mirror as the driver of the SUV got out and approached the listing agent, I said to my agent, "he missed it!". On my way home my agent called me back and said that the listing agent let her know that the SUV driver was very interested in the property and wanted to know if I'd be interested in flipping it? She gave me his number and said he'd be waiting for my call. After a 10 minute conversation, he had offered me $40,000 more than I was buying it for, I politely declined. Looks like that listing agent needs another 35 years of experience!

Both units were empty, so I took the opportunity to renovate and renter proof both sides. One side had fresh paint and new carpet so I worked on that side first so I could get it rented and have some money coming in. I did a bunch of little things like, changing outlets and switches from dirty looking off white to pure white, replaced the 1990's blinds, gold hinges and door knobs, and some bigger ticket items like glass mosaic backsplashes and quartz counter tops. While renovating the other side, I was blessed with a great tenant who is still there to this day. A couple of months later I had finished the other side and got it rented.

After all expenses, the property cash flowed $968 a month or $11,616 per year. The property was worth at the time, $275,000 and at a 3.5% annual appreciation rate would return $9,625 in year one. The tenants would also pay down the principle by around $3,600 a year. If we add all of those up we find that the property generates $24,841 in year one and if we divide that by the $72,000 that I had used to buy and renovate the property, we find that this duplex provides a return on investment of 34.5%, BOOM! So, with selling the farm and continuing to save, around $48,000 over two years, I was able to buy three properties in under three years. Not bad for an average wage earner.

THINK ABOUT THE BIG PICTURE

To do a fair comparison I'll have to back out the last duplex because I had a little over two years to save additional money, but don't misunderstand the opportunity factor that having the cash to acquire two more properties in such a short period of time gives a person. Without having the cash flow and equity of the other properties I wouldn't have been able to buy the last duplex! That said, I used $123,000 from the sale of the farm to buy a SFR which at the time of this writing is worth over $500,000 and a duplex that is worth just over $400,000 (over the period, Orlando experienced a higher appreciation rate than the 3.5% I used in my initial calculations, it pays to be conservative!). The SFR cash flows zero because I live in it and can't rent out any of the land for agricultural uses and the duplex now cash flows $1,062 a month, has its principle paid down by around $3,500 per year and appreciates by $14,175 per year, in total generating $30,419 per year. My primary residence, the SFR, has gained $258,000 in value since I bought it and the duplex has gained $155,000.

So lets total those up and see how we did. In 6 years since selling the farm, the SFR gained $258,000 in value and cash flowed zero, and the duplex gained $155,000 in value, had an average annual cash flow of $10,572, and an average annual principle paydown of $4,000. Without taking tax write offs in consideration, the two properties had a total return over 6 years of $500,432. So, did my gamble to sell the farm pay off? If we remember, I used around $40,000 to get just under a $140,000 back in just two years which is an eye popping 87% annual return! Now, I didn't get that rate of return because I'm smarter than the Oracle of Omaha, two important factors played into that rate of return, 1. I didn't know it at the time, but I bought at the very bottom of the market and 2. I still bought it at a significant discount to fair market value at the time because it needed work and was an REO.

Relative to that kind of performance, I failed miserably! Sarcasm aside, my original dilema was whether to keep the farm for the additional 8 years for a maximum potential return of $268,000 in appreciation and $76,800 in pasture rent, for a total of $344,800, or sell to lock in around $100,000 and reinvest in multiple properties. So, total investment time period if I were to keep the farm would be 10 years and my projected best case scenario was to have $344,800 in total returns which equates to a 24% annual return on my initial $40,000 invested, pretty damn good!

Now, taking the total profit of $100,000 from the sale of the farm plus my initial investment of $40,000 and using it to buy a SFR and a duplex allowed those two properties to generate a total income over 6 years of $500,432. If we take $140,000 and plug it into a compound interest calculator for 6 years to come up with $500,432 we find an annual rate of return of 23.65%. Hmm, looks like I missed the mark on this one. Let's look at the nominal return. Over 10 years the farm was expected to return a total of $344,800 in the best case scenario. Over a 6 year period, the SFR and the duplex generated $500,432, a 45% increase over the farm. If we want to extrapolate that out for another 4 years we can. Using rough numbers I'll just take the difference between the two, $155,632 and divide it by 6 years to get an average annual nominal difference of $25,939. Multipling that by another 4 years gives us an additional $103,756 on top of the $500,432 for a total of $604,188 or a 75% nominal increase! As far as actual cash in the bank, the two properties beat the farm, by a fairly wide margin, even though the rate of return was lower.

So my point to this is to 1. Illustrate how blessed I've been and give thanks to God and 2. make you think about the big picture and make a grand plan, not just focus on the rate of return. The banks will allow you to get 100% of the returns on a property with only buying 20% to 25% of it. If the total asset value is five times higher than what you put down, you can get a smaller return but still make more money because there's a bunch of extra dollars working for you! As some of you are probably tabulating, the more equity that you build up in a property, the lower the rate of return that you're going to get. That said, once you hit a certain percentage of equity, it will be to your benefit to go buy another property with some of that equity.

In summary, it's your job to spend the time and give the attention that it takes to become an "expert" in your area. Understanding the reasons behind all of your observations over time will allow you to pick winners, time and time again. Your time and your investments time has value which changes over time, try to have a plan that includes the big picture. In Ch. 11 I'll go over in more detail the calculations that I suggest you run on a prospective property.

CHAPTER 10

SOME OF MY PERSONAL EXPERIENCES WITH TENANTS

A quick takeaway from this chapter.

- **You want to know what it's really like to be a landlord – read on**
- **Attitude is everything!**

THE GREAT A/C LEAK OF 2016

Taking that into consideration, most of the professionals that you expect your tenant to vet and hire, only know slightly more or are trying to get in and get out as fast as they can and their work or lack there of, will show it. I can think of a few examples of tenant blunders that have happened to me over the years. As I recall these events, just think about how well the tenant would handle the situation including the hiring of a repairman.

I get a call at 7:30 pm and the tenant relates that water is leaking from the air conditioner. That's not usually too big of a deal. The tenants were moving in that day and they probably had the door open a lot allowing a bunch of hot, humid air in. I asked her how bad was it leaking? She said, really bad, there's water all over the floor. OK, hold on…. there's water all over the floor. Is she exaggerating? The A/C would have to leak for a weak to have water all over the floor. So I ask her how long it's been since she noticed it leaking to which she replies, a few minutes. Hmmm, and you say it's coming from the A/C, and it's all over the floor, the apartment is 750 sq. ft.

Let's ponder this for a minute. With what's transpired so far, do you think just because you have a solid lease, it will be prudent to just sit back and say, not my problem, it was working when you signed the lease, call someone and have it fixed. Remember the screwdriver comment a little while ago? I'll continue. I tell the tenant to please turn of the A/C, put a bunch of towels down to absorb the water, and I'll be right there. Luckily for me, and the only reason I didn't continue the questioning, was because I was just leaving the area and I'd be able to get back there in about 5 minutes. As I pull up the front door is open and there's water rolling out of it while the tenant and her boyfriend are scrambling around with a broom and towels trying to corral the water. As I open the door to my truck I can hear the hiss of pressurized water spraying everywhere. I immediately grab my water T that I always have in my truck, take the lid off of the main water valve (you should know where it is) and shut off the water to the unit. The hissing dies down and the water stops.

Would a residential air handler have pressurized water plumbed to it? Would you think that most people would be able to recognize pressurized water spraying onto the floor? Remember the screwdriver comment! It is now clearly obvious that the air conditioner is not the cause of the leak. As I walk past the tenant and her boyfriend, through the standing water towards the closet that the air handler is, I notice a medium sized box on the floor that is wet on three sides and the bottom of course. I look into the air handler closet and below the air handler is a pvc pipe which runs to the water heater that's on the other side of the wall, that is broken. Very conveniently as luck would have it, about three inches below the break there's a shut off valve on the pipe. Too bad it wasn't used.

So I asked what happened? Well, we were just minding our business, putting some boxes away, when all of a sudden the A/C started leaking water everywhere. I asked, was it right after you put this box in the closet? The boyfriend, by the look on his face, was starting to see where this was going. She replied, yes, with a confused look on her face. I bring them both over to the closet and have them squat down and look at the broken pipe. I asked her how hard she shoved that box in there? She said, not THAT hard. I spent the next four hours, getting all of the water out of the unit with tenants, buying box fans to dry whatever water got under the baseboards, cutting out and replacing the broken pipe and building a small section of wall with an access door to protect that pipe in the future. Before I left, I gave instructions to the tenant to leave the box fans where I had them, leave them running for the next two days, and to PLEASE be gentle with the property going forward.

A few points to glean from this experience,

1. Before you rent a property, go through it and make it as simple to understand and bomb proof as you can. I should have seen that coming and built that protective wall in the first place.
2. This example should illustrate just how ignorant a large majority of the population is to the systems in a house. I'm not trying to be mean or rude, but if you think about it, most renters grew up in a house that they knew nothing about and had no responsibility to maintain or repair, I did. Then they moved out to a rental under the same circumstances. If something is wrong, call someone.
3. That said, when you get the phone call that I did, are you really going to say, not my problem, you're responsible, get it fixed? There's water gushing into your property for however long it takes your tenants to call the right person, which in this case is not an A/C guy, wait for them to get there and then hopefully figure out what the problem is. I installed air conditioners for a little while and would venture to say that most A/C guys don't carry a water T with them and may not have any idea where your properties water shut off valve is.

Maybe the A/C guys gets paid for the visit regardless of what he does and tells the tenant this is a job for a plumber, I'm out of here. So your tenant calls an emergency plumber who takes however long to get there and finally resolve the problem. During all of this time, maybe hours, water has been inundating your rental. Who knows how much has seeped under your baseboards and into the walls. Do you end up with a bunch of mold growth in your walls over the next three months? Do you end up having to cut out the lower third of all of your drywall, have the mold mtigated professionally, then new drywall put up and the texture hopefully matched so you can't tell?

Will the tenant have the wisdom to know that there's probably water soaked into the baseboards and walls and that they need to get fans and leave the fans on full blast for 2 to 3 days? If they can't figure out the difference between pressurized water and water dripping from an air handler, I think you have your answer. Will they be able to take a step back, or in this case, squat down and take a look at the problem to see if they can mitigate it? There was a shut off valve 3 inches below the break in the pipe that they could have immediately solved the problem with.

I'VE LOOKED AT IT FOR 1 SECOND, YOU WON'T BE ABLE TO FIGURE IT OUT

The next example is similar, but not nearly as bad. I was mowing the lawn at one of my duplexes when I notice the boyfriend of the late 20's couple that lives in the other side is jogging over towards me with his hand up waving. I shut down the mower and remove my ear protection, what's up man? Hey man, I'm sorry but I think we broke something under the sink, it's leaking water. As I open the front door I can hear water spraying under the sink, the girlfriend is standing in the middle of the kitchen looking at me and the boyfriend won't shut up. He keeps telling me, "I don't think you're going to be able to stop it, I looked under there." I look under the sink and shut the quarter turn valve off in all of about 2 seconds. I can see what appears to be a small gouge in the plastic hose that comes from the hot water valve to the faucet. As I stand up I see a wire mesh basket with cleaning supplies in it on the floor. The look on the girlfriends face was priceless as she says, "I told you there was a way to shut it off!" I'm pretty sure that she revoked his man card that day. God takes care of me again! I happened to be right there when the problem happened and was able to mitigate it quickly and without too much damage. God is good!

THE GREAT ELECTRICAL MYSTERY OF 2019

I get a text message one afternoon relating that there must be something wrong with the electricity in this persons unit because their dining room and child's bedroom lights keep burning out. The tenant continues by saying it's been happening for months now and it's bad, it's hurting their eyes. Mind you, this property has 12 ga. copper wire with a ground and has professionally upgraded meter bases and breaker panels. There hasn't been a problem like this brought to my attention by that tenant in the prior three years.

Unfortunately for me I was at my day job when I received this text and was not able to go investigate for myself. This tenant cooks with a lot of spices which tends to set the smoke detectors off which leads him to take them down, I constantly have to visit the unit and put them back up, reminding him that most people die in fires of smoke inhalation. That said, if there was a problem and a fire occurred, they may not become aware of it until something bad happens. Because this was electrical in nature and a potential safety issue, I had to call an electrician to go check it out right away. A couple of hours later I get a call from the electrician and what do you know, he relates that the property appears to have brand new meter bases and electrical panels that are installed correctly and the service voltage coming into the house and going out to the branch circuits have no fluctuations. Everything checks out A OK.

I stop by after work and the tenant shows me the lights that keep burning out as proof that there's something wrong. They're incandesent candelabra fan lights. I ask how fast they're burning out? I can tell by his face that he's not too sure. He replies, "uhhh, like every couple of months." Well, I'm sorry to hear that Mr. Tenant, as you know the elctrician stated that the electrical service is functioning properly, let me see if I can help you. I went to the store and bought eight LED candelabra style bulbs, installed them and never heard another thing about it. I had adopted that tenant and their lease when I bought the duplex. When his lease was up I did not renew it based on his constant removal of the smoke detectors. My leases have a clause in them that relates if a tenant removes or disables a safety device it's considered a breach of contract and they can be evicted.

THE SUPER HIGH UTILITY BILL

I get a call from a tenant advising me that their electric bill is super high and that I suggested it should be somewhere between $80 to $120 a month according to the previous tenants usage. First of all, what I said during that conversation was that depending on her usage, and if it was similar to the previous tenants, it should be somewhere between $80 and $120 per month, acccording to them. Anyway, I tell her that I'm very sorry to hear about her high electric bill and ask her if she has a current bill that I could look at. She replies, yes and sends me a picture of her current utility bill. I look at it and immediately see the problem, she was looking at the total utility bill which, at this property, has water, sewer, and recycling on it is as well. Up at the top of the bill is the electric portion which showed a charge of, wait for it, $84.

Again, I'm not trying to be mean or rude to anyone. I didn't pop out of the womb knowing everything I do today and I've made plenty of mistakes over the years. I'm simply trying to illustrate a trend that I've noticed over the years. That being said, there seems to no longer be any algorithm that people follow when faced with a problem. Well, maybe a better way to put it would be, the alglorithm starts at, I have a problem, and follows a straight line to, call someone else to fix it. Any business that you're going to get into is, in my opinion, going to involve a lot of hand holding.

INCREDIBLE CASH FLOW

I have a friend in the biz who owns 44 mobile homes and grosses well north of $300,000 a year from those rentals. I thought that I may be overlooking this segment of the market so I asked her if I could check out her operation. She politely obliged and drove me around a number of units while explaining her operation. We stopped at a mobile home that she had just finished renovating. While inside, I noticed a stack of envelopes on the counter with different names and addresses on them. I asked what they were for. She replied, "they're 3 day notice to quits." In Florida it's an official way to say, pay the rent that you owe in 3 days or move out in the company of the county sherriff. I counted them real quick, there were nine letters. I asked how often she has to do that to which she replied, "that's about average every month." 9 out of 44 units, 20% of her units require that notice, EVERY MONTH!

I asked her about the eviction process in her neck of the woods. As I would find out, she was intimately familiar with it. I asked her about maintenance issues and problem tenants, her stories didn't sound fun to say the least. Managing those 44 units was her full time job and she employed a full time handyman. She had clearly evolved to be an expert in her field and earned more money on her rentals than I did by a wide margin. As the saying goes, there's no free lunch and she definitely paid a price for that income. That said, for her it was a good value, it was her only job and she had a lot of experience with it. When she goes to sell it, she will be looking for a buyer that has similar strengths and a desire to earn money in that fashion. Her buyer won't be the part time investor with a full time job.

CHAPTER 11

RUNNING THE NUMBERS

A quick takeaway from this chapter.

- **All models and assumptions are wrong – but some can be useful**
- **What rate of return do you want?**
- **Find a quick and accurate way to calculate a properties ROI & Cash on Cash return**
- **Commercial loans are for 5 or more units and are expensive!**
- **Value add and forced appreciation is where the big money is!**
- **Remember, one day you're going to sell it – who's your buyer?**

You understand construction, insurance, local laws and regulations, what is desireable to people and why, what your customer looks like, what your future buyer looks like, how to view your investment time horizon, and how much time and effort you want to put into your investment. Now comes the easy part, running the numbers. I've been giving brief examples of how to run the numbers throughout this book, so hopefully this chapter wil be more of a review than anything. This chapter will be fairly short and will include random examples of different properties to give you a better idea of how to calculate returns. To do this I suggest that you get a pad of paper, a pen or pencil, a calculator, and have access to a mortgage calculator with an amortization table like the ones that can be found on the internet.

This book is intended for the average person who's looking to get into rental real estate and with that said I'm going to assume that most of you will start off with a SFR, duplex, triplex or quadplex. For the examples I'll use some values that I've experienced in the Orlando area, like property taxes and insurance premiums. Obviously your numbers will vary as time goes by and in different parts of the country, but this is how you do it.

OWNER OCCUPIED DUPLEX

Example 1 – Owner occupied duplex, meaning you're going to live in unit and rent the other unit. The duplex is a 2/1 with a garage on each side and rents for $750 per unit. It's for sale for $230,000. Let's say that you plan to use an FHA loan and only put 3.5% down.

To calculate your down payment:

$230,000 x .035 (3.5%) = $8,050

To calculate the amount you will need to finance:

$230,000 x .965 (96.5%) = $221,950

*To calculate your FHA Mortgage Insurance Premium because you're putting less than 20% down, closing cost:

$221,950 (loan amount) x .0175 = $3,884.13

**You may be able to finance this cost.*

To calculate your typical closing costs (CC) not including MIP or your down payment:

$221,950 x .02 = $4,439.00

Total cash from you to close on this loan:

Down payment:	$8,050
MIP:	$3,884.13
Typical CC:	$4,439
	$16,373.13

Now we have to use our mortgage calculator and punch in our financed amount of $221,950. Then we're going to set our loan term to 30 years and for this example we'll use a 4.20% interest rate that is fixed for the life of the loan. You should get a principle and interest payment of $1,085.37. If you remember, we abreviate this by using P&I or just PI.

Now unfortunately, we have to add in the ongoing MIP monthly payment that is required by the FHA because you didn't put down at least 20%. If you remember the average is about .85% depending on credit score.

To calculate this:

$221,950 x .0085 = $1,886.58

Now we need to divide this by 12 to get a monthly payment:

$1,886.58 / 12 = $157.22

Now we take our PI payment and add it to our MIP monthly payment:

$1,085.00 + $157.22 = $1,242.22

Note: *PMI or MIP on FHA loans – FHA lenders no longer cancel your MIP once you reach a certain home equity percentage. The amount of time you'll need to pay MIP depends on your down payment. If you put down at least 10% at the time of your purchase, you'll pay MIP for 11 years. If you have less than 10% down at closing, you'll pay MIP for the entire length (term) of the loan.*

Now you have to calculate your property taxes. Remember, **DO NOT** assume the current taxes listed on the property appraisers website or what your mortgage originator gives you is going to be accurate after year one! I can't stress this enough, the taxes will change and sometimes drastically for reasons that I explained earlier in this book.

In my area the property tax rates range from 1.5% to 2.4% of assessed value, so I use 2% most of the time unless I know that I'm looking at a property in that higher taxed area. Now, as stated earlier in this book, the taxing authority looks at arms length real estate transactions and then taxes them on a value that is some percent less than this amount, presumably to avoid conflict between taxor and the taxee. For example, it would look like this:

$230,000 (sale price) x .88 (taxing authority's discount) = $202,400

Your taxable value (without any exemptions) would then be $202,400, and your expected yearly property taxes, which we abbreviate as T, would be:

$202,400 x .02 = $4,048 per year.

Now we have to break this down into a monthly escrow payment which we'll do by dividing the annual amount by 12:

$4,048 / 12 = $337.00 per month.

Now we have to add homeowners insurance, which we abbreviate as I. For this example we'll use $1,500 as an annual premium. To get a monthly escrow payment we'll just divide by 12:

$1,500 / 12 = $125.00 per month.

$125.00 + $337.00 = $462 a month in Taxes and Insurance, TI.

Now we add everything together:

PI	$1,085.37
TI	$462.00
MIP	$157.22
	$1,704.59 Total PITI plus MIP

Your total monthly mortgage payment will be $1,704.59 per month.

So, we have a total monthly mortgage payment of $1,704.59 a month, the monthly rent we hope to receive is $750, and we used $16,373.13 of our cash to buy the duplex, not counting emergency cash because this may be semi-illiquid assets like a retirement account. Let's look at what our return will be in year one:

PITI + MIP	$1,704.59
- Rent	$ 750.00
	$ 954.59 Your portion of the mortgage.*

**We have to remember in this scenario that you are living in one side which has a certain value. Your basically paying $640.09 a month for your duplex because in year one, your principle paydown equates to about $314.50 a month which goes back to you when you sell it. So to compare you'd have to look around to see what equivalent rents are to give you an idea of how valuable your side of the duplex is, to you. If we use this example, you're paying for a duplex AND getting shelter for about $110.00 a month LESS than if you were renting alone, which of course would return you NONE of what you paid into it.*

Now we'll compute the total capitalization of the duplex:

Property value – $230,000 x .035 (3.5% annual appreciation rate) = $8,050 Year one appreciation

Principle paydown – $314.50 x 12 = $3,774.00 Year one principle paydown.

Cash flow – $0.00 Year one cash flow. (I'm not counting this as negative because you're living in one side.)

	Year one appreciation	$,8,050.00
+	Year one principle paydown	$3,774.00
	Year one capitalization	$11,824.00

Now to find the capitalization rate we take the properties income and divide it by the cash we used to buy it:

Income $11,824 / $16,373.00 cash to close = .722 or 72.2%

Let that sink in for a second, you took $16,373 of your hard earned cash and invested it in a duplex, you got to live in a rental unit for about $110 a month under the going rate, and your investment made $11,824 in returns, in the first year! Your $16,373 investment had a 72% return, in the first year!

Another way to look at it would be:

Property Income in Year one – $11,824 / 12 months = $985.33 a month.
Your out of pocket monthly costs to buy the duplex – $954.59 a month.

	$985.33	Income
-	$954.59	Your expenses
	$30.74	

The duplex paid you $30.74 a month to live there AND own it!

Now let's look at the tax implications of your investment. We'll assume that you're a regualar guy or gal like I was and are making around the median household income, which as of 2019 is $69,560 per the St. Louis Federal Reserves website, which would put you in the 22% tax bracket.

Let's first find out what your effective tax rate would be:

2019 Tax brackets	
0 - $9,700	10%
$9,701 - $39,475	12%
$39,476 - $84,200	22%

The first $9,700 of your income gets taxed at 10% giving you a tax liability (what you owe for that portion of your income) of **$970**. Your income from $9,701 to $39,475 gets taxed at a 12% rate which would look like this:

$39,475 – $9,701 = $29,774

$29,774 x .12 = **$3,572.88** in tax liability on this portion of your income.

The next portion we need to compute is your total earned income of $69,560 minus the beginning threshold of your final tax bracket or $39,476 and multiply it by that brackets rate of 22%:

$69,560 - $39,476 = $30,084

$30,084 x .22 = **$6,618** in tax liability for the final portion of your income.

Calculating your effective rate would look like this:

$970
$3,573
+ $6,618
$11,161 total tax liability.

Now we take your total tax liability and divide it by your total income to get your effective tax rate:

$11,161 / $69,560 = .16 or 16%.

So, even though your income put you in the 22% tax bracket, your actual rate of income taxation was only 16%, pretty cool.

Let's take a look at our legal tax write offs. Again, I'm not a CPA and this is not meant to be legal tax advice! That said, If you live in one side of a duplex and rent the other side you may write off, among other things, half of the mortgage interest, half of the homeowners insurance, and half of the property taxes. If we recall, we have a year one property tax bill of $4,048, and an insurance premium of $1,500. We have to go back to our mortgage calculators' amortiztion table to find out our year mortgage interest which in this scenario is $10,013. So without going into supre detail with the unknowns of what repairs and maintenance and other expenses you might have, we'll just use these three write offs:

T	$4,048	
I	$1,500	
+ Mortgage Interest	$10,013	
	$15,561	Total of write offs

$15,561 / 2 = **$7,781** Total allowable write offs in this scenario. You get to reduce your taxable income by this much.

Let's see what this does to your taxable income for the year.

Annual income $69,560 - $7,781 = $61,779 in adjusted taxable income.

The amounts don't change until our highest bracket so we can just add the two lower bracket totals and go from there:

$ 970
+ $3,573
$4,507 for the 10% and 12% brackets.

In our top bracket we're going to recompute:

Total taxable income $61,779 - $39,476 = $22,303

$22,303 x .22 = $4,907

Add all the brackets together:

$970
$3573
+ $4907
$9,450 is your new tax liability after your write offs.

So we take the total income taxes that your employer took out of your paychecks which was $11,161 and subtract your new tax liability to get your tax refund:

$11,161
- $9,450
$1,711 owed to you.

If we want to be more detailed about our assessment of this owner occupied duplex we can then apply this tax refund to its income in which case the duplex would have paid you the refund divided by 12 or $142.58, plus the original $30.74, for a total of $173.32 a month to live and own the duplex.

I picked this example to do first for a reason. At first glance, it doesn't look like such a great deal, you bust your backside to save up $20,000, get to become a landlord, and have to pay about $200 a month more than your tenant to live in the same size unit! From talking to people over the years I realized that I needed a quick, and easy to grasp message about this so I didn't have to break out a spreadsheet. I started asking people, "If someone told you that you could buy a house for $200 – $300 a month, would you do it?" The answer is always, "Of course!" followed by a look of what a stupid question.

That said, there are always those with big dollar signs in their eyes that tend to blow this investment off. I warn them not to overlook the fact that this investment is returning a whopping 72% per year, which any hedge fund manager on wall street would kill to have, and will return even more once you move out and rent the other side. Also, in this scenario, you effectively went from paying $750 a month in rent to getting paid $173 a month to live, a swing of $923 a month! That's like getting an $11,076 a year raise!

I can't stress this enough to would be rental property owners, when you don't make a whole lot of money, like I didn't, this is your ticket on to the bus, that takes you to the big leagues! You're not gonna be hanging out with A-Rod anytime soon, but you'll be on your way there! Remember what Warren Buffet said, don't pass up a good deal, for a great deal!

OWNER OCCUPIED DUPLEX 5 YEAR PERFORMANCE

Let's move out a bit on the timeline to see how this investment performs. We'll assume that your pay is relatively constant and you've decided to get deeper into the game and get another income property. Unfortunately you're having to come out of pocket every month by about $200 which, on the surface will reduce your savings rate. Let's say that you want to put 20% down on the next property so you're not stuck with MIP. We'll assume that you can save 25% of your take home pay and you've calculated that it'll take you about 4 years to be ready to buy another one. You should have a good idea about the math that I'm going to do so I'm going to speed this up a bit.

Your gross income $69,560 – $11,161 taxes = a net income of $58,399
Net income $58,399 x .25 = $14,599 a year in savings
Year one savings plus tax refund = $14,599 + $1,711 = $16,310.

Year two: You raise the rent by 3% to $773 a month, you save $14,599 + $276 from the increased rent and your tax refund of $1,711 which equates to $16,586, the duplex went up in value by 3.5% or $8,331, and you paid down another $3,700 in principle.

Year three: You raise the rent by 3% to $796 a month, you save $14,599 + $552 from the increased rent and your tax refund of $1,711 which equates to $16,862, the duplex went up in value by 3.5% or $8,623, and you paid down $3,900 in principle (remember, it increases each year).

Year four: You raise the rent by 3% to $820 a month, you save $14,599 + $840 from the increased rent and your tax refund of $1,711 which equates to $17,150, the duplex went up in value by 3.5% or $8,925, and you paid down $4,300 in principle.

Let's look at what you have at the end of year four:

Your duplex is now worth $263,930, you have a remaing balance on your mortgage of $205,488 which gives you $58,442 in equity, and you've saved a total of $66,908 which is enough for a 20% down payment plus 1% in closing costs and leaves you with $11,483 for emergency cash and whatever else. If you wanted to buy the next duplex as an investor and put 25% down you'd only be about $1,700 short of having the down payment and closing costs covered!

With appreciation and principle paydown, minus your initial $16,373 investment, your duplex made $42,069 for you, your increased rents earned you $276 + $552 + $840 = $1,668, and your tax write offs earned you $6,844 for a total of $50,581 in 4 years which averages out to be $12,645 a year or $1,054 a month, for 4 years! Your duplex paid you, $1,054 a month, to live in and own it, not bad!

Let's look at it in terms of your initial cash investment over the 4 year period:

Excluding the value of you living in it, your initial $16,373 investment returned $66,954 in 4 years, ***a 42.2% annual return!***

$66,954 / $16,373 = 4.09 You quadrupled your initial investment in 4 years!

Should I drop the mic now or keep going?

Let's look at the year 5 performance of your investment after you've bought your second duplex and moved out of this one or decided to buy a house. You're now renting both sides and have raised your year 4 rent of $820 by 3% to $845 a month. To be fair we're going to increase your taxes and property insurance from $1,500 per year $1,700 per year, $4,048 per year to $4,556 per year. So we're going to add these together and then divide by 12 to get our adjusted TI monthly payment of $521 per month. Now we're going to add in our PI and MIP of $1,242 to our TI escrow of $521 to get our new total monthly mortgage payment of $1,763.00.

$845 x 2 = $1,690 a month

$1,763 Total mortgage
- $1,690 Total income
- $73

Well that's a bummer, we're still paying $73 a month for a duplex, I'm being sarcastic, that's less than a phone bill! Let's do some quick math and see how it works out for the year:

Current value of your duplex is $263,930 x .035 = $273,168 value by the end of year 5.

$273,168
- $263,930
$9,238 Year 5 total appreciation.

After year 5, the balance on your mortgage will be $201,009, and your TENANTS will have paid down $4,470 worth of principle.

$9,238
+ $4,470
$13,708 total income in year 5

Let's see how that relates to a return on your initial investment of $16,373.

$13,708 / $16,373 = .837 or 84%. An 84% annual return in year 5!

But wait, there's more, let's see how it affects your taxes. Let's assume like many median income earners that you haven't received many raises and your income sits at $72,000 a year. If we remember, the lower tax brackets aren't going to change, so we'll compute the final one:

$72,000 - $39,476 = $32,524

$32,524 x .22 = $7,155

$ 970
$3,573
\+ $7,155
$11,698 total income tax that will be taken out of your pay in year 5

Now let's look at your write offs:

$1,700 Insurance
$4,556 Property taxes
\+ $7,840 Mortgage interest for the year
$14,096 taxable income reduction.

Now, you also had negative cash flow of -$73 a month:

-$73 x 12 = -$876

$14,096
\+ $876
$14,972 total taxable income reduction.

$72,000 - $14,972 = $57,028 in adjusted taxable income.

$57,028 - $39,476 = $17,552

$17,552 x .22 = $3,861

$ 970
$3,573
\+ $3,861
$8,404 tax liability after write offs.

$11,698 total income tax that was taken out of your pay in year 5
\- $8,404 your adjusted tax liability
$3,294 year 5 tax refund

$3,294 tax refund
$4,470 principle paydown
+ $9,238 property appreciation
$17,002 total income in year 5

$17,002 / $16,373 = 1.038 or a 104% return on investment in year 5 all while being cash flow negative!!

***A BIG note here, If you purchased another property like a SFR or another duplex, you'd have even more write offs, and they would be significant! Let's take an educated guess, I'm going to use round numbers that are close:*

Duplex 1 write offs are – $14,972
Duplex 2 that you live in are – $8,000 (because you can only write off half of your expenses)

$14,972
+ $8,000
$22,972 in total taxable income reduction

$72,000 - $22,972 = $49,028

$49,028 - $39,476 = $9,552

$9,552 x .22 = $2,101

$970
$3,573
+ $2,101
$6,644 in adjusted taxable income

$11,698 total income tax that was taken out of your pay in year 5
- $6,644 new tax liability
$5,054 year 5 tax refund!

That's like getting a $421 a month raise in year 5 by tax write offs alone!

Don't underestimate the power of this!! It's how the little people like us make it to the next level!

TURNKEY INVESTOR ONLY DUPLEX

The next example that I'll use is a more expensive turnkey duplex that commands higher rents. This one will be a larger, 2000 sq. ft. 2/2 with a 1 car garage on each side and each unit rents for $1,350. We're going to be in full investor mode on this one which means we're not going to live in one of the units. That said, the banks feel, and they're probably right, that the loan is more risky. I spoke about this earlier, if you remember, the banks figure that if anything goes bad in your life that you'll stop paying on that duplex before you stop paying on your primary residence. Therefore, they require more money down, like a lot more! If you're going to rent a SFR you're going to need 20% down plus closing costs, and don't forget about 6 months of emergency cash! If it's an income property, duplex, triplex, or quadplex, get ready, you'll have to put 25% down!

SOME THOUGHTS ON COMMERCIAL LOANS

When you decide that you're ready for the big leagues and want a 5 unit or larger building, you're going to have to get a commercial loan. If you guessed that commercial loans are more risky, give yourself a pat on the back. As we've learned, banks don't like risky and with that said, be prepared to put 30% or more as a down payment and you're going to get a variable interest rate loan that they'll be nice enough to amortize for 15, 20, or maybe 30 years, but will have a balloon payment due in 5 to 7 years.

You didn't think this was going to be easy, did you? So, there have been many popular, and successful, internet talking heads that will tell you not to waist your time with 4 or less units, that there's an economy of scale to be had with a dense number of units under one roof at one location etc. and they're absolutely right! I'm not sure who their audience is, although it seems like their message is directed at the "newbie", presumably to stir excitement. The average wage earner is not going to be able to buy a 5 to 20 unit building by almost any stretch of the immagination and will be biting off an enormous chunk of risk. Being thrown to the lions would be an understatement!

Just remember, when there's more potential money to be made with more units, there's also more potential money to be lost. Imagine if you had a 25 unit building and in one year 20% of the units (5 units), had to have the A/C system replaced at $5,000 each, I hope you have $25,000 laying around! Slow and steady, get warmed up and build up a bunch of emergency cash before jumping into something like that. That said, I'd definitely encourage you to shoot for the stars when your experience and income get to safe levels, so I'll continue with a brief description of a small commercial loan.

Commercial loans can become a little tricky and as stated before are riskier for both the bank and you so I'm going to breeze over them. We should know by now what amortization means but I'll review. Amortization is the process of paying off debt with regular payments made over time. The fixed payments cover both the principal and the interest on the account, with the interest charges becoming smaller and smaller over the payment schedule. A simpler way to look at it would be the number of payments that the loan is divided into. If you're getting a $100,000 loan and I tell you that you can have the payments divided over 180 months or 360 months, which term will give you the lowest monthly payment? The longer term, of course.

So, the longer the term, 30 years, the lower the monthly payment and greater the total interest paid. The shorter the term, the opposite. Typically, people are only exposed to simpler loans like the ones for cars and a little more complex being the loans for houses but there are many ways to slice a loan. Commercial loans will have a relatively long amortization, the loan divided by a larger number of payment periods so to make the monthly payment lower, but will have a short repayment period of say 5 to 7 years when the balloon payment is due. A balloon payment means that at the end of the balloon term of 5 to 7 years, you owe, in full, the remainding balance on the loan. Yikes! Commercial loans like this will also frequently require you to report your financial situation quarterly to the lender. If your idea of accounting is writing your bank balances on a napkin in crayon, sorry Charlie, you're in the big leagues now, you'd better come to the bank with professional vacancy rate and profit and loss information. Let's take a look small loan.

Say that you have a commercial property that you want to buy for $500,000. Your lender has told you that you'll need 30% down or $150,000 in cash. That means that you're going to finance 70% or $350,000. This loan would have a 70/30 Loan to Value or LTV. Now, because this is a commercial loan and is more risky, the bank of course is going to whack you on the interest rate as well as the down payment, and the term. I would, depending on the economic environment, expect the interest rate on a loan like this to be at least a full point higher than the prevailing 30 year, fixed, SFR mortgage rate. So it turns out that you're going to finance $350,000 that will be amortized over 20 years, at a variable interest rate starting at 5.25%, that adjusts quarterly based on the prime rate that is printed in the Wall Street Journal, and will have a balloon payment due in 5 years.

We're not done yet, a commercial loan requires much more due diligence like environmental studies etc., than a 4 unit or less conventional loan. For this example we'll just use 2% for the closing costs, which means that you'll need to bring another $10,000 to the closing table. In total you're going to need to bring $160,000 in cash to close on this loan. Oh, let's not forget emergency cash, we'll assume 6 months worth of payments. We'll figure that out in a few. Your monthly PI payments are going to be $2,358.45. Insurance on a commercial building is also going to be more expensive, we'll assume for a 5 unit building it will be $4,000 a year or $333 a month. For property taxes we'll assume that there are no special assessments, residual permits or fees, and your tax rate is 2%. You're buildings assessed value will be $500,000 x .02 = $10,000 for your yearly tax bill. If we divide that by 12 we get a monthly payment of $833. Your total monthly PITI on this commercial 5 unit building will be $3,524. Back to our emergency cash, 6 months worth of payments equates to another $21,144 in cash that you'll need to close on this loan for a total of $181,144.

After 5 years of making all of your scheduled payments and assuming that interest rates never change during that period, you will have paid $87,175 in interest and your remainding principle balance will be $292,309. In total, during those 5 years you will have made $211,440 in payments to the bank, the insurance company and the local taxing authority, you will now have to stroke a check to the bank for $292,309, your balloon payment. I hope you've been eating Ramen noodles and taking cold showers for the past 5 years! So, it is possible that the original lender will refinance you into another loan, or they may not.

Either way you're going to have to go through all or some of the loan process again and will have to pay closing costs, again. The lender will usually give you a 45 to 60 day grace period to find another loan, I hope the economy is doing well when you need to find another loan. As you can see, it's a great thing that lenders will take the risk on commercial loans but it also puts tremendous pressure on the debtor. It is my opinion that if and when you decide to take on a commercial loan, that you eat Ramen noodles and take cold showers so you can hyper aggresively pay down that loan or pay it off completely within the repayment period!

Back to our 2000 sq. ft. 2/2/1 duplex. It's for sale for $350,000 and rents fro $1,350 per unit. You'll have to put 25% down plus 2% in closing costs for a total of 27% or $94,500 in cash to close.

$350,000 x .27 = $94,500

You'll be financing 75% or $262,500 on this 75/25 LTV loan.

$350,000 x .75 = $262,500

If we go to our mortgage calculator and punch in a loan amount of $262,500 financed for 30 years at a fixed rate of 4.25% we come up with a monthly PI payment of $1,291. Because this duplex is more expensive we'll assume a more expensive DP3 insurance premium of say, $2,000 a year. We'll calculate our property taxes like this:

$350,000 x .85 (discount) = $297,500 x .02 (tax rate) = $5,950 year one tax bill.

$2,000 DP3 + $5,950 tax bill = $7,950

$7,950 / 12 = $662.50 monthly TI escrow payment.

PI \$1,291.00
+ TI \$ 662.50
\$1,953.50 total PITI monthly payment.

So, your total monthly payment is \$1,954 and your rental income is \$1,350 x 2 = \$2,700 a month.

\$2,700 monthly rental income
- \$1,954 total monthly mortgage expenses
+ \$ 746 monthly positive cash flow

So this duplex is cash flowing \$746 a month or \$8,952 a year, not bad. Let's see what kind of cash on cash return it's generating. Your cash to acquire the property was \$94,500 and in year one it paid you \$8,952 cash back:

\$8,952 / \$94,500 = .0947 or 9.5% cash on cash return, not bad.

Now let's look at what our total return would be excluding tax benefits because they are too specific to the person:

Asset value \$350,000 x .035 (3.5% year one appreciation) = \$12,250

Principle paydown in year one was \$4,320
Cash flow in year one was \$8,952

\$12,250
\$4,320
+ \$8,952
\$25,522 year one capitalization

\$25,522 / \$94,500 = .27 or 27%

A 27% return on your investment in year one, BOOM!

At that rate, in 5 years this asset will have made you $217,712 ***and*** gave you back your original $94,500 for a total return of $312,212! Are you excited yet? Well, I have to bust your bubble just a little bit. Some of you may have noticed that parts of my calculations have some assumptions in them like annual price appreciation and most importantly, occupancy rate. As stated earlier, the 50 year annual home price appreciation is 3.1% and in my area is much higher due to population growth. I touched on occupancy rate earlier in this book and told you that, at the time of this writing, banks were using a 70% occupancy rate.

If we remember, occupancy rate is the percentage of time during the year that your rental unit is occupied and earning money. We went over the easiest way to calculate this by multipling your monthly rent by the occupancy rate, whatever that might be in your area. For the past 12 years my area has hummed along at a 94% occupancy rate, gotta love Florida! Anyway, whenever I look at the viability or profitability of a potential property I apply a worst case, best case, and base case scenario. If after running the numbers I'm ok with the worst case scenario, I know it's a good deal for me. After that I will average the best case and worst case returns to see how the asset will likely perform.

INVESTING IN OUTSIDE AREAS

At some point you'll have to go outside of your home area where you've become an expert in real estate trends to find your next property. At that point you'll have to consider the economy and direction of the new unknown area that you're thinking about investing in. As an example, Florida has been able to support strong property price growth and low vacancy rates for many reasons. Florida has typically had good leadership and is very business oriented. It has great weather which is a major reason for it being such a huge tourist destination. It has a diverse economy that is attracting new companies in the fields of Fin-tech, healthcare, aerospace, and manufacturing, from high tax states like New York and California. There's also no personal income tax which everyone, including retirees like! The culmination of the above has led to the state averaging ***22,500 new residents every month, for the last 10 years***, BOOM! In 2010, Florida had 18.8 million residents, by the end of 2020 it was 21.5

million! Suffice to say, it's a good place to own a rental! So when you're researching new economies to buy properties in, Floridas economic model is probably a pretty good one to compare it to.

ASSUMPTIONS AND MODELS

I heard a saying a long time ago that, all models are wrong, but some can be useful. If you think about it, it's true, to some degree we're always guessing at data points. Anyway, I use two assumptions in my models that I believe to be fairly accurate and repeatable. The first being the annual price appreciation that I spoke about earlier which can of course, depending on your assets time horizon, be extremely volitile as witnessed in the 2008 crash. If you sold in 2006 you were laughing all the way to the bank. If you wanted to sell after 2008 you'd be locking in severe losses. If you think about it, those unfortunate people had to hang on to their assets for another 8 to 10 years before the regained their values, they lost 8 to 10 years worth of time!

The second assumption that I use is occupancy rate. I've carefully studied this in my area for a long time now and I'm blessed enough to maintain an occupancy rate that so close to 100% that I use that number for my best case scenario. For my probable worst case scenario I use what the banks use, 70%. On a side note, for a 2008 style, the world is collapsing model, I look at what my total monthly mortgage payment is and divide it by the number of bedrooms there are in the property, in this case, four. So, \$1,954 / 4 = \$488 a month per room. A person making less than \$23,000 a year could afford that. Anything beyond that point I'd have to come out of pocket for. So if I have six months worth of emergency cash or \$11,724 and I had to lower the room rent by \$100 down to \$388 a month, I'd have to come out of pocket \$400 a month. \$11,724 / \$400 = 29.31 or 29 months. At \$388 a month for room rent, which is the equivalent of a 43% decrease in the current rents, I'd be able to keep that property for 29 months before I had to start paying the difference out of my salary. I'd have almost 2 ½ years to whether any storm or sell the property.

So, if we take our current rental income of $2,700 and multiply it by .70 we get $1,890 a month. Oops, we just went negative! We just went from making $746 a month to having to pay $64 a month!

- $1,954 total mortgage expenses
+ $1,890 total rental income
- $64

Now before you get too fired up remember the duplex in the first example. Number 1. – even if you had to pay $64 a month for a while it'd probably still be a decent deal. Number 2. – it could happen for some period of time so you'd better be prepared! Number 3. – your vacancy rate will most likely not be that high for any sutained period of time, but you do need to research it before you buy something. You are watching the rentals around you as they come available and noting how fast they go off of the market, right? You have to put the work in to protect yourself!

So let's look at this calculated out:

Asset value $350,000 x .035 = $12,250

Principle paydown $4,320

Negative cash flow -$64 x 12 = -$768

$12,250
$4,320
+ -$768
+ $15,802 total income in year one at a 70% occupancy rate.

$15,802 / $94,500 = .167 or 16.7% return on investment, I'll take it!

Note: *Most people will breeze over the numbers of this deal and as soon as the cash flow turns negative, they'll be done. By doing so, they will have missed a good deal, searching for a great deal. If you want to be like everyone else, do like everyone else! I know you're* *smarter than that, because you're reading this book trying to speed your learning and learn from the mistakes of others, keep it up!*

So, then we take the worst case scenarios return of 16.7% and add it to the best cases return of 27% and divide by two to get the average:

16.7% + 27% = 43.7 / 2 = 21.85% average year one return.

TOTAL ROI VS CASH ON CASH RETURN

I don't know about you, but I love it when my investments make 100% returns every 5 years, just sayin'. If we want to look at different aspects of this investment, and you should, we can look at the total ROI versus the cash on cash return. As mentioned before in this book, different investments can have different purposes. Say that you don't need monthly cash flow and you're going to pay a management company to manage the property which ends up eating all of its free cash flow. The plan may be to hold this investment for 10 years and not have to deal with it much because you're super busy. In 10 years you sell it and pocket a $200,000 payday which translates to an annual return of "only" 14%. I'd take it!

On the other hand, say that you have more time than money and need the cash flow. Maybe you save up and buy four mobile homes for $10,000 each that need a bunch of work. You fix them up and rent them for $500 a month each. You have no mortgage, your taxes and insurance are ridiculously low and you're making an extra $24,000 a year in cash. You're most definitely going to work harder for that return than the first investor worked for his/her return, but in the same time frame the two of you will have made about the same amount of money!

That said, I want to share a concept or rather, a way of looking at things if you haven't thought of it already. The first investor worked however hard, for however long to have the money that he/she earned, invested, and saved, work for him/her. They cultivated this money which now, with some guidance, works hard for them. In the other scenario, the mobile home guy was just getting started in his journey, having more time than money and had to spend a lot of time, effort, and stress, to make his money. If you're just starting out, this is usually the case. You will have to work for your money for a good while before your money can work for you. If this is the case, do what you have to do and get after it! If you work hard and smart, you'll be in the first investors position before you know it! Don't forget, you have to have money so it can work for you, if you don't save it…eeee pobrecito!

OK, back to our ROI vs. Cash on Cash return comparison. So we have a total average ROI of 21.9%, let's see what our cash on cash return is. If we use the average of the difference between 100% occupancy and 70% occupancy we get 15%. So we'll take the worst case scenario of 70% occupancy and add 15% to it to get an occupancy rate of 85%. Our total rents are $2,700:

$2,700 x .85 = $2,295

$2,295 adjusted rental income
\- $1,954 total mortgage expenses
$ 341 monthly free cash flow

$341 x 12 = $4,092 yearly average free cash flow

$4,092 / $94,500 = .0433 or 4.33% cash on cash return.

If you want to look at it like a dividend yielding stock, this property provides a year one cash dividend of 4.33% at an 85% occupancy rate. If it's rented continuously for the year:

$2,700 100% rental income
\- $1,954 total monthly mortgage expenses
$ 746 total monthly cash dividend

$746 x 12 months = $8,952 in year one cash dividends

$8,952 / $94,500 = .0947 or a 9.47% cash on cash return or dividend.

QUADPLEX

Now let's look at a quadplex listed for $475,000. Each unit is a 950 sq. ft. 2/2, it's concrete block with a hip roof that is 6 years old, it was built in 1992 with grounded 12 ga. copper romex, has copper pressure piping and PVC DWV piping. It has decent windows that all have screens and are functional. Each unit has a standard lower effeciency split A/C system with the air handler inside and the condensing unit outside. All of the A/C units are 4 years old and are in good condition. The stairwell to the second floor and the balcony are steel with lightweight concrete and are in good condition with no signs of rust or structural degradation.

The balcony is appropriately sloped away from the building for proper drainage. The "pad" that the quadplex was built on is sufficiently high and appropriately pitched for proper drainage away from the structure. You've also looked at the lot as a whole to see where the engineer decided to send all of the property's water run off (towards the street, to one side, or the back of the lot) and you don't see any issues. You've also looked at the street to see where the water collected on it drains and/or collects. You've determined that it doesn't collect or run off into the quadplexes lot based on the direction of the slope and the lack of dirt and debris build up from prior standing water.

The building is connected to muicipal water and sewer, you've identified the water shutoff(s) and the main sewer cleanout and the most probable path that these pipes take out into the street. You've also determined that there's nothing that could or is interfering with those paths out to the street like a big tree. There's no evidence that tenant "X" is consitantly parking his big work truck on or across that pathway either. There's also no trees near the building or driveway that could cause any problems. The parking area is not pitched or raised in any locations that would cause water to drain back against the building. If the building has a gutter system, the downspouts lead well away from the buildings foundation, say 24" or more.

The building itself is PSL, Plumb, Square, and Level. Plumb being vertical, Level meaning flat, and Square meaning that intersecting joints are 90 degs. This easiest to tell by paying close attention to how windows and doors line up with their frames and if they operate smoothly. Moving inside we find basic rental property finishings like, basic cabinets, formica countertops, linoleum in the wet areas and carpet everywhere else. Everything appears to be clean and in good working condition, just basic. If the area supports it, there's potential for forced appreciation and increased rental income from upgrading.

After looking through the attic you don't find any evidence of randomly spliced wiring and there are no signs of water or structural damage from say, a big tree limb that crashed through the roof 6 years ago and Joe Blow roofer repaired the damaged trusses using his own engineering. Back inside, all of the toilets are solidly attached to the floors, the faucets for the tubs and sinks don't move and are functioning. The areas around the tubs were they meet the walls sounds and feels solid. The floors themselves feel solid and don't have any weird slopes or dips in them. You know from your research that this building, in it's current condtion, and in this area, should command rents of $900 to $950 a month and should have an occupancy rate of 94%. You also know from being an expert about rents in your area that if you renovate this property, you can easily get $1,300 a month in rent per unit. So let's look at what this property should yield:

$475,000 x .27 = $128,250 in cash to close

$475,000 x .75 = $356,250 to finance for 30 years at a fixed interest rate of 4.25% gives a monthly PI payment of $1,753

$475,000 x .85 x .02 = $8,075 year one tax bill

$1,800 DP3 insurance premium in year one

T $8,075 + I $1,800 = $9,875 / 12 months = $823 monthly TI escrow payment

PI $1,753
+ TI $ 823
$2,576 total monthly mortgage payment.

$925 x 4 units = $3,700 in total rental income

$3,700 rental income
- $2,576 total monthly mortgage expenses
$1,124 free cash flow

$1,124 x 12 = $13,488 in year one cash flow

$13,488 / $128,250 = .1051 or 10.5% cash on cash return in year one, nice!

Let's look at the total return or cap rate:

$475,000 x .035 = $16,625 in year one appreciation

Principle paydown in year one = $6,012

$16,625 year one appreciation
$13,488 year one cash flow
$ 6,012 year one principle paydown
$36,125 year one total capitalization

$36,125 / $128,250 =.2816 or a 28.2% total return on this property in year one.

How does this property perform in our worst case scenario of a 70% occupancy rate:

$925 x .70 = $648 a month in adjusted rental income per unit

$648 x 4 = $2,592 in total adjusted rental income

$2,592 total adjusted rental income
- $2,576 total monthly mortgage expenses
$ 16 total monthly adjusted free cash flow

$16 x 12 months = $192 in year one adjusted cash flow

$16,625 year one appreciation
$ 6,012 year one principle paydown
+ $ 192 year adjusted cash flow
$22,829 year one total adjusted income or capitalization.

$22,829 / $128,250 = .178 or a 17.8% total cap rate.
Pretty damn good!

RENOVATING THE QUADPLEX FOR BIG RETURNS

Let's look and see how it performs if we upgrade the property. I'm going to breeze over the details as this is just for conceptual purposes. The cabinets are good but we're going to put nicer doors and hardware on them. We'll put fancy quartz countertops and nice tile backsplashes in all of the wet areas. We'll pull out the linoleum and carpet and tile the whole place. We'll upgrade the appliances to the nicest looking, in style, base models. We'll paint with trendy but neutral colors and make sure that the trim has a nice, crisp, complimentary, but different paint color. If need be, we'll change all of the outlets, switches, covers, fans and lights so that they're in style, neutral enough and match each other. I'll assume that you're going to do some of this work yourself and hire a professional for some. Obviously prices will vary with time and place and so will each readers ability and experience. So, for exercise we're going say that all of this will cost around $15,000 per unit or $60,000 for the whole building. That's a pretty substantial number isn't it? It's almost 50% of your cash to close. Remember, you don't have to do all four units at once, you can do one at a time. Let's see how the completed building performs at a 100% occupancy rate:

$1,300 x 4 units = $5,200 in total rents after renovation

$5,200 in total rent
-$2,576 in total monthly mortgage expenses
$2,624 in total monthly free cash flow

$2,624 x 12 months = $31,488 in year one cash flow

$31,488 year one renovated cash flow
$16,625 year one appreciation
+ $ 6,012 year one principle paydown
$54,125 year one total renovated capitalization

$128,250 in down payment and closing costs + $60,000 in renovation costs = $188,250 in total cash into the property

$54,125 / $188,250 = .2875 or a 28.8% year one total cap rate.

$31,488 / $188,250 = .167 or a 16.7% cash on cash return in year one.

Cash on cash return is up from 10.5% to 16.7% and the total cap rate is up to 28.8% from 28.2%. Now, some of you might be scratching your heads in disappointment about the total cap rate not going up that much. That's a tough one to answer because I have no idea how much the building increased in value after it was renovated but I can give you an idea using my area and my level of input (work) as an example. Because I do every bit of work that is legally acceptable, I'm able to save a substantial amount of money. Just based on input costs and from experience with doing this exact renovation that for every dollar I spend, I get two dollars back. But let's cut that back by 25% and see what happens:

$60,000 in renovation costs x 1.75 = $105,000 increase in value

$475,000 original asset value + $105,000 after renovation increase = $580,000 after renovation value.

$580,000 x .035 = $20,300 year one appreciation.

$31,488 year one after renovation cash flow
$20,300 year one after renovation appreciation
+ $ 6,012 year one principle paydown
$57,800 year one total after renovation capitalization

$57,800 / $188,250 = .3070 or a 30.7% year one total cap rate, BOOM!

Let's look at this building over the next five years. After year 5 the building will be worth $688,858 and you'll have a principle balance of $322,895. You'll have $31,488 per year of cash flow assuming you don't raise the rents:

$688,858 - $322,895 = $365,963 in equity after year 5

$31,488 x 5 years = $157,440 in cash after year 5.

$365,963 + $157,440 = $523,403 of total capitalization after year 5, without raising rents or taking into account any tax benefits. That's an average annual return of 22.7%* over five years! *Remember, as your equity builds up, your return on that equity goes down and we didn't raise rents.

QUICK FORMULAS TO SAVE TIME

I think by now you understand how to run the numbers and you should be able to apply your numbers, to your situation. That said, depending on the market that you're in, you may want or need to, find a faster way to see if a property meets your criteria and is worth further investigation. For instance, there were 1,000's of properties listed at any given time and the good ones would go in a matter of hours. Because I was an expert on my area and I knew what things would rent for I came up with a quick calculation exercise. Whatever the prevailing interest rates where, I'd find out how many thousands of dollars financed, over 30 yrs in my case, equalled $100 in monthly payment. Say that $20,000 financed for 30 years at a 4% ***fixed*** rate equalled a monthly payment of $100. If I had a property that I was considering, that was listed for $250,000 with two units that would rent, as is, for $875 each, the equation would look like this:

$250,000 x .75 = $187,500 / $20,000 = 9.375 or $938 a month in PI.

Because I had run the numbers on so many properties I knew what price ranges of properties had what price of property taxes and insurance and at that time it happened to be between $400 and $600 a month TI. So, I would just add The PI and my averaged TI together to get a pretty accurate idea of what the total monthly mortgage would be:

$938 + $500 = $1,483 in total monthly mortgage costs.

I would then use a 100% occupnacy rate and use the going rent times however many units, in this case, two, to find out what the properties income would be:

$875 x 2 = $1,750 in total monthly income.

$1,750 total monthly income
- $1,483 total monthly mortgage expenses
$ 267 monthly free cash flow

You know where I'm going with this:

$267 x 12 = $3,204 per year in cash flow

$250,000 x .26 = $65,000 cash to close

$3,204 / $65,000 = .04929 or a 4.93% cash on cash return.

That's no bueno! As a rule of thumb and depending on market conditions, I look for a minimum 10% cash on cash return. Another way of doing it which is less accurate but faster is taking the total monthly rents and multiplying them by 12, and then by 10, to get what the sale price should be so the property returns roughly, 10% on cash, which would look like this:

$875 x 2 = $1,750 x 12 = $21,000 x 10 = $210,000 sale price.

This can also be done another way by multiplying the sales price by 1% to see if it is more, less, or equal, to the monthly rental income:*

$250,000 x .01 = $2,500 in required monthly income

$1,750 total monthly income
- $2,500 total monthly mortgage expenses
- $ 750 negative monthly cash flow

**I have found that this method is not nearly accurate enough for me for the time that it saves, which isn't much. Using the above method, it tells you real quick that either the income generated is not enough to cover the mortgage expenses or the price is too high, but not much else and therefore requires further calculation. In the end, you're going to have to find out what fair value is at your rate of return to see how far off your idea of price is versus the sellers. If you guys are close enough it's worth negotiation. So, I'll do my calculations real quick to show you:*

$250,000 x .26 = $65,000 I can use 10% of this number to do quick math if I want.

$250,000 x .75 = $187,500 / $20,000 = $983 + $500 = $1,483

$875 x 2 = $1,750 - $1,483 = $267 x 12 = $3,204 / $65,000 = .04929 or 4.93%

My cash to close is $65,000 so in order for me to get a 10% annual return I need a yearly cash flow of $6,500.

$6,500 / 12 = $542 a month in needed free cash flow

$542 - $267 = $275 a month in extra income needed.

Oh, that's fairly easy, if $20,000 equals $100 a month, this property is over priced by almost $300 a month so the price needs to come down by $60,000:

$20,000 x 3 = $60,000
$250,000 - $60,000 = $190,000 what the new sales price should be, easy!

Let's see how accurate this is:

$190,000 x .26 = $49,400 cash to close

$190,000 x .75 = $142,500 / $20,000 = $713 PI

$190,000 x .85 (appraisers discount) x .02 (tax rate) = $3,230 year one tax bill

$1,500 year one DP3 policy

$3,230 + $1,500 = $4,730 year one TI

$4,730 / 12 = $394 a month in TI

$713 PI + $394 TI = $1,107 total monthly PITI

$875 rent x 2 = $1,750 - $1,107 PITI = $643 a month in free cash flow

$643 x 12 = $7,716 year one free cash flow

$7,716 / $49,400 = .1561 or a 15.6% cash on cash retrun.
Way off of our 10% guestimate!

This should be a prime example that there is no super quick and accurate way to find out what sales price is needed for what return, no matter what method you use. Any time that you change the sales price, the down payment, taxes and the PI change. The farther you go, the bigger the difference. So, I end up having to do the math anyway which is what I suggest that you do. The researched methods I've been using in this book as far as an average insurance and property tax rate, the property appraisers discount, and how much money equals $100 a month in payment is about as easy as you can make this process without having wild differences in results. It's up to you to research and qualify the results of your area.

As you become an expert on your area you'll be able to slice up a potential property however you'd like to see if it looks like a good return and is worth further investigation. You can slice it up into purchase price per square foot, price per bedroom, or price per door. You can then apply a ratio to those metrics if you want. The point is, play with the numbers to get some practice and find an accurate way that you like to run the numbers.

FORCED APPRECIATION

As you begin to expand your real estate empire you'll start to notice, and be able to take advantage of, new opportunities in the rental real estate game. The 800 pound gorilla in the room is called, "forced appreciation". Although the majority of U.S. rental real estate units by a wide margin, are run by little folks like us, we should remember, that it is still a business! We've put a bunch of blood, sweat, tears, and, oh yeah, money, into our businesses, so we should try to get the highest performance from our properties. That said, as your cash reserves grow, you'll be able to take advantage of "value add" deals, which is a fancy way of saying, the property needs a bunch of work to achieve top performance but the seller isn't willing to do it, so the property ***should*** be offered at a discount.

It doesn't take a rocket scientist to figure out that if you buy something at a discount and fix it up, you can sell it for more profit, but that's only part of the equation here. We spent an additional $60,000 in cash in the last quadplex example that we upgraded, which added intrinsic value to the property of around $105,000, bringing it's value to $580,000 from the $475,000 that we purchased it for. It makes sense, nicer cabinets, counter tops and tile floors etc. As a bonus, it also brought in much higher rents which made us very happy! Let's take a look at how this increased rental income fits into the value equation of our rental property.

From the last duplex example that we just went over, we were looking for a minimum 10% cash on cash return for our invested money. If we remember, the return on investment was related to the price of the duplex and the rental income it generated. If it could generate a 10% return on rents of $1,750 per month and at a purchase price of around $220,000, what would the purchase price go up to get that 10% return if rents increased by 50%? If the buyer is buying this as a business, they're going to be looking at it like this and comparing it to there other investment options. Let's see how this works with our prior quadplex example:

$1,300 x 4 units = $5,200 in total post renovation rental income.

$5,200
- $2,576 PITI
$2,624 year one monthly cash flow

$2,624 x 12 months = $31,488 in year one cash flow

So, just looking at this real quick, we can see that if an investor is looking for a 10% cash on cash return on their investment, this property would support that with a $314,880 investment, meaning, using all of the same numbers like our 27% cash to close, our quadplex would be worth $1,165,000! Before you get too excited, remember I warned you about using "quick" formulas and as the numbers get higher, so do the discrepencies. I'm going to use a more conservative number like $680,000 for our theoretical after renovation value. Let's see how this plays out:

$680,000 x .27 = $183,600 cash to close

$680,000 x .75 = $510,000 for 30 years at a fixed rate of 4.25% = $2,509 PI

$680,000 x .85 x .02 = $11,560 T

$2,000 DP3 policy because our building is worth more now I

$11,560 T + $2,000 I = $13,560 TI yearly / 12 months = $1,130 monthly TI

$2,509 PI + $1,130 TI = $3,639 PITI total monthly mortgage expense.

$5,200 total monthly income
- $3,639 total monthly mortgage expenses
$1,561 total monthly free cash flow

$1,561 x 12 months = $18,732 in year one free cash flow

$18,732 / $183,600 = .1020 or a 10.2% cash on cash return. Pretty cool!

As you can see, the next buyer that is willing to accept a 10% cash on cash return, just like you did when you bought it, will now pay $205,000 more than you did, because you spent an extra $60,000, a 242% one year return! Now you understand why the big boys and girls look for these value add properties. Think for a second if we had the same situation, but with a 30 unit building. We renovate the property and achieve a $375 per unit increase in rental income, times 30 units equals an extra $11,250 a month in income, or an extra $135,000 in yearly income! What about a 200 unit apartment complex, $375 times 200 units equals an extra $75,000 a month, or an extra $900,000 in yearly income!

Forced appreciation is huge, but as I've stated before in this book, there are no free lunches! When I was first getting into the game, almost every property was a value add property. I would have the, "everything is so easy, why don't you just..." people explain to me that if they were doing it they would only buy value add properties and make gozillions. Oh, if it were that easy. They seemed to forget that I wasn't rich at the time and in order to make a value add property work, you need the cash to renovate it, ***along with all of the cash required to buy it!*** This annoying little detail always seemed to escape them. Suffice to say that I had to watch a painful number of incredible deals, like the breeze through my fingers, slip away! That's the way it goes. If you don't pass up on all of those good deals, eventually you'll build up enough cash to buy ***and*** renovate that value add property.

WHO'S YOUR BUYER

One more thing I want to mention is, even though the numbers may work out to a $680,000 sales price, it doesn't mean that you're going to have a buyer at that price. If you remember farther back in this book I suggested that you know who your renter is going to be and who your future buyer is probably going to be. As you move up higher on the income scale things that were outrageously expensive to you will become understandable and reasonable. You'll end up building up a significant amount of cash and you will most likely not be interested in "smaller" deals like a quadplex. God willing, you may have half a million dollars that you're looking to put to work and through your experience you'll know that you want that 20 unit value add building, not a few duplexes.

That said, I've noticed that generally, things move in price ranges and each price range has its buyers. You always want to make sure, if at all possible, that you're in the sweet spot of the range, where you have the biggest supply of would be buyers or you're in a niche market. That quadplex at $680,000 may be way out of reach for the "small" investor who doesn't have the $183,600 in cash to close and the extra $21,834 in emergency cash. So now you're hunting for that person who is transitioning from small to medium investor ***and*** wants your quadplex. How soon you want to, or have to, sell that quadplex will determine whether you realize that huge forced appreciation. Be careful and don't get lazy, put some thought into it!

The higher you go in the price range, the more sophisticated your pool of buyers are likely to be. The sheer fact that your prospective buyer has a few hundred thousand dollars laying around to buy something with is an example of them being able to navigate this challenging life with a higher degree of success. They will have most likely faced the same challenges and had similar experiences to what you're going through. I know I can sell any one of my duplexes to an owner occupant who will accept a much lower return than a higher end buyer. The owner occupant will most likely be buying on emotion because of how upgraded the duplex is and they will be comparing the cost to live in one side of that duplex with the cost to buy a similar condo or house. The condo will be about the same price as one unit of the duplex but will have high and unpredictable HOA fees. A house that is average size will be same price or more than the entire duplex. They look at it like a stepping stone to home ownership, which it is, where someone else is helping them pay for it. They will most likely be willing to buy it at whatever the market rate is for a house.

That said, the higher wealth buyer is not looking for a place to live in or a stepping stone to home ownership. They're looking for the highest return on their investment and they most likely have many different investment options other than your $680,000 quadplex, it's just a fact of life. At almost every rung of the economic ladder there's going to be someone above and below you. I know people with private jets that cost $5,000 an hour to operate and a couple thousand dollars a month to store in a hangar. I remember when it took me an entire year to save $5,000. Those people have shared experiences where they've been at a business conference and met half a dozen people that make as much money in one month, as they do in an entire year! Know who your future buyer is and don't pay for things that you won't get a return on! If the area and the future buyer doesn't support quartz counter tops, keep the formica!

So, set up your economic model carefully and make sure to the best of your ability that your research data is realistic. Always keep your eye on the broader economy like , interest rates, unemployment, average earnings, home ownership options, and anything else that may affect your investments value. When you look at your models remember that, all models are wrong in some fashion and magnitude, so be conservative and be prepared for deviations. Once you solidify your model and price range, stick to it! You're not trying to win an online auction for a sweater, if it's outside your range and the seller wont come down, ***walk away!*** He that fights and runs away, may turn and fight another day; But he that is in battle slain, will never rise to fight again – Tacitus. Hit a home run on your first property!

CHAPTER 12

MAKING AN OFFER

A brief reminder from previous chapters BEFORE you make an offer.

- **Know your financial position**
- **Know your product - value**
- **Know the area**
- **Know your customers wants and needs**
- **Know the areas rents**
- **Know the value of recently sold properties in the area**
- **Know your customers options**

A quick takeaway from this chapter.

- **Research your sellers position on the property**
- **Run your numbers**
- **If your market supports it, make a lowball offer**
- **Remember, you make your money on the buy**

You've done your research over the last six months to a year and have looked at every listing for sale, for rent, and that has sold. By doing this you know what sold and for how much and what rented for how much, how fast it rented, and most importantly, why? You have a real good idea about what people want and how much they can and are willing to pay for it. You've run the numbers on a bunch of different properties at different price points throughout the last year for practice and you've come to realize what you can afford and what return you're likely to get. You've gotten your financial house in order by cutting way down on your debt, cutting out non essential items, and maybe working some extra hours or getting a second job. You've been confirming what is written in this book by speaking to different lenders and seasoned investors. You have your down payment and emergency cash saved up, along with a pre-approval letter and when asked, you can quickly provide proof of your funds.

You're looking sharp and by now, probably know more than your real estate agent. You're 90% of the way there, don't quit now! It's probably going to be tough and may take many months or more, to find "the one". Remember, you've made it much farther than most and no matter how many reps are in your workout, the last one is always the hardest! Stay sharp! Stay motivated! When the time is right, it will happen!

You're up early one morning doing your normal routine, checking to see what's for sale and boom, there it is! You've driven past it probably a dozen times over the last year. It's in a great area, rents are good and the economy is doing well. It definitely needs updating and has some deferred maintenance but it's structurally sound. Lucky for you, the current owner has owned it for the last 15 years and hasn't kept up with the going rate on rents. The property has long term tenents on both sides for the last 8 and 11 years, because of course, the rents are $300 a month under the going rates. Hopefully the realtor doesn't deal much with MFR's (Multi-Family Residential) and is only basing value on the SFR market.

RESEARCHING YOUR SELLER

The real estate agent may not see the potential value in some moderate upgrades and the increased rents that it will bring. Hopefully not. You quickly scan through the listing pictures online looking for any areas of hidden potential or red flags (aluminum branch circuit wiring etc.). It's looking good so far. You do a quick property appraisers search to see if you can find out who owns it and confirm that indeed they have owned it for the last 15 years. You then put the owners name into your local authoritys database that keeps records on mortgages (our's is the county comptroller) and see if they have a mortgage on the property, for how much and when the mortgage was first recorded.

You find that he indeed has a mortgage on the property for \$157,000 that was originated 15 years ago. You don't find any mortgage satisfactions or new mortgages that have been recorded after the original one indicating that he has not paid off his original mortgage nor has he refinanced. We have to assume that he put 25% down on the property 15 years ago because the property appraiser and comptrollers sight indicate that he has owned and lived in his primary residence, which is not this duplex, for the last 22 years because he's had the homestead exemption for that entire time. Doing some math you assume that he bought the property for around \$210,000 15 years ago. You punch his mortgage amount into a mortgage calculator and enter the prevailing interest rate at the time of his purchase.

You scroll down the amortization table to the 15 year mark and find that he only owes \$111,517, assuming he didn't pay any extra towards his mortgage which he may have. You then check the property tax authoritys website to see what his tax rate is, how much his property taxes are and if he is current or behind on his taxes. Everything looks good and he's up to date on his property taxes. You make a quick call to your insurance agent to find out how much a policy on that duplex will be. The real estate listing agent knows that it's a bit ugly, has some deferred maintenance, and needs some upgrades so they list it for \$305,000 which is about \$20,000 below FMV (Fair Market Value).

RUN YOUR NUMBERS

If the duplex sells for \$305,000, after real estate commisions and closing costs, he should profit around \$169,083:

\$305,000 x .92 (6% RE comm and 2% closing costs) = \$280,600

\$280,600 Profit after fees
- \$111,517 Principle mortgage balance owed
\$169,083 Gross profit before income taxes

Current rents in the area are \$1,050 a month for the way the property sits but he's only getting \$750 per month per side. From your research you know that he's probably paying somewhere around $944 a month in PI and from checking the tax assessors sight and current insurance rates you calculate that he's paying around $431 a month in TI, for a total PITI of $1,375 a month. So, if your calculations and guesstimations are correct, the duplex is bringing in $1,500 a month in revenue and his total monthly mortgage expenses are $1,375:

$1,500
\- $1,375
$ 125 monthly free cash flow

From what we can estimate about the circumstances of the seller and the property, keeping in mind that all models are wrong to some degree, it looks like this seller may have run out of steam on being a landlord in regards to the low rents and deferred maintenance, and he's not cash flowing a whole lot. If he has a lawn service, his cash flow will effectiviely be zero. The rents may be low because he wants tenants that know what a good deal their getting and don't bother him. This seller may just be done being a landlord. That said, we may have a fairly promising environment to work with.

THROW A LOWBALL OFFER - MAYBE

We have to look at the big picture though, which would be demand for this product. The bargining advantage is in your favor if there's a balance of supply and demand, and it's most definitely in your favor if there is over supply. If however, you happen to be in a hot market where there's a lot of demand for MFR's, prices and rents are rising, you're going to have to move fast and present a strong offer very close to full asking price. If the market is weak and demand to be a landlord is low, that duplex might sit on the market for 6 or 8 months. If that's the case, I'm going to significantly low ball him to see where he's at. In this case, I'd offer him $30,000 less, or $275,000, citing in writing, the poor condition of the property, a list of needed upgrades and its low curb appeal. I'm then going to let him stew over the fact that he has a qualified buyer with proof of funds, that's ready and able to close, who has a fair list of concerns, who will be his ticket out of the landlord game, and he'll still profit around $141,483 for his years of trouble. He'll be out of the landlord hassle, put $141,483 in his pocket, and won't have to lift a finger to fix anything on the property.

$275,000 x .92 (8% closing costs) = $253,000

$253,000 - $111,517 (remaining mortgage balance) = $141,483 gross profit.

I would definitely expect some back and forth and plenty of B.S. from the real estate agent citing the endless awesomeness and potential of the property. If he ended up not coming off of the price enough I would ask for repairs and or upgrades. In this case I'd all but guarantee that he's not going to do any repairs or upgrades and after he sees that I'm not compromising on the value and he's not getting any other full price offers, he'll come back to me with something like $300,000. I would then come back at $280,000 and the deal would probably end up somewhere near $295,000. That said, if it was an ice cold market like back in 2009 – 2012 , I'd let that sucker sit on the market for another year and then resubmit an offer that's $25,000 lower than my original low ball offer. If he didn't want to come off the price it'd be obvious that he doesn't really want to sell and I'd move on to the next property.

YOU MAKE YOUR MONEY ON THE BUY

The point of that exercise was to get you to think about evaluating your position and the sellers position, through research, and finding out who, has what kind of leverage. You can definitely learn this through trial and error but you'll likely miss out on some good deals in the process. One key point to remember is, ***you make your money on the buy!*** In this example, there are two ways that we can make money on the buy. 1. Buy at full asking price, remember, we determined that it was listed $20,000 under FMV and let the property operate as it is. 2. Buy at full asking price taking advantage of the $20,000 discount and raise the rents to fair market value.

This is just an abbreviated example to get you thinking. Don't forget that there are a lot of things involved in valuing a property and just because the price is $20,000 lower than the other duplexes doesn't necessarily mean that you are getting a good value. It might need $20,000 worth of work and the seller isn't willing to pay you for the hassle of getting this done or the down time while your unit is empty. In that case, depending on the market, I'd walk away from that deal. Remember, knowledge is power!

CHAPTER 13

KNOW YOUR CONTRACT

A quick takeaway from this chapter.

- **Read and understand your contract and it's time frames carefully**
- **Be very careful with wire transfers**

Up to this point you've put a lot of hard work into being prepared for this deal and luck favors the prepared! You've run your numbers on this deal, done your research, set your minimums, done your initial inspection, calculated your offer, and submitted it. The realtor calls you a day or two later and says that your offer has been accepted, congratulations! Take your time and ***carefully read and understand the contract and all of its time frames!*** If you miss a timeline, you could lose that good deal and your deposit. You definitely don't want to go through all of the work that you did only to lose the property to a back up offer because you didn't know that it would take 3-5 business days to transfer your own money! It's going to be a game of hurry up and wait. Don't expect others to keep you on track, know your contract and be prepared for delays.

You'll eventually get a number of calls from your lender, real estate or closing agents, requesting that you get this paperwork emailed and that payment done right away. You'll go from sitting in your recliner to running around like a chicken with its head cut off trying to get page 11 of your retirement accounts rules emailed only to find out that it is intentionally blank, which is why you didn't send it in the first place, but they need it anyway. A week later you'll be going through your bank statements trying find out what that $400 transfer was so you can write a letter to your lender expalining it. I'm not exaggerating, remember, after 2008 and depending on the economic conditions, the lender could care less if you get your loan or not. Be prepared to run around.

The inspection period that you agreed to is 10 days but you didn't realize that the inspectors are so busy that their three weeks out. Do you skip the inspection? Will your lender allow you to skip the inspection? Know your contract! You should be able to find a sample contract that is commonly used in your area so you can study it and ask questions ***before*** you ever have to sign. If not, a local real estate agent should be able to provide you with one. It turns out that you were able to get an inspector in the time frame alotted and the property has passed. You've gotten your loan commitment, your inspection period has passed and all parties accept the fact that your chance for getting out of the contract without losing your deposit has expired.

WIRE TRANSFER – BE CAREFUL

Around this time you'll be getting some sort of settlement statement that will give a breakdown of the estimated costs and proceeds of the sale and who that money comes from, and goes to. Understand that this is an estimate and the numbers will probably change as payments and interest is calculated daily. This statement will also give you a good idea of what your cash to close will be, which you will most likely have to provide via wire transfer. I can't stress this enough, ***BE EXTREMELY CAREFUL WITH WIRE TRANSFERS!*** Wire transfer fraud is up exponentially! With everyone having so much personal information online, the chances of having someone in the email chain of your transaction (lender, real estate agent, lawyer, closing agent ect.) compromised, greatly increases. I've mentioned this before in this book and I'm mentioning it again.

When hackers compromise a professional in your email chain they just sit silently in the background reading all of the emails and indentifying those that they can use to their advantage. They see that real estate agent "X" has a closing coming up and from reading the assorted emails and attachments, they know that the cash to close on this upcoming transaction is $76,000. They then hijack that group email chain from one of the professionals and tell you that these are your wiring instructions and the wire transfer needs to be done on "X" date, which happens to be a day or two earlier than the real date. They provide you with a bunch of attachments that were already in your email chain, so it looks legit. These bad actors are typically overseas and if you fall victim to this fraud you willmost likely not get your $76,000 back! $76,000.....that would be a really bad day! So, we NEVER wire funds without personally talking to the closing agent and any others involved to confirm the instructions on the wire transfer. Don't trust emails!

CHAPTER 14

CLOSING

A quick takeaway from this chapter.

- **Make sure your wire transfer instructions are legitimate and accurate**
- **Confirm that you're going to get all keys and leases at closing**
- **Read carefully and understand all of your closing documents**
- **Bring an approved I.D.**
- **Bring an approved color pen**
- **Make sure you sign and date all of the documents the same way**

So your cash to close is ready to be wired, you know your wiring instructions are legit, you've spoken to your bank about it and are waiting to close. You wire your money on time, have all of the identification that they require, and head to the closing. You've double checked and confirmed with your real estate agent that you'll be receiving all of the keys to the property along with all of the original leases and deposit monies held, after you sign. I have a friend of mine that bought a duplex and didn't receive the keys until **three weeks** after closing! The owner was out of town and the tenants were gone most of the time. If a pipe broke and the tenant wasn't there, what would he do? Break in? Not a good situation to say the least! My friend now owned it, the seller had gotten paid, and was in no hurry to get the keys over to him.

READ CAREFULLY AND SIGN CAREFULLY

At closing, take your time to read and understand everything that your signing. The closing agent and lawyer will most likely be annoyed that you want to study the closing documents and the mortgage because most people just sign away. You'd better believe that if anything is wrong and you go back to them that they'll say, we told you to read and fully understand everything before signing and in fact, you signed a paper saying that you were warned and that you did in fact read it all and understand it. At my first closing, I found so many mistakes in the closing documents that they had to reprint all of the paperwork 3 times. When I made the lawyer aware of the third mistake, $452 that was supposed to go to the older couple that were selling me the duplex, but was allocated to me, he literally took all of the closing paperwork and threw it on the floor in the corner of the room. It was almost 5pm by the time everything was squared away and all was signed. I lived about 40 minutes away and headed home. Just after I got home I got a phone call from the lawyers office saying I needed to come back and resign everything because I didn't sign with my middle initial. So I went back the next day and resigned everything, using my middle initial. As stated before in this book, bring your ID, find out how they want you to sign and sign the same way on every paper with the same color pen!

CHAPTER 15

TITLE INSURANCE

When you're done, you'll receive a packet with all of your signed paperwork, the survey of the property, the deed and the title insurance. The title insurance, insures against any defects that may be found after a title search has been done. Basically, you or the seller, paid a title insurance company to research the historical chain of custody and transfer of the property that you are buying. They research and determine that the current seller lawfully owns the property and can lawfully sell it to you. Nowhere along the line did anyone come to unlawfully possess the property and then sell it.

For example, the land that your duplex is on was originally owned by a guy in 1885. He died, and the property just sat for a while. Someone privy to the situation forged a document that states the guy sold him the property just before he died, and brings it to the local authority. For whatever reason, this document is accepted by the local authority and the land is transferred to Mr. Dirtbag. Over the years the property gets bought and sold several times. One day, the great, great, granddaughter of the original owner finds a piece of paper like a will, in an old chest that states, when Mr. Original owner dies, he wants the property to go to his grandson. She asks everyone in the family if they can remember this property but no one can.

So she decides to do some research and finds that in fact, there was a property that he owned, but was never given or transferred to his grandson, it was sold to someone that the family never heard of. His will was never enforced and therefore his lineage now has rights to the property. Oops! I'm sure there are some flaws in my example, but you get the idea.

One can't sell something that is not legally theirs, nor can you legally own it. That said, the payout on the title insurance policy is usually the full amount of your purchase. In this case, the title insurance would pay off your mortgage, give you back your down payment, and the property would return to the family.

CHAPTER 16

DEEDS

A quick takeaway from this chapter.

- **What deed you have will determine if you're protected from title defects**
- **What deed you have may affect how your property sells**

In Florida there are four basic types of deeds. I will breeze over them to give you an idea of what a deed is so you can research further in your area. Different deeds provide different benefits to the buyer. I'll describe them from the greatest to the least benefit to the buyer.

THE WARRANTY DEED

The "Warranty Deed" or "General Warranty Deed" conveys fee simple title and also provides certain covenants, like a warranty of title, to the buyer. The Warranty Deed has five covenants; 1. The right to convey – asserting that the owner has the right to convey or transfer the property. 2. The covenant of seisin – which asserts that the seller does in fact own the property, and is the only owner of the property. 3. The covenant against encumbrances – Which asserts that there are no undisclosed or non-visible encumbrances, ie; liens, restrictions, or limitations, on the use of the property. 4. The covenant of quiet enjoyment – where the seller promises that the buyers use, possession and enjoyment will not be disturbed by a title defect. 5. The covenant of general warranty – that states the seller will protect the buyer from harm caused by title defects and will defend the buyer against any claims to the contrary.

STATUTORY WARRANTY DEED

Then there's the Statutory Warranty Deed, which is basically the same as the above, only in shorter format. I guess typing all of that back in the day on every deed was too much, so instead of it being the size of a paragraph, it's a long sentence.

SPECIAL WARRANTY DEED

The Special Warranty Deed basically gives all of the same benefits as the General Warranty Deed, but limits its coverage soley to the time that the buyer owns the property, not all the way back to the time of the dinosaurs.

THE FEE SIMPLE DEED

The Fee Simple Deed, like the other two, conveys title to the buyer, however, it gives no covenants or warranties of the title to the buyer.

ESTATE OR TRUSTEE RELATED DEEDS

Estate or Trustee related deeds allow a legally designated person to sell a property that they don't own.

QUIT CLAIM DEED

Lastly, there's the Quit Claim Deed, which, in essence says that the person selling is not guaranteed to have ownership of the property in whole or in part, or what kind of ownership they have, but if they do have any ownership, they're conveying it to the buyer. As with most things, be careful, try to learn what you can, and try to protect yourself by using a lawyer.

CHAPTER 17

YOU BOUGHT AN INCOME PROPERTY, NOW WHAT?

A quick takeaway from this chapter.

- **Make the property safe and renter proof**
- **Address any initial tenant complaints**
- **Tidy up**
- **Analyze your rents**

Well first, Congratulations! You've been able to accomplish something that most others will not! Now you have to finish strong! I would love to be able to give you an example of every possible situation that you may come across but as I'm sure you know, there are just too many variables involved. That said, I'm going to try to convey some concepts to get you thinking and you can apply them to your specific situation.

MAKE IT SAFE AND RENTER PROOF

With all that you've read so far combined with all of your research, you probably already have some solid ideas on the next steps to take but I'll go ahead and share some of my thought processes for you to compare. Depending on the type of buyer that you are (blue collar worker trying hard to save for their first place, or Dr. So n' So who makes $400,000 a year and wants to diversify some of your built up cash into real estate), will typically dictate the type and condition of your income property. The blue collar worker will most likely only be able to afford a property that needs some level of repair, maintenance, and updating, whereas the Dr. will probably buy a turn key property. That said, and by the title of this book you may have guessed, I'm going to focus on the blue collar worker.

Your first order of business is to address any safety issues, electrical, structural, common area problems like trip hazards etc. The next step that I'd take would be to "renter proof" the property. Hopefully you noticed most of these potential issues during your initial inspection of the property. Anything that's loose, tighten it. If it looks like it needs support, or more support, ie; bar tops, knee walls, towel racks, cabinet shelving etc, do it. If something, "most of the time doesn't give me any trouble…", fix or replace it. If anything is funky, weird, or a challenge for the tenant to use, make it simple. If anything, drips, shakes, or makes an unusual noise, fix or replace it. Place proper fire extinguishers in the kitchen, the laundry area, and the carport or garage and let the tenant know where you put them, and go over how and when to use them.

If there are pipes, fixtures, or wires that look like they could get smashed or have something hooked on or hung from them, protect or hide them or if possible change their configuration. If the unit is occupied, I wouldn't ask them what is wrong with the place. I know this may sound weird, but I have noticed that they'll use this opportunity to grossly exaggerate things that affect their own neuroticism. An example would be a very nice tenant I acquired after buying a duplex that was super worried about any environmental factors like dust, mold, pesticides, or herbicides being used. The bath tub in their unit had a small drip from the tub spout that would release one drip every 4 to 5 seconds. I had noticed this during my initial inspection but didn't think much of it. Also, when I asked the tenant how they liked living there and if there were any issues with the unit, they replied, "nope, everything is fine".

ADDRESS ANY INITIAL COMPLAINTS - WITHIN REASON

After I became the owner and asked again if there were any issues however, the tenant advised me that I had to fix the dripping tub spout because the prior owner did nothing and it's been making them sick. They continued, "it's probably due to mold from it constantly being wet." We're talking about the drain in the bathtub being "wet" people! It was clear that the tenant had no understanding that every drain in any house has what's called a "P-Trap" or something similar that is designed to hold water in it to prevent sewer gases from coming back up the pipes and infiltrating the house. With that knowledge they'd have realized the pointlessness of their concern.

Without wanting to go down the road of, "your place is making me sick", I simply replaced the rubber gasket on the cold water shower valve and fixed the leak. To my surprise, it was less than 24 hours when the tenants symptoms had disappeared. Miraculously, they were no longer sick and thanked me for getting rid of the mold problem. I didn't mind fixing something that annoyed them when I had the time, but I definitely didn't need the drama and having to fix it right away. So, if there is an issue that is important enough to them, there's no need to ask, they will let you know, I promise! That said, during your scheduled quarterly inspections, you need to look for potential problems like leaks.

GET EVERYTHING NEAT AND TIDY

Next, I would clean any rubbish from the exterior and clean up the yard and landscaping. Once you have the property stabilized and all systems functioning properly, then you can turn your attention to maximizing cash flow and further increasing value. If there are tenants in place you need to honor whatever lease that they have in effect. Once their lease expires, you can put your lease into effect, which I suggest that you do. That said, if your newly acquired tenants have been in place for some time and happen to be paying substantially lower than market rents, take it easy on them, they probably aren't aware of the going rates. When their lease expires, don't come knocking on the door with your new lease that's $300 a month more. Remember, they're working people just like you!

RAISE THE RENT?

Give them as much notice as possible saying something like, I'm sorry to have to raise your rent but keep in mind that I bought this property 15 years after your last landlord and have a mortgage for quite a bit more than they. I know your previous landlord didn't keep your rental rate current, which was good in the fact that you were able to pay much less in rent for such a long period of time, but is also bad in the fact that you're not aware of the current fair market value and may not be prepared for it. Let them know them know that they're currently paying $300 a month under the going rate but you're willing to eat some of the increase to give them time to adjust. Let them know that when their lease expires, if they choose to stay, you'll only raise their rent by $100 a month and in the lease cycle after that, you'll have to bring them to fair market value which will be an additional $200 a month.

Give them time to adjust and or time to find another place if they can't afford your new rate. Remember that most people earn only slightly more than it costs them to live, so be cool! I can definitely tell you that what goes around, eventually comes around, and at some point your product is not going to perform up to expectations. If you demand perfection and are heartless towards your tenants situations, they will treat you the same! Try to do the right thing, be nice and considerate and God will take care of you!

CHAPTER 18

REPAIRING AND RENOVATING

A quick takeaway from this chapter.

- **Figure out if renovating will be a good return on investment**
- **Select finishings and appliances that are appropriate for the area**
- **Run post reno numbers to get an idea of your ROI**
- **Adjust your rents post reno**
- **Cash out refi to get your money back**

TO RENO OR NOT

Next, I would start thinking about what upgrades will give you the most bang for your buck in your area. In reality, you've probably already thought about this during your first walk through at the property. If there's an oddball room that you could add a closet to and make a bedroom out of, that'd be a big money maker. If you could close in a carport and make it secure storage, that could save someone $200 a month. They would gladly pay you half of that or more to have their stuff secure and only steps away. If you have pink formica counter tops, change them. If you don't have the money to do fancy new cabinets and quartz counters, just change out the pink formica for a better looking, more up to date formica. If you don't have the money to do a big renovation and the property is liveable, wait and save up the money. You don't want to piece meal some nicer things here and there and delay a big return renovation for another 2 to 3 years.

When you do have the money for that big reno, wait until the current tenant leaves to do it so you don't have a big time crunch to worry about on your first renovation. Remember that people love pretty, fancy things but they usually don't want to pay for them, so don't go top of the line unless your property will support the subsequent rental price increase. Also, on average, your tenants will definitely take better care of a nicer, fancier property but at the end of the day, it's still not their stuff which means that they will be hard on it. It's a lot easier on your sanity and your wallet, if you have to pay $800 to replace a refrigerator, rather than $2000.

CABINETS

In my experience, I've had good luck with all wood cabinets and quartz countertops. They're definitley not cheap but I feel there's a breakover in value versus a big box store cabinet and any of the other upgrade countertops. If you look carefully at the cheap, and by cheap I mean how they're built, big box store cabinets, you'll see that they use some sort of compressed fibre board material for the structural panels with plastic brackets that are secured by staples. Relative to the price of all wood cabinets that have dovetailed drawer joinery and use metal brackets with screws, the cheap cabinets aren't that cheap. If you were installing them for your own use knowing that you'd be gentle with them and keep them from getting wet I'd say go ahead, but for renters, I'd say that they'll probably be junk in a few years.

GRANITE IS COOL, BUT....

As far as counter tops go I prefer either basic Formica for lower end rentals or quartz for upper end. As stated earlier in this book, Formica is amazingly tough stuff, you just have to keep the wood that's underneath it from getting wet. When everyone and there brothers wanted granite countertops, quartz was half the price. Now that they've come out with quartz products that look very close to natural stone, granite has fallen behind quartz in price. As of the writing of this book, the price of quartz is around double the price of granite. Granite can be very beautiful, but unless you're getting black granite, it stains easily. Granite requires a decent amount of care and maintenance with cleaners and sealers. I can tell your from experience that I have yet to find a reasonably priced sealer that works. That said, care, maintenance and rental property don't go together. Anectdotely, many people say they don't like the level of maintenance that granite requires which points them towards quartz. That, combined with the newer, better looking quartz options have undoubtably raised its popularity and price. The oldest quartz countertop in my inventory is almost 12 years old and looks the same as the day it was installed.

APPLIANCES

As far as appliances go, as stated earlier, I get the cheapest name brand models in the current style as long as that style is neutral enough. I'm not buying a seafoam green mid century style fridge for a rental whether it's in style or not. As far as paint colors, I follow the same rule. I almost always put some type of tile backsplash in the wet areas to add a touch of fancy and to protect the walls and underlying cabinets from water damage. If the water heater and air conditioner(s) are in good working order, leave them. If and when they do fail, upgrade to more efficient units, but don't go too fancy, you want it to be easy and affordable to fix!

If the roof leaks a little bit here and there, patch it until you have the money to do the whole roof. Remember, when you have some leaks and you call a roofer out to see if you need a new roof, the answer is usually yes! That said, I've had roofs that, "wouldn't last another year", last for another seven years! If the unit is empty, take advantage of this time to fully renovate it and make any layout changes that you know tenants are going to like, as you can afford it of course.

DON'T SET YOUR RENT TOO LOW

Once you're done stabilizing and updating the property as your budget allows, I would list the property for rent about $50 to $100 below the going monthly rate. My philosophy on this is, give them a bit of a good deal on the rental and they'll be more inclined to appreciate you and your rental and stay longer. This has worked for me, most of the time. Don't get too carried away with your charity though. The tenants who were the biggest pains in my backside were the ones that I was being the nicest too by grossly undercharging. Find a good balance between nice but firm.

To give you an idea of what I'm talking about, one of my tenants that I acquired through a purchase was paying $650 a month for a unit that, as-is, would rent for $950. At the time I hadn't raised her rent in the last 7 years. One day I gave her a heads up, that in about a year and a half, I'd finally have the money to renovate her unit. She seemed pleased with this until I said that I would have to raise the rent after the renovation. I asked her if she wanted to pay more for a renovated unit. The answer was a strong, no! I said that was fine, but I would have to find another tenant when the time comes.

I asked her to please start looking for another place to rent and when she did find one, please give me as much notice as possible. I also told her that I knew this was a tough market to find a rental and if all she could do was let me know that she vacated and left the keys in the mailbox, that'd be fine too. A year passed and she saw me outside mowing the yard. She approached me and asked how my timeline was on th renovation. I told her I was a little bit behind, but should be close to my original date, which was about 6 months away. Three months later, I asked her how the search was going? She shrugged her shoulders and said, "ehhh." I said OK, I'm still planning on the date that I gave her three months ago.

About two months later I asked her how the search was going? I got the same reply, "ehhh." I told her more matter of factly, OK, but I'm going to have to start the renovation on the previously mentioned date which is right around the corner! After that conversation I ceased to see her out and about around the property. I texted her a week later and asked how the search was going, no reply. Then again a few days later, radio silence. OK, I guess we have to start getting official. She had been a month to month tenant for the last 6 plus years so I posted the official notice to vacate in the time specified on the front door. I also mailed the same notice via certified mail. The certified letter got returned of course and I all of sudden started getting a lot of hateful, nasty text messages from her loaded with false accusations. I told her that I understood that she was upset about having to move, I have no idea what she is referring to in regards to her accusations, and that I would need her to be moved out by the date listed on the notice. I also reminded her that over the past 8 years, I'd saved her roughly $18,000 by not charging her market rent.

D-day came, and she was out. When I went inside I found a note from her stating that she was sorry for the nasty text messages, she never realized how much the rents had gone up, and thanks for taking care of her for the last 8 years. I sent her a text message that said, thanks for the note, and I wish you well in your future endeavors. I fully renovated that unit with fancy cabinets, quartz countertops, new floor tile, a new bathroom and new stainless steel appliances. All totaled, I spent about $23,000 renovating that unit. Two weeks after it was finished I rented it for $1,486 a month, an $836 a month increase on one unit! Excluding my generosity of only charging $650 a month when the unit would rent as-is for $950 a month, it's a $536 a month increase:

$536 x 12 = $6,432 year one revenue increase.

$6,432 / $23,000 reno cost = .27965 or a 28% cash on cash return for the remodel.

RUN YOUR POST RENO NUMBERS

A year and a half earlier I had done the same renovation on the other unit which went from $900 a month to $1,450 a month. All totaled I spent $42,000 and a lot of sweat and sleepless nights renovating both sides, which returned an extra $1,086 a month in cash flow. A few months after the last unit was renovated the property appraised for $160,000 more than its pre-reno appraisal. The interest rates were still low so I did a cash out refinance to get back the money that I had spent on renovations. Doing this reduced my monthly cash flow somewhat but it allowed me to buy another duplex about 8 months later. Lets look at the new returns after the renovation:

$900
+ $650
$1,550 pre-reno rental income

$1,550 total monthly income
- $1,407 total monthly PITI
$ 143 monthly free cash flow

$1,486 Unit A
+ $1,450 Unit B
$2,936 post reno monthly income

$2,936 total monthly income
- $1,621 total monthly PITI after cash out refinance
$1,315 post reno free cash flow

$1,315 post reno cash flow
- $ 143 pre reno cash flow
$1,172 post reno net cash flow increase

$1,172 x 12 = $14,064 year one free cash flow increase

$14,064 / $42,000 = .33485 or a year one cash on cash return of 33.5%

$42,000 / $14,064 = 2.986 or 2.99 years to return my capital investment on the project, in cash (assuming no rent increases)

Now lets look at the total return on the renovation:

$230,000 pre reno appraised value x .035 = $8,050 in appreciation

$143 x 12 = $1,716 pre reno yearly cash flow

$3,700 in pre reno yearly principle paydown

$ 8,050 appr.
$ 3,700 PP
+ $ 1,716 CF
$13,466 total duplex yearly income

$13,466 / $13,800 total cash invested in duplex to that point including purchase = .9757 or a 98% total cap rate or ROI. Incredible isn't it?

$390,000 after reno appraised value x .035 = $13,650 in year one post reno appreciation.

$1,172 x 12 = $14,064 year one after reno free cash flow

$3,500 year one after refinance principle paydown

$13,650 Appr.
$14,064 CF
+ $ 3,500 PP
$31,214 year one post reno total income

$13,800 + $42,000 = $55,800 total cash invested in duplex including purchase

$31,214 / $55,800 = .5593 or a year one post reno total return of 55.9%, BOOM!

If I use total revenue for the duplex, the renovations pay for themselves in less than a year!

RENO, CASH OUT - REFINANCE, AND BUY ANOTHER ONE

Do I have your attention yet? If I calculated out the forced appreciation on this duplex for a 10% total return, its value would be well north of $475,000. At $475,000 and current interest rates, this duplex would still give an investor a 20% total return! Don't underestimate these "ugly" value add properties! They're no fun and expensive in the beginning but, man do they pay off! I know when you're first starting out, $42,000 is a huge amount of cash, it took me 5 years before I could renovate my first unit and another year and half before I could do the other side. If the rents in the area will support the renovation, do it!

CHAPTER 19

LISTING THE PROPERTY FOR RENT

A quick takeaway from this chapter.

- **Make sure the place is clean**
- **Take good photos in a logical order as someone would walk through the property**
- **Highlight any upgrades**
- **Accurately describe the unit and the area**
- **Accurately list your rental requirements and restrictions**
- **Get to know your prospective tenant**
- **Make sure the property is a good fit for the tenant**
- **Beware of Red Flags and Professional Tenants**

For now, you're all done busting your hiney and spending all of that hard earned and saved cash. You now have a shiney new rental unit that needs to get leased so it can start paying you back! Now you get to swim through yet another area infested with sharks. But not to worry, with some disciplined techniques you be able to swim with confidence. At this point you should absolutely be an expert in the rents in your area. As I've mentioned earlier in this book, I would set your rents to a reasonably fair level if not slightly lower, so that your freshly renovated unit will look like a good deal. By now your unit has been empty for a good bit of time so you want to get it rented to a quality tenant quickly. Setting your rent

$50 to $100 a month below the going rate, depending on market conditions of course, will drive a tremendous amount of traffic to your rental. This is good and bad. It's fantastic because your unit will get rented fast. It's bad because it will probably be your first time being exposed to this process and, depending on market conditions, can hit you like a tsunami. I'm going to give you some tips to prepare yourself a little later, for now I suggest that you confirm your proposed rental price by acting like you're shopping for a rental unit in the same area as yours.

By doing this you're also going to notice what websites list residential units for rent. I would suggest that you list your unit on the major websites like, Costar group which will list your unit on all of their residential sites like Zillow, Hotpads, and Trulia. Pictures, Pictures, Pictures! People love pictures, so give them plenty of ***quality*** pictures, ***after*** all work and cleaning has been completed. I know you'd think that I wouldn't have to emphasize that, but I do.

LOGICALLY ARRANGE YOUR PHOTOS

After your unit is clean enough to do surgery in, take some quality pictures with good lighting of all the areas that prospective tenant would want to see. Don't get lazy now. What would you want to see if you were looking? When you upload your pictures, put them in an order that represents a prospective tenant approaching and then entering your unit. Then order them as if the tenant was walking through your unit. What are they going to see first, the kitchen? If so, take a broad picture of the kitchen and then move in for close ups. After the kitchen, what's the next room to grab their attention, the living room? Arrange your pictures so that they show the natural flow through the unit. This will give the prospective tenant and idea of the size and the layout of your unit. Don't have the first picture show the kitchen, then the next picture show the garage, then the bedroom, then the back porch. You get the idea. Absolutely bring attention to unique and upgraded items like cabinets, countertops, appliances etc. If there are very few units with garages in your area, highlight this.

DESCRIBE THE AREA

Next, accurately describe the unit and the area. You're absolutely starting off on the wrong foot if you lie or greatly stretch the truth about your rental. Would you want your tenant to lie to you? That said, some listing sites pull information from the local property appraisers site and may not allow you to adjust things like square footage. For example, some duplexes have two unique identifiers or addresses on the property appraisers website and each unit can be sold individually. Others have one address listed on the appraisers website for the whole building. In this case the listing website will show your rental units square footage along with the numbers of bedrooms and bathrooms equal to the entire building even though it should be half of that.

Just make a note of the discrepency along with the reason and the correct measurements. In other cases the unit or building square footage that is listed is wrong for whatever reason. If it's only off by a few percent I wouldn't bother mentioning it. Also, the listing site may not have an option in its drop down menu for "duplex" or "quadplex", it may only have "apartment" or "condo". Again, just make a note of it in the listing description. If you took good pictures, they should tell the whole story. That said, any other items of possible concern that may not be obvious from the pictures like, being in the flight path of a major airport, tell them. You will definitely get less attention but the ones who do stop by and eventually rent the unit will know 100% what they're getting and will be much less likely to complain about it later. Again, you want to be honest with them, you want them to be honest with you, and you want them to make an informed decision and be happy in your unit. You also don't want to go through all of the work of listing your unit, fielding phone calls and emails, showing the unit, doing background and credit checks, and signing leases to have your tenants move out in four months and have to do it all over again.

MAKE SURE THE PROPERTY IS A GOOD FIT FOR THE TENANT

Another reason that I mention this is that over the years I've noticed that prospective renters will fall in love with some aspect of the rental unit and breeze over other aspects that could be negative like the fact that there bed will not fit in the bedroom! Another good one is they work the third shift at the hospital so they're going to be sleeping during the day. They're looking at a unit that is directly across the street from an elementary school yard. I ask the tenant if they're a light sleeper to which the tenant replies, "yeah." I go on to say that maybe this unit isn't the best choice for you because the kids are out all day yelling and screaming and having a good time. "Oh no, it'll be OK, I just love what you've done with the place and the location." Well, four months later it wasn't OK, and the tenant broke their lease. I didn't feel bad about charging the early termination fee because I had repeatadly brought the potential noise issue to their attention. Like I've mentioned earlier in this book, to a certain degree, try to think for them because in the end, you may have a tenant that doesn't want to be in your unit which will definitely affect how they view and care for your unit and or they'll leave early and you'll have to go through everything again while your units vacancy rate stacks up.

BEWARE OF THE PROFESSIONAL TENANT!

So you're doing your part to be honest, forthcoming, and provide a quality product at a good deal, now it's time to make sure your prospective tenant will do the same. The product they are delivering to you is, themselves. Believe it or not, there are "Professional Tenants" out there who are deceptive, unscrupulous, and know how to work the system. These Professional Tenants prey on excited new landlords. They know that once they take possession of, or move into your unit, you'll have to evict them to get them out. Because this isn't there first rodeo, they'll know that it may take 5 to 6 months to get the Sherriff to kick them out, depending on your laws in your area.

So they gave you first months rent plus a small security deposit which you accepted because they seemed so nice and you didn't run any background or credit checks on them. Month two comes along and crickets. Three days goes by, then five, then seven, and you haven't heard a peep from them. So you text them and say very nicely, "hey just checking in, I haven't received the rent check yet, get back to me as soon as you can." They reply the next day and give you some long sob story and express how sorry they are and that this "thing" just happened and caught them off guard, could you be nice and give them a bit more time or could they just pay double the amount next month?

You bite, feeling bad for them and let them go until next month or maybe ask them what they can pay this month and take a couple hundred dollars or something. Month three comes along and they didn't come through on their promise to pay month three plus the rest of month two. Again you play the text message/voicemail phone tag game with no response for days and days. You're starting to really get annoyed now because you were trying to be nice and you feel like they're now trying to take advantage of you. Maybe they get back to you and pile on the original sob story and promise to pay you $300 in cash tomorrow. Maybe you accept this partial rent payment and maybe you don't. Maybe you've finally had it and decide to get them out. Maybe there's a twinge of compassion left in you and you simply ask them to leave. They're not going to by the way. Maybe you're afraid of the whole eviction process and you offer to pay them to leave.

This is becoming a real hassle and maybe your thinking about doing things to get them out that probably aren't legal and would land you in hot water. During all of this time, you've not been able to get into your unit to see what the condition of it is because they are "never there" and always request that you come another day when they can be there. You can't just unlock the door and go inside without their permission unless it's an emergency so you're up the creek without a paddle. You finally talk to some investor friends that tell you to start the eviction process immediately. You go through the process and depending on the timing of notices, a few months later, they get kicked out by the Sherriff.

So, you've received maybe 2 months rent for the last six to eight months that your unit has been active. With your ex tenants being the good people that they are, I'm sure they were kind enough to take good care of your freshly renovated unit during their stay, right? You're so mad now that you're going to sue them for damages, and, get nothing, because they have nothing, which only make you more mad. I know in my area, law enforcment considers this "a victimless crime" and will pursue the infraction when everything else in the municipality settles down – read, never! Number 1. As mentioned earlier in this book, avoiding a problem is most often the easiest on your wallet and your emotions. Number 2. Find out what the whole eviction process looks like in your area and what remedies you might have.

RED FLAGS!

Now is probably a good time to go over some of the red flags that I've witnessed over the years. Any correspondence that you may receive similar to this should raise questions, " I saw your place online and I just love it, it'll be perfect for me so I'd like to move forward because I need to move right away." Why do they need to move right away? Are they professional tenants, poor planners, or did there landlord spring a huge rent increase on them with no warning. Maybe their current landlord is selling the place and only gave them a month to find another place. In either case you need to be cautious about anyone who is willing to promise to pay rent for a year without seeing your place in person.

Another good one is when a prospective tenant during an abbreviated walk through literally waves a wad of cash in your face wanting to move in right away. It may be two, three, six months or an entire years worth of rent. Don't do it! Depending on the laws in your state, the number of months rent that you accept can determine the time fram of the rental term which will influence the the time frame of any notice to vacate. In my state, Florida Statute 83.46 (2) states – If the rental agreement contains no provision as to duration of tenancy, the duration is determined by the periods for which rent is payable. F.S. 83.57 goes on to say – ...terminated by either party by giving written notice of... year to year, 60 days.... If you handshake on a deal where the tenant gave you six months of advance rent, you may have to give that tenant 45 days notice to terminate his/her tenancy versus 15 days if they only paid one month at a time. In the case of our professional tenant this would give them another month in your unit. Definitely know your local rental laws and ***NEVER*** rent to anyone without doing full background and credit checks and signing a lease!

These professional tenants will want to move in quickly and get possession of your rental unit so to not give you time to think about it or do your normal checks. As just mentioned, they can do this by offering you cash up front or offering to pay a higher rent than your asking because they love the place so much. During their walk through of your property, they will breeze through it without really looking at anything or measuring anything to see if there stuff fits and won't have any questions for you about you, the unit or the lease. I've had people tell me within 10 to 15 seconds of walking into a unit that it's perfect for them and they'll take it. Don't do it!

TENANT SCREENING

You need to come up with a process that is both fair to every prospective tenant and thorough. Have this process set up ahead of time and don't play it by ear. Once you have this process set up, impliment it the same way, every time, for every person. To help with this I list all of my prerequisites at the bottom of my rental listings. I spell out the process in detail for the prospective tenant. That way, there are no surprises and in a way, they accept the process by moving forward with an application. Doing it this way also allows them to see that I'm not picking and choosing which prerequisites that I want to follow.

The required qualifications that I currently list are as follows: A minimum credit score of 705, must have a gross monthly income equal to or greater than three times the monthly rent, must have verifiable employment and income, must submit to and pass all background and credit checks, all persons over the age of 18 must fill out an application and qualify, and then anything that is specific to that unit like, no pets, no smoking, no cosigners etc. Think about the information that you put in your listing as the first step in a weeding out process. This is not meant to sound like tenants who don't qualify are bad, it simply allows you and the prospective tenant to save time. I'm not going to start the loan process on a $3 million dollar boat because I know I won't qualify. If they don't like small bedrooms, they'll skip it. If they smoke, they'll skip it.

That said, you'll be amazed at how many people don't read part or any of the information in your listing.

With population growth in Florida over the last ten years being so high and construction being so low, rental demand is very high. On any unit that I list I am fortunate to typically receive 20 to 30 emails a day and about half as many phone calls. Over time I realized that the majority of prospective tenants did not read my lisiting or requirements in it. I spent plenty of wasted time showing a unit to a tenant who was never going to rent it for any number of reasons like they smoked or had a pet that wasn't allowed. After learning this, I have a saved reply email that repeats nicely, but in bold lettering, all of the requirements of that unit and to please make sure that you qualify before setting an appointment to see the unit. This greatly reduced the time wasted for the tenant and myself.

That said, you're going to have to set your rent and your requirements in accordance with local laws and the market conditions at the time. On top of the above mentioned requirements for my prospective tenants, I also do an internet search on them. If you have "non-smoker required" on your application and you find that two days ago there's a picture of them smoking at a bar, you can disqualify them for lying on the application. I also require that the tenant do a walk through of the unit so they can confirm that it is acceptable to them before signing a lease. During this showing, as mentioned before, I highlight the good and the bad of the property. I encourage them to take their time, look around, measure the rooms, and ask any questions that come to mind. During this process I try to find out about them, where there from, what they do for a living, why their moving, what they like and don't like about the area, what their hobbies are, if they have any pets etc.

PETS

Oh, if they have a pet, ask to see a picture of them and if need be, ask to meet the pet in person to gauge its demeanor. Schedule a time to meet the pet, usually a dog, when you know there's going to be a lot distractions like cars and people moving around nearby. Does the dog look comfortable and calm or do they look skittish, afraid, or aggressive? After you've OK'd the pet, have them fill out on your pet addendum, what breed it is, a description of the dog, its weight, and name, and whether it is current on all of its required vaccines. This should eliminate the possibility of them bringing you their friends dog and then sliding their pitbull in afterwards.

ENGAGE IN FRIENDLY CONVERSATION

You'll definitely want to engage in conversation with your prospective tenants for all of the above mentioned reasons. If something about your unit seems to displease them, find out how much of an issue it's really going to be. I've had people rent from me knowing full well it's 45 minutes from their job or hobby, only to later hear them express their unhappiness, repeatedly, about their 45 minute commute to their job or the boat ramp that they love to use every weekend. Again, it's helpful to try and make sure that they're going to be happy in your unit. As they get comfortable talking with you in a friendly way, you may hear things that may cause future conflict like, as one prospective tenant said to the other in front of me, "yeah, you can turn this garage into your art studio, you just have to cut a hole in that A/C duct to get A/C in here, it's easy." Uhhhhhh, ***NO SIR!***

CHAPTER 20

SIGNING THE LEASE

A quick takeaway from this chapter.

- **Generic internet leases are just that - generic**
- **Take part in the design of your lease and run it by a lawyer**
- **Fully understand your lease**
- **Have all of your addendums in place**
- **Check their ID**
- **Don't give possession of the unit before the lease start date**
- **Be able to give them a receipt**

PLAYING AN ACTIVE ROLE IN YOUR LEASE

You've listed your unit, processed whatever number of applicants and have finally been blessed with, "the one." It's now time to sign a lease and collect some money. So let's talk a little bit about leases. I defintiely recommend having a real estate attorney write your lease or at the very least, review it. That said, I want to give you some points to think about when writing your lease. First, don't assume that the lawyer is going to think of every last detail. In their realm, it's a low payout item that they most likely have a generic version of in which they handout and charge for. Take it home and go over it then ask any questions that you may have, but don't get carried away, because they charge by the minute for phone calls, seriously!

LEARN FROM MY MISTAKES – ADDING LEASE PROVISIONS AND ADDENDUMS

I have learned that everyone is as nice as can be until they really want something, then it's, "what does it say in the lease?" Don't be rediculous or unconscionable with your lease, but spell out all of the details. To give you some ideas, here are some of the provisions that I have in my leases:

"If the initial funds, herin known as the first and last months rent, plus any security deposits due, fail to clear or fund, this contract is null and void." If someone signs a lease and gives you a check for these funds and the check bounces after they've taken possession of the property, you now have to eveict them!

"Only paper sanitary tissue manufactured for use in public and private sewer and septic systems is allowed to be flushed down any toilets. No pre-moistened wipes may be flushed down any toilets at any time, regardless of the manufacturers claims of appropriateness of use in public and private sewer and septic systems." These wipes are a huge problem for both septic owners and municiple sewer systems. Don't believe me, research it!

"You shall not overload any system…"

"No lifting devices shall be attached to the structure…"

"No greases or oils of any kind shall be allowed to pass through any drain pipe…"

"No driving, parking, or standing, on any part of the grass, for any reason, at any time…"

"_____ is the maximum number of cars that are allowed to be parked on the premises…"

"If you have a pet, you shall take care of your pet in a humane manner and keep the pet in good health and maintain all vacinations and licenses…"

I also have addendums about no crime, no drugs, bed bugs, what to do and what not to do in the event of severe weather – no, you can't hook up a generator to the dryer outlet in the garage, a mold addendum, and a move in – move out checklist. I also videotape the property a few minutes before the tenant takes possession of it.

Basically, you want to write your lease for the one percenters. There's a one percent chance that after all of your precautions that you'll get a bad apple, but if you do, you'll be ready. That said, when writing your lease, think about how whatever situation can go bad. For example, "You said I could have a dog, you didn't say I couldn't chain it to a tree in the backyard all day and night." Again, I'm not saying there's no remedy for this, but if you have it in your lease, it's a violation and the process will be much easier and things will happen much quicker!

"You didn't say I couldn't run an automotive repair side business out of the driveway." Because most of the "Mom and Pop" landlords will have basic, generic leases, your tenant may inquire about the strict nature of your lease. Reassure them that you're not trying to be over bearing, the nature of the lease is for the one percent chance that you get a bad tenant and you've never had to enforce any of these provisions to date. The odds of you getting a bad apple is truly low because of all of the research and checks that you submit your prospective tenants to. So remember that you have a great tenant and make sure that you take care of them in the event that they have a little stumble here and there!

BE COOL YOLANDA!

Congratulations, you've come so far! You've got a great unit, in a great location, for good rent, with a great tenant in place! Now you're going to establish a working relationship with your tenant. You're going to be courteous and prompt to any issues that may arise and they're going to pay on time and take care of your place. Don't get caught up in the minutia, don't be on there backs, give them freedom to enjoy their rental. Lets say that you drive by one Monday morning and see that it looks like they had a party sometime over the weekend and the yard is a mess. Don't be so quick to send a text message or phone call about the mess. Maybe they finished up their little soiree late and had to be at work early on Monday. I can tell you that it's great that they have the discipline to party late on

Sunday and still get their butts into work on Monday morning. It's better than not going into work, and that work of course pays their rent, to you!

Give them another day or two at the max to get things cleaned up, be understanding. At some point in their tenure, they're most likely going to forget to pay the rent on time. Find out why, and if it's legit, don't charge them the late fee. Have you ever forgotten to do something? Now, if it happens two months in a row without some kind of communication as to why, that's a different story. The big thing to remember that I see many people seemingly forget is, we are all human and prone to mistakes. We have ultra high demands on others, but not so much on ourselves. One day, you or your property will mess up and they will treat you how you've treated them. As the great Samuel L. Jackson once said, "**...BE COOL!**"

Be firm when it's required ie; every time you drive by their truck is parked on the lawn and you've asked them nicely not to do that three times already. Be cool when they happen to not pull their car in the garage all of the way and close the garage door on their bumper causing it to break the master link of the door openers chain. Be firm when the tenant you inherit decides to test you in month three of your ownership by not giving you any heads up that they aren't paying the rent on time, three days goes by, then five, then seven, nothing. Good morning Mr. Tenant, it's seven days past your rent due date and I have not received the rent payment for this month or heard anything from you, what's going on? Tenant; "Oh, yeah, sorry about that, I had to fix my car." Hey, that's OK, stuff happens, next time please give me a heads up and understand that I'll have to charge you a $50 late fee if the rent is not received within the three day grace period. Next month they test you again of course and one minute past the three day grace period you post a 3 day notice to quit on their front door along with sending one by certified mail. You text and call to notify them of the situation along with their breach of the lease agreement and the late fee that will be charged. Oddly enough, after the tenant receives these test results, the testing stops. Be firm! You have a good tenant that has to change jobs suddenly and informs that their going to be about two weeks late on the rent while being very apologetic about it. Two weeks goes by and they make good on their promise and the following months rent are all on time. Be cool!

THEY'RE GOING TO WANT A RECEIPT

So it's lease signing day and you're headed over to the unit to meet your new tenant, receive the initial monies and sign the lease. You're going to want to bring your keys and their keys to the unit, some pens, your lease which has been pre filled out by you, and some sort of official receipt that you can give them in return for their move in money. Some tenants will pay their move in money, first months rent, last months rent, and security deposit, in cash. Depending on the rental, this can be quite a bit of cash and their going to want a receipt. Cash is good because you don't have to worry about a check bouncing which means you can have the start date of the lease be the same day that you both sign.

MOVE IN - MOVE OUT CHECKLIST/VIDEO

Regardless of how they pay, give them a receipt. While the tenant is looking over the lease and signing, I'll let them know that I'm going to take a quick walkthrough video of the unit and that I might get them in the video, and do they care? I've never had anyone care that they were in the walkthrough video. When they do offer concern, I advise them that the video is for their protection and mine, and if they still don't want to be in the video, they can just step outside. Your lease will probably have certain parts of it that you want to emphasize and I suggest that you have your tenants initial these sections. I also suggest that you have a section that can be notarized in case they are out of town and need to sign the lease remotely. On one of the signing pages I suggest that you have a section where you can record what kind of I.D. they presented to you on the day of signing.

KEYS PLEASE - UH, NOT JUST YET

Now, unless they've given you cash or given you a check that has cleared prior to today, they don't get the keys to the unit. The date when the lease is signed is just that, it is not indicative of when the lease begins, that is the lease start date. That said, if the aforementioned conditions are met, they can be one in the same. When you do get a tenant that signs the lease on one day and the lease start date is sometime in the future, you may get the follwing request. "Hey, I was wondering if I could get the keys so I can slowly move my stuff in over the next few days?" I do apologize but unfortunately I cannot give you possession of the unit before the official lease start date. After all of your interviews, research and background checks it most likely won't be a problem, but why take the chance. During the process, tell them when the unit will be available and ask them when they would like to move in. Set that date on the lease and give them possession of the unit on that day.

CHAPTER 21

PROVIDING A GOOD PRODUCT

A quick takeaway from this chapter.

- **Maintain your property**
- **Have scheduled inspections for your benefit and theirs**
- **Stay on schedule with pest control**
- **When things get tough, maintain a good attitude**

Hopefully you've cleaned, fixed, and renovated the unit in a thoughful manner. As the saying goes, you have a tight ship, now it's up to you to keep it that way! OK, maybe I just made that up, but you get the point. As mentioned earlier in this book, I highly suggest that you maintain the property and not leave it in the hands of the tenant(s). You're providing a product and a service to the tenant, and the service is the manager, which is you! Be prompt and courteous when addressing questions and concerns. Be an advocate for your tenants when needed, for example, a parking issue on the street in front of the unit.

Change the A/C filters yourself and when you do, check under all of the sinks, by the toilets, the dishwasher, tub, washing machine and water heater for any signs of leaks. You will most likely notice a leak long before a tenant does. This protects you and gives the tenant a quality product with few disruptions in service. Show that you care and they will care in return.

MAINTENANCE

As far as maintenance goes, I'll share what I do and you can decide what you'd like to take on and what you'd like to pay to have done. Every time the lawn gets cut I blow off the windows, doors, soffits and overhangs. This keeps debris from building up in these areas and holding moisture or harbouring insects. While doing this I inspect the soffits and attic vents to see if there are any insects or animals getting in the attic space. I remove any loose or built up debris from around all of the A/C units. Loose debris, like dust, dirt, lint from the dryer vent, and grass, will all get sucked up into the A/C condenser fins greatly reducing effeciency which causes the units duty cycle to be longer increasing wear and tear. This debris can also collect in the condensate drain causing the system to shut off or worse, leak inside of your unit. While doing this I like to listen to the A/C's to see if their running normally or making any unusual noises that require further investigation. I also check the condensate drains to make sure they are clean and if the system is operating at the time, that they are in fact draining condensate.

When blowing off the windows and doors I look for degrading caulk and weatherstripping and check to see if anything has become dislodged like screens. If you have an irrigation system, now is the time to see if any heads are broken or if there's evidence of over or under watering. Next, I glance up at any trees that are on the property to see if any branches look like they can come down and damage anything or hurt anybody. Sometimes you'll find big branches that have broken off, fallen a few feet and have been caught by another branch. Sometimes these branches hang so precariously that it would only take a ladybug landing on it to send it crashing to earth.

KEEP THAT ROOF CLEAN - YES, I SAID THE ROOF

I then turn my attention to the roof. Depending on the situation, dirt and debris from trees can build up and stop or divert water drainage and allow fungus and other plant life to grow in it which can degrade the roofing material and of course attract bugs. If I have built up debris on the roof, I head up there and blow it off. In my opinion, blowing it off is better than using a broom because a broom tends to remove a lot of aggregate if it's a shingle or rolled roof. However you decide to do it, do it very carefully and be ***EXTREMELY CAUTIOUS*** of power lines!

While I'm inside the unit I also look for any unsafe practices like smoke detector removal, a jamb packed dryer lint screen, 50 electrical loads plugged into one outlet, and the scented candle that is basically touching the curtains. You gently want to encourage safe habits. I also check under the front of the refrigerator for any built up dust or debris that may make the compressor work harder or not at all. This is the area where most refrigerators draw in air to cool the compressor and the condensor grid. I also look for anything that may be loose like, doors, cabinets, cabinet pulls, toilet seats, faucets, and switches. Tenants will leave the items loose and continue to use them which can turn an easy 3 second fix into a pain in the rear!

SCHEDULED INSPECTIONS AND PEST CONTROL

I inspect the interior of each unit every few months depending on use and whether the tenants have any pets. Conditions permitting I spray for bugs once every year. Depending on the environmental conditions in your neck of the woods you may have to spray more or less frequently. Speaking of environmental conditions, I have a property where the address side of the building faces due south and gets no natural shade. The exterior paint on that side degrades twice as fast as the the shaded north side. The north side will have a nice sheen to it and the south side after about 4 years, will look flat and chaulky and come off on your hand, time to repaint!

CHECK YOUR ATTITUDE!

I have another property that has landscape bushes planted very close to the building that look very nice, but also retain or emit a lot of humidity through respiration resulting in fungus growth on the walls directly behind the bushes. This fungus needs to be removed every 4 to 6 months by hand washing or pressure washing, fun! All of this maintenance can seem like a lot of work, and when it all decides to gang up on you, it can be. If you've prepared your property like I've suggested, 99% of the time your maintenance work load will be cursory. As for the 1% when everything gangs up on you, just remember that for your 2 to 3 days of misery in the last 6 months, you're probably getting paid a sizeable amount of money! For example, in total, one of my duplexes pays me just shy of $3,000 a month. For 6 months that's $18,000. If I divide that over 3 days of hard, miserable work it comes out to $6,000 a day. I think I can suck it up for $6,000 a day, don't you? So remember that, no matter how inconvenient the "thing" is or how hard or disgusting the work.

That mentallity is the difference between the amateurs and the pros. The amateur will get into the game with dreams of easy money and no headaches. They'll own a property for a short time and one day when they're walking out the door to go on vacation, they'll get a phone call that informs them of some big problem that needs to be taken care of right away. It will totally screw up their plans, they'll have a terrible attitude about it which will of course make the whole process worse, and they'll end up saying, "this isn't worth it!"

They'll then put the property up for sale and lament to their friends about how terrible it is to be a landlord. Attitude and perspective is ***EVERYTHING!*** I was listening to an interview of an active Navy SEAL and the interviewer was giving the SEAL's what I would consider to be a commensurate level of praise and respect. I'll never forget what the SEAL said in reply, "It's not that we're that good, it's just that everyone else sucks!" I thought, profound indeed, as I laughed. Through further conversation he expressed that everyone thinks the SEALs are flawless and although their performance is measurably and consistently better than the average enlisted man, it is seldom perfect. He went on to say that the difference is attitude or mental toughness. He said most people make it 95% of the way to their goal and then quit. He said it gets hard or miserable, and they quit. He went on to say that, they make mistakes on any given training exercise or mission which makes things harder or more miserable for them, but they recover from those mistakes and complete the mission. He said, they deal with whatever hardship comes their way and they keep moving.

So, remember, your mind is an incredibly powerful weapon that can work for you or against you! Keep your eye on the prize and don't make decisions based on emotions. Look at your failures as learning opportunities. The list is long of successful people who've suffered tremendous and repeated failures in their lives, but they kept going, and now we read about them or see them on TV. Abraham Lincoln, Albert Einstein, Henry Ford, Walt Disney, Oprah Winfrey, Sochiro Honda, Thomas Edison, Michael Jordan, The Wright Bros., Maya Angelou, Kieran Behan, Bethany Hamilton, Single Mom's and Dad's who just keep going, the list goes on! It's really the only thing that we have control of in this life, attitude!

Don't ever let anyone tell you what you can or cannot achieve, including yourself! God only knows what you're truly capable of, and he wants you to find out! There can be no success without failure, no happiness without sadness. You have to know one, before you can recognize the other. No one can break your spirit unless you allow them, and there is truly, only one failure in this life, and that's the failure to try! So get out there, take your licks, and see what you're made of, you may be surprised!

CHAPTER 22

RAISING RENTS

A quick takeaway from this chapter.

- **Remember, your tenants are people too**
- **Make sure your rent is competitive**
- **If you need to, raise the rent**
- **Try to give as much warning as possible in regards to rent increases**

So everything is going great so far, the year is coming to an end and you're wondering if you should raise the rent. On the one hand, you've done a ton of work finding and placing those great tenants and you don't want to lose them. That said, you want to get a fair rent for all your blood, sweat, and tears. In my opinion there are two ways that you can look at it and two ways your tenants can view it. For you, you can raise the rent "X" percent and after only one year has passed since they had to move, the tenant will probably deal with it and stay, rather than go through the hassle of trying to find a new place. This does of course depend on how crazy you get with the rent increase!

PERSPECTIVE ON RENT INCREASES – DEPENDS ON WHO YOU ASK

For the tenant, they may be used to renting from corporate landlords who raise the rent 3% every year like clockwork or they may be used to Mom and Pop landlords where they never raised the rent. They may understand that your costs as a landlord typically go up every year or they may not be aware of that and get sour thinking that you're trying to nickle and dime them.

I didn't raise the rent on a tenant for 5 years once and when I finally came to them in year 6 and explained that I had to raise the rent by $100 a month, they were shocked and mad, even though in total, it was less than if I'd had raised the rent every year by 3%. I guess that's what I get for trying to be nice.

The other way that you can view it is, I want this tenant to stay as long as possible. I want them to feel as if they are getting a great deal. It takes a lot of time and effort to place a new tenant and every month that the unit goes unrented reduces the effective rent that you get every month, as discussed earlier in this book. So maybe I'll raise the rent in year three or year four. You have to ultimately decide how you want to run your rental(s) and people generally don't like surprises so communicate your intentions with your tenants before they sign a lease. Educate them on the fact that just because you're a "Mom and Pop" landlord, doesn't mean that your expenses don't go up every year. Let them know that your taxes, insurance and any other costs that you may have, go up every year due to inflation and that when you raise the rent you're not doing it to fleece them of their money.

CHAPTER 23

PREPARING FOR THE NEXT PROPERTY

A quick takeaway from this chapter.

- **If you're ready, go for it!**
- **Remember what got you here**
- **It's the same process but you'll be making more money and need more money**
- **Don't get too far over your skis!**

SLOW YOUR ROLL ELON!

Everything is going great, you're collecting rent and starting to recoup the money you've invested. If you want to expand your real estate empire, you're going to have to be careful and calculating going forward. Don't get too excited about your real estate mogul status and go buy a boat or a car.

CASH OUT REFINANCE?

Remember what you've learned and had to go through to get to this point in your journey. If the economic environment is right, stable economy and interest rates, forced appreciation and cash out refinancing tremendously accelerates your ability to purchase another property. You can literally buy a property, renovate it, and do a cash out re-fi to get all that reno money back and go do it again on another property. Just remember, don't get too far over your skis, your properties need to cash flow to make you lendable. You're still going to have to fit into the lenders DTI box, have the down payment money and now you're going to need even more emergency cash! It really is an awesome deal, but it's no free lunch.

If you're hungry for more, keep your head down, keep living frugal, working hard, and saving that money! If you're not that hungry and don't care if you get another property next year or five years from now, relax and enjoy some of the fruits of your labor. In either case, I suggest that you don't add to your reportable debt load. If you want to reward yourself, do it using cash. If the numbers on the next property that you want end up being close, that new car or boat you got a loan on may push you outside your lenders DTI box and disqualify you. Think about it, make a plan, and stick to it!

CHAPTER 24

LEARNING ABOUT YOUR PRODUCT

******There is too much information in this chapter to give bullet points. That said, this is a very important chapter to read so you can understand what you're buying and how big of a headache (read – money), or not, the property might be. You just can't rely on sellers, realtors, or home inspectors to protect you. Have an oversight and it could cost tens of thousands! If you want to protect yourself and your wallet, read on.******

Because for most of us, saving for a down payment on a property is going to take some time, you might as well be efficient and learn about your product while you save. I have to tell you that in high school, I could care less about anything regarding building construction. Sports, girls and cars ruled my thoughts and not always in that order. I liked cars and wanted to understand how they worked, and make them faster of course! So I started reading everything I could on the subject. After years of reading, trying and doing, I've been able to maintain all my vehicles without having to pay a gazillion dollars to the stealership, and do a number of interesting projects.

Fast forward to the early 2000's, I'd gotten tired of being a slave to the dollar and finally started to think about how to make my money work for me instead of the other way around. After much thought I decided real estate was the way to go for me. So I applied the same techniques I'd used to learn about cars, to real estate. The only difference was I liked cars, they were fun and exhilarating! A concrete block and a 2" x 4" aren't very exciting. Knowing myself, I had to make it interesting or I'd never learn what I needed. At first I focused on the benefits of owning real estate; everyone needs a place to stay, very few moving parts (relative to cars), only 12 transactions a year, huge tax benefits and as inflation goes up so does the value and the rents! Pretty awesome deal!

BETTER MAKE THE FIRST ONE COUNT

So, I hit the books with tenacity. I wanted to know everything I could so I could stack the deck in my favor. That said, I knew I had to make my first deal a homerun or at least a triple, or it could really set me back time wise. I don't want to scare you with that statement. You can make mistakes on your first deal and survive and even make money. However, at this stage in your journey you're most likely cash flow limited so it might take you 2-4 yrs to save up for your first place. If your first deal is a dud and cash flows zero, it'll take you another 2-4yrs (or more if it cash flows negative!) to save up for property number two. If your first place is a dud it will most likely make it harder for you to qualify for property number two when you do finally save up the down payment money.

You may be thinking, I have little knowledge and no experience and I have to hit a homerun like the big boys! Unfortunately, yes! The big boys actually have more room for error, go figure. I've noticed over the years that the majority of real estate investors have "extra" money that they want to put to work or get some sort of tax shelter from. However they acquired the money, they have $150,000 - $300,000 (or more) in cash to play with. If you're like I was, you have debt. Suffice to say, if they made a not so good deal and ended up losing $50,000 they sure wouldn't be happy about it, but it wouldn't crush them and set them back 7-10 yrs. You, like I didn't, on the other hand, don't have that luxury and hopefully you're picking up what I'm putting down, TAKE IT SERIOUSLY! You'll most likely have plenty of time to learn while you're saving money. Make that first punch count! Know your product!

BUILDING CONSTRUCTION

Let's talk building construction! Most structures in the U.S. are built from 3 main materials, concrete, wood and or metal, with the first two winning by a landslide. Each, as one would expect, has its advantages and disadvantages. Also, different areas of the country will have predominant construction types based on climatic conditions and the cost or economic conditions at the time of construction. Live along the coast and concrete block or concrete masonry units may be the best choice. If there's a recession happening at the time however, like in the '70's, concrete block may be too expensive so they end up building with wood. You'll start to recognize this as you learn more and look at properties. You may see homes that were built with EQ metal studs for non-load bearing interior walls instead of the more common wooden 2"x4"s you're used to seeing at your local big box store. I've noticed that at different times, the same builder will use steel studs in one phase of a development versus another. When I asked why, the reply was, price! There may be a huge wildfire out west that destroys the raw product for studs and or a big uptick in the number housing starts causing more demand than supply, in turn driving up the price for wood products. You will also find this in the electrical portion of a property. From approximately 1965 to 1973, single strand (one solid wire) aluminum wiring (not to be confused with tin coated copper wiring) was used in houses in some locations due to the rising cost of copper by the significant growth in the Japanese economy between the end of World War II and the beginning of the Cold War, the U.S. and other countries stockpiling, among many other materials, a lot of copper and the oil embargo from 1973-1974. In a nutshell, supply and demand caused the rise in copper prices and as we humans do, we adapt. So aluminum branch circuit wire became the alternative (more on aluminum wiring later).

WOOD FRAME

Most people are familiar with wood framing or dimensional lumber. You see at the big box stores and probably have seen a home being built using wood framing. Wood framing has its advantages and disadvantages. Wood framing, depending on the circumstances, is usually cheaper than Concrete Block, it's lighter and easier to transport and handle. It's relatively easy to cut to any desired length or shape and there are multiple ways you can fasten one piece of wood to another. Lumber is very strong for its weight and in some cases rivals steel in its tensile strength. Yellow pine has a compressive strength (measured parallel to the grain) of around 8400 psi and a bending strength (measured perpendicular to the grain) of more than 14,000 psi. Compare that to a CMU (concrete masonry unit) or concrete block which has around 2000 psi of compressive strength. In the rental property owners world, wood frame is easier for us to modify or repair and concrete block is much more resilient to weather and insects. That said, most homes that are built with concrete block have interior walls and a roof made of wood frame and unless you're getting really deep into modifications or additions you're not going to be messing with the exterior block walls. I can only think of two disadvantages of wood framing, 1. It's response to moisture in regards to movement, swelling and shrinkage and 2. It's decay from biotic agents like mold, fungus, bacteria and insects. Designed and built correctly, a wood frame house should be just as strong (and most likely more flexible) than a concrete block home. One thing I don't like is when I see a wood frame home being built and it pours rain on it EVERY afternoon for almost a month until it's dried in. One part of the wood gets soaked and the other is dry. I wonder how much movement and stress occurs from those repeated cycles.

Wood frame construction after an afternoon shower.

An impressive wood frame 2 story home under construction.

CONCRETE BLOCK

Concrete block is man made under controlled conditions. It has a compressive strength range from 1000psi to 5000psi depending on the type, won't burn, rot or be destroyed by insects and is unaffected by moisture. It can be stored for long periods under various conditions without ill effect. Although concrete block has good compressive strength, one disadvantage is its poor tensile strength. In other words, it doesn't stay together very well when you try to bend it. There are a lot of variables, but for comparison sake, concrete blocks flexural or bending strength before it breaks is only about 260 psi or about 10% of its compressive strength. Another disadvantage is the fact that you can't just run up and easily attach something to a concrete block wall. You need special drill bits and special anchors or screws. Another disadvantage is shaping it. You can't easily cut it into whatever shape you need. If you need to fill a space that's 6 7/16", with wood it's no problem, just cut it, concrete block, not so easy!

After reading that concrete block might not sound so awesome, but hold on. If we add some metal to the concrete we significantly increase its ductile strength. If a piece of rebar is placed vertically at every corner, around window and door openings and every 4 feet horizontally, we end up with a very strong wall in all directions that is also very resistant to degradation from most things that nature throws at it. This is probably why it's used in tropical environments that are subject to high moisture and potential high wind loads. Given the advantages and disadvantages of concrete block, my first choice is a home built from concrete block.

Concrete block home under construction. Notice how thick the concrete block is compared to wood frame construction.

Sounds good! Now how are you supposed to identify a structure that is built using concrete block versus wood frame? If the outside is covered in an attractive finishing product (stucco or siding) and the inside is finished in drywall, how are you supposed tell the difference? One easy way to identify the construction type from the street is to look at the windows. Concrete block doesn't require an exterior protective coating aside from paint. Wood frame on the other hand requires a protective barrier like tar paper back in the day, or house wrap (made from high density polyethylene fibers) that is predominantly used today. This house wrap supposedly allows the house to "breathe" while keeping moisture away from the wood. The house wrap is usually white in color and feels similar to a tough but thin plastic sheet. It is not designed to be an exterior cladding and may suffer rips or tears so it must be covered by something more durable which is why wood frame homes are usually covered in some sort of siding or stucco. The house wrap needs to wrap into the raw window openings to give protection to those surfaces and the window is designed so that it has a flange that surrounds the window, allowing it to be nailed or screwed to the house wrap covered wall sheathing. This flange is formed into the window allowing the exterior surface of the window to stick out just past the thickness of the typical siding material. This is why, 98% of the time, the windows are flush with the exterior walls on wood frame construction. If the windows are inset into the exterior wall by a few inches, it's concrete block. Unfortunately this isn't guaranteed 100% of the time because builders/designers can purposely try to make the structure appear a certain way. I've seen entire neighborhoods that were built with concrete block but the front of all of the homes had the windows flush mounted with the cement board siding. If you were to look at the sides or rear of the home you'd find the windows recessed as you'd expect. Another confusing sight you might come across is a two story home where the first floor windows are inset and the second floor windows are flush. In this situation the first floor is built from concrete block and the second floor is typically wood frame. Keep this in mind especially if you're doing a google street view drive by.

Concrete block ordinary construction home with slab, exterior block walls, and wood trusses installed. You can see the roughed in plumbing sticking out of the slab. Interior wood frame walls will be added later.

Windows set into concrete block.

Window set proud (sticking out) on a wood framed second floor. High Density Polyethylene protective house wrap attached to the exterior wood sheathing. Window to the left is temporarily screwed to the inside so it can easily be removed to load drywall onto the second floor through the window.

Wood frame window flange (red arrows) that is used to secure the window to the house. The exterior surface of the window frame sits proud in the expectation of matching the thickness of exterior siding.

This is a precast concrete window sill for a flush flange window (not to be confused with a flush mounted window on wood frame). Windows for concrete block will have a much smaller flange that is flush with the outside surface of the window. This flange is not used to mount the window like in a wood frame application, rather locate it properly and act as part of a seal. Note the vertical wooden "buck" that the upper arrow is pointing to and how it aligns in the same plane as the cast ledge of the window sill, lower arrow. The installer will put a bead of caulk on the interior side of the window flange and push the window into place. The installer will then head inside and screw through the window frame into the wooden buck to secure the window.

A good view of 1st floor windows inset into concrete block and 2nd floor windows flush or slightly proud on wood frame after stucco siding has been applied.

Flush mounted windows with wood siding and trim.

Flush mounted window with vinyl siding.

TIMBER FRAME

This next segment is for the smaller possibility that you're buying in an area that has very old structures, pre-1920's. Post and beam joinery or timber framing was widely used from the 1600's to the middle of the 19th century. Timber framing uses locally sourced wood that is cut down, hewn or debarked, smoothed to some degree then cut to the desired finished size. Once roughly sized it is cut so it can be joined to another post or beam. This can be as simple as just stacking beams on top of each other or cutting very tight fitting V-notches or dovetails into the pieces being joined. If done well, these techniques have proven to last for centuries! Another joining technique is called Mortise and Tenon which involves cutting a slot or hole (mortise) in one piece of timber and using a corresponding loose piece of wood that is cut to the exact dimensions of the mortise, like a key going into a key hole, to join the two pieces.

An example of incredible craftsmanship and precision in this new construction, heavy timber home.

Usually there are one or more corresponding holes drilled through the combined joint and then a corresponding peg or dowel is driven through the holes in the joint. This makes for a very strong joint. Timber framed structures are very strong and have lasted for literally hundreds of years. Being so old, it should be obvious that most of the systems that you'll find in these structures will have been added at a later date so, caveat emptor!

BALLOON FRAMING

Timber framing required a lot of time and effort to construct and as we all know, time is money! So, people began to look for faster and cheaper ways to build. In the early 1900's saw mills began to produce dimensional lumber like 2" x 4" and 2" x 6" we are you used to seeing today in our big box stores. Increasing demand for construction lumber after World War I drove this response. Construction using these new smaller, "light" wood components was originally met with criticism and a lack of confidence from those in the industry. They initially gave it the nickname "Balloon Framing", meaning, it was so light it would just blow away like a balloon. There's one constant in the world, change, and we humans aren't always welcoming of it. As it turns out, these salty old dogs were wrong in their assumptions as one can find 100+ year old examples of balloon framing all over the country. Here in Florida those balloon framed structures have survived every major storm to hit them for the past 100 years, not bad. For us as investors, the biggest concerns with this type and age of construction are, insurability (or lack of), the support system below the house, the electrical and plumbing systems in the house and the most worrisome, fire! Using a two story home as an example, balloon framing used very long 2" x 4"s in lengths of 20 feet which run vertically from the sill plate (the floor) all the way up to the top plate (where the rafters connect to the wall). The interior walls were attached to the interior face of these 2" x 4"s and the exterior walls were attached to the exterior face of these 2" x 4"s.

This style of construction leaves an open void from the first floor sill plate all the way to the attic. 100 years ago there really wasn't any insulation in walls and if a fire started or got into an exterior wall, the vertical void space would act like a chimney pulling in fresh air from the bottom feeding the fire and sending super hot gases up against the top plate and into the attic. Those exterior 2" x 4" studs that make up the walls each have a notch cut out of them to hold a horizontal ribbon plate or ledger board that the second floor, floor joists rest on.

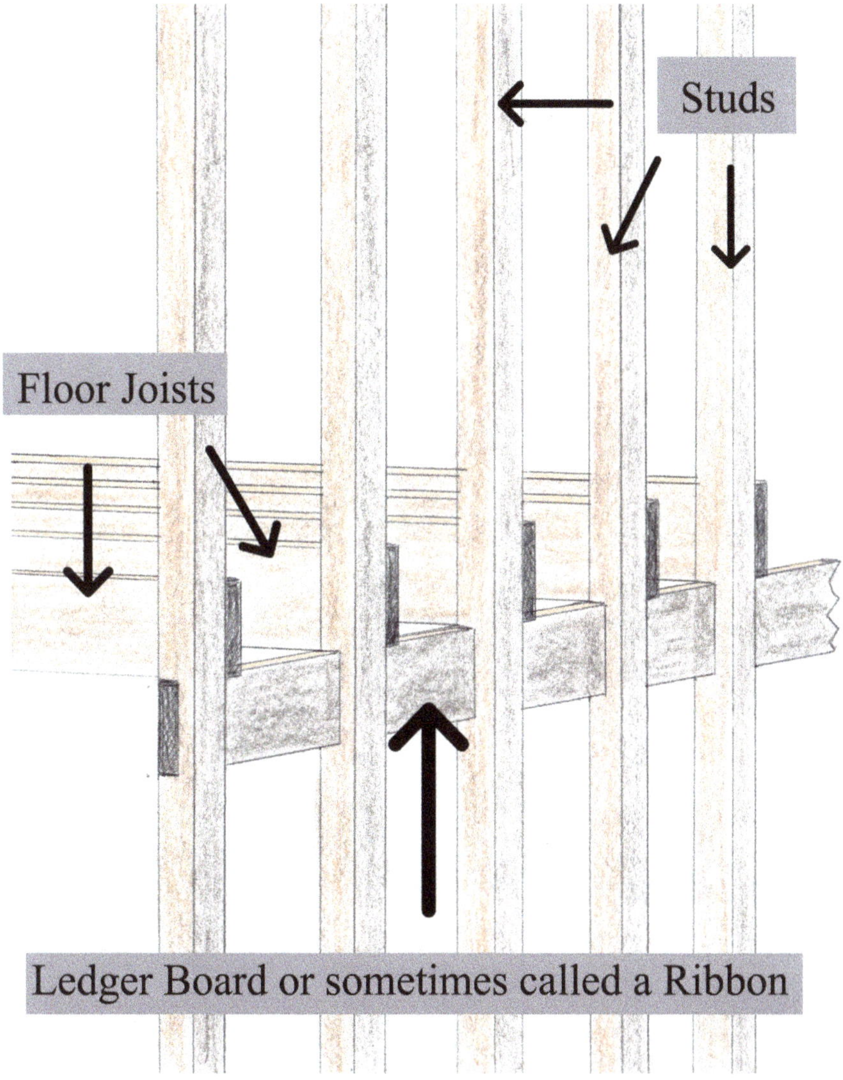

As you can see, any degradation by fire to the exterior wall studs will compromise the integrity of the entire structure, possibly causing collapse. From my knowledge, typically the roof would burn off before this became a factor. Either way, not good! Adding fire blocking to this type of construction is highly adviseable. Understand however, that this is not easily or cheaply done. You must remove, at least sections, of all of the interior walls to add this blocking.

Looking at a balloon frame house from the exterior, with the exterior sheathing removed. As you can see, there's an unobstructed void space between the exterior and interior walls.

Looking from the interior of a balloon frame house, with the interior wall removed, at the backside of the exterior wall. Again, notice the unobstructed void space running from the first floor to the roof.

Balloon frame construction with Knob and Tube wiring.

TRUSSES

Now that we have an idea of what wall construction we're looking at, let's turn our attention to the roof construction. Roofs can be flat or pitched in multiple fashions or a combination of those two general types. The object is to keep mother nature, mostly rain, out of the house. The flat roof can basically be designed like a floor with rows of joists that support the expected loads for that geographic area and the roof decking which is usually plywood or OSB (oriented strand board). A pitched roof design that is typically called a shed style roof will have similar components that are simply pitched from one exterior wall to another. Aside from those just mentioned are pitched roofs that have 2 or more sections that are pitched away from each other towards an exterior wall, a common example being the gable roof. A gable roof can be supported by either rafters or trusses. Trusses are engineered wood products that support live and dead loads (live loads are loads that can move like flowing water or a person walking. Dead loads are loads that don't move like solar panels or, more commonly found on commercial roofs, air conditioning units.) by efficiently transferring the loads to the building walls or supports.

This roof system appears to be under quite a bit of stress from this environmental load.

Examples of dead loads (Air conditioning units) on a pitched residential group home and flat commercial roof. If I had to guess, the A/C units on the group home were installed long after the structure was built. Do you think the roof structure was designed for this additional load?

It is suggested that the first use of trusses were in primitive dwellings dating back around 2500 b.c. and the Greeks were well known for using trusses to support their roofs. The modern truss design came as a response to the high demand for covered bridges in the early 19th century. The two systems most commonly used were the Pratt and Warren trusses. The Pratt truss, invented in 1844, includes vertical members adjoined to diagonals that slop down towards the center of the truss. The Warren truss, patented in 1848, is basically alternating right side up and right side down, triangles.

Pratt truss bridge.

Warren truss bridge.

The advantage of the truss system allows much less material to support much more weight. Less material equates to lower cost. A major disadvantage of the truss design is, if one portion of the truss system fails it greatly reduces the load carrying capacity of the truss and in some circumstances, unfortunately, can cause the entire system to fail instantly, as witnessed in the I-35W bridge collapse in 2007, killing 13 and injuring 145 and the I5 Skagit River bridge collapse in 2013. A single gusset plate failed in the I-35W collapse and a truck hit and damaged a single member of the I5 bridge.

I-35W Bridge after collapse.

Residential roof trusses have a few main components, a bottom chord, two top chords, a number of "webs" between the top and bottom chords and some kind of fastener to connect all of them together, usually a gusset plate.

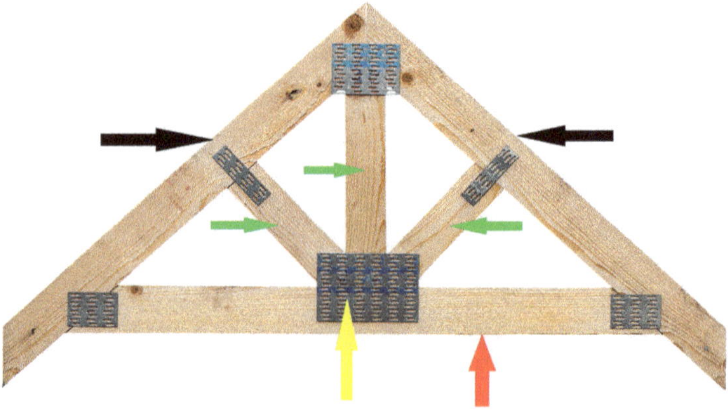

Top chords (black arrows), Webs (green arrows), Bottom chord (red arrow), Gusset plate (yellow arrow)

Modern lightweight wooden roof trusses with gusset plates.

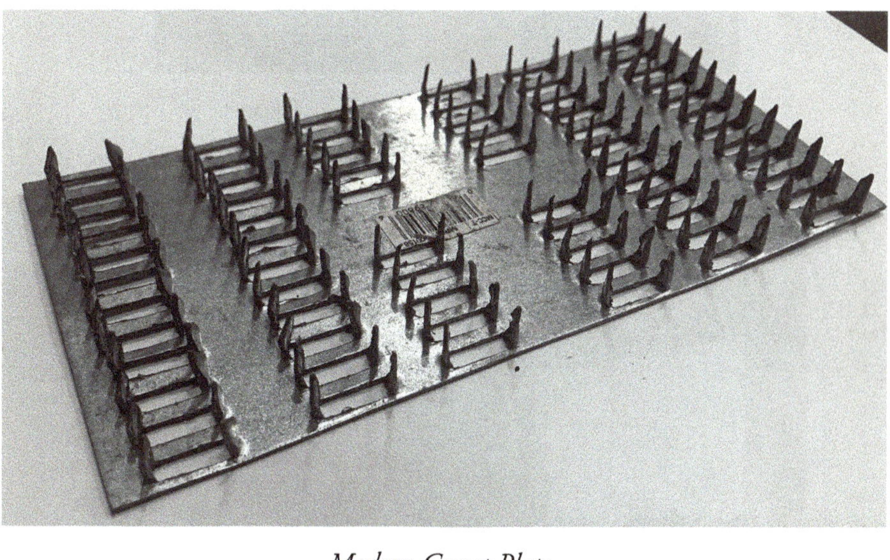

Modern Gusset Plate.

Gusset plate installed at the truss factory.

Don't get them too hot because they tend to pull out, yikes!

ROOF SHAPES

Before we go any deeper into roof construction, we should probably talk about roof shapes, and what style or shape roof insurers prefer. The hip style wins hands down. A hip roof is one that has all sides or planes of the roof, slope down and connect to an exterior wall. Shed, Gable, Butterfly and Gambrel (in other words, all other styles of roof) roofs, they don't like. These roof styles more easily allow horizontal winds to get under the edge of the roof without allowing an equal or greater force of wind pushing down on the roof, hence making it easier for the roof to be lifted off the house and be placed in your neighbors' yard!

> ***Note:*** *A big factor in the insurance cost of a property is the shape of the roof and how it's attached to the building. The thinking of old was, most of the forces a roof had to deal with were downward and some lateral. That said, nails used to attach the roof decking were relatively short, thin and spaced far apart. The trusses themselves were simply nailed to the top plate of the exterior walls.*

Example of a Hip Roof.

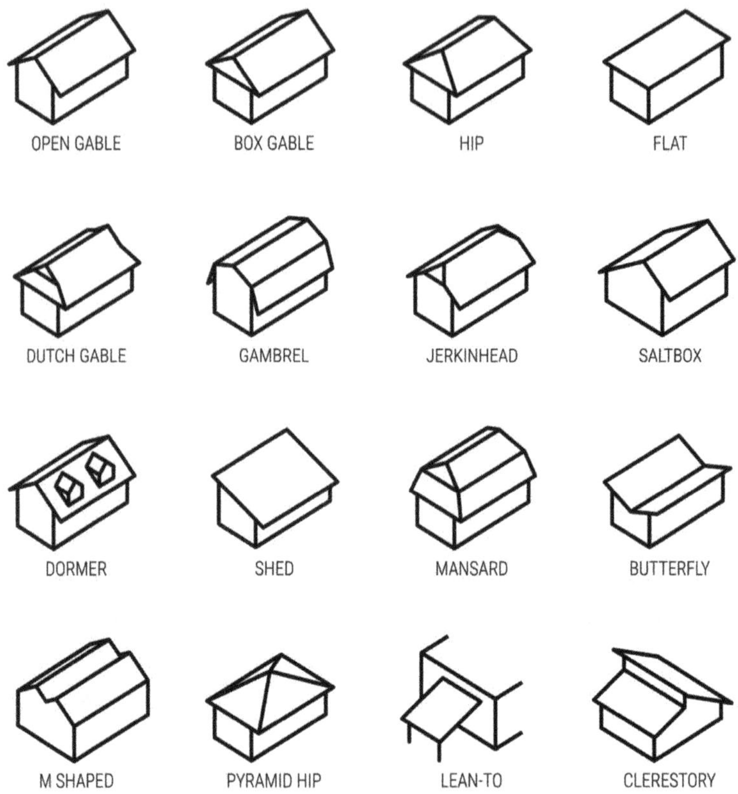

As time would show, not only the shape of the roof, but the way the roof was attached to the walls would become a key factor to whether a roof would stay on in a big storm. Uplift, forces trying to lift the roof off of the building, would become a major concern during storms. I'm sure you've seen videos of what appears to be a complete roof being blown right off of a building. The nails used to hold the roof to the rest of the structure would simply pull right out. As these events happened with more frequency building codes began to change, especially in locations subject to hurricanes. The new codes required the trusses to be "clipped" or better, "strapped" to the top plate with longer, thicker, nails or preferably with screws. The roof decking would also get longer, thicker nails that are spaced closer together.

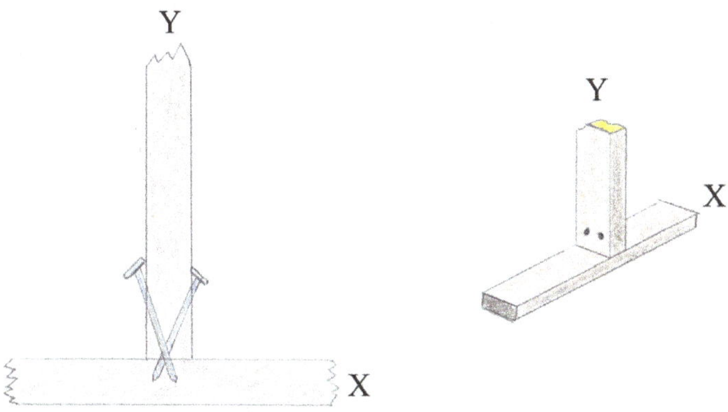

An example of the nailing technique used to hold down roof trusses or rafters called Toe Nailing.

In this picture, a rafter is sitting on the top plate of an exterior wall. A downward load on the rafter (red arrow) also generates a lateral load (yellow arrow). Push down hard enough and the rafter will slide outward across the top plate. In years past, builders would toe nail the rafter into the top plate. This adds some downward clamping force to the rafter and top plate increasing the friction between the two and also adds resistance to shear via the metal nail (blue arrow). This works very well for downward loads, however does little to resist upward loads. The nails only resistance to uplift is the friction between the portion of the nail that is in the top plate and the top plate itself.

Rafter ties.

Rafter strap.

Truss strap embedded in concrete wall.

Just thought I'd throw this in here, toe nailing joists or ledger boards for your deck is not such a good idea either. Look up deck collapses on the internet.

ROOF DECKING

Roof decking is the material that is attached to the trusses. Decking serves a few purposes, it's a structural component tying all the trusses together giving the roof lateral stability, it provides a surface to attach the waterproofing, water shedding material ie; shingles, tiles, metal panels etc., lastly it provides a surface to walk on for construction, inspection and maintenance. Generally speaking, there are a few common types of roof decking. Most common, depending on the age of the property, is 4'x 8' sheets of plywood, 4' x 8' sheets of OSB and 1" x 6" x 8' or 1" x 8" x 8' dimensional lumber. The 4' x 8' sheets of plywood and OSB are typically found in newer homes post 1970's and usually range in thickness from 3/8" to 1/2". The dimensional planks are usually found in older homes, pre-1970. In my opinion the 1" x 6" or 1" x 8" boards make for the strongest roof.

Oriented Strand Board with its distinctive flakes.

Plywood with its smoother finish

1x8 decking as viewed from the attic.

1x8 decking as viewed from the roof.

Most of you are probably familiar with plywood and understand that it is many layers or plys of wood that are coated with glue, typically oriented 90 degs. to one another and then pressed together while being heated until the glue cures. Oriented Strand Board or OSB as it's commonly referred to was invented in the 1960's but didn't come into broad use until the mid 1980's. OSB is made by putting wood in a gigantic shredder where flat pieces or flakes of varying size and shape come out. These pieces are then "sprinkled" down onto a forming mat or conveyor. The chips or flakes land on the conveyor at many different angles providing strength in different directions. The whole "mat" of material ends up having engineered levels of heat reactive adhesive and wax and is put into a press where it's compressed to a desired thickness and heated to around 400 degs. F. for "X" amount of time. It is then finished to final size and branded. In my experience, OSB takes longer than plywood to absorb water but also takes longer to dry out, which I believe is what causes it to degrade faster than plywood. In my opinion, a plywood roof is more desireable than an OSB roof.

I just wanted to add purlins to this discussion on the small chance you might see them on an ancillary structure or carport. I wouldn't classify purlins as decking or sheathing by any means, but they do perform a similar job. Purlins, in my experience, are dimensional lumber, metal or formed light gauge metal, that is attached on top of rafters, or trusses at a 90 degree angle to the aforementioned for the purpose of securing the waterproofing material (which is usually metal panels) and structural stability. Because there are large gaps between each purlin and each truss or rafter, the metal roofing panels (and its fasteners) have to be able to support whatever loads may occur in those gaps. Be very careful if ever attempting to walk on this type of roof!

Purlins (red Arrow).

Purlins on a re-roof (horizontal 1x4's).

WATERPROOF ROOF COVERINGS

There are many types of roof coverings, rolled asphalt, 3 tab asphalt shingle, architectural asphalt shingle, cement tile, clay tile, metal tile, metal panel, membrane, tar and gravel, and wooden shakes(shingles). As would be expected, the more demand there is for a given product over time, more companies offer it increasing supply and driving down prices. That said, asphalt shingle roofs have the lions' share of the market and relatively speaking is the cheapest form of roof covering with the exception of rolled asphalt. Why is rolled asphalt cheaper? My guess is partly the way it has to be manufactured so it can be rolled which makes it thinner and reduces its life span in relation to asphalt shingle and its appearance. It just doesn't look as good as asphalt shingle to most people. In my experience, rolled roofing will be your cheapest form of roof covering, followed by 3 tab asphalt shingle, architectural asphalt shingle, metal panel, metal tile, concrete tile then clay tile. Tar and gravel, membrane (usually reserved for commercial flat roofs), and wooden shake (shingle) roofs are almost non-existent on homes anymore, at least in Florida.

Let's talk about the pro's and con's of the most common. Rolled roofing as mentioned before, has a thinner, lighter felt or fiberglass mat which allows it to be rolled for packaging and easy application. Rolled roofing is typically reserved for low pitched roofs of 2:12 and less. If you're wondering what a 2:12 pitch is, allow me to explain. A roofs pitch or angle is usually described in terms of how many inches it will rise for every 12 inches it will travel horizontally. For instance, from the peak of the roof, horizontally and outwards to the edge of the roof that overhangs the exterior wall is 20' or 240" and the distance vertically from the top of the exterior wall to the peak of the roof is 10' or 120".

Rolled roofing on the jobsite.

Rolled roofing being installed.

This roof would have a pitch of 6:12. For every 12" of horizontal run, the roof would rise 6" vertically, giving you a pitch angle of around 26 degrees. The reason rolled roofing is usually reserved for low pitch to flat roofs is because it comes in very large sheets of around 100 sq. ft. and those sheets are basically glued or cemented down to the felt covered decking where the sheets overlap, allowing it to be waterproof-ish. So water can pool, for a short period of time, say 24 hours, on the rolled roofing and it won't penetrate to the decking. Shingles on the other hand are separate pieces that have fairly large gaps in them which would never keep water out in the scenario above. That said, most shingle manufacturers I'm aware of recommend a pitch of 4:12 or greater with the absolute minimum being 2:12. However, I personally would not recommend going that low from my experience helping a friend with his roof leak on a shingled 2:12 pitch roof.

With rolled roofing having a thinner mat, less asphalt and surface aggregate, its useful life, from my experience in the southeast, is only 8-12 years. Some factors that conspire against rolled roofing is the fact that it's used on a low pitch roof. Although a low pitch roof sheds water more gently reducing aggregate erosion, it also doesn't do a very good job of removing debris from the roof. Depending on the situation of course, this leads to a build up of organic material on the roof, especially if there's a lot of tree cover. Most people don't do a great job of getting on their roofs and cleaning them so this organic material builds, retains water and things begin to grow in it. These things will actually degrade the rolled roofing and as a bonus will further reduce the water shedding ability of the roof. If this is left to get worse (have you ever seen an old house with what appears to be weed garden growing on the roof?) it can cause ponding or standing water on the roof which, being bad enough, can add significant weight to the roof.

"A good example of rolled roofing used on a flat commercial roof.

In my neck of the woods where the sun is long and intense, it absolutely beats the crap out of the roof. Roof temperatures in Florida can exceed 160 degs. F for hours! Combine that with heavy afternoon thunderstorms during the summer and I'd plan on a reroof every 8 years and if you make it to 10 years, be happy. In terms of cost, as of the writing of this book, a 2500 sq. ft.(or 25 square- roofers use roof measurements divided by 100 sq ft.), 1.5:12 pitch, simple, gable roof, as quoted to me by 5 separate roofing companies, was $8500.00.

> ***Note:*** *Many construction jobs in Florida were lost during the great recession of 2008. Some moved to other states, some were at the end of their careers and just retired and others changed their vocations. Now that Florida is once again large population gains due to the very favorable tax environment, relatively inexpensive real estate and the weather, construction has picked up significantly causing a shortage of workers. This supply=demand imbalance has caused labor costs to rise significantly. So, in the early 2000's, those quotes would've been in the $4000-$5000 range.*

ASPHALT SHINGLES

Asphalt shingles are very common and the roofing companies have a lot of experience installing them. They are thicker than rolled roofing and have more aggregate allowing them to withstand Mother Nature for much longer than rolled roofing. The general consensus says, an asphalt shingle roof will last approximately 15-30 years.

> ***Note:*** *As of late I've noticed the insurance companies not accepting 18-20 year old architectural (the top of the line shingle) shingle roofs that are in great shape. More on this later.*

NAIL POPS

I can only think of a few cons to architectural shingle roofs; 1. Being poor installation, ie; the roofer with the machine gun nailer going as fast as he can, trailing off of his line as he reaches far out for those final nails causing the nail to be exposed on the next course of shingles or another good one is when the pressure in the compressor for the nail gun starts to drop for any number of reasons (gets unplugged, seen it!) and the last 7 nails haven't been driven in far enough, allowing the heads to stick up just above the decking and felt paper. I'm sure he notices it but eh, its no big deal right, the job must go on! Remember I told you about those gaps in the shingles? Well water does end up getting under portions of the shingles. This water finds its way to those nails, underneath the head of the nail and into the roof decking. A few months later, if the nail pop isn't that bad, you go in your attic and notice some dark spots and what appears to be water stains. If the nail pop is bad you're probably up in the attic because you noticed a water stain on the ceiling. If the roofing company is still in business and you have a warranty you call them back and HOPEFULLY they find all the nail pops (in that section, because I can guarantee you they're not going to inspect every one of the 3000 nails on your roof) and fix them. On the other hand, if you're reading this book you're probably buying a used home or multifamily, don't have a bunch of money and the warranty and or the company is long gone. This being the case you're going to have to get your butt up in the attic, find the leak and then try to find that spot on the roof! So much fun! Then you'll have to gently lift up a bunch of shingles looking for a nail that is slightly raised. Once you find the nails, if you can, without destroying the shingle, tap the nail all the way in. You usually can't do this because it's under a stiff shingle so you have to fill it with a roof patching compound and repeat. Yes, it is as much fun as it sounds, especially with the summer sun beating down on you!

If you're lucky, you can see the nail pops from the ground.

Hot and cold cycles can also have deleterious effects on screws.

The aggregate that is on the shingle to protect it from the sun, immediately begins to wash off with every rain. In Florida on a typical 95 deg. F. day, the roof gets to be 150+ degrees which happens to be in the range of when asphalt softens releasing its grip on the aggregate. Then comes the torrential rain from the typical summer thunderstorm which falls at a rate of 2"-3" per hour on up to 5" per hour for bad storms. Per the USGS, one inch of rain is equal to 6 gallons of water per square yard. To get a reasonably accurate measure of just how much water a Florida roof has to deal with on a daily basis, we'll say the average roof size is 30 square (3000 square feet), divided by 9 (to get square yards) equals 333.33. Multiplying that by 6 gallons equals 1,999.98 gallons of water, per inch of rain, per hour. Multiply 1,999 gallons times our rainfall of 2.5" per hour and we get 4,997 gallons of water per hour! That's just one storm! In Florida this happens just about every day in the wet season, which runs about 5 months a year. If you're ever curious about just how much water is rushing off of your roof or what this does to a shingle roof, just take a peak in your gutters and look for the shingle aggregate that has accumulated.

In heavy winds, the shingles tend to lift up and sometimes break off. This is not such a big deal to fix so the roof is weatherproof again but it is hard to do it and have it look good. As you can probably imagine, a roof that has been weathered for say 6 or 7 years gets some of its shingles blown off and then those shingles are replaced with new ones. Sticks out like a sore thumb!

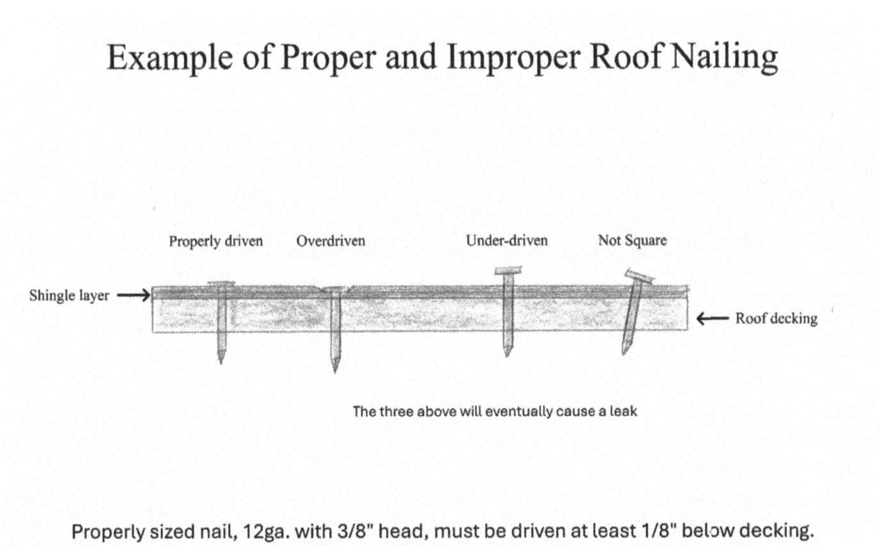

3 tab shingle roof. Notice how flat the shingles appear vs. the Architectural version.

Architectural shingle roof.
Notice how the shingles appear to overlap and some sit taller than others.

METAL ROOFS

Metal roofing is my favorite. It has long uninterrupted panels for water to flow off of. The seams where the panels meet are raised and overlapped making it difficult for water to blow up into. It's very durable, lightweight, requires minimal maintenance, will last 50+ years and in light colors reflects a lot of the suns energy. Compared to asphalt and aggregate shingle or rolled roofing, metal roofing will not degrade from water running off of it (which is cool because that happens to be its main job!). Metal roofing can be painted and repainted for maintenance or if you just feel like changing the color. If metal roofing is damaged (assuming no underlying decking damage) you can just unscrew the damaged panel(s), screw in a new one and no one will know the difference. All that said, I can only think of two cons to metal roofing; 1. Being the price. It's expensive, especially if you're not installing it yourself. If you get a quote for an architectural shingle roof and it's say, $10,000, multiply that times two for a basic metal roof and times three for a standing seam metal roof.

> ***Note:*** *Check your local codes to see if you can install the roof yourself. In Florida this is only allowed on owner occupied properties. Doing it yourself will be a challenge, but it will save you in the neighborhood of 50%-75%. You'd be paying yourself $15,000-$20,000 to install the roof!*

The noise and possible cellular signal disruption. This is very situation dependent but it's worth mentioning. Some metal roofs are screwed directly to the felt paper or peel and stick underlayment and some are installed on purlins which elevates the metal to allow for an air gap. The concept is the metal is allowed to expand and contract with rubbing the underside on the underlayment and also allows another layer of insulation. Some have noted that this has a "tinny" sound effect during rain. The metal doesn't buffer the sound as well as a shingle roof. For reference, I have metal roofs on two of my buildings and in 12 years no one has had any complaints.

There are many different styles of metal roofing. Common styles for average priced homes and rental properties are 5v crimp, Ribbed or Corrugated and at the high end, Standing Seam. If you're curious about price, a rule of thumb is, if you can see the fasteners, it's cheap-er.

Mucho expensive Standing Seam metal roof (no visible fasteners).

Although I have seen this corrugated style of metal roof on some homes, it's usually reserved for out buildings like sheds and barns.

FYI, they can make metal to look like just about any other roofing material.

FYI, they can make metal to look like just about any other roofing material. Believe it or not, this is a shingle look metal roof.

SPANISH STYLE ROOFS

I won't spend too much time on Spanish style, Mediterranean or Clay roofs because they are exorbitantly expensive, relatively delicate and very expensive to repair if you get storm damage. As of the writing of this book, expect to pay around $15 per square foot (yes I said square foot!) for a clay tile roof. A 3000 square foot roof would cost you $45,000! Suffice to say, I'd stay away from this type of roof unless you come across an outstanding deal, like a 40% return on cash!

Looks beautiful, just don't have to fix or replace it!

Spanish tile roof being repaired.

BASIC ELECTRICAL THEORY (VERY BASIC)

So, for informational purposes only, now would be a good time to talk about the basics of a residential electrical system. First and most important, just about every book or article I've ever read about the subject talks about "electrical theory", so keep that in mind! Beginning at the power plant, in basic terms, electricity is generated by passing a closed loop wire through a magnetic field or vice versa. As a child in school you may remember science experiments involving magnets that had north and south poles. If you have two magnets and you hold the north pole of one close to the south pole of another, the magnets will want to attract and stick together. Conversely, if hold the north pole of one magnet and push it towards the north pole of the other magnet, they will want to repel each other. This invisible force is what makes or pushes electrons in a copper wire in one direction or another.

If we take this magnet, attach it to a shaft and spin it around inside a tunnel of wires (or vice versus) we can induce electromagnetic force in these wires and thereby produce alternating current electricity.

Simple a.c. Generator

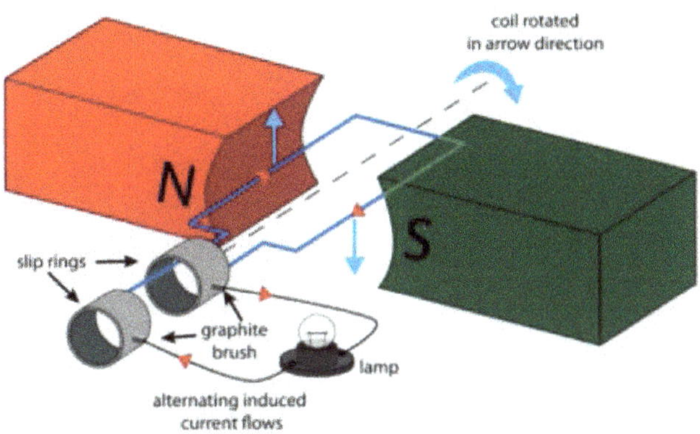

In this case we're spinning a single wire through a magnetic field.

The direction of the flow of electrons in the wire(s) depends on the relationship of the magnetic field and the loop(s) of wire. If we move, in this case spin, the magnet near the wire(s) or spin the looped wire(s) near the magnet, we will impart a force on the electrons in a positive direction for half of the rotation and a negative (or opposite) direction for the other half of the rotation.

Formation of Alternating Current (AC)

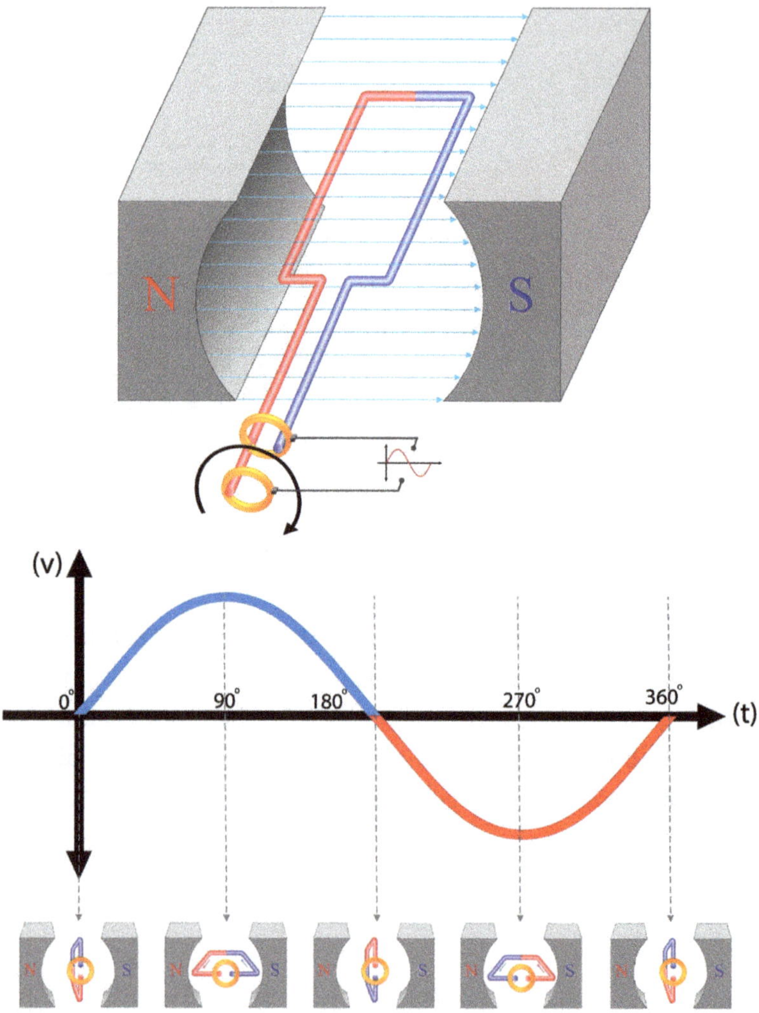

This diagram shows how the direction of the current changes as the wire is rotated through the magnetic field.

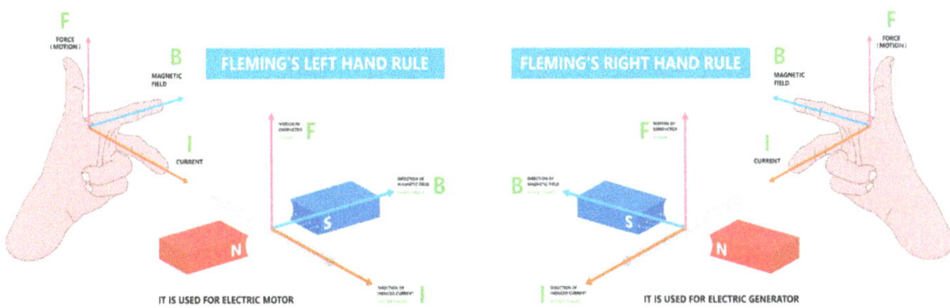

Fleming's hand rule is another way to look at current direction.

This is a very basic description of how alternating current (AC) is produced and illustrates how the electrons in the wires of your kitchen light are changing polarity or moving from the black or "hot" wire to the white or "neutral" wire and back again, at 60 times every second (60 hertz). This is not to be confused with direct current (DC) that is used in batteries, where one side of the battery has an excess of electrons (the negative side) compared to the positively charged side, and when connected, the electrons flow from the negative pole to the positive pole until the charges on both sides of the battery are equaled out and the battery is "dead".

So, we have a generator that produces an alternating push/pull force on the electrons in wires that travel across power poles to a transformer (which reduces the voltage from the power plant down to what is used in your house), then through wires into the main service panel in your house, through an Overcurrent Protection Device or breaker and through your house to your kitchen light. We use a light switch to open (turn off) or close (allow) the flow of those electrons through the light. So what happens inside the light switch? There's basically a metal draw bridge (imagine a bunch of cars waiting for the bridge to close so they can drive across to the other side) that is attached to the power source side of the "hot" wire and when this bridge is up, it doesn't make contact with the kitchen light side of the "hot" wire. The switch is off, the bridge is up and no electrons (cars) will flow. When we close the switch (draw bridge) we connect the wire making a continuous circuit for the electrons (cars) to flow back and forth.

Now, one might ask, "if there is a considerable force always pushing on the electrons (cars), why don't they just jump across the bridge to the other wire?". Well, air, under certain conditions, with voltages that we use in our homes, has a tremendously high resistance to electron flow. So that little air gap in the light switch between the raised draw bridge and the other end of the wire is good enough to prevent the electrons from jumping over to the other wire. So, how does lightning travel through the air? Great question! The answer could probably be a book on its own and if you have the time it's an interesting read, but for this book we'll just say that the extreme differences in charge between the cloud and whatever the lightning ends up hitting is tremendous (a typical lightning bolt has 300 million volts and 30,000 amps!) and this allows the electrons available in the air to be ripped off and used to complete the pathway.

So, what is all this voltage and amperage stuff? The movement of electricity is often related to the movement of water. Let's say we have an electrical circuit that provides 4000 volts (our houses have a maximum of 220 volts). Voltage is often described as how much push or pressure the electrons are under. Let's think of a pressure washer. You can use a pressure washer that provides 4000 psi to blast away dirt and grime but you may notice that it doesn't actually put out a lot of water. This leads us to amperage, which is the measure of how many electrons are moving in a circuit. In this example, the push behind the water is high but the amount of water moving is low, so the pressure washer would have high voltage but low amperage. On the other hand, let's say we're at the beach standing in the surf. Every eight seconds or so, a wave rolls onto the beach. Relatively speaking, it's not moving very fast but if you try to stand in front of it, it knocks you down like a rag doll. It does this because a tremendous number of those little water molecules are ganging up against you. On their own they don't exert much pressure (voltage) but the 5000 gallons that hits you really packs a punch. This is amperage and amperage kills! Only 10 milliamps across the heart is enough to stop it from beating in a fashion that is compatible with life. I shouldn't need to say it but I will, BE EXTREMELY CAREFUL WITH ALL ELECTRICITY!

The power company has to send electricity over very long distances so it needs to impart a lot of pressure (voltage) on the electrons. The really tall power transmission lines can have hundreds of thousands of volts in order to overcome losses in the hundreds of miles of line.

As we get closer to your house you can find power lines that are mounted high, medium and low on the telephone poles. A good rule of thumb is the higher the line, the higher the voltage. The top lines can have upwards of 7200 volts. Depending on the local needs, you may find any number lines at various voltages. Typically, the very lowest lines are reserved for phone and cable lines but don't bet your life on it!

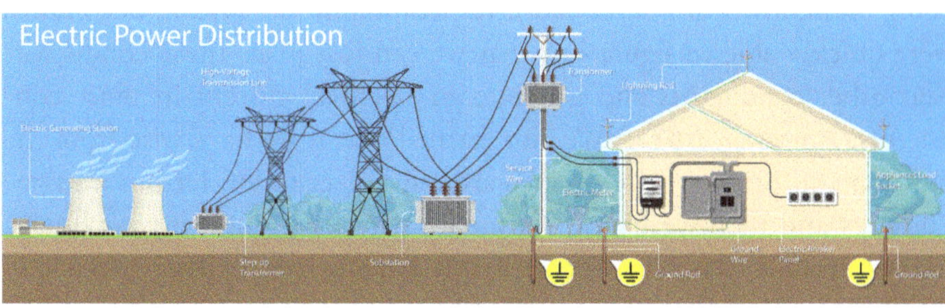

This 7200 volts is obviously too high to use in our homes so it must be reduced or stepped down, by a transformer.

Single phase pole mounted transformer.

If we think back to our generator, it produces electricity by moving a magnetic field through a wire or vice versa. Well, conveniently we can produce a magnetic field by moving electrons through a wire. So, our power source generates high voltage alternating current which in turn generates an alternating magnetic field around the conductors. Humans, being blessed with the most powerful weapon on the planet, our brains, were quickly able to figure out that we can just place these conductors near other conductors and generate an electrical current in those conductors. Amazing, isn't it! We also learned that if we have wire from the power plant (primary wire) looped around a piece of soft ferrous iron say, 10 loops and then we have a secondary wire (that goes to your house) looped around that same piece of soft ferrous iron (without touching the primary wire) say, 5 loops, that whatever voltage we put through the primary wire we end up getting half the voltage in the secondary wire. If we have 10 loops of primary wire and 20 loops of secondary wire we double the voltage of the primary wire. Pretty cool! It may be easier if we view the piece of soft iron in the shape of a picture frame. The primary wire is looped around the left vertical part of the picture frame and the secondary wire is looped around the right vertical part of the picture frame.

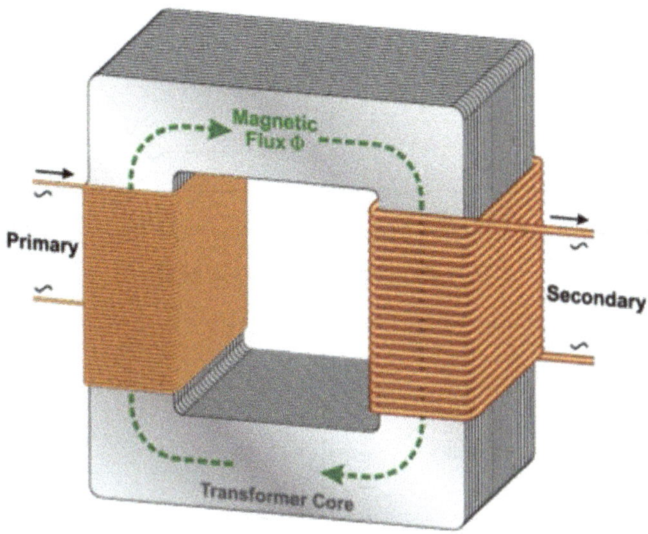

So, basically speaking, if the primary winding has 100 turns in it and carries 440 volts and the secondary winding that goes to your service panel has 50 turns it, you get 220 volts at your service panel. But wait a minute, you say! Our houses have 220 volts and 110 volts, what gives? If we run a wire from the secondary winding that only uses 25 turns of the winding, we get 110 volts. If we then run another wire from the secondary winding that only uses 25 turns of the winding and run a neutral wire back to the middle of the winding, we get two 110 volt pathways of alternating current. This is why you have L1, L2 and the Neutral wire coming into your service panel. L1 is 110 volts, L2 is 110 volts and neutral is the return path for both of these lines or legs. Remember, this is just general information to give you a BETTER idea of how this stuff works, don't get too carried away!

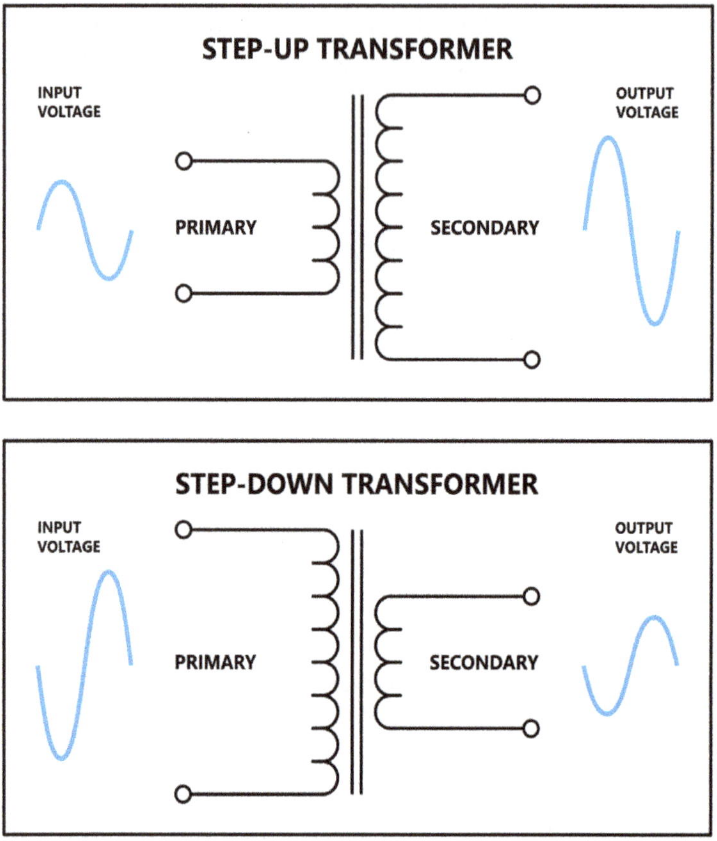

Primary wire coming from the power company on the left, secondary wire (L1 and L2) going to your house on the right with a center Neutral tap. The voltage difference between the top right lug and the bottom right lug is 240V. The voltage difference between either lug and the center tap is 120V.

Transformers can also be on the ground like this pad mounted one.

This next section is going to confuse some and anger others with how "wrong" I am. This is my opinion based on a good bit of research so, here goes. Contrary to popular belief, electricity (the alternating kind) does not want to go to ground or earth. It wants to go back to its source. The next shocker is, the ground wire in a cable is not meant to send errant alternating current to the ground or earth. It is meant to be a low resistance alternate pathway back to the source. I know, I've heard, and believed for years, that electricity wants to go to ground. An example of this would be, you have a drill with a metal case, somehow the hot wire inside the drill gets detached and is touching the metal case, you pick up the drill, squeeze the trigger and the electricity travels through the case, which is connected to the ground wire, which then travels into the ground via the ground rod where it causes such a high amperage draw that it trips the breaker and saves your life. It made sense at the time, electricity wants to go to ground right? Well, as I started to learn more about the systems in houses I began noticing things that didn't make sense based on my prior beliefs, so I hit the books!

So, if the ground wire doesn't go to ground, what does it do? The green or bare ground wire that is in the drill, connected to its metal case, is connected to the ground prong on the drills plug. When plugged in, that ground prong is now connected to the green or bare ground wire in the cable that travels back to the service panel where the overcurrent protection devices or breakers are located. The ground wire is then connected to the ground bus bar (makes sense) in the main service panel. This ground bus bar is also attached to a bare ground wire that runs outside the house and is usually attached to an 8' ground rod that is driven into the earth (again, makes sense). This is where it gets fuzzy for some people. The ground bus bar is bonded (connected) to the neutral bus bar which allows a path back to the source (transformer).

Now wait a second, you might say, if electricity wants to go to ground and the return path for this electricity is also connected to a ground rod, why doesn't the breaker of whatever circuit being used immediately trip? The answer, it doesn't want to go to ground (although it can), it wants to go back to the source. The earth apparently, isn't such a good conductor (situation specific I'm sure), so we'll agree with the old adage, that electricity takes the path of least resistance. On top of this, if you check out the pole that your transformer is mounted on, you'll find (should find unless it's a 3 wire system) a ground wire traveling from the transformers' neutral wire to a ground rod. This would seem to allow two paths back to the source (transformers secondary winding). You have the path of least resistance being the neutral wire ("grounded conductor" in National Electric Code speak and not to be confused with a "grounding conductor" sheesh!) and another path from your service panel, down the ground wire, into the ground, across to the pole, up the ground wire on the pole, to the neutral wire and back to the source.

Hmmm. As I tell my wife and kids all the time, I don't make things complicated, they get that way all on their own! So as stated before, the ground (actual ground you walk on) is not such a good conductor and if you want proof of this I suggest you look up a guy named Mike Holt, read his literature and watch his videos on Youtube. He is considered an expert in his field and has testified as such in legal proceedings. He is an excellent learning source and explains things very well.

For this topic I suggest you check a video he has on grounding and bonding and an older one on ground resistance measurement. ***What he does in this video is dangerous, so if you're not an expert, don't do it!*** In the older video he's at his office that has a grounded system (which has been standard for about 40 years) where he drove a ground rod 10' into the ground and via an extension cord, directly connected the hot wire to the ground rod. And nothing happened. No fireworks, no tripped breaker, 105 volts and just 4 tenths of an amp going into the ground.

He then drove the ground rod another 20' into the ground for a total of 30' deep and did it again to find only 1.3 amps travelling into the ground. At 40' deep it jumped up to 5.5 amps. At 50' it jumped to 8.4 amps. When he put two 50' deep ground rods in parallel he got 13.24 amps going into the ground. On the final test he disconnected the neutral wire that allows a low resistance path back to the source, made sure the neutral and the ground bus bars were connected and ran an 1800 watt hair dryer. Did the breaker trip? Nope.

This is a good example of why you should try to educate yourself about how things work. Just going off of what everyone else says can get you in trouble. I think a key takeaway is there's no safe place to send errant electricity. The only safe option is to turn off the electricity, which oddly enough, is what breakers are designed to do. As is clear from Mr. Holts' video, if the system isn't configured correctly, it won't work! *More about this in the next section.*

In a grounded system, imposed high frequency direct current (DC) from a nearby lightning strike or similar event is dissipated into the ground instead of possibly arcing from wires to pipes in walls or damaging electronics. Grounding also (hopefully) reduces the touch potential in any metal objects. As stated above, the best way to eliminate errant electrical flow is to turn it off and turn it off quickly. In order to do this we need to provide a very low resistance, uninterrupted pathway back to the source so the fault can draw as much current, as fast as it can, to make the breaker trip and shut off the electricity.

Why do we need to draw a bunch of current? Won't my 15 amp breaker trip at anything over 15 amps? Not necessarily. Over Current Protection Devices or breakers have a couple basic jobs to do. First, turn off the electricity in the event of a fault and second, turn off the electricity in the case of an overload. Aren't those two one in the same? Uhh, no. An overload current is an excessive current flow relative to normal operating current, but still confined to the normal circuit paths provided by the conductors. A short-circuit or ground fault current flows outside of the normal circuit paths.

The concept to think about in an overload situation is controlling heat in the circuit. Fire is bad! That said, low magnitude or short lasting overloads really aren't a big deal. Say, your pool pump fires up and draws a ton of amps for a couple seconds, no big deal, not enough time to build up a dangerous amount of heat. Let's say you're air conditioner is old and draws a little bit more amperage than the circuit is designed for but cycles on and off every 30-40 mins, no big deal.

A Short-circuit or ground fault differs from overloads as they can be hundreds to thousands of times greater than the normal operating current. So the breaker needs to, not trip, any time it gets a little fluctuation in current and needs to trip immediately in a short circuit or ground fault. A 20 amp breaker for example, must trip at a sustained current of 27 amperes (135 percent) at less than one hour, and at 40 amperes (200 percent of wire rating) in less than 120 seconds. Oh and the ambient temperature affects when the breaker will trip too. In a short to ground the breaker will trip in milliseconds, if it has a low resistance, uninterrupted path bask to the source! If not, it can kill you. If your eyes are already glazed over I won't go any further.

Now that we have some basics covered, let's say we've come across a super deal on an old house that we need to put an offer on, in the next 30 minutes. We took off some of the outlet covers to find a jumper wire was connected from the outlet to the metal outlet box. We went in the attic to find that the house (from what we can see) uses flexible armored cable. That said, it looks like that hack should work, maybe. A few questions we need to ask are, what is the condition of the flexible armored cable? Has it been physically damaged somewhere along the run? Is it still an uninterrupted run or has someone changed out one of the metal outlet boxes for a fiberglass or plastic one sometime in last 50 years? Let's say we test for continuity and find it is an uninterrupted run. Is it low resistance? If so, how low does it need to be in order trip the breaker fast enough? It only takes about 200 milliseconds to cause fibrillation in the human heart.

During the mid- 2000's there were a number of DIY and Flip shows on TV. In the span of 30 minutes a couple of newbies would totally renovate a house "by themselves". Everybody was doing it. The housing market started to heat up due in part to policies the Clinton administration put into effect, mainly, the repeal of the Glass-Steagall Act which was part of the 1933 Banking Act, and later G.W. Bush, more on this a little later.

So everyone and there brother was now a real estate investor and apparently a construction guru too. Like I've mentioned earlier, I've physically looked at thousands of properties over the past 14 years and the number of those properties that had major and terribly executed DIY modifications was significant, probably in the 30% range. Keep in mind I live in the Orlando area so I was in one of the hot beds for investment at the time which is probably why the numbers were so high.

Looking at so many properties allowed me to see "modifications" that were done, how they were hidden and how well they worked even though they weren't done correctly. Back in those days, I hadn't earned my own respect yet so I hired many a home inspector, only to find that very few of them (at the time anyway) knew much about how things worked. They only knew that a certain gauge wire has to have a certain sized breaker on it, the air coming out of the air conditioner should be colder by 15-20 degrees and if they put an outlet tester in an outlet and it shows two yellows, you're good.

I'm not bashing all home inspectors, this is just my experience and from what I've seen recently there is a much greater depth of education in this industry. That said, you have to know enough to check the checker! If I plugged in a circuit tester to our "modified" outlet, it would show that it's wired correctly! You're about to spend a lot of hard earned money, so to be safe, you're going to want to be able to check the checker!

So, if you really dig into that property and find that all of the old stuff is in good and proper condition, is safe and insurable, pull the trigger! If you find things that raise big red flags, regardless of what the home inspector finds, walk away! Try to learn as much as you can about your product so you minimize the chance that you end up with any big surprises like a $10,000 re-wire.

ELECTRICAL SYSTEMS

In 1882 Thomas Edison formed the Edison Electric Illuminating company of New York which brought electric lighting to parts of Manhattan. It would take another 43 years for electricity to make it into about half the homes in America. Early electric service provided between 30 and 60 amps of power and did not offer 220 volts. These service panels (where electricity from the source comes into your house) had screw in fuses made of glass with a brass or copper element that would melt if too much power was drawn through it essentially turning off the flow of electricity. These early electrical systems from about the late 1800's to the earl 1940's used a wiring system called "knob and tube".

Ceramic Knob (red arrow), and where a ceramic tube should be (yellow arrow), allow the wire to be held in place, electrically isolated, its direction changed (knob), and passed through (tube), in this case, a wall stud.

In my opinion, knob and tube wiring worked well for its time, using thick gauge copper suspended in air and low amperage draws allowed this wire to operate at cooler temperatures. Unfortunately, the protective covering on the wires, usually a rubberized cloth, tended to break down and become brittle (depending on circumstances) after only 25 years. This would allow exposed, live, current carrying electrical wire. Not the safest scenario, but in the 6,000 plus properties I've looked at over that last 14 years, I have found many early 1900's properties with accessible, live, knob and tube wiring happily living in, some wall spaces but mostly in attics. As long as no one touches it and nothing falls across it or gets placed on it, it's fine. Obviously, this isn't safe and should be rectified immediately.

An old glass fuse and disconnect box.

Another problem you'll run into is simply the age of the property. I don't mean its structural integrity per se, but the amount of time it's been around to have every Tom, Dick and Harry mess with, modify, and damage it. Knob and tube is usually fully exposed (insulation intact but not concealed behind a wall) in unfinished spaces like attics and basements. This leads people to do all sorts of things like hang things from the wire, add their own circuits with newer wire and damage the wire, knobs and tubes.

Other issues arises as people modernize their properties and add fiberglass or blown in, insulation. Knob and tube was not designed to be covered with insulation. It was designed to be in free airspace to dissipate heat, covering it may cause the wire to get too hot further degrading the protective covering. The biggest issue by far, as mentioned before, is insurability. You probably won't be able to insure the property for a reasonable price or at all unless it's been professionally rewired, a newer roof has been put on, a modern HVAC (Heating, Ventilation and Air Conditioning) system has been installed and probably a complete re-plumb. Remember that when these homes were built, the electrical system was only designed to provide lighting!

To have a property re-wired professionally means, a new service drop, new meter base, new breaker panels, new conduit, new wiring, new outlets, new switches and light boxes and you may have to bring the number of outlets up to code (meaning add more). To do this the electrician(s) will have to tear apart sections of the walls and ceilings to run the new wires and no, they usually will not replace what they've torn apart so you have to get a drywall or plaster guy to fix this and try to match the finish of the original walls and ceilings.

Suffice to say it's a lot harder to re-wire a house than to wire it during construction and that means money!! I got a quote in 2016 to rewire a house where no demolition work was required, all the walls and ceilings were down to studs and I was going to re-drywall the 1700 sq. ft. three bedroom, 2 bathroom house. The lowest quote I got was $10,000! As you can see, these older properties present a lot of challenges and if you plan on buying one, and unless you're very handy I'd suggest against it for your first one, it should be priced accordingly!

Old cloth jacketed wire.

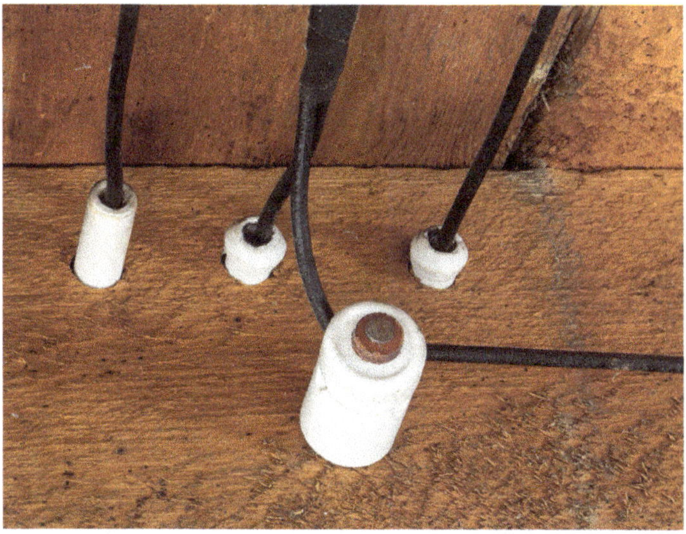

Old cloth jacketed wire, in pretty good condition. Look at how the splices were made back then. Cut away the insulation of one wire, wrap the other wire tightly around it, and tape it all up! Notice that this is "wire" and not cable. There was one separate hot wire and one separate nuetral wire.

Hmm, what's hiding behind that wall? New cable mixed with old cable.

New cable spliced into old cloth jacketed wire. Don't get lazy by just pulling an outlet or switch and looking at the wire! Really dig through that house because once you sign the papers, it's your problem!

Note: *In the early days of the housing crash, people who made fast, poor buying decisions with the intent of flipping the property, tried to get out of their positions by any means possible with zero regard for the new buyer. In my travels I've found many an old property that had a foot or more of new Romex cable wired to outlets and switches that was subsequently stuffed up inside the wall. This would throw a red flag after I found old cable elsewhere in the house, so I'd gently pull the cable out of the wall through the outlet box. What do you know, it's wire nutted to old cable!*

FLEXIBLE ARMORED CABLE

Towards the end of the knob and tube era and running from 1920 to 1940, flexible armored cable came on the scene. Flexible armored cable is frequently called Greenfield, BX (B experimental), AC (armored cable), and there was an AX (A experimental) but it never made it to full production. We humans like to make things simple so, depending on the age of the person you're talking to, they may refer to it simply as BX cable (even though when it went into production it was no longer experimental) or Armored Cable. Flexible armored cable was designed to be an upgrade to knob and tube and began to be the wiring of choice. Flexible armored cable offered a number of advantages over knob and tube. The flexible metal that covered the cable didn't really degrade over time like knob and tube and it offered impact and abrasion resistance.

> ***Note:*** *Many homes built before the mid 1960's only had 2 wires in the cable, a "Hot" and a "Neutral" and no third wire to offer grounding. This becomes an issue with newer appliances, equipment and tools that have a three prong plug.*

Good condition, two wire, flexible armored cable or commonly referred to as BX cable.

You may have seen some adaptors on outlets that have a protruding three prong style receptor on one end and only two prongs on the end that plugs into the two prong outlet.

This was an old bandaid which allowed you to use that equipment but still didn't offer true grounding protection. There's a lot of scuttlebutt amongst the DIY community and some old school electricians in regards to the protective metal covering being used as an equipment ground and or a system ground. The idea being that the protective metal covering of the armored cable is connected to an outlet box at one end of the circuit and also being connected to the metal service panel at the other end. So, in their theory, to achieve a grounded system, where the cables are protected or shielded from induced super high voltage from a nearby lightning strike by carrying that voltage down the flexible armoring to the service panel that is grounded to earth (because lightning, direct current, wants to go to earth) via a bare wire that's attached to a ground round driven into the earth. Now to achieve a "3 wire equipment grounded" system, they postulate that they can remove the old two wire outlets, install a 3 wire outlet like you're used to seeing in homes today and run a ground jumper wire from the outlet to the metal outlet box or use the metal frame of the outlet that ends up being screwed to the metal outlet box. On the service panel side of the system they would run a jumper wire to the neutral bus bar (because Alternating Current wants to return to the source which is the transformer on the power pole) if the service panel isn't already bonded to the neutral bus bar, to complete the "equipment grounding" circuit. While this seems to be logical on the surface, and may work most of the time, there are some sketchy aspects that I'll go into later.

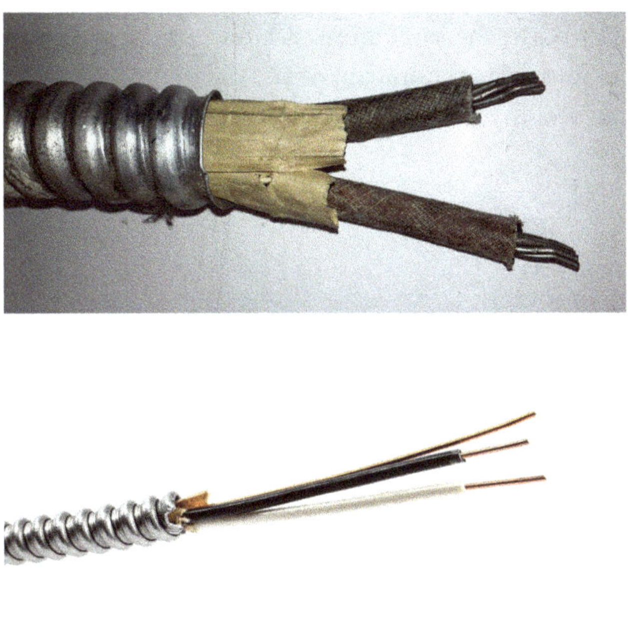

FAC from different periods. Notice the different cable jacketing.

Disclaimer time! I am not a certified, licensed electrical anything and I'm only sharing my limited knowledge and experiences to help you make better decisions when it comes to interviewing a contractor on the potential work and costs involved when you have to make a quick decision on a property that looks like to be a great deal. That said, hire a professional, have a good idea of the work being done and keep them honest!

ARMORED CABLE

Didn't we just talk about armored cable? Yes, but not this armored cable. New armored cable (AC) is allowed by the NEC (National Electric Code) Sec. 250.118, to be used as an EGC (Equipment Grounding Conductor) in accordance with Sec. 320.108 because it must have an armor of flexible metal tape with an internal bonding strip of copper or aluminum in intimate contact with the armor for the entire length. As of the writing of this, Listed Flexible Metal Conduit cable must meet certain conditions to be up to code and this one condition seals the debate about using AC as an EGC. "The combined length of FMC, Flexible metallic tubing and liquid tight FMC in the same ground fault current path cannot exceed 1.8m (6 ft.). So the maximum run of the circuit you can safely have is 6 ft. As you can see, if you're trying to do it right, it's pointless.

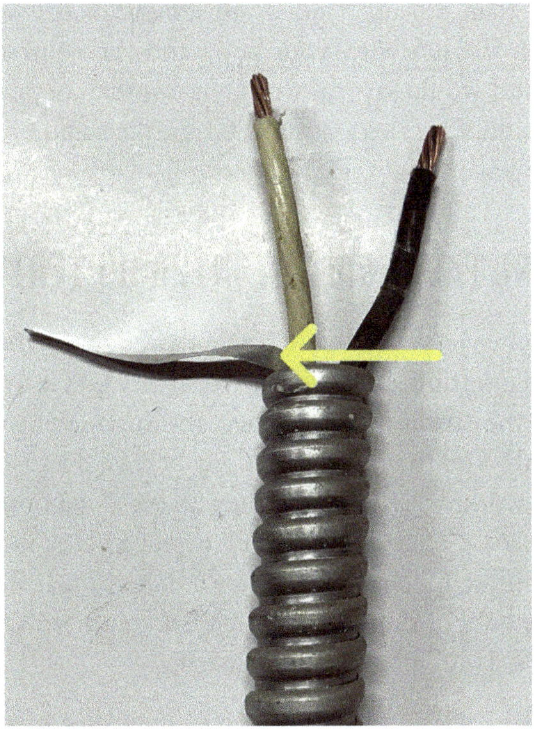

So, our original problem was we have an old property that has armored cable wiring with no ground, 2 prong outlets, and we want to make it both user friendly and safer. We basically have 3 options; 1- Rewire the entire house at significant expense. This is the best option for functionality and safety and will add some value to the property. I say some because it depends if the buyer understands what it means to have a similar property with the old armored cable system and how much it costs to perform the upgrade.

A buyer that understands all these things including the reduction in homeowners insurance will pay you for the work. A buyer who doesn't, either won't or will buy the similar property that's listed for $10,000 less. 2- Install GFCI (Ground Fault Circuit Interrupt) outlets in all locations or at the 1st location of a branch circuit that feeds other outlets and you will have to label each outlet with "no equipment ground". Keep in mind a GFCI outlet will not prevent a shock, but should render the shock harmless, **should**. If you happen to contact both conductors somehow and there's less than a 5 mA (milliamp) difference between the current flowing through the hot wire, your body and the neutral wire, it won't break the circuit. I would say this would be less than desirable! 3- Replace all the branch circuit breakers with GFCI breakers and or do a combination of GFCI breakers and GFCI outlets.

GFCI (GROUND FAULT CIRCUIT INTERRUPTER)

You may be saying to yourself, "self, what voodoo do they use in these GFCI's?" Good question, I like your curiosity! A GFCI works by continuously sensing the current flowing back and forth along the "hot" wire and the "neutral" wire (which many falsely believe doesn't carry current). If everything is working as designed, the current along both wires is equal or balanced. If some of it tries to go someplace other than that circuit, there will be a difference between the two conductors. If this fault current exceeds the trip level of the GFCI, which is around 5mA, the GFCI will trip in as little as 1/40th of a second! Amazing!

AFCI (ARC FAULT CIRCUIT INTERRUPTER)

An AFCI is designed to prevent arcing electricity from starting a fire. Wiring, be it in the walls or attic of a house or the electrical cords of appliances, can get damaged allowing electricity to jump or arc through the air. This arcing can make things a little toasty, like 10,000 deg. F. toasty and can obviously melt insulation, vaporize metal and start fires in surrounding materials. An AFCI monitors the current flow through itself and uses detection circuitry to discern between normal and unwanted arcing. Arcing produces a current signature or waveform that the AFCI recognizes and then turns off the flow of electricity.

AFCI breakers with indicative white pig tales and test buttons.

NM (NON-METALLIC) SHEATHED CABLE

Non-metallic sheathed cable (NM), was invented by the Rome Wire company in the early 1920's and trade named Romex. The Romex trade-name is now registered to the Southwire Company which can be found at most big box stores. Although invented in the early 1920's, NM cable was not broadly used until the 1950's. Early NM cable had a varnish like impregnated cotton jacket. As you look at properties from around the mid 1940's to the late 1960's, you're likely to find this cable with only two conductors and jacketing dry and brittle. Starting around 1950, synthetic rayon replaced the cotton braided jacketing. The 1960's gave way to a thermoplastic protective jacketing. By the 1970's, PVC (Polyvinyl chloride) jacketing was being used.

Modern 12 gauge, 2 wire with a ground, Romex NM PVC sheathed cable. (notice the sheathing color).

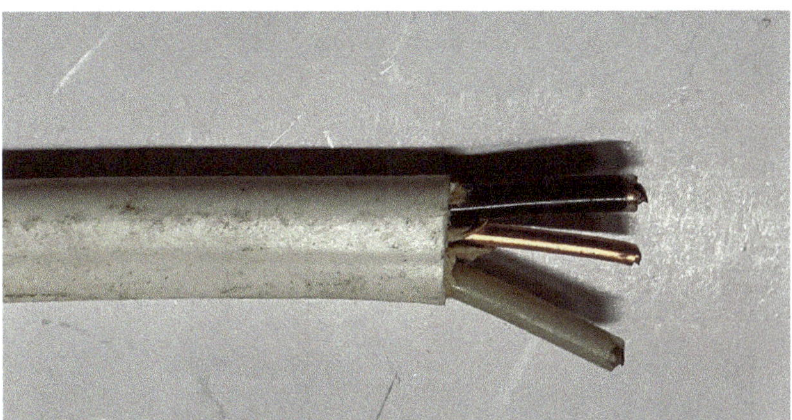

Modern 14 gauge, 2 wire with a ground Romex NM PVC sheathed cable. (notice the sheathing color).

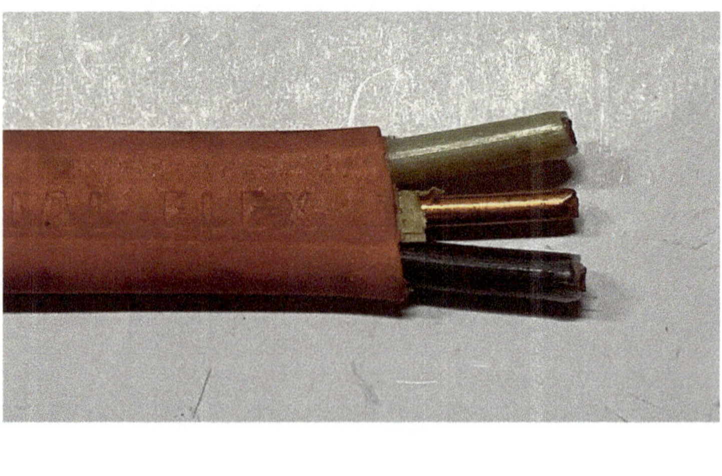

Modern 10 gauge, 2 wire with a ground Romex NM PVC sheathed cable (notice the sheathing color).

> ***Note:*** *Braided jacket NM cable was allowed to be used until the mid- 1980's. Prior to 1962 most NM cable had no EGC (Equipment Grounding Conductor). After being mandated by code, a bare copper EGC was added. As you inspect properties you may notice the EGC is a smaller gauge, sometimes 2 sizes smaller, than the CCC (Current Carrying Conductors). It wasn't until around 1969 that the grounding conductor was made the same size or gauge that the Current Carrying Conductors were.*

After looking through thousands of attics, I've seen all of the above mentioned cable in various conditions. Some of the older silver/gray fabric jacketed cable I've seen is in fantastic shape and still pliable without cracking or flaking. That said, I've seen at least an equal number that have been very dry and brittle with complete sections of the outer jacket missing, especially were the cable makes a hard bend around or over a 2" x 4". Unfortunately I haven't been able to find a correlation as to why some properties have pristine fabric jacketed cable and some don't. Did one roll of cable sit on pallets in the yard of a business, exposed to the sun for six months while another happened to be delivered and used right away, who knows? You'll find this conundrum with some plumbing pipe also. The best thing to do is get up in the attic and look!

Maybe a furry friend was nibbling on this.

> ***Note:*** *Wire is expensive and electricians try to use the bare minimum amount of it to complete a job. When you're up in the attic you'll find the wire pulled very tight, over, across and around objects. Being an old, car guy, we would never do something like this as any movement of the vehicle/engine would eventually abrade through the wire. I don't think there's enough movement in most items in the house or the house itself to be worried about this however, in my opinion, it most certainly reduces the life of the jacketing as I've witnessed many, many times.*

In my opinion, NM sheathed cable was invented as a way to reduce the cost of manufacture and speed up installation, while giving an acceptable level of protection to the Current Carrying Conductors. Modern NM cable, ~1969 and newer, will have two insulated Current Carrying

Conductors, one black, one white, and one bare Equipment Grounding Conductor that are all the same size or gauge, jacketed with a thin but durable and flexible, PVC sheathing.

> **Note:** *When people or a manufacturer speaks of the size of a wire, they refer to it buy what gauge it is, 10 gauge, 12 gauge, 14 gauge, etc. Assuming the wire is round and solid, gauge refers to its thickness. The thicker it is, the more efficiently it will conduct electricity. The NEC establishes codes as to what size wire will be required for a given circuit ampacity. For example, the circuit your bedroom light is on is only designed to carry a relatively light load of current, say 15 amperes. The NEC relates, depending on the type of wire, accompanying equipment and enclosures, this circuit which could carry a maximum of 15 amps continuously, requires a minimum wire size of 14 gauge. Why does the NEC care what size wire we put in? Well, the concept here is to conduct electricity and keep heat under control. Your typical copper wire will melt at 1,984 degs. F. so, we can run a ton of amperage through the wire before we have to worry about it melting. The protective insulation on the other hand, will melt at a much, much lower temperature, the highest that I'm aware of is only rated to a maximum of 194 degs. F. So, if we melt the insulation away, now we have, at minimum, a shock hazard and probably a fire hazard because the now bare wire can impart its 200+ degs. F. of heat on any surrounding insulation or wood. That said, the system is only as good as its weakest link, the insulation. Scientists have figured out that the thicker the wire is, the more current it can carry without heating up too much. Thus, the reason behind the rules on wire size and ampacity. So, a 14 gauge wire should carry more current than a 10 gauge right? Um, no, it's the exact opposite, until of course, you get down to size 0 wire (referred to in the profession as "aught") where it makes sense again and the higher the number, the more current it will carry. You'll find this written as 1/0, 2/0, 3/0 etc. This size wire can carry a lot of amperage and is typically reserved for the wires that feed your entire house. The branch circuit wiring in a house will typically*

range from the biggest, 6 ga, or 8 ga. for the oven and heating, 10 ga. for water heaters and dryers and 12ga. to 14ga. for everything else. Circuit ampacity will range from 50A to 60A for the oven and heat, 30A for the dryer and water heater and 15A to 20A for everything else.

This is the cable you're used to seeing at your local big box store. These cables will have single strand wire that is solid (except for 6ga. and 8ga.) and different color sheathing for the different sizes or gauges. 14ga. cable has a white sheathing, 12ga. cable has a yellow sheathing, 10ga. cable has an orange sheathing, 6ga. and 8 ga. wire will be stranded (multiple smaller gauge wires bundled together to make one wire in the cable, this allows the wires to move over each other when bending it) to make it easier to manipulate around objects and has a black sheathing and finally outdoor wire listed for underground use will have a much thicker gray sheathing.

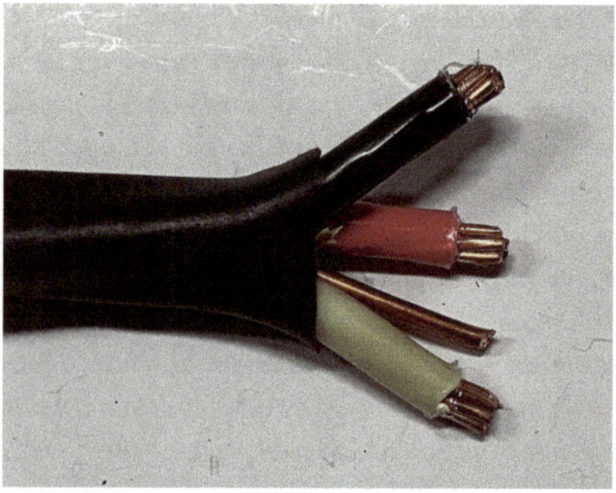

Modern 8 gauge, 3 wire with a ground, Romex NM PVC sheathed cable (notice the sheathing color).

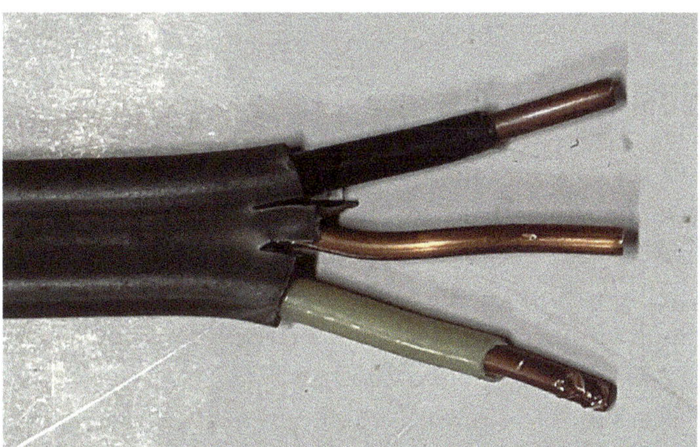

Modern 14/2 with a ground Romex NM PVC sheathed cable for direct underground burial. The sheathing on this is extra thick and the wires are isolated from each other via the sheathing and not by paper wrapping like the normal Romex (notice the sheathing color).

ALUMINUM WIRE

Now on to the big one, aluminum wiring! There was a presidential ad campaign in the 1980's that said, "Just say no to drugs!" What they meant to say was, "Just say NO to aluminum wiring!". Specifically, aluminum branch circuit wiring. As mentioned earlier in this book, aluminum branch circuit wiring came to be as an alternative to prohibitively expensive copper wiring from around 1965 to 1974.

So, what's the big deal with aluminum wiring? Aren't those 500,000 Volt transmission wires made of steel covered aluminum? Isn't the wire coming from the power pole into my main service panel aluminum? Well, yes to both. So, why did the Consumer Product Safety Commission state that houses wired with single strand aluminum branch circuit cable before 1972 are 55 times more likely to have one or more connections reach "fire hazard conditions" than homes wired with copper?

One reason is aluminum is less ductile than copper which means as the electricians yank the wire through holes, over trusses and around obstructions, the metal fatigues which increases its resistance, in turn increasing how hot the wire gets during normal use. Aluminum also has a higher electrical resistance than copper under normal conditions even without being fatigued. Aluminum also suffers from galvanic corrosion and oxidation that makes the connection points an even higher resistance, causing more heat buildup. Aluminum is also more malleable (soft), has greater thermal expansion and contraction, and has excess vibration or harmonics as current passes through it.

These last three things are, in my opinion, what put the final nail in aluminum wires coffin. To visualize this, let's use the outlet that your refrigerator is plugged into. The aluminum wires insulation is stripped back by the electrician and either pushed into the holes in the back of the outlet or wrapped around the terminal screws that are then tightened down pinching the aluminum between the underside of the head of the screw and the side of the outlet. The compressor in the refrigerator cycles on and off maybe 100 times a day. The wire excessively (compared to copper for which the outlet was designed to use) expands and contracts during these cycles causing the connection between the screw and the wire to loosen. This causes more electrical resistance at the connection which causes more heat. The hotter it gets, the more it expands and contracts making the problem worse. Add in the oxidation that's taking place and it gets worse. If part of the exposed wire arcs to the outlet or screw it will cause a tremendous heat event that can actually vaporize (remove more aluminum making the gap and the problem bigger) and cause more oxidation. Consequently, this combination of events was responsible for 50% of the house fires in the United States, yikes!

So, how can one tell if the property they're looking at has aluminum wiring? First, you'll want to find out when the property was built and or added on to. Next, when you visit the property you'll CAREFULLY remove the outer cover of the main service panel or have someone do it so you can look at the wiring inside of it. With the panel cover off you'll be able to see all of the branch circuit wiring and their connections to the breakers. It's at these connections you'll be able to see if the wire is aluminum or copper.

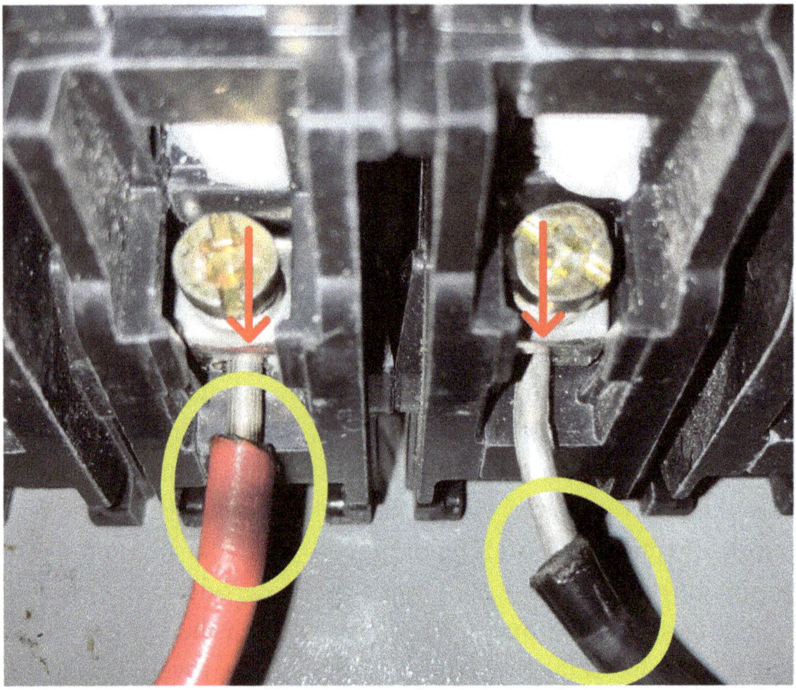

In this picture you can clearly see the shiny aluminum wire (red arrows) and also see where the wire has gotten hot enough to slightly burn the insulation (yellow circles).

You're only concerned with the branch circuits, the wire from the Over Current Protection Device (breaker) out to the house, ie; "living room, west wall" etc. If taking the cover off of the panel is not an option, go into the attic and look at the cable sheathing. Look for the word(s)"Aluminum", "Kaiser Aluminum", the abbreviations "AL", "ALCAN" or "KA-FLEX" stamped into or printed on the sheathing.

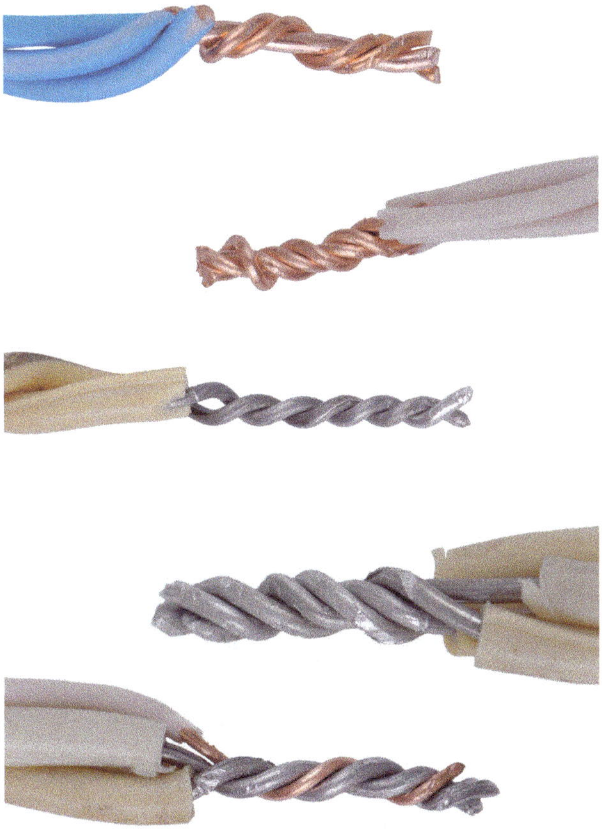

This is a pretty good side by side comparison of copper and aluminum wire.

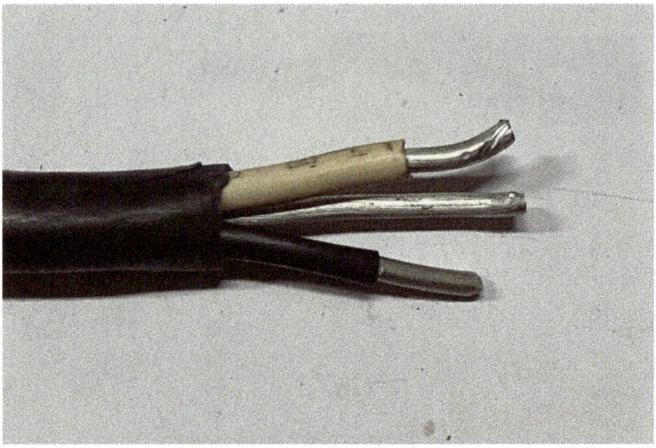

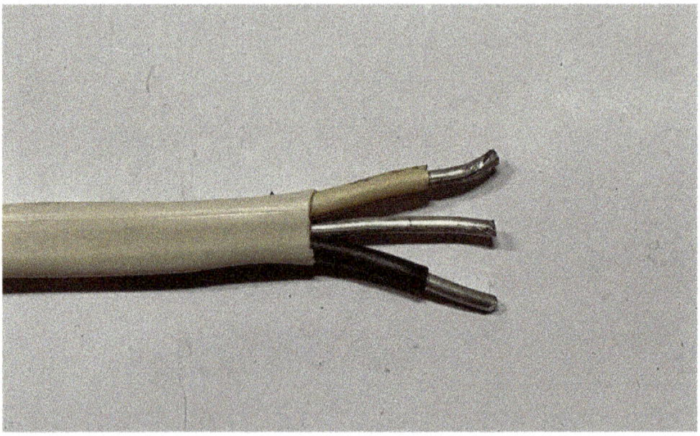

Some examples of Aluminum cable – Look for "Kaiser", "KA-FLEX", and "Alcan".

Removing outlet and or switch plate covers then looking in with a flashlight is another option. The aluminum wire will be obvious, it's thicker and much lighter in color than copper. You may see an "adapter" so to speak that looks like this.

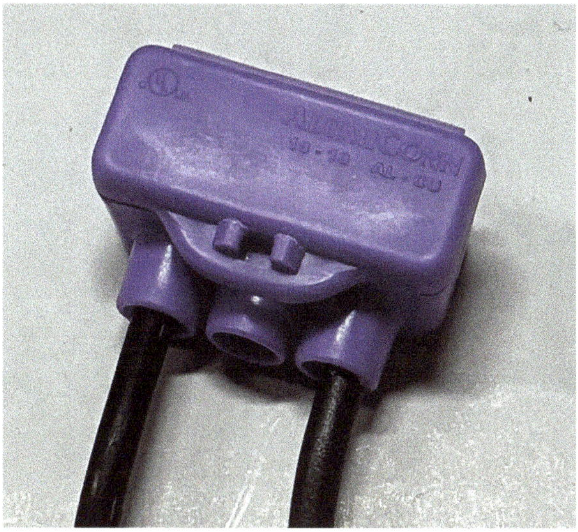

Certifed Aluminum to Copper Adapter

These specific AL/Cu (Aluminum to Copper) connectors are the only approved option I know of that will make the circuit safer. Your insurance company however, will most likely not care and either drop or not give you insurance or raise your rates to an astronomical level. Remember, if you don't have insurance, you're in default of your mortgage and they can foreclose on you!

I've seen homes with aluminum wiring that are 46 years old, have not been modified and are still working fine (from what a person can tell) and I've seen some, where the top part of a duplex outlet shows no voltage and after further inspection the wire to the top part of the outlet is found to be burned up and still live. The corrosion is so bad that electricity won't flow through the outlet but the wire still has voltage. At the end of the day, unless you're paying cash, it really doesn't matter how you feel about aluminum wiring because most if not all insurance companies won't insure a property with it. My advice, stay away from aluminum wiring, it's too much risk, cost and hassle for someone looking to get into the game!

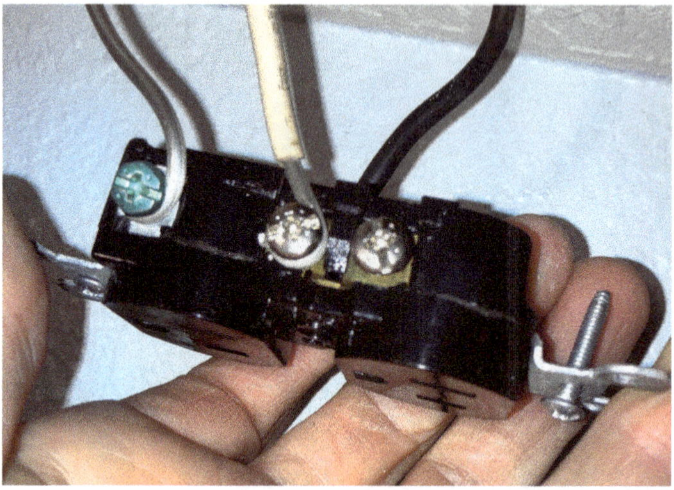

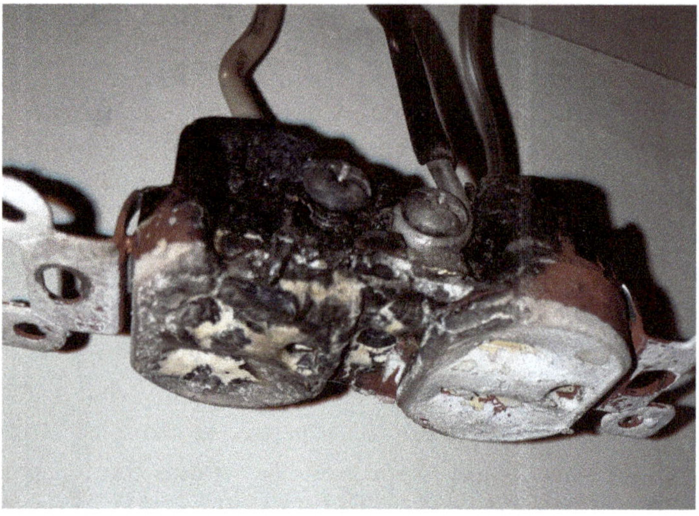

Aluminum branch circuit wiring at a functioning and not so functioning outlet.

ELECTRICAL PANELS

In the electrical panel world there are basically two that are of major concern. The first is the Federal Pacific Electric, or FPE, main electric panel including the "STAB-LOK" breakers. These panels were installed in millions of homes from the 1950's into the 1980's. Unfortunately, our good friends over at FPE falsified testing data allowing them to obtain the needed safety certifications to sell to the public. The gist of the matter is that these breakers will fail to trip reliably. As such, when overloaded or shorted, they keep the current and heat flowing until a fire starts. That said, there are plenty of older properties today that are still functioning with FPE panels and breakers. My first duplex, built in 1958 had them until I replaced them, around 2010. Regardless, most insurance companies won't insure a property with them and they will have to be replaced. I apologize, but I don't have a picture of one.

The next one is Zinsco. Unfortunately Zinsco breakers and panels were also rebranded to GTE-Sylvania, Magnatrip, and Challenger. Any of these panels, which oftentimes has multi-colored breakers, may suffer the same fate as the FPE panels, breakers not tripping, but may also have the connections at the bus bar becoming loose. The only way to know this would be removing the breakers and inspecting the bus bar. Suffice to say, most insurance companies will require you to replace thes panels. Challenger may be accepted after inspection because after about 1981, they stopped manufacturing the Zinsco style panels, but continued to sell the breakers. It is estimated that around 9,000 properties nationwide have these bad breakers.

PLUMBING

There a five main types of plumbing pipe used in homes today, PEX, PVC, ABS, Copper, and galvanized cast iron. As with most things, they all have their pro's and con's. More importantly, insurance companies like and don't like certain ones regardless of whether the pipe is junk or the poor assembly is to blame. I'll go over the pro's and con's and give you some things to look out for.

PEX (POLYETHYLENE CROSS LINKED PIPE)

Invented in the 1950's and originally marketed in Europe, PEX or polyethylene cross linked pipe didn't arrive in the U.S. until the 1980's and was initially used for radiant floor heating. PEX won't leach (supposedly), rust, corrode, pit or get pinholes, suffer from scale buildup, has better freeze tolerance, reduced heat transfer, is lightweight and easy to work with, comes in 10 foot sticks and rolls as big as 300 feet, and is cheaper than copper. It's flexible yet strong allowing fairly short radius 90 deg. bends reducing the amount of fittings (that could possibly leak) needed. It's about one third the cost of copper, although copper will last about 70 years vs. 50 for PEX. It can be color coded for easy identification in random parts of the house. Typical colors are red, blue, white and a sort of translucent.

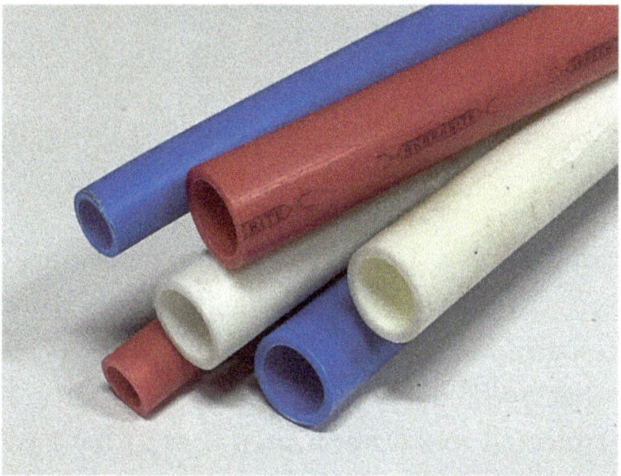

PEX's long, uninterrupted runs and relative ease of installation made it affordable to have a manifold system installed. Manifold systems have one main plenum that all of the runs to the house are attached. At the plenum or manifold, each run has its own shut off valve. So, if you need to change the cheap gate valve that supplies the toilet because it will no longer turn the water off (ask me how I know), you can turn the water off to that bathroom only while you work and the rest of the house can remain in service.

Now for the bad. PEX has a relatively high expansion rate, so thought needs to be given as to how you're going to run the hot water lines. It has a shorter lifespan than copper which is typically 70 years. It has temperature limits that need to be considered. For instance, it's not allowed to be directly connected to a water heater, it must have an 18" copper or metal lead. Relatively speaking, the aforementioned aren't that bad. The next few things are big ones. PEX does not hold up well when exposed to UV (Ultraviolet) light. Assuming this exposure time is limited I wouldn't worry too much about it. That said, I've seen plumbing trucks with rolls of PEX hanging on the back of the truck fully exposed. How long does that roll hang out in the sun? I don't know. It could've been completely used that day on a job(s). I've also seen rolls of PEX sitting on pallets out in the sun behind plumbing businesses. How long are they sitting there? Does this decrease the life of PEX enough to be concerned? Who knows? I own a property that was re-piped with PEX in the mid-2000's and I can tell you from personal experience I've had PEX that just split longitudinally causing a pressurized leak. On the same property I had the main water pipe coming out of the ground that was exposed to sun day in and day out split in the same fashion. The main feed coming out of the ground was exposed to at least 3 hours a day of direct sunlight and down here in Florida, that sun is angry! I was going to change out that feed pipe but it burst on me before I got the chance. I can't be mad because that pipe was used well outside of its design parameters. The pipe in the wall split in the same fashion although God was very graceful and allowed it start small when I was on property. I noticed a little bit of water creeping out from under one of the baseboards. I turned off everything that was making noise and I could hear the slightest hiss coming from the wall. I immediately shut the water off.

> ***Note:*** *If you're going to be a landlord, and especially in the beginning of your journey, always have a water T in your vehicle! There's nothing worse than finding a leak and having to scramble around trying to make something work or worse, make a 30 minute round trip to the store while water is gushing out inside your property.*

Blessings come in many forms and sometimes, initially, they don't resemble a blessing at all! This is a good time to bring up attitude. I was on my way home after a very hot and hard days work. Something told me to stop by the aforementioned property and replace the garage light that wasn't working anymore, so I wouldn't have to worry about it tomorrow. It would only take me about 15 minutes. As it would turn out, I ended up having to do another 4 hours of work that day, which was night by this time. Many people would have gotten very mad at this situation, but you have to keep it in perspective. If I would have just cruised home, that leak, if it didn't get any worse, at best would have done a ton of damage if it wasn't noticed by the tenant. It was evening time and the oozing water was in a corner that they probably wouldn't have paid any mind. They would have gone to bed and either called me in the middle of the night or not until they woke up the next morning and found a pool of water on the floor that had damaged a bunch of their stuff and mine. Needless to say I was very thankful to have found the leak while it was still small!

I had to cut out a section of drywall to locate the leak. I noticed streaking in the pipe just like on the pipe that was exposed to the sun and burst. I cut out that section of pipe and made an emergency repair. That got me thinking about the rest of the pipe in the house. Was it a ticking time bomb? During my pre-buy inspection it was evident that pride in workmanship wasn't a big concern but other than some loose fixtures, the pipe I could see in the attic looked ok. I decided to do another inspection this time using a bore scope which is a pen sized digital camera with a light that is attached to a long flexible conduit. I let the tenant know I'd be back first thing in the morning to do the inspection and to please call me if anything happens before then.

An example of a bore scope

When I arrived the next morning I checked the previous nights work and then headed up into the attic to scope down into the walls that the plumbing ran through. Well what do you know, those geniuses installed the hot and cold pipes going to the bathroom, right over and across, the metal vanity light support that's in the wall. Upon further inspection, I can see that over time and presumably due to water hammer (the back and forth movement of an unsupported pipe from turning the water on and off), a notch has been cut into the surface of the pipe. To make a long story short (I know, too late), when that piece of pipe was removed it only had a sliver of life left in it. When I flexed the pipe by about an inch, that notch split open. So you see, many of your problems are blessings in disguise and actually prevent you from a worse problem in the future! The pipe in the wall that failed in a similar fashion to the feed pipe made me wonder if there was any correlation to UV overexposure. As of now, I don't know, but it's something to keep in mind.

The next biggy with PEX is the fittings that are used to connect the pipes. The crimp ring style fittings (there's basically two kinds, a copper and a stainless steel ring) have to be installed fairly precisely. The rings need to be installed 1/8" to 1/4" from the end of the pipe which will place pressure directly over the two raised rings of the fitting that the PEX is sliding over. This is not that easy using the copper crimp ring as the ring, while sitting in the crimp, tool will easily slide down the pipe. Watching plumbers perform this task, I noted that they would locate the ring and the tool, then quickly clamp the ring. Some plumbers are precise at this and others are down right bad! They're supposed to check the crimp with a gauge specifically designed for this. I have yet to see a plumber do this. Honestly, the good ones don't need to but the bad ones definitely need to. In my opinion, the stainless steel crimp rings are a far better choice. They allow slight pressure to be put on the ring to hold it in place on the pipe before maximum pressure is applied to finish the crimp.

> ***Note:*** *I've noticed recently while renewing and getting new Homeowners Insurance that the insurance carriers are asking more questions in regards to PEX piping and in many cases requiring on-site inspections. From speaking with several agents, it seems as though the insurance companies are experiencing more claims due to PEX failures. As mentioned earlier, these failures could be due to the fittings used or the installation techniques. Some agents I've spoken to have noted pipes in attics splitting. Could be from UV exposure through attic vents, who knows. It doesn't really matter because if the insurance company won't accept it, unless you're using all cash, you can't buy it!*

Copper crimp ring.

Stainless crimp ring

THE DREADED ZURN FITTINGS

On to the last, but biggest concern with PEX plumbing, the Zurn F1807 or Qpex yellow brass fitting. These fittings were manufactured and sold from 1996 – 2010 and had Qpex or F1807 stamped in them. These fittings were designed and manufactured using UNS C36000 and C37700 brass alloys in accordance with ASTM F1807. Unfortunately these fittings will degrade over time and leak regardless of whether they were installed correctly or not.

When brass pipe fittings are manufactured, zinc is added to the copper alloy to increase the strength of the brass. The corrosion of brass is dependent on the amount of zinc in it. It is recommended to keep the zinc content between (15%-19% of the total alloy). However, to reduce cost, manufacturers began using higher zinc levels in the alloy. When water flows through the fitting, the zinc leaches from the brass and creates a powdery buildup. This process is known as dezincification. This buildup can cause a blockage within the fitting, so keep this in mind if you're looking at a property that has unexplained low water pressure. The fitting also becomes structurally weak as the zinc is removed from the alloy. This weakness can cause the fitting to leak and or completely fail.

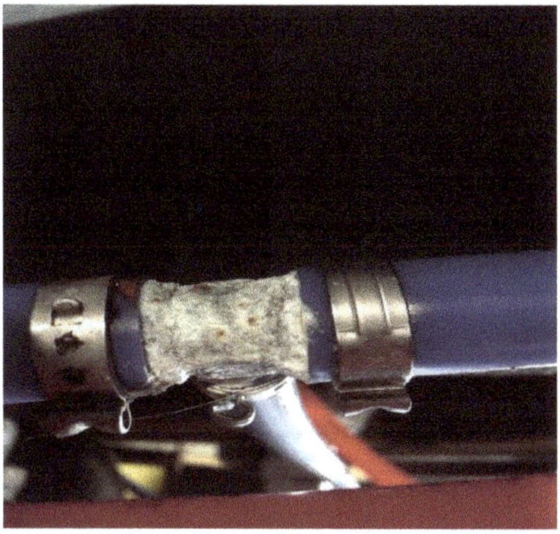

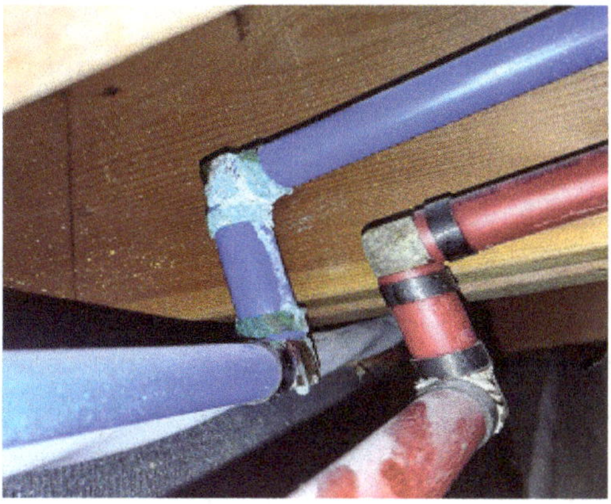

Another problem that can arise is chlorine degradation of the pipe itself. You'll need to check with the water authority that serves the property you're looking at to find out how much chlorine they add into the water supply. I have found some information on the internet from plasticpipe.org that relates water used in PEX piping should have no more than 4 ppm (parts per million) of chlorine.

There are also different grades of PEX pipe. As with all the plastic pipe I can find available in stores, PEX has printed manufacturing information on it. This information includes what standards the pipe complies with, and the grade of the pipe. The grade of the pipe is indicated by a series of four digits. The pipes resistance to degradation by hot chlorinated water is indicated by the first digit. The manufacturers use 1, 3, and 5 to indicate how much exposure time the pipe can have and last for 50 years without failing. If the first digit is 1, the pipe will not (read-should not) fail when exposed to hot chlorinated water 25% of the time, 3, 50% of the time and 5, 100% of the time. That said, I would only buy grade 5 PEX regardless of whether it's for cold or hot water! The second digit in the 4 digit code on the pipe refers to its UV resistance. "0" means not tested, 1 means the pipe should be good if exposed to UV for up to a month, 2 up to three months and 3 up to six months. The last two digits in the 4 digit code are reserved for hydrostatic design stress. Basically, whatever the last two digits are, multiply them times 100 to get the HDS. For example, a pipe reads 5308. The 5 indicates it has the highest resistance to chlorine, 3 indicates the highest resistance to UV and 08 indicates its HDS is 800 psi.

So as this complicated world would have it, not only are there different grades of PEX piping, there are also different types, with different grades. No need to say anything, I know your pain. That said, there are 3 main types, PEX A, PEX B and you guessed it, PEX C. Without going crazy, their differences lie in how they're manufactured, PEX A with peroxide, PEX B with Silane, and PEX C with irradiation. PEX A has the highest flexibility or softness may be a better word for it. If you kink PEX A you can use a heat gun to repair it. Unfortunately it's about double the price, has a lower burst pressure and may leach chemicals. PEX B has the highest burst pressure, the highest oxidative and chlorine resistance and is the lowest price of the PEX types. It's more rigid than the other types, has coil memory (when it's wrapped in a coil for shipping it wants to stay in that shape), and kinks have to be cut out and a new section of pipe spliced in. Now, I couldn't find a whole bunch of data on PEX C, but here's what I could find, it's softer than PEX B and doesn't have coil memory but, and this is a big but, apparently it's prone to cracking. I have no personal experience with PEX C so I can only pass on information. That said, when I see prone to cracking, I'll pass on PEX C.

If you're going to use PEX piping, you're going to need PEX specific tools and fittings. You basically have three somewhat affordable options. Two crimp ring types and a much more expensive, tube expanding method, which I can see professionals using. As previously mentioned, I'm partial to the stainless steel crimp ring. You will most likely use one of the two crimp ring methods due to cost. Regardless of which crimp method you choose, keep in mind when planning your plumbing repair that the great force required to crimp the rings onto the pipe requires considerable mechanical advantage from the tool. Thus, when fully opened to start the crimp, the tools handles have a spread of about two feet. While this is of no concern when you have plenty of room to work, when working in a tight space, which is more the rule than the exception, you may have to crimp the pipe onto the fitting first and then fish the assembly into place. This lack of room to work can be a serious impediment and may require you to buy an expensive tool or switch to a different pipe that either brazes or glues together.

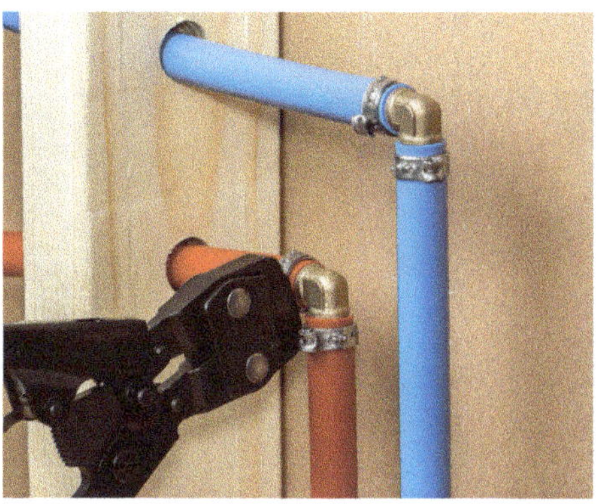

Stainless steel crimp rings and tool.

Copper crimp rings, tool and gauge.

Powered crimper (can be usueful in tight spots).

There are basically three types of fitting you can use, two metal and one plastic. I'm partial to metal as I feel, anecdotally, that metal is stronger and will last longer. This may or may not be the case of course. Either way, there are two relatively cheap fittings that appear the same except one is metal and one is plastic. There is another, super user friendly fitting that is made of metal that is named after the company that produces it, Sharkbite. Remember, super user friendly equals, super expensive. They're really amazing fittings that can join many types of pipe together, pipes that are the same and pipes that are completely different, like joining PEX to copper! These fittings or maybe more appropriately, couplers, are orders of magnitude more expensive. They're much more complex, have more material in them, are easily removable and make it almost fool proof to make a water tight connection, which is reflected in the price. They're great for one time quick fixes. However "easy" these fittings may be to use, you should ALWAYS carefully follow the manufacturers installation and use instructions!

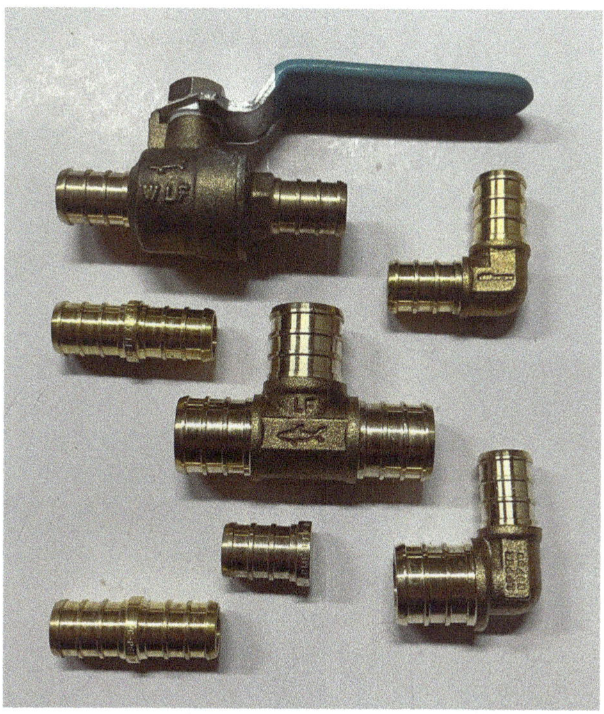

Metal PEX fittings.

Plastic PEX fittings.

Sharkbite fittings used to join PEX to PEX and Copper to PEX.

PVC (POLYVYNIL CHLORIDE)

Although the compound was discovered around 1835, it wouldn't be until 1932 in Germany, when it was first formed into a pipe. It would take a few more years to improve the production process enough to offer piping for use in residences. Although the new processing technique was inconsistent, around 400 homes had this piping installed from 1936 – 1939. The main attraction of this new piping was its resistance to a wide range of chemicals, its light weight and its smooth interior finish offering little resistance to flowing liquids. With the early success in Germany, the pipe would eventually make its way to North America by 1949 and be introduced in the United States in 1952.

> ***Note:*** *In my experience, PVC has a much better resistance to UV vs. PEX and PEX has a much better resistance to bursting under freezing conditions.*

With its physical toughness, chemical resistance, smooth interior and a life expectancy of 100 years, PVC pipe would proliferate throughout the United States. By 1983, around 30,000 miles of PVC sewer pipe was in the ground, making its share of all sewer pipe 80%. Exhumed sewer pipe in Germany would show that after 30 years, the pipe looked and tested like new. A truly amazing material it may be, if you've been paying attention, you've undoubtedly noticed that I've only mentioned PVC sewer pipes. From research and speaking to construction professionals, it appears that most codes do not permit the use of PVC for water distribution in a residence. From what I can tell, the main concern is the pipe leaching carcinogenic materials into the water and secondly its reduced performance as the liquid flowing through it gets hot. The EPA noted in the late 1990's, that samples taken from PVC water mains in the Midwest over 6 years showed that 55% of the samples taken from 4 unique test sites exceeded the VC (vynil chloride) MCL (maximum contaminant level) of 2 ug/L. During my research I found a number of plastic pipe manufacturer/suppliers refuting, scientifically of course, any idea that plastic piping can leach any chemicals. Suffice to say, I wouldn't chance using PVC for water distribution in a residence.

The maximum operating temperature of PVC is 140 deg. F. and the hotter the fluid gets, the less pressure the pipe will hold. At its maximum operating temperature, PVC will only hold 22% of its 73 deg. F. pressure rating! Also, the pressure ratings of the molded or cut threads of PVC fittings are only 50% of solvent systems. With solvent welded (glued) joints being twice as strong, it's a no brainer, use solvent welded joints when you can. There are three different schedules of PVC pipe that you're likely to find at your local store, Schedule 30 (thin wall for low pressure), Schedule 40, Schedule 80. These schedules refer to the wall thickness of the pipe, the higher the number, the thicker the wall.

The difference between Schedule 40 and Schedule 30 (thin wall) PVC pipe.

Different diameter PVC pipe.

Different size Schedule 40 PVC pipe.

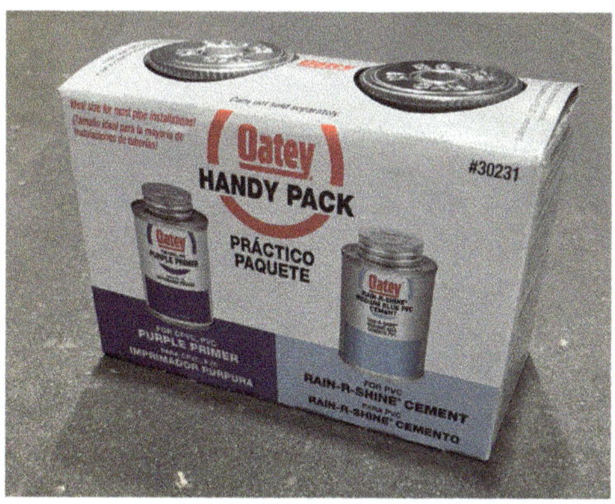

PVC primer and cement.

Special PVC pipe cutter for small diameter pipe.

For larger diameter or thin wall pipe you will need to use a fine tooth saw.

PVC pipe being primed before the application of cement.

GALVANIZED STEEL PIPE

Galvanized pipes are steel pipes that have been dipped in a protective zinc coating to prevent corrosion and rust. Galvanized piping was commonly installed in homes built before 1960. Galvanized pipe was invented as an alternative to lead piping that was used in water supply systems, which I think we all can say was a good thing! Today, however, we have learned that after decades of use, galvanized pipes corrode and rust on the inside. As you may be starting to figure out, it's a bit of challenge to transport water from the source, to a point of use and keep it uncontaminated. Metal is strong and will last a decent amount of time but it rusts. If you add a protective coating to prevent the oxidation you end up trading one contaminant for another. Use some sort of plastic and it'll end up leaching some level of chemical into the water.

Used primarily from the 1930's into the 1980's, galvanized pipe will suffer from internal rust, clogging and or low water pressure due to internal rusting, discolored water, water that tastes bad and has an odor, and can release lead into the water from the zinc dipping process. Galvanized pipe should be easily recognizable as it has a large diameter relatively speaking, it's strong enough to do a pull up on it (assuming it's attached securely), the runs of pipe thread or screw into the junctions or fittings and a dead give away is, it's magnetic (assuming it's not layered with paint, dirt dust etc.).

Section of galvanized pipe

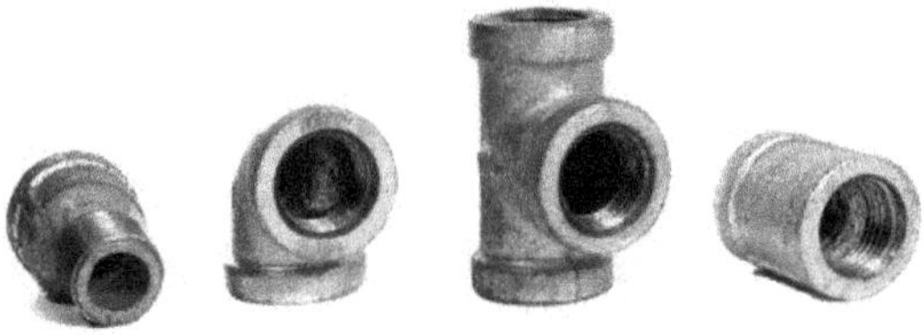

Galvanized pipe fittings.

As you can see from the picture below, iron or steel pipe has large, bulky looking fittings which make it easy to differentiate from other types of piping. The pipe used in this picture is the same as galvanized but without the galvanic coating. The pipe used here is called black iron. Black iron is uncoated pipe that has formed an oxidized coating on it that appears black. Black iron pipe is not allowed to be used to transport water and is typically designed to carry gas like propane or natural gas, as in the picture below. If you were to see this during a walk through it may confuse you as this piping is running to a water heater. From looking at the picture, the first clue that this is a gas pipe is the black color of the exterior of the pipe. The second clue is the yellow pipe sealing tape that's specifically used for gaseous applications. The third would be the contaminant drop out pipe that hangs straight down below the feed pipe and finally that this pipe is directed towards the lower part of the water heater, as every water heater I know of has the water in, and water out connections, at the top of the water heater.

Gas fueled water heater with black iron pipe feeding gas into the meter (left side). Notice the dropout below the horizontal line.

If I came across a property with galvanized water supply and or sewer piping, I would strongly consider having it re-piped. That said, the piping may give you some time before actually needing to be replaced but I would definitely replace the supply side of it due to the possible chemical leaching. Something to consider with any metal underground sewer pipe like cast iron or galvanized is how you're going to remove, replace, or repair the pipe. It's not like the supply side piping that runs in the walls, crawl space or attic that is, relatively speaking, easy to get access to. Drain and waste piping in a monolithic concrete slab (one big solid pour of concrete to form all the floors in the structure) home are pre-arranged and buried in the ground, then covered with concrete. In order to change these pipes you'd have to cut out big, long, sections of the concrete floor, so budget accordingly if you come across this pipe! One other option that

I know little about but seems promising is pipe lining or sleeving where they basically line the inside of the pipe with resin using a bladder that unfurls through the pipe eliminating the need to dig up the pipe.

CPVC (CHLORINATED POLYVINYL CHLORIDE)

CPVC, the other PVC pipe you find in the big box stores. It looks a little bit different, instead of bright white (pressure tested and typically used for cold water plumbing, drain, waste water, and vent systems) or dark grey (not pressure tested and typically used for electrical conduit) it has an off white to yellowish hue (Sched. 40), or a light grey appearance (Sched. 80 pipe). It can also be made in purple which is typically used for non-potable irrigation systems. In reality, plastic pipe can be made in just about any color so always check the pipe information that is usually printed on it.

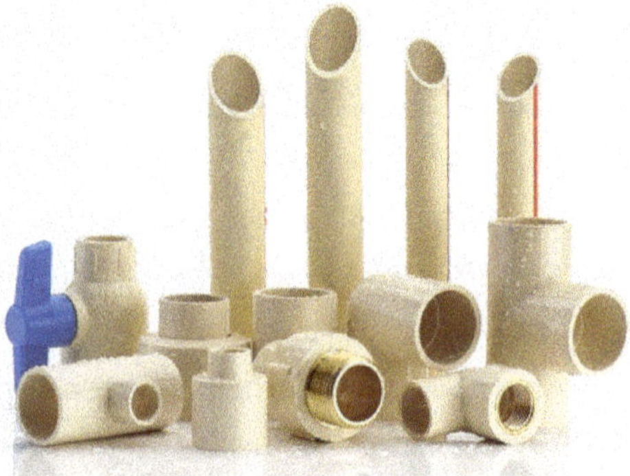

Schedule 40 Off white/yellow CPVC for hot and cold water supply

Schedule 80 Gray CPVC for high pressure use

Purple CPVC for non-potable use only

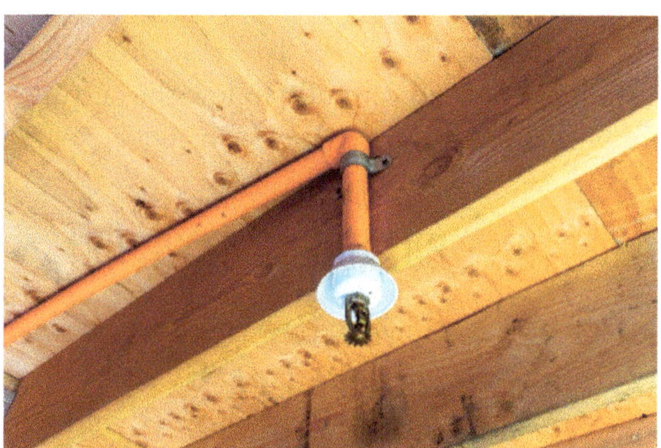

Orange, flame resistant, CPVC used in fire sprinkler systems

As you can see, you can't totally rely on pipe color. It can be gray because it's higher pressure Sched. 80 CPVC or it could be gray PVC that indicates it's UV (Ultraviolet Light) resistant. So, definitely check the pipe before you buy and DO NOT mix and match the pipes unless the strength of the bond between the pipes doesn't matter, ie: a lawn ornament.

The main difference between CPVC and PVC is the range of temperatures each is capable of withstanding. CPVC can handle temperatures up to 200 degs. F., while, as mentioned before, PVC maximum rated temperature is 140 degs. F. Above those temperatures, both CPVC and PVC will begin to soften, increasing the risk of joints and pipes failing. CPVC is a thermoplastic made from a base PVC polymer with additional chlorine molecules. The chlorine added to PVC gives CPVC higher temperature and pressure performance and improved fire and corrosion resistance.

As stated earlier, PVC was invented in the 1930's, and around 1942, scientists learned how to increase the performance of PVC by adding extra chlorine to the slurry. The first field trials started in 1960, as CPVC pipe was installed in plumbing in an experimental home built by the National Association of Home Builders. The success of that project led to the start of commercial production in 1962. Similar to PVC, CPVC was found to be in almost new condition after 30+ years of use.

Being much cheaper than PEX or metal piping systems, CPVC is a good choice for repairs or upgrades. CPVC is fairly flexible relative to metal piping making it more forgiving during installation. As with any plumbing system that uses multiple joints, there are many points of potential failure if it's not installed correctly. Make sure you use the correct cleaners, primers, cements and carefully follow the cutting and assembly instructions for whatever pipe system you're using.

ABS (ACRYLONITRILE BUTADIENE STYRENE)

ABS pipe and fittings are made from a thermoplastic resin called Acrylonitrile-Butadiene-Styrene. ABS pipe was originally developed in the early 1950s for use in oil fields and the chemical industry. In 1959, an Arizona builder, used ABS pipe in an experimental residence. More than two decades later, an independent research firm dug up and analyzed a section of the drain pipe and had similar results to PVC/CPVC. Similar to the other plastic pipes, it's durable, won't corrode or rust, has a smooth interior for good product flow and has a maximum working temperature of 140 degs. F. ABS pipe however, comes with no pressure rating relegating it drain, waste water or vent use. ABS pipe contains a chemical called bisphenol A, also known as BPA. BPA is used in various types of plastics and resins because it creates durable (hard) pipes.

I've only come across a few properties containing ABS pipe and in all cases the pipe appeared to be in good working condition with no cracks or leaks noted. That said, I haven't had enough exposure to give you an opinion on it. If you've been paying attention, you've probably noticed that I've mentioned that PEX, PVC, CPVC and now ABS all have these amazing qualities as related from third party tests and in many cases, my own experience. That said, if you study history, in particular a man named Edward Bernays and his rebranding of propaganda as "public relations", you will quickly call into question the validity of third party tests. After reading about his conquests, the old saying, "believe none of what you hear and half of what you see" comes to mind. A company invents or discovers a new product and they test it for "x" amount of time and then tout how amazing it is so they can sell a lot of it. I don't believe companies set out to produce dangerous or poorly performing products, but when flaws are discovered, they're usually in too deep and must do damage control.

ABS pipe manufactured from 1984 to 1990 by Gable Plastics, Inc., Centaur Mfg., Inc., dba Phoenix Extrusion Co., Polaris Pipe Co., and Apache Plastics, Inc. contained plastic resin that could cause the ABS pipe to crack and ultimately leak. In many cases hairline cracks were found with only minor seepage, but these small cracks still allowed sewer odors to escape into the structure. The pipes that failed significantly were identified fracturing near the joints and in some cases completely shearing off, allowing the wastewater to pour out. Lawsuits began to be filed in the mid 1980's with a big class action lawsuit being awarded to the plantiffs in 1998. The cause was identified as a production issue and manufacturers ended up covering the damage costs to consumers. The sunset for the settlement was in 2009 and since there is no more class action settlement money, the informative websites that dealt with the ABS pipe failures are now disappearing from the web.

> ***Note:*** *From my general life experience and research I've noticed that often times, operator or installer error can be attributed to a product being labeled as defective or junk, (like the poor installation of the PEX fittings) whether it's on a house, a vehicle or is a tool. Unfortunately, a trait of many is, to not read and follow instructions. Not to preach from the pulpit of perfection, I too have fallen victim to laziness in my youth and fortunately for me, it's always quickly taught me a lesson. That said, after studying pictures of failed ABS piping, there seemed to be a buildup or*

excess of cement around the joints that failed. The instructions for the ABS cement (and PVC, CPVC for that matter) specifically states that excess cement or puddling can cause weakening and premature failure of pipe or fitting. Just sayin'.

COPPER

This is the pipe you're probably the most familiar with. Its shiny color, like that of a new penny is a dead giveaway. The history of copper pipes being used to deliver water and remove waste, goes back over 4,000 years. Ancient Egyptians used copper pipes to distribute water around 2150 B.C. followed by the ancient Romans who used copper for water pipes and cisterns. By the 1940s, copper became the most used material for plumbing in the developed world. Copper has many useful attributes such as corrosion resistance, formability, durability, recyclability and safety as it actually has antimicrobial properties. It has been shown that bacteria, yeasts, and viruses are rapidly killed on metallic copper surfaces and copper has recently been registered at the U.S. Environmental Protection Agency as the first solid antimicrobial material.

Raw copper tube

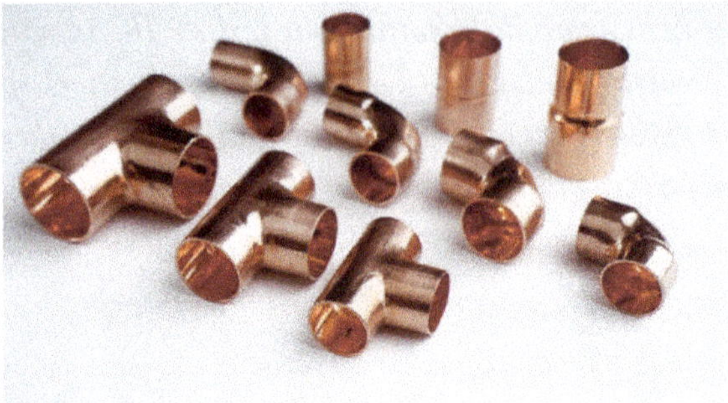

Assorted copper fittings and pipe

One potential point of concern is the lead used in brass fittings, solders and fluxes in properties that were built prior to 1978. Lead in brass components for plumbing has been steadily reduced over the years with today's new components mandated to contain less than .25 percent lead content in surfaces exposed to water. All copper alloy plumbing components have to pass the NSF 61 criteria (just like the plastic drinking water piping) for drinking water safety. The copper industry purports, "unlike other materials used for service lines, copper is completely impervious—it keeps outside chemicals from contaminating the water system. Chemicals such as petroleum products may be spilled on nearby streets and insecticides and fertilizers intentionally spread on yards—places where service lines are located—can permeate through the walls of plastic service lines, weaken them and contaminate the water within."

In the 1990's in Florida there were many new construction communities suffering water leaks from copper piping. Homes that were only a few years old had, what was found to be, pinhole leaks in the copper piping. Anywhere along the pipe, you could find oozing or leaking from several "pin holes" that were grouped in a certain area. Of course people were upset, builders were concerned and lawsuits began to fly. Builders blamed the corrosive municipal water supply and the municipal water supply pointed to poor quality piping and assembly. Some tests by local utility suppliers postulated that poor electrical grounding of the structure could be responsible.

Pinhole leaks in copper piping

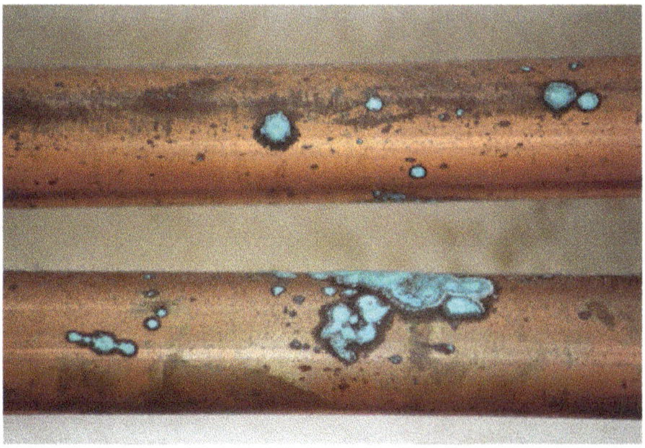

Pinhole oozing or weeping in copper piping

So, after 30 years what did they find as the cause for all these leaks, uhhh, nothing. So there you have it! As I stated earlier, it's my opinion that a manufacturer will try to make a good product and be the first to market with it after "x" amount of testing, a builder will most likely use the cheapest allowable product, and an assembler will put it together as fast and as cheaply as he/she can.

Copper pipe comes in three types, M, L, and K. These types refer to its wall thickness, like schedule refers to the wall thickness of plastic pipe. The thicker the pipe, the longer it will last and of course, the more expensive it is. Type M has the thinnest wall thickness at .028" and should be used for drains. Type L is thicker at .040" and can be used for pressurized water. Type K at .049" is the thickest and is usually reserved for underground service. If type M is allowed by code, the builder will probably use it.

If you're like me, the deeper you go into all this, the more you realize that you really aren't going to know what you're going get. Did I get a house plumbed with thick wall copper that was assembled in the best possible way? Did the roofer do a good job at driving the nails in to the proper depth and along the correct line? Did the electrician run out of cable on Friday afternoon and decide to use a 4 wire cable and common neutral on a run? Why does it say on the final inspection form of my septic system that the drain field was installed too low, but still passed? It's a bummer, but that's how it works. Houses would probably be 50% more expensive if everything was done the old fashioned way. I changed my thought process from, find the property with the best materials to find a property that is the easiest to repair. Big crawl space with exposed plumbing, great! Big tall attic that makes it easy to access electrical and HVAC systems, awesome! Plumbing entombed in the slab and a super low pitch roof with no access, not so bueno! Keep reading, I'll do my best to help you out!

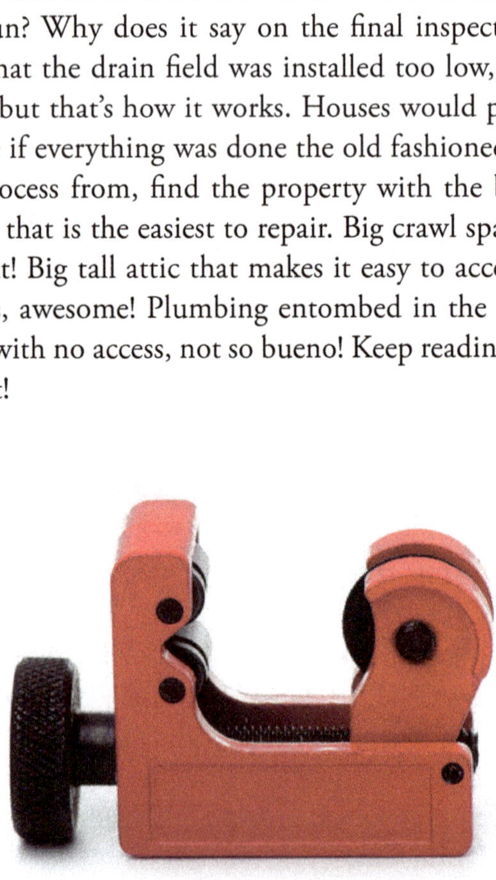

Small diameter copper pipe cutter

Larger diameter copper pipe cutter

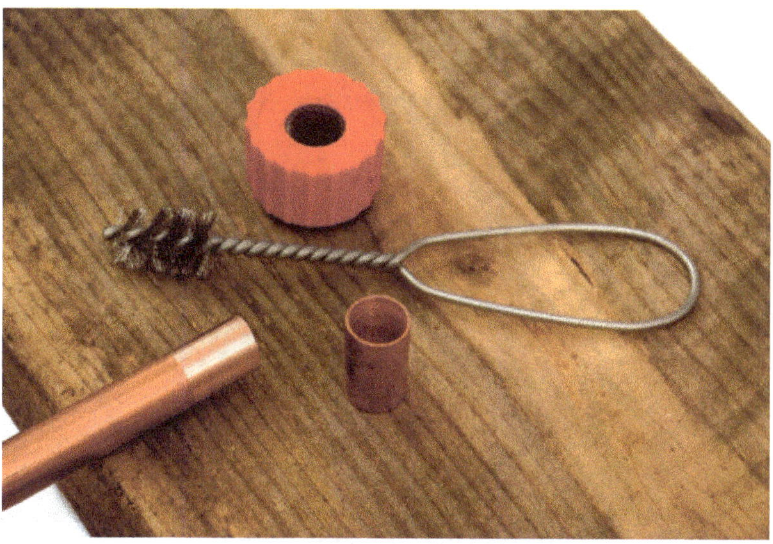

Brushes and deburring tools for copper pipe

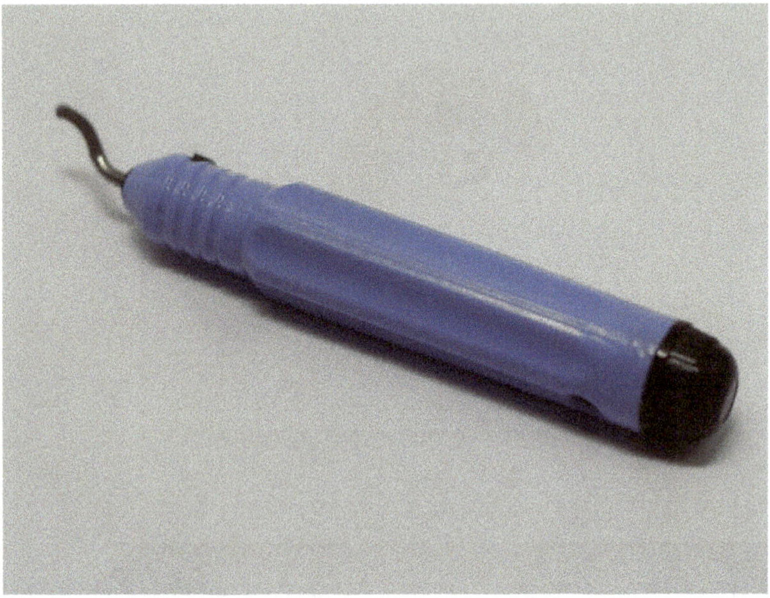

Edge reamer pen

OxyAcetylene Torch kit for brazing and welding

Unless you're going to use the aforementioned, very expensive Sharkbite fittings, plumbing repairs on copper is best left to the professionals. Using an Oxyacetylene torch to braze copper pipe takes research, good pipe finishing techniques and a good bit of practice brazing. I won't tell you that you can't do it, just remember, that pipe is going to full of pressurized water behind that nicely finished wall.

CAST IRON

Cast iron pipes date back to the 17th century and were quite expensive at the time. Only the wealthy, like King Louis XIV of France, could afford this new pipe system. King Louis XIV had approximately 15 miles of pipe connected to his palace and surrounding buildings in the area from the Seine River. In the United States, cast iron pipes date back to the early 19th century. In the 1930's, indoor plumbing became more common and cast iron piping was the only available option, but still only affordable to the wealthy because the manufacture and installation of cast iron was highly labor-intensive. Cast iron became more common for sewage piping use years later and outperformed other pipe materials. Cast iron didn't face any competition until the 1970s when plastic pipe became more common.

New cast iron pipe

Fairly clean and possibly painted cast iron sewer pipe

Cast iron sewer pipe as is more typically viewed

I've owned properties in Florida with 60+ year old cast iron sewer pipe that have shown to be in great shape, and have inspected numerous properties with fully exposed (mounted on an outside wall) cast iron sewer piping that functions well and appears to be in great shape. That said, problems you may encounter with cast iron sewer piping are, pipes being broken by nearby tree root activity, clogging due to internal corrosion, and in severe corrosion cases, failure of the pipe (I've never witnessed this). Cast iron is very strong and very quiet, especially in two story homes were the sewage travels some distance down through the house (or in some cases outside the house). Its durability however, makes it difficult to install, remove, or repair and usually requires big, expensive tools. I think failing cast iron pipe would be a good candidate for the previously mentioned resin pipe relining system.

POLYBUTYLENE

Let me start by saying, **THIS PIPE IS UNINSURABLE!** Now that we got that over with, let's look at a little history of polybutylene piping. Polybutylene or "PB" was a plastic pipe manufactured between 1978 and mid-1995 for use in home plumbing systems. As is usually the case, it was less inexpensive than the current offerings and offered advantages over other materials, such as flexibility, ease of installation, and resistance to freezing. So, remember the trend, if it supposadly works as good or better and is ***easier to install***, builders are going to use it. As such, polybutylene was installed in around 10 million homes in the U.S. during it's run. After an exhorbitant number of claims of ruptured pipes and subsequent property damage, the manufacturer(s) decided to shut it down, and production ceased in mid-1996.

"PB 2110" printed on the pipe

As you can see from the pictures above, Polybutylene pipe has a very distinctive dull gray color which is most common, but can also come in white, silver, black or blue, is fastened similar to other plastic pipe like PEX and if it's still readable, will have "PB 2110" printed on the pipe. Polybutylene is also fairly "soft" and flexible. During your inspections you may find the pipe is actually deformed from being so soft to begin with and further degrading over time. From my experience, PB will show longitudinal cracks or fissures and will fail shortly after. When the pipe does fail there is usually a good sized split in it allowing a significant amount of pressurized water to come out. Polybutylene is no longer an accepted pipe in the U.S. Building Code. After some independent research, it turns out that PB fails due to exposure to disinfectants that are common in municipal water systems. The chemical reaction causes the pipe to fail from the inside out. I'm not going to spend a whole lot of time on PB pipe because it is uninsurable and will need to be replaced immediately. If you find this distinctive gray pipe in a house you're looking at, I'd either walk away from it, or if I had the money, would negotiate a lower price and have it replaced. That said, look for prior water damage! At the time of this writing, in Central Florida, a typical replumb will cost

$3,000- $5,000. As stated before, the easier it is to access the attic space or crawl space/basement the cheaper it will be.

In my humble opinion, in general, other than having a bad pipe like PB or someone who didn't properly connect/install the piping, there's not too much to go wrong with the pressure side of plumbing. Unfortunately, however, if the piping wasn't fastened properly within the hidden spaces, there's really no way to tell until it fails. You won't be able to see most of the plumbing in a home and nor will your inspector. Your inspector may note some issue such as, low or differing pressures throughout the house but he/she most likely won't be able to tell you why it's happening. They'll tell you what it could be, like poor pipe routing, improperly sized fittings, or foreign material built up in the pipe. Unless the two of you are going to tear open the walls or the slab, it's just going to be an educated guess. I'm not knocking inspectors, there's just only so much you can see in a house.

One of the other unknowns is how much and what kinds of chemicals are being used in the municipal water supply? Did they use a chlorine concentration of 7ppm for the past 14 years and just recently drop it to 3ppm? As stated above, all piping is designed to operate under certain conditions and although you may have veiwed 20 homes that have original copper piping that is 100 years old, the next house you look at it may have had its copper relaced after only 3 years. What was different? I'm sorry to report, you'll probably never know.

DRAIN WASTE AND VENT PIPING (DWV)

As its names imply, this piping is designed to ***drain*** gray water from showers, sinks, dish and clothes washers, remove ***waste*** water from toilets, and ***vent*** the entire DWV system. In the context of what can be found inside the typical home, DWV piping can be made from Cast Iron, Galvanized Steel, PVC, and ABS. Although the piping used for these purposes can withstand a certain amount of pressure, and in some cases may be made of the same material (ie: PVC) as pipes designed for pressurized use, they are not designed to be used in a pressurized system. In this section we'll be focusing on the piping inside a typical dwelling.

I'll go over the piping from the dwelling to the connection at the street or spetic system a little later.

You already have a pretty good idea of the pro's and con's of each piping material so I won't revisit the topic. In this section I want to give you a general concept of how the DWV system works to help you troubleshoot and identify potential problems. The general concept to understand with drian pipes is, you want the water and waste to move at a certain speed, not too slow to avoid last nights dinner from settling in the pipe and having the water flow around or over it and not too fast to avoid it smashing into and building up against the wall of a turn. The way I think about it is, we want whatever is in the pipe to float just enough, and have the water impart enough force so it won't get stuck. That said, a pipe that has a smooth interior surface is highly desireable. Big, smooth, gentle turns or changes of direction are good. Where two pipes meet or converge we want a very smooth easy transition. At your local big box store they sell many different drain fittings that may appear to be interchangable but in certain circumstancs are not.

A sanitary tee looks similar to the letter 'T', while a Wye looks similar to the letter 'Y'. A sanitary tee is used for a horizontal to vertical transition, and a wye is used for combining 2 lines into one horizontal line. Remember the concept is to maintain a flow (greater than 2 feet per second is considered self cleaning) without causing clogging. That said, how these fittings are oriented also matter. There's also wye's that have short and long sweeps or radius'. Both of these fittings have different usages and can not be switched. So before doing plumbing work, make sure that you have a good understanding of using a sanitary tee and a wye. In my humble opinion, the DWV system is more complex in design than the pressurized portion of your plumbing and therefore requires more knowledge and careful installation or repair.

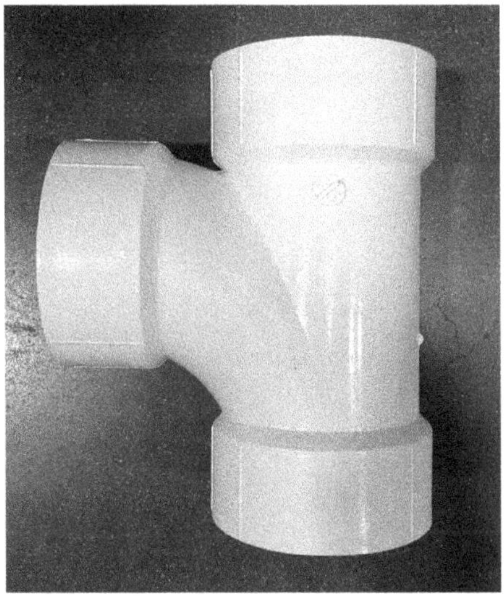

Sanitary Tee

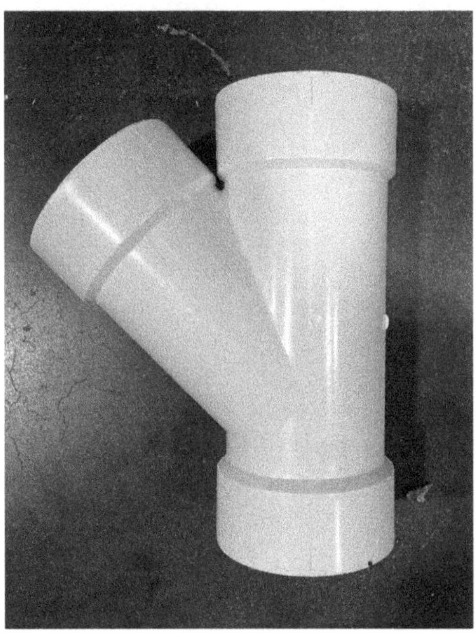

Sanitary wye

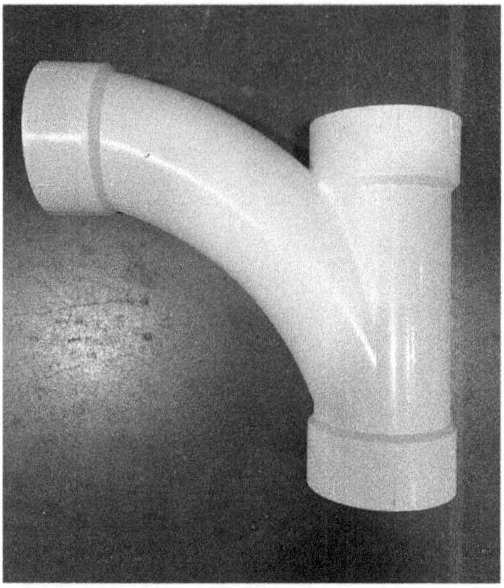

Long sweep sanitary wye

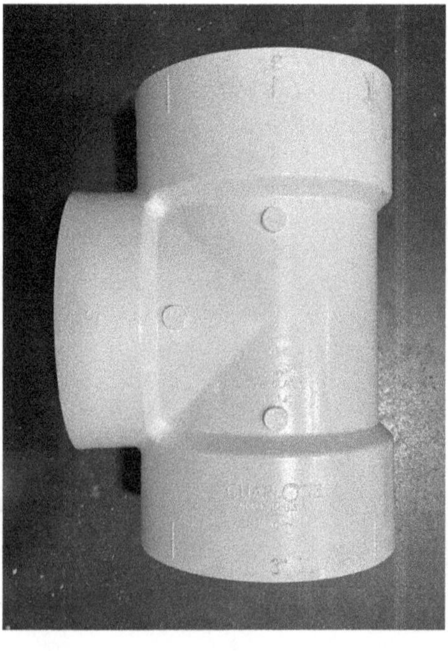

Non-waste tee

There's actually a lot of things going on in the DWV system and they all have to work together correctly or you'll have constant problems. Remember, most of the time, the pipes are filled with air and when you suddenly add a big bolus of water and or waste, you have to allow the air that is displaced to go somewhere, if not, the waste and water won't move. Think about when you've tried to pour out a big 2 liter soda bottle by holding it upside down. Soda or whatever is inside the bottle comes out but it's very slow and every now and then the bottle takes a big gulp of air. You learned from experience that if you angle the bottle just right to allow an equal amount of air into the bottle, as soda is going out of the bottle, you'll get a smooth flow of liquid that actually empties the bottle faster than if you were to hold it upside down.

So we've flushed the toilet and a big bolus of water and uh, other stuff, is on it's way to the sewer or septic system. The pipe is tilted a specific amount called it's fall, flow or pitch. This "fall" (typically between ¼" and ½" per foot) is designed to allow this bolus of stuff to maintain that certain speed we talked about before. While this bolus is on its way to the abyss, it's taking up about half the inside diameter of the pipe and air is taking up the other half. This bolus is displacing air as it travels down the pipe and if the air had no place to go, given the right circumstances, last nights dinner would just come to rest in the pipe. No bueno! Plumbers know they have to allow this air, which is usually very stinky, and in reality, not very good for us, a place to go, and not go! We want the air being pushed to go outside the house where it'll just disipate away and not fill our nostrils while allowing outside air to flow in behind this bolus so it doesn't create negative pressure. When there's nothing going on in the system we don't want this air to float out of our drains and toilets into our house. They achieve this by putting in a trap seal to keep the sewer gases from entering the structure and venting the system just above the roof.

The next time you're outside a home, look at the roof from the street, you'll notice several pipes sticking out of the roof by about a foot or so. These pipes are the different plumbing vents for the different "fixtures" in the house, ie; laundry room, bathrooms, kitchens etc. Basically, where ever something is going to enter the drain/ waste system, a vent needs to be nearby to facilitate the escape of any sewer gases and also allow air to flow in behind the moving bolus so it doesn't create a suction effect in the drain line and pull the water out of the trap seal (remember the soda bottle example). Wash your hands in the sink and all that water enters the system, a vent needs to allow the balancing of pressures in the system. Flush the toilet, same thing. Clothes washer dumps a bunch of gray water into the system, you guessed it, you need a vent. The diameter of the piping is all carefully considered in relation to how much water and or waste is expected to enter the system and at what rate. If a large volume of stuff enters the system rapidly, we're going to need to balance the movement of a large volume of gases. If design of the structure doesn't allow a vent to be placed nearby, like a kitchen island, we may have to place an air admittance valve under the sink in the island to allow air to enter in behind the bolus of water so it doesn't pull the water out of the trap seal.

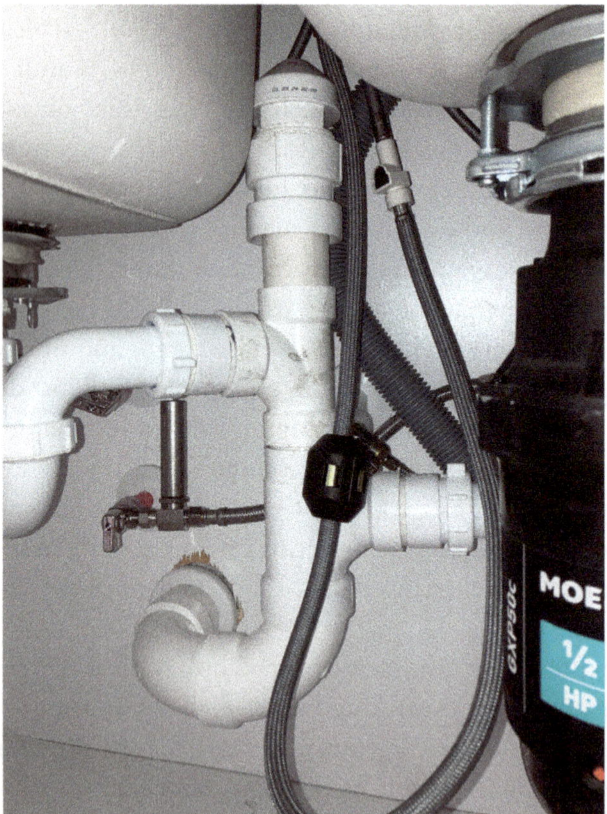

Air admittence valve under a sink

What the heck is this trap seal thing you keep talking about? The appliance water trap seal was invented in 1770 by Alexander Cummings and was incorporated into Victorian drainage designs to eliminate odors and reduce the potential spread of infections. This trap/seal basically uses a given amount of water that is always present in the pipe to block the flow of gases that build up in the system from entering the home. You've undoubtably seen this before but may not have known what it was. Called a "P Trap" because of its shape, it is the curved pipe underneath every sink. You may have have dropped something down the drain and had to remove part of this p trap to retrieve it. This "P" shaped pipe, which should probably be called a "U" pipe, under the correct circumstances, always maintaines water in the "U", which prevents sewer gases from escaping into the home. When a given amount of water is added to the "U" shape, an equal amount of water leaves the "U" shape into the drain system.

How the P trap gets its name

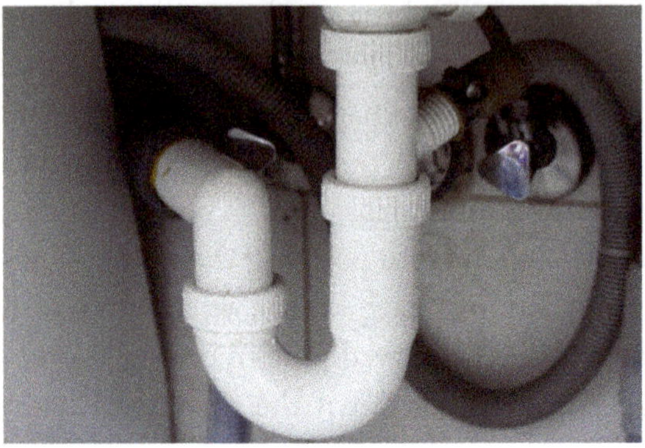

Typical P trap under a sink

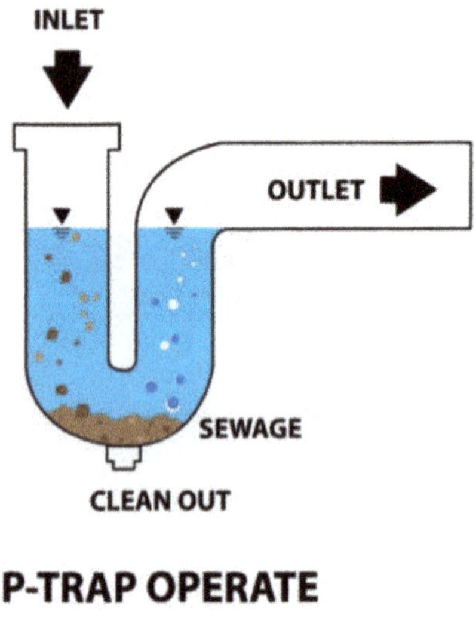

Illustration of a P trap with water in the trap

Not to get into too much detail, but the trap is designed to have a specific size so it can hold a specific weight of water in it so it may resist the momentum of water flowing out of it and into the system and normal fluctuations in system air pressure. If you're a Curious George like me and may have spent a significant portion of your childhood staring at things and wondering how they worked, you may have noticed that the water level in the toilet bowl will move up and down sometimes. What the heck would cause that? I mean, the water is just sitting in there like it would sitting in a cereal bowl, albeit a dirty one. The milk in my cereal bowl doesn't grow and recede unless I'm adding to it or eating it. After making mental notes of this phenomena over however long, I started to notice a pattern. On windy days, the water in the bowl would undulate. That was about the extent of my curiousity at the time as my attention span at that young age would prevent me from thinking any further about water in the toilet bowl. It wasn't until many moons later, when I knew the architecture of the plumbing, that I was able to put it together. On windy days, when the wind would blow strong enough across the top of the systems open vent pipes on the roof, it would cause the pressure within the system to drop (Bernoulli's Principle) causing some water to be sucked out of the bowl. When the wind would relax, the pressure in the system would increase, moving the water back into the bowl. I couldn't wait to tell all the other kids! Seriously people, I'm kidding!

The point of that whole trip was to illustrate that the DWV system is failry complex and even seemingly small changes in pressure can affect how well the system will work. If you DIY a portion of the system and you don't use the correct size piping, fittings, fall etc., you may cause the pipe to become full during a drain event reducing or eliminating the effectivness of the vent stack which can cause your fixture to constantly lose its trap seal. So, if you're having drainage problems, check the drains and the vent stacks for blockages. That said, as with anything, you should learn how to do it right before you dive into a project.

SEWER PIPES

Sewer pipes leading from a dwelling to the main sewer in the street can be made of many different materials and or a mixture of materials. What I mean by that is, you may have an old home that originally had a vitrified clay sewer pipe and a section of this pipe was damaged somehow and a section of PVC sewer pipe was spliced in using rubber couplings. So, depending on the age of the dwelling, you really could have just about any type of sewer pipe. That said, before you go crazy worrying about it, I haven't come across any dwellings out of the thousands of properties I've looked at over the years, with any main sewer line problems. The main thing you want to look for before any deeper investigation, is, anything that would exert a significant amount of pressure on the sewer line. Does the construction worker who rents the place park his enormous work truck right over the sewer line everyday? Are the roots of a big nearby tree exerting pressure on the pipe? Have the roots penetrated the pipe? When you inspect the place and turn on every faucet and flush all the toilets in succession, does the sewer back up or is it slow to drain? Is there a big depression in the ground near the sewer line where a big tree once lived? If so, you may want to have the line checked with a camera.

How do you find the sewer line you ask? First, do your best to locate the main sewer line cleanout. Depending on the building it could be in a basement, in a garage, in a crawl space, attached to the exterior of the structure, or directly outside the dwelling in the ground. They can be tough to find when they're outside in the ground. Some cleanouts stick out of the ground a foot or so and some are at ground level. Over the years, soil and vegetative buildup can completley obscure the cleanout. Depending on how old the dwelling is that you're looking at, it may not have a cleanout at all. You'll have to check in your area to see when cleanouts were mandated. Once you find the cleanout, look from that point out towards the street, assuming a typically sized structure on a typically sized lot, a straight line from that cleanout into the street should be the path that the sewer line follows. Of course there are many variables, but the concept to keep in mind is, the shortest, straightest path is the cheapest. If you end up having the sewer line scoped (inspected with a camera), the plumber will most likely start at the cleanout. If you end up not being able to locate the sewer line/cleanout and your concerned about it, a plumber or utility locater should be able to locate it for you.

Outside ground level cleanout

Irrigation valve box cover for cleanout

Buried ground level cleanout

Cleanout in an exterior wall

SEPTIC SYSTEMS

Since the dawn of mankind, humans have needed to figure out what to do, with their doodoo. If there's not that many people in your group and a lot of land around you, it's not that big of deal, just don't do your business by the water or near camp. As our numbers began to grow and we began to live in ever more crowded conditions, this became a major health issue.

Although it appears natural for most complex organisms to groom or clean themselves and not defecate where they sleep, it seems that humans during the 14th century either forgot this critical trait or made the conscious decision that the benefits of living in a crowded city with open sewers in the street, just outside where the slept, outweighed the risks.

This oversight or decision would prove to have quite painful consequences. It's estimated that 25 million people across Europe died from disease from 1347 to 1352. That's considered to be 40% of Europes population! In the city of Paris it's estimated that half the population died from disease. You may know this as the Black Death or Bubonic Plague. As far as I know, the Black Plague consited of three different plagues, the Bubonic being the most common and affecting the lymphatic system, the pneumonic being the next most common affecting the lungs, and the septicemic being the third most common although this may be just a progression of the lymphatic version that has spread to the bloodstream. Of those who contracted the Bubonic version, 4 out 5 died within 8 days! This may explain the reason the septacemic version was the least common.

It probably wasn't a good sign if you saw this guy coming.

14th century Plague Doctor

How much of a role the terrible waste management played in the spread of the plague is unknown, but I'm sure it didn't help. Almost 500 years later, around 1860, a Frenchman by the name of Jean-Louis Mouras, built the first concrete septic tank. Tired of running outside every time he needed to go, he ran clay pipes from his home to his new tank. Supposedly he used it for 10 years before deciding to dig it up and see what was happening inside. What he found, to his surprise, was mostly liquid with a layer of scum on top. Impressed with his findings, he decided to work with a scientist to understand what was happening and solidify his invention. In 1881 he applied for and was granted, a patent. It would only take a few years for his invention to reach the United States.

As with any of the other systems in a dwelling, we should try to understand how an on site sewage treatment and disposal system works. Knowledge is power and can help you avoid a property with a septic problem or tell the lying, deceitful, septic contractor that your drainfield does not need to be replaced for $10,000. Septic systems are underground wastewater treatment systems and are typically permitted, inspected and governed by the local department of health.

Basic home septic system

Concrete septic tank with its lid off

Ready to be buried concrete septic tank with raised access ports.

Plastic septic tank

Chamber style drainfield

Chamber style drainfield with fabric cover to prevent silt infiltration.

The typical system is made up of a tank, a drainfield, and the piping to connect the two to each other and the house. A person in the house goes number two, flushes the toilet and some liquid, some number two, and some toilet paper (notice I said toilet paper and not wipes!) makes its way down the sewer pipe via gravity and out into the septic tank.

> ***Note:*** *It's common today for people to use wet wipes to clean their backside. The manufacturers of these wet wipes produce them to make money. That said, they advertise them as septic and sewer safe. On the surface, I don't know how a wipe that comes wet and remains so in its package without breaking down, is supposed to magically breakdown once it hits the toilet water. I can tell you for a fact that municipalities are having problems with wet wipes clogging lift stations and other equipment so much so, that they've appealed for the secession of such on the local news. Over the years I've dealt with a number of plumbers and they all say not to use wet wipes. From my own personal experience I had a tenant that used wet wipes and when I noticed this, I asked her to stop using them and of course explained why. As it turns out, she continued to use them, because, what do I know? I get a call a few months later saying the toilets and other drains are backing up.*

I drive over to find she is still using wet wipes, confirm the whole system is backed up and call for a septic tank pump out. When the septic company arrived and pulled the lid off of the tank, what do you know, a disgusting, floating mass of used wet wipes. The pipe leading to the drainfield was clogged with wet wipes and as it would turn out, wet wipes had made it all the way into the drainfield. When she came to investigate what was going on, she noticed the mat of wet wipes in the septic tank, I just looked at her, but hey, what do I know! After replacing the drainfield and adding a filter to the drainfield side of the tank, I now have in my lease a statement prohibiting the use of any wet wipes, regardless of the manufacturers claims of appropriteness and the tenant is financially responssible for any damages occuring from such use.

The pipe entering the tank should have a "T" shaped section of pipe attached to it, in the 6 to 12 o'clock position, with additional lengths of pipe extending up towards the tank lid and down towards the tank floor. This "T" helps dissipate the energy of the flushed waste, allows gases and pressurized air to escape towards the top of the tank and the septage to enter the tank in the middle of the liquid layer. This allows any solids to fall to the bottom of the tank where it forms the sludge layer. In this layer, anaerobic bacteria consume the organic materials in the sludge, giving off gases in the process. Any liquid portion remains in the liquid layer and any lighter than water items such like fats and oils, float to the top of the liquid layer forming the scum layer. Yummy topic, isn't it? This scum layer reduces the exchange of gases between the liquid layer and the headspace in the tank, and vice versa. This scum layer is degraded over time by aerobic bacteria.

The tank itself usually has a vertical baffle to further conatin solids and scum and keep them away from the outlet of the tank. The liquid layer in between the scum and sludge layer is known as the effluent. This clarified wastewater then flows out of the tank via gravity through the outlet baffle or outlet "T". This "T" is similar to the inlet baffle "T" except that it is placed lower in the tank to allow drainage. The open portion of the dscending leg of the "T" is well in the liquid layer, allowing, under proper working conditions, only effluent to leave the tank and enter the drainfield. The upper portion of the "T" allows gases and pressure to be released and is high enough not to let the scum layer leave the tank.

Once the effluent leaves the septic tank, it either travels out to the drainfield via gravity or travels to a dosing tank via gravity. If the conditions allow the tank to be higher than the drainfield, then we can simplify the system and just let gravity carry it out to the drainfield for dispersion. We must pump the effluent out to the drainfield if it's higher than the septic tank. Inside the dosing tank is a pump with a float switch that activates the pump when the effluent gets to a certain level. The pump then sends a certain number of gallons, a dose, of effluent out to the drainfield also known as the leachfield, for final cleansing. If you've got your thinking cap on, you probably already see a disadvantage to the dosing system. If the pump stops working, the system will eventually back up into the house. There is typically a visual and audible alarm at the power source for the pump to alert the homeowner of this.

A look inside the dosing tank

Dosing system alarm

There are a couple of different common drainfield designs, one is called conventional – a number of perforated pipes laid in gravel which is then buried, and the other is called a chamber system – which has a number of chambers, like train tunnels, buried in the ground. There are a few other systems that are less common, and specialized to a specific use or location, which I won't cover. If you come across a property with an aerobic treatment unit or a sand filtration system, do your homework on these systems and start adding dollars to your maintenance fund.

Perforated hard PVC drain pipe

Perforated pipes wrapped in foam peanuts for graveless installation.

Perforated hard PVC drainfield being installed.

The conventional drainfield has been around for a number of decades and basically consists of one big trench or a number of trenches, filled with gravel, then having perforated pipe laid over top of that gravel. The pipe is then covered with a fabric that allows water to penetrate but keeps most of the soil out of the pipe. This pipe is then covered over with more gravel and topped off with remaining soil. As mentioned earlier, the effluent is either gravity fed or pumped into this system of pipes where it is allowed to slowly percolate down through the gravel and eventually the soil. The microbes present in the gravel and soil breakdown the remaining yucky stuff as the water makes its way to the aquifer.

The chamber style system is very similar to the conventional system except they use rows of connected chambers in place of the perforated pipes and gravel. The chamber style system basically provides a long open tunnel for the effluent to gather and then slowly percolate. This eliminates the need for gravel thus greatly reducing the cost of the drain field. These chambers are open on the bottom and have slits in their side walls allowing effluent to flow out into the soil along the bottom and both sides of the chamber, thus decreasing the horizontal footprint required for the drain field. You may need 500 sq. ft. of horizontal space for a perforated pipe system, but only need 275 sq. ft. of horizontal space for a chamber system. Another advantage of the chamber system over the perforated pipe system is it's purported resistance to clogging. This makes sense but is purely my opinion based on conversations with contractors and those who've had their perforated pipe drain fields fail. That said, this type of failure may be implied by contractors because it's easier and cheaper to install the chamber system and then regurgitated by customers. It does however, make sense that it would be easier to clog a series of half inch diameter holes in a 4 inch pvc pipe versus a 30 inch wide by 30 foot open chamber. I chose to install a chamber style system in one of my multifamily properties after a drain field failure.

Some things to consider with these types of systems are the actual footprint or size of the drainfield, perforated pipe systems usually being much larger than a chamber style systems, they may not be suitable for higher water tables or allowed near bodies of water. In Florida there is growing concern that septic systems are leaching nitrogen and other materials into local waterways. Depending on the size, these systems can cost from $5000 to $10,000 to replace and for some odd reason, most of us are very concerned about the cost of things. That said, if you were replacing a drain field at your house, I'd be ok with you cheaping out because you'd do the research on the do's and dont's and would manitain your system. If you're replacing a drain field at a multi-family property, I'd go as big, simple, and easy to maintain as you can.

You see, 98% of renters have no clue what a septic system is or how it differs from a sewer system, and in reality, they have no idea how a sewer system works either. In the last big building they lived in, they could just flush whatever they wanted down the toilet and put whatever they wanted down the the sink drains, grease, oil, bleach, plastic femanine products, paper, rings, small stuffed animals, whatever, and it just, went away! If anything about your rental property differs from their previous "normal" life, it will be your responsibility to educate them. Unfortunately, half of the remaining 2% that have have an idea of the do's and dont's, won't care and will play the odds that nothing will happen during their 2 to 3 year stay.

So how can renters possibly mess up a drain field? It's just dirt over pipes and gravel or plastic chambers. Two words, PARKING LOT! For some unexplained reason, a certain percentage of renters love to drive over and park on, grass. There's a perfectly good concrete driveway right there, nope, gotta park right up by the front door or in the back yard.

Whatever their reasoning, you have to prevent this. Just telling them not to, isn't good enough. Shortly after you leave, they'll be back at it and their affinity for off roading will lead to compaction of the drain field which will, oddly enough, greatly reduce the ability of the drain field to, well, drain. If you're lucky, their 4000 pound chariot won't collapse the lid of your septic tank during their excursions. All of this of course is no bueno, as a reduction in the percolation rate of the drain field will eventually cause the stinky stuff to back up into your property and replacing a tank lid is expensive and dirty!

You'll eventually get a call that the toilets are backed up and won't drain. It'll be Sunday and you'll have to have a septic company come out on the weekend and pump out your tank for $300 to $600 because you want to keep your property safe and habitable. If any of their stuff gets ruined by the back up they will undoubtably blame you. Hopefully you required renters insurance! You'll probably have two to four people living in your multifamily and the septic tank will probably be around 1000 gals. With the average person using about 50 to 100 gals of water a day, in 3 to 5 days your tank will be full again. On a positive note, your drain field will have gotten a 4 to 5 day break to fully drain. This will buy you another 2 to 5 days, depending on how compacted your drain field is, before the drains start backing up again. To remedy this, I prefer physical barriers like fences, bushes, big rocks or decorative wooden posts that will cause great damage to their vehicle if they drive over them.

Besides extra-vehicular activities and flushing the moving van they showed up in down the drain, you'll have to be aware of the environmental conditions around your drainfield. For some reason plants love moist bacteria laden soil which means they will love your drainfield. That said, their should be no bushes or trees near your drainfield. A general rule of thumb is, however wide the canopy of the tree or bush is, that's how far the root system will reach.

This is a rule of thumb so I'd give a substantial buffer just to be safe!

Roots from trees and shrubs will penetrate the drainfield causing a substantial decrease in its flow rate eventually leading to back ups and drainfield failure. Unlike the few months it takes to cause failure from being used as a freeway, failure from root infiltration may take a few years.

This shouldn't be a problem.....

That's not hair.

Lastly I'd like to talk about drainfield surface management. It's very important to maintain the grass that is over and around the drainfield. Other than looking nice, the grass helps maintain the soil above the drainfield so that it doesn't erode away and helps absorb rainfall to lessen the impact on the drainfeild. The roots of the grass aren't long enough to get into the drainfield but help absorb rainfall and then transpire the moisture out of the drainfield and back into the atmosphere. Remember, there's only so much water per day the drainfield is designed to handle, if it's getting deluged every day for hours by heavy afternoon thunderstorms or your neighbors sprinkler head is broken flooding your yard, it's capacity will be reduced.

So, you're going to want to pay careful attention to the location and grade of the drainfield. Is it near a big driveway or road that slants towards it? Does the storm drain at the corner constantly back up flood part of your yard? Does you or your neighbor have 2000 sq. ft. of roof with no gutters that will just dump all that water on it? Maybe you do have gutters but they dump out onto the drainfield. No bueno! Is there a slight depression over your drainfield that will collect rainwater? Your specific location will dictate how much attention you need to apply to this. If you live in Arizona it's probably not worth being on your radar but I can tell you, here in Florida the rainfall amounts can be absurd.

There is usually evidence of drainage issues, rings of grass clippings or leaves and or dirt. I suggest if possible, you visit the property multiple times under different atmospheric conditions.

This would be, shall we say, a less than ideal location for a drainfield.

As of the writing of this book, and the current climate cycle we appear to be in, I would seriously consider the affects of surface water, especially if you happen to be buying property in the dry season. I have noticed in Florida that the intensity of the wet season rainfall has significantly increased. Rainfall rates of two plus inches per hour are happening in afternoon thunderstorms. That slight depression in the ground over your drainfield could become a big headache and expense a few months later.

Overloading the drainfield with water can come from mother nature or inside the property. If everything looks good outside, head inside and start to investigate. In my experience, running toilets are the biggest culprit in secretly overloading a septic system with excessive water use coming in a close second. If one or more of your toilets flapper valves aren't sealing, the toilet will constantly drain into the system and the tank will constantly try to fill itself up. You're tenant may or may not notice and may or may not care and or forget to tell you, especially if you're paying for water. During your quarterly walk throughs carefully look and listen to how things are running, the A/C, the washer, the fridge, flush the toilets and listen. It can give you advance notice of a problem.

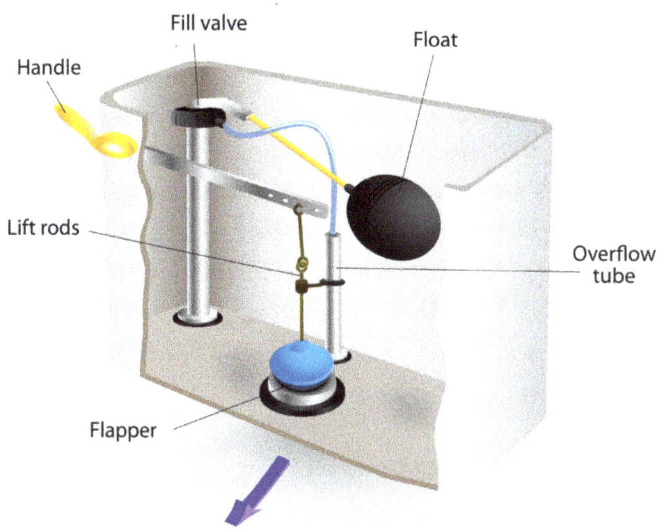

If you are having a septic problem and you pay for water, you can usually call the utility to find out what the usage is, sometimes on a daily basis. This can help pinpoint which unit is causing the problem. Remember that each person is going to use 50 – 100 gals. of water a day through consumption, showers, washing clothes and dishes, and finally using the toilet. If you're system is designed to accommodate two people per unit and there's four per unit, you just doubled the amount of effluent going into your drainfield! There should be specific rules in your lease about how many people are allowed to live in each unit, how many people can visit and for how long.

We previously mentioned the other few killers of the septic system, fats, greases and oils. Fats, greases, and oils that are in a liquid form in hot water can turn to a more solid state when cooled. They often stick to the sides of plumbing and septic pipes where other types of debris can get caught up and form a blockage. Fats, greases, and oils also collect in the top of the septic tank to form a layer of scum. The biological treatment going on inside of the septic tank relies on bacteria to digest and breakdown sewage. Since bacterial action does not easily digest these fats, greases and oils, it will need to be pumped out. The fats, greases, and oils that aren't cleaned out of the septic tank before it becomes too thick can get lodged in the septic tank outlet valve or travel out to the drainfield in the partially treated wastewater. Scum collecting in the soil beneath the drainage pipes can cause the whole system to come to a halt. Your lease should have strong, specific language as to what can be passed through a drain.

> ***Note:*** *If there's no garbage can nearby, some tenants seem to believe that anything they flush down that toilet will magically get transported into the Sun where it's incinerated. Childrens toys, femanine products and plastic applicators, grease, oils and basically anything that is not biodegradeable should not be passed through a drain into your septic system.*

Until now we've looked at the inner workings of the septic system, things to do and not to do. Now let's take a look at how this all looks when you show up to view the property. The realtor may not know whether the property your looking at is on septic or sewer and if it's a rental property like a duplex or quadplex, it's likely that you won't meet the owner until closing. The best way to tell is by going on the property appraiser or local health department site and trying to find permits that were issued. They will tell you what kind of system, how large, when and who installed it.

Sometimes you don't have time or can't find this information so you'll have to do a little investigation on site. As mentioned earlier in this book you'll want to find the main sewer line cleanout.

Next you'll want to look in the street to see if there are any manhole covers with an "S", "SANITARY" or "SEWER" on them. If you find these nearby, there's a good chance the property is on sewer. If you look down the street and as far as you can see you don't find any manhole covers, with the exception of storm drains, the property is most likely on septic.

Examples of storm sewers or drains that transport rainwater.

Don't just glance at a manhole cover because it may not be what you think.
This is a cover to an underground electric vault.

Once you've determined the property is on septic and you've found the cleanout, the septic tank should be within a direct shot from the cleanout. You may or may not be able to find the tank as it is buried and may not have a visible inspection port.

Visible plastic tank lids.

Visible iron tank lid vs. a buried concrete lid.

This style of inspection port will be fully buried and not visible from the yard. You'll need a long metal probe used to poke into the ground to generally locate the septic tank. Then you'll have to start digging!

Next, you'll want to try and find the drainfield so you can assess it. This may be super easy in the case of a mound system.

Raised drainfield next to residence.

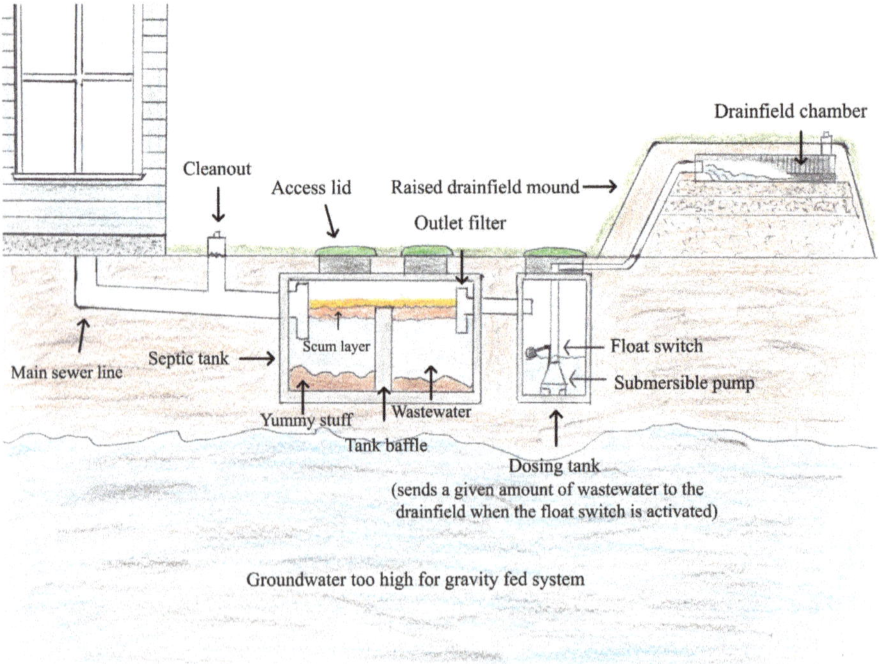

There are a few drawbacks to a mound system, aesthetics being one, mound systems just aren't that attractive and the added complexity being the other. As with any drainfield, code calls for a specific size drainfield and tank system based on how many bedrooms, bathrooms, the number of people expected to live in the dwelling, square footage or any combination of all those. Code requires certain setbacks from property lines, wells, and structures. When you're dealing with a mound system you need even more room around the drainfield to accommodate the mounds "shoulders" which have to be a given size.

Due to space and most likely budget limitations, these mound systems are very obvious.

Most people either don't have, or don't want to spend any more money than necessary on something so utlitarian as a septic system and I definitely don't know any contractors who, out of the goodness of their hearts, offer to pay for the extra fill dirt and labor required to disguise the mound gently into the surrounding area. So what you end up with is a smack you in the face, oddball, obviously man made, rectangular mound of dirt somewhere in the yard. More complexity also costs more money and requires more maintenance, which of course, costs more money in the long run.

Regardless of the system the property has, it had to be designed right, installed right, inspected and passed. Overworked and or lazy inspectors and contractors aside, for the most part, the aforementioned should provide you with a good working system, that, with proper use and maintenance, will last decades. That said, one of the big questions is, did the prior owners/occupants use and maintain the system properly? How can you tell, it's buried underground! Now that you have a better understanding of how the whole thing works, you should be able to test it.

SIGNS OF WATER DAMAGE

The fixtures – sinks, tubs, and toilets are all connected to the septic tank via sewer and drain pipes. These connections should be solid and leak free, so check where you can for these things and look for signs that there was a problem in the past. Is the sink, tub, or toilet loose, wobbily, or moeveable? Is it leaking? Do the baseboards near it look discolored? Do they have bubbling or peeling paint? If you poke them with a small flathead screwdriver, does it go through the baseboard like it was a piece of paper? Is the caulking or grouting missing? Are there any of these signs on the wall in the room directly on the other side of the fixture? Are any of these signs under the sinks?

These are obvious signs of water damage but gives you locations that are common problems. Usually the underlying support medium degrades causing the exterior to begin to fail. In these cases it was the drywall. If you were to gently poke the drywall near the tub with a screwdriver (top picture) it would go right through it. If the tiles on the tub (bottom picture) sound hollow or feel loose when you bump them with the side of your fist, suspect water damage behind them.

These are more subtle signs and are right outside of two stand up showers. Again, note these common problem areas.

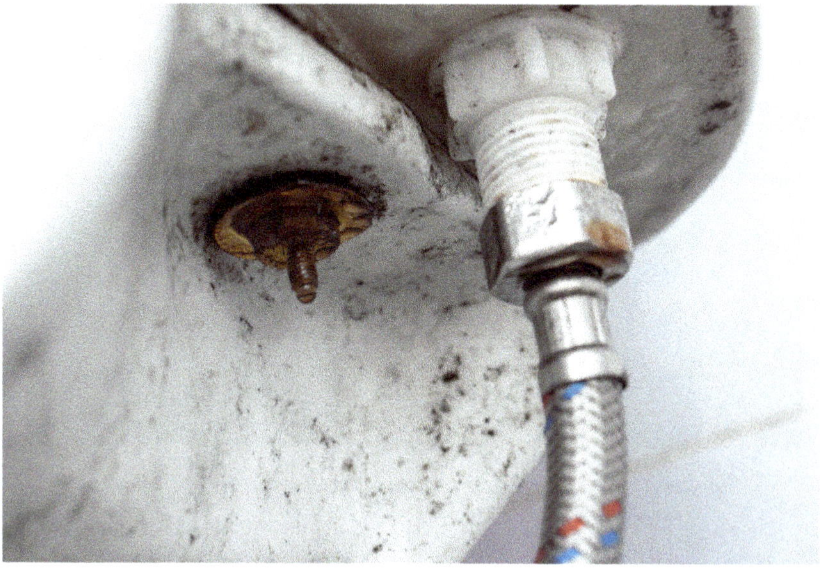

Most likely caused by leaking from the water supply to the toilet.

Swollen (top) and peeling (bottom) baseboards in bathrooms.

Let's talk about basics, with the fixture fully open and water flowing full blast, does water freely drain without gurgeling? Test this on all the fixtures and drains. After I do a cursory walk through, I make sure all the drains are clear of obstructions I can see, (I don't want to flood someone's property) then I turn on all fixtures full blast (all faucets, all showers, flush all toilets), one at a time, eventually having all of them on at the same time, full blast. While I'm looking at other things in the house, I'm listening to what's happening and occasionally checking all the fixtures.

TOILETS

I watch how the water drains, I check around the drains and pressure fittings for leaks. I check around the walls where the pipes come out of. I flush the toilets, repeatedly, ten to fifteen times each, while I'm running this test. Again, listening and watching how the water drains and looking for leaks around the base of the toilet where it attaches to the floor, where the tank attaches to the toilet, the pressure pipe and fittings and the wall and baseboards near the toilet. I let this continue for about fifteen to twenty minutes. With each fixture flowing about ten to fifteen gallons a minute and whatever the toilets add to the total, you will have dumped about seven hundered to a thousand gallons of water into the system in a very short period of time. If everything continues to drain well with no slowing or gurgeling drains, things are looking good.

> ***Note:*** *Gurgeling or slow draining in only one drain is usually indicative of a clog in that drain only. If all of the drains are slow or gurgeling it is probably an issue with the main run from the house to the septic tank, the filter in the septic tank, if it has one, or the system itself including the drainfield and or dosing pump if it has one. Remember, check the dosing pump for simple fixes like a tripped breaker or it being unplugged.*

I continue my inspection as normal and when I'm done with the inside, I head out to the drainfield. Are there any funky smells filling your nostrils? Are there any damp or wet areas over and around the drainfield or septic tank? If there is an inspection port in the drainfield, check it. Is it slap full of effluent (that's a technical term – just kidding)? Check the main cleanout. Is it mostly empty or about full? If everything checks out, the system is probably in pretty good working order as you just put it through a pretty good challenge. If you want to carry this further you can also have a professional inspection. If the system is on the edge, doing all of this will most likely reveal problems either immediately or over the next week or so. Always talk to the current tenants, nicely and carefully, to find out about any previous or ongoing problems. By the time you're ready to do your final walk through you should be able to notice any signs of hidden issues that have popped up and of course you're gonna ask the tenants how everything has been since the last time you spoke to them. Maybe the drains backed up a week later and the tank had to be pumped out. If so, I'd halt the closing and ask for an explanation and further negotiate.

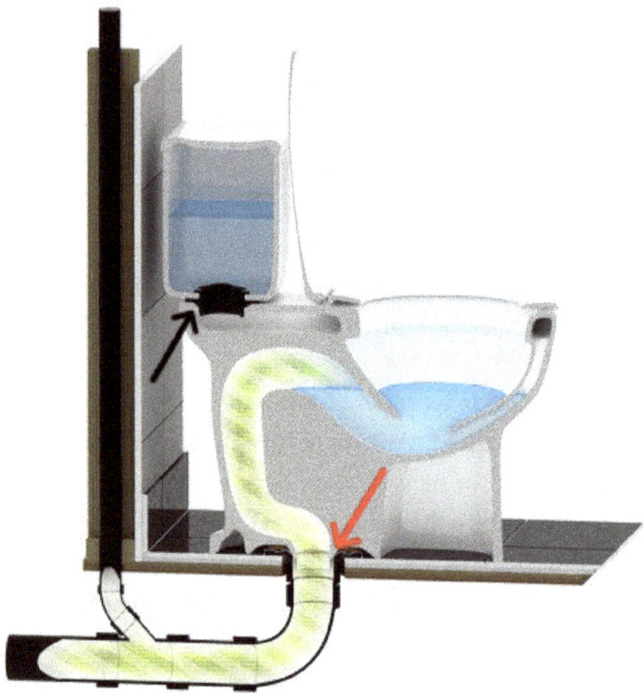

Tank to Toilet seal (black arrow) and wax ring seal (red arrow).

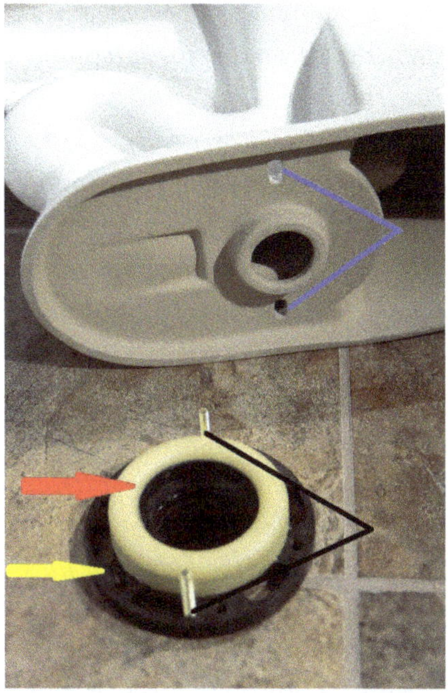

Toilet flange fixed to sewer pipe (yellow arrow), Wax ring seal (red arrow), Toilet flange bolts used to secure toilet to flange and floor (black lines), corresponding holes in toilet for flange bolts to pass through (blue lines).

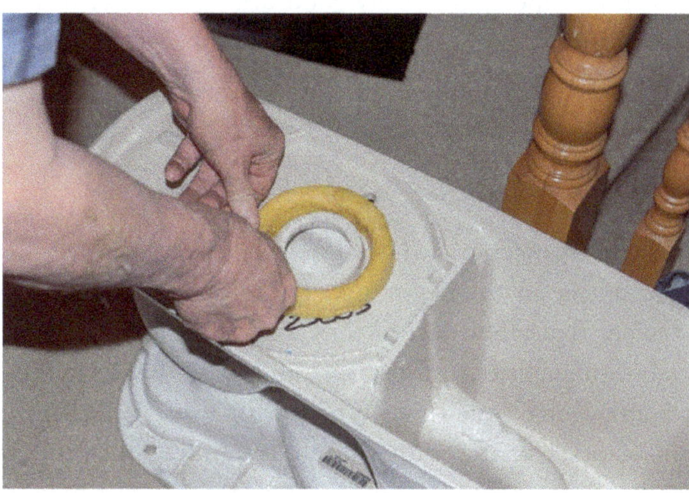

Another view of how the wax ring fits on the toilet before installation.

> ***Note:*** *Toilets seal to the sewer pipe via a wax ring that gets compressed between the bottom of the toilet and the toilet flange that is fixed to the sewer pipe. The toilet flange has two bolts that are 180 degs. apart and stand vertically. The toilet base has two corresponding holes for these bolts to pass through. The wax ring is placed on the flange with the flange bolts in place. The toilet is then carefully lowered into position, being careful not to twist or tear the wax ring. Once in position, the toilet is then pushed straight down until it makes complete and solid contact with the floor (the floor may not be level and the toilet would require shims). Supplied nuts are then spun onto the bolts that protrude through the toilet base. These nuts are then tightened (but not too much or you'll crack the toilet base) to secure the toilet and then decorative caps are placed over the bolts and nuts.*

In general, for your first property, you should avoid getting a rental with a septic system if possible. A municipal sewer system is much simpler, cheaper, and more reliable. Your tenants bascially pay for the system maintenance (by paying for the sewer service) from the street all the way to, and including the sewage treatment plant. All you're responsible for is basically one pipe that runs from the house out into the street. If you have no choice or the property is a really good deal, get it! I've owned several properties with septic systems, you just have to be prepared for surprise expenses and have a strict policy that you enforc with your tenants.

WATER VALVES

I though I'd add this section as I don't believe it's given much thought by most, including me in the beginning. I'm talking about those wonderful little devices that allow you to turn the water on and off to faucets, toilets, washing machines, refrigerators and water heaters. They just sit there, for a long, long, long time. Whoever first installed them probably chose the cheapest version with the understanding that they're pretty simple devices. Being relatively simple, one would expect them to have a failry long service life, and they do, as long as you don't try to use them!

When you do need to use them, chances are, it will either not shut the water off at all, mostly shut it off, or shut it off but leak excessivley from the valve stem. Hopefully you don't need to shut it off in an emergency, if you do, you better know where the main shutoff valve is! Is it on the outside wall of the house or buried in the ground? If you haven't previously thought about this it's a very fun task while water is spewing out inside your property, at night, on a weekend! Hopefully you're pick-king up what I'm putting down. Know where that valve is and make sure it's in good working order before you have a problem, oh, and you do have that water T I mentioned earlier, right?

When old, these valves will leak when you try to use them.

Back to shutoff valves inside the house. As you run back inside you're greeted with the pleasant sound of silence indicating that you've solved your gushing water problem. As you round the corner and find the mess that was created you say a few choice words, in your head of course, and get to work cleaning up. Your focus then turns to the original problem, say there was water leaking from the supply hose where it enters the tank. You take it apart and find that the rubber or plastic seal on the supply hose has failed. No big deal you say, I'll just run down to the big box store and grab another hose, that's the right length and connection size. But wait, that stupid shutoff valve is leaking too. OK, I guess you'll just have to change that too. This is where it can get really fun!

Do you have an older house and the valve is soldered onto the pipe? If so, I guess it's safe to assume you have your torch with you, yes I'm being sarcastic.

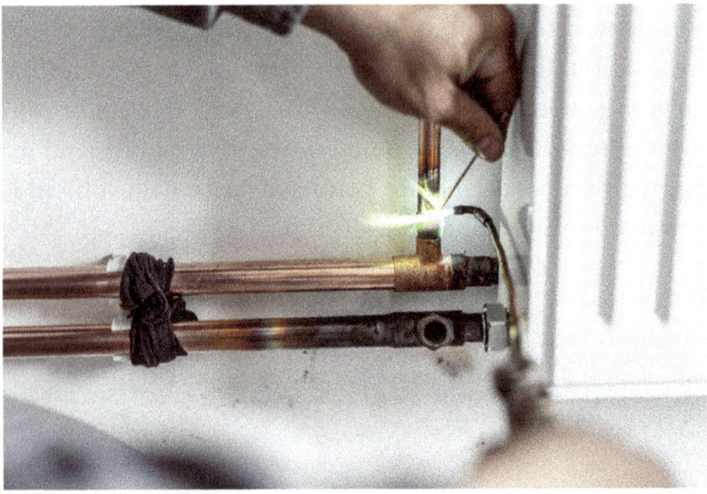

As you can see, there is usually very little space to work with, which of course, is what makes it fun! Clearly I'm being sarcastic!

If you do have to sweat out an old valve and braze in a new one, make sure that you have protection for the surrounding materials like this flame proof mat.

Has it been replumbed with PEX and the the valve is crimped on? Did the original rough in or subsequent plumber(s) leave enough length of pipe for you to remove and replace the valve? Is the valve lammed right up against the finished wall? Is it a compression valve and you feel like you might twist the pipe into a pretzel trying to get it off? If the valve is the sharkbite removable kind and you have enough room to fit the special tool or something similar back behind it to remove it, cool! If you have to cut the pipe to remove and replace the valve and you have enough pipe, cool! If not, guess what, you're cutting open the wall to get access to the pipe so you can add enough length onto it to place the new valve! Better get your "stuff" together because now it's 9:30 pm and the big box store closes at 10pm! No big deal, you've done this hundreds of times before and you know exactly what to get and where to get it in the store. On top of this, you have plan B ready in case Store A doesn't have everything you need. It's really not a problem because it's not like you have all the water to the property shut off!

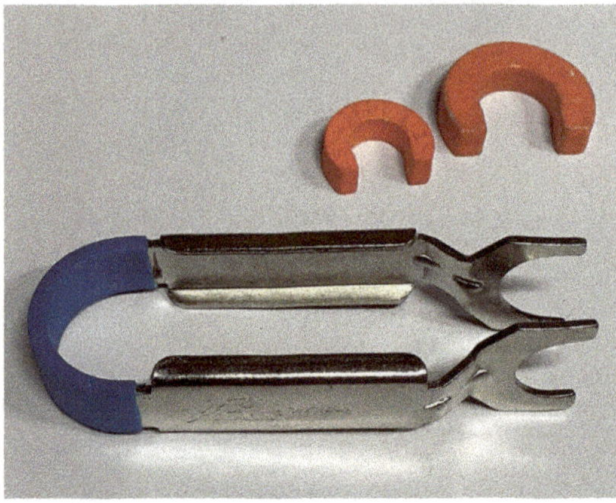

Sharkbite removal tools.

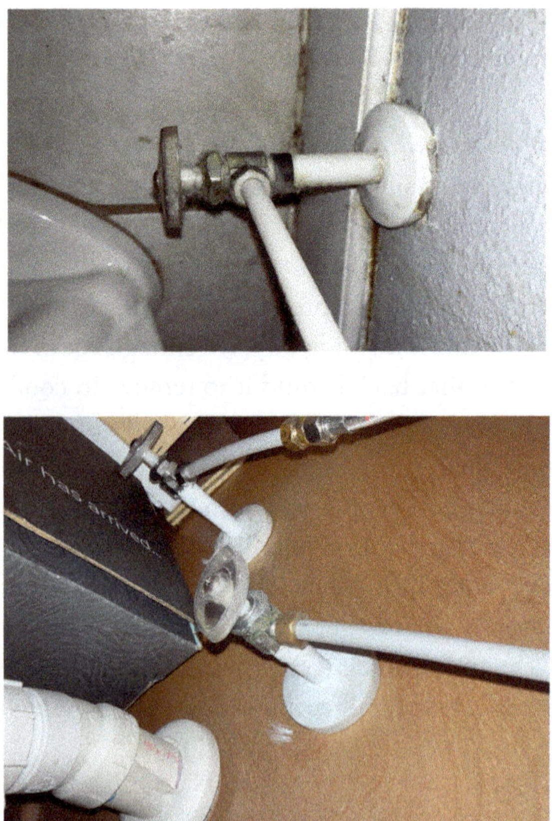

Both of these stubouts have enough room to easily replace the valves.

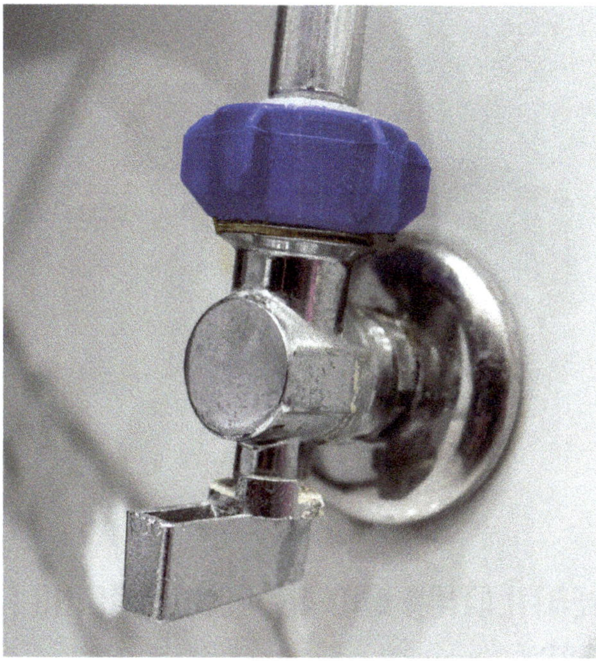

If this was a crimp ring or a soldered valve you'd have a long night ahead of you.

If you can't get the valve fixed, what are you gonna do? You can't leave the water off all night. Can you cut off the valve and put a cap or plug on the pipe? Is it a small leak where you can use underwater tape to slow or temporarily stop it? Put a bucket or tuppeware underneath it until first thing in the morning? Hopefully the store will have what you need and you'll get it all fixed. This story was designed to give you an idea of the troubles you can run into with something so simple and some of the tools necessary to fix it. After you buy your first property, go through all of the shutoff valves and figure out what you'll need to do to replace them. Then as they fail, replace with all metal, quarter turn, ball valves. I've had very good luck with these.

Quarter turn, ball valve.

HEATING VENTILATION AND AIR CONDITIONING (HVAC) A BRIEF HISTORY

Technically, HVAC has been around since humans discovered fire. Fire would heat the air and other solid objects around it like rocks that would then slowly release or radiate that stored heat energy back into the cave, teepee, or whatever. The ancient Greeks and Romans dug channels underneath their marble flooring to spread heat from adjacent fires. Around the 14th century, chimneys and stove piping was used to direct and radiate heat.

The AC part of the acronym didn't truly come into existence (with the exception of fans) until the 20th century. In 1902, Willis Carrier, (sound familiar) invented the "Apparatus for Treating Air". His machine utilized large fans blowing across coils that circulated coolant and was first used in a printing facility in Brooklyn, NY to control humidity. As a byproduct it also helped control temperature and circulate air throughout the building.

1914 saw the first residential air conditioner at the home of Charles Gates who was fortunate enough to be the son of barbed wire manufacturer, John Wayne Gates. The 1920's and 1930's saw more big businesses and theatres install air conditioning but this new invention was insanely expesnive at the time. The first room air conditioners invented by J. Q. Sherman and H. H. Schultz, according to a Popular Mechanics article, cost anywhere from $10,000 to $50,000 dollars at the time! The 1940's saw increased electrical demand from air conditioning use as many skyscrapers began to add this feature.

After WWII, average wages increased sharply resulting in an equal rise in residential air conditioners being sold, around 1 million units annualy. By the 1970's, central air conditioning became mainstream. From the 1970's on, is what I would consider "modern" air conditioning. The basic concepts would remain the same with changes in various refrigerants for various reasons, ozone depletion being a big one, and changes to system controls to maximize effeciency.

Generally speaking, a modern HVAC system is the most complex system in a home. It involves plumbing of both liquids and gases at varying temperatures, pressures, and humidites along with a multitude of items that use both low and high voltage alternating current and more frequently today, direct current too. You're A/C technician has to be able to understand electrical theory, rules and codes, some plumbing rules and codes, general construction techniques, gas welding of copper piping, some physics, thermodynamics, fluid dynamics, and chemistry of the refrigerants along with all the equipment specific to HVAC.

If you want a decent knowledge of this system, it's going to take some time, but I encourage you to do it! Remember, you're trying to make this real estate thing your business or at least your side business and there are a lot of expensive things that go into this business, knowledge is power! The more you know, the less they can take advantage you, even if you never plan on working on an HVAC unit. One thing to keep in mind for the studious types, even if you have a deep understanding of how the whole thing works you will still lack the experience and exposure to all the different types of equipment, controls, and the all important, "I've seen this a bunch of times before on this model". That said, continue to educate yourself and work to find a good, honest HVAC company!

SYSTEM OPERATION AND THEORY

So how does all this voodoo work? The heating portion of the HVAC system is the simplest (unless it's a heat pump) so we'll start there. The air handler (the big rectangular box that is somewhere inside the structure) 99% of the time, will be in the garage, the attic, the basement, or in a closet of some type inside.

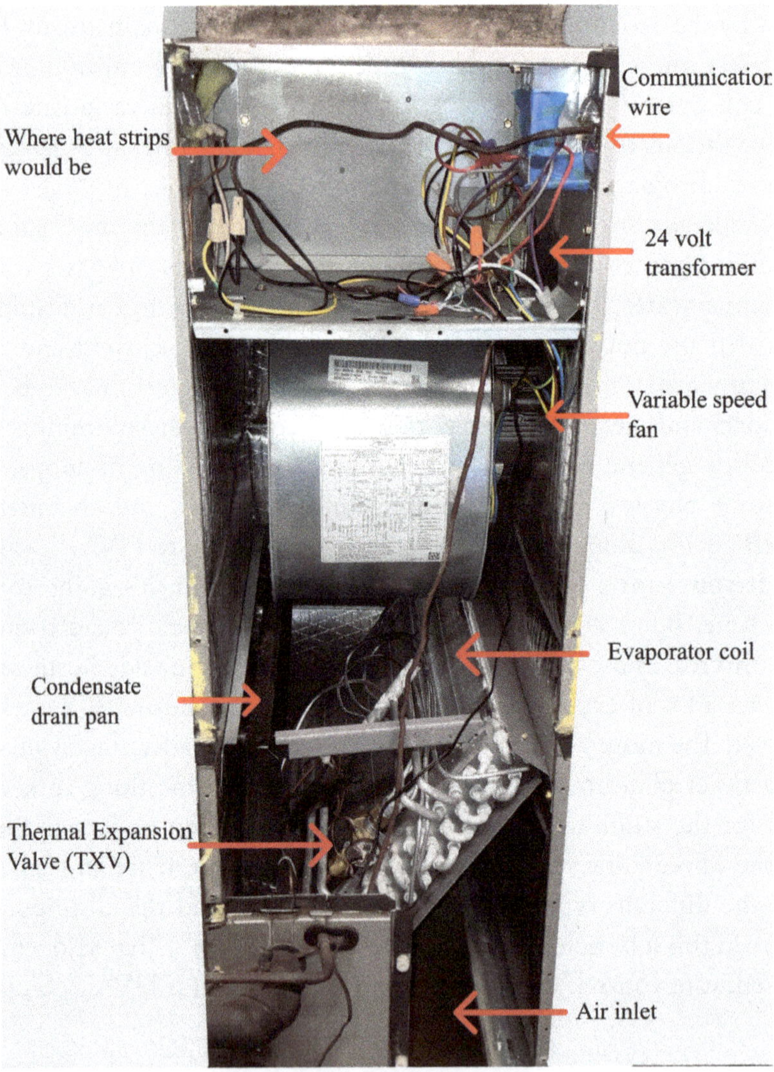

Typical air handler components.

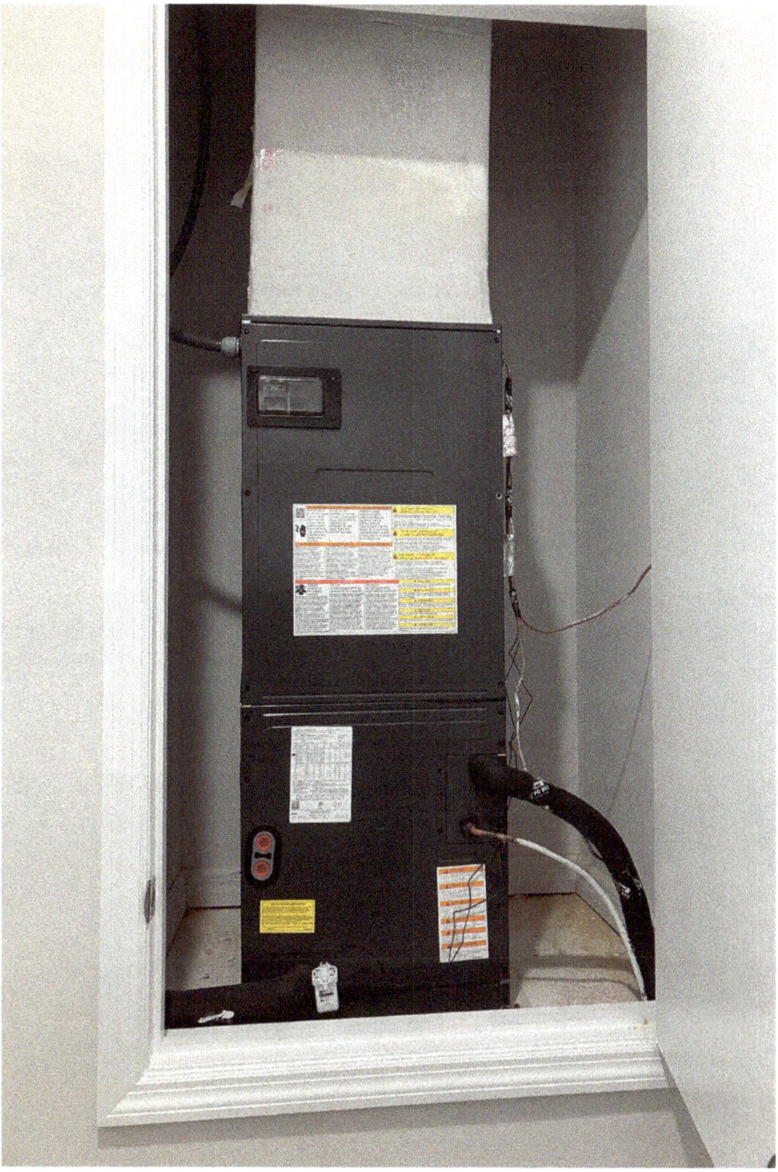

Fairly typical air handler in a closet.

Typical attic air handler installation. Air handler positioned horizontally due to space limitations. Condensate drain pan and pipe (black arrows) draining to the outside for added protection of the ceiling below.

Air handler suspended from the ceiling in this garage.

A more typical garage installation.

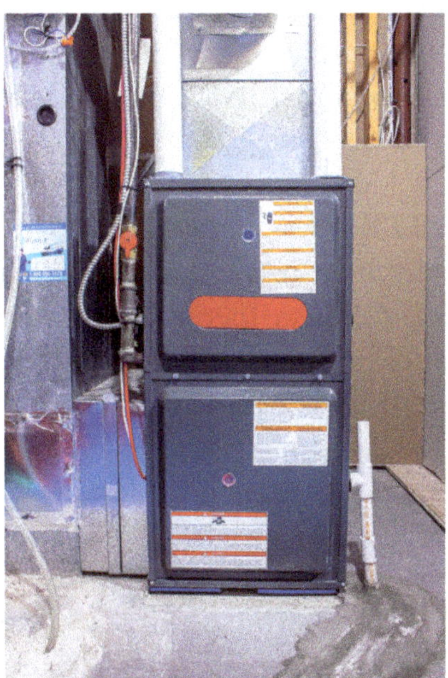

Typical basement installation.

This air handler, handles the air inside your home. It sucks the air from inside your home through the "return", typically a big square or rectangular grate, and then a filter, up through the evaporater, into the fan which then blows the air past the heating coils (if any), and out into the "supply" ductwork to each room of the house. Each of the aforementioned are carefully designed for a specific amount of flow volume, speed, and pressure. In this case we're trying to warm the air in the house. Typically, this will be achieved by burning some kind of fuel, natural gas or propane, electrical resistance via heating coils, compression of a gas in the case of a heat pump, or any combination of the three. The fan pulls in the cool air and forces it over and across the aforementioned heating elements. Heat moves from hot to cold or higher energy to lower energy. As the air passes over these elements it takes heat away from them, in turn becoming warmer. In fancy talk, the distribution of the energy in the air handler is unbalanced (entropy) and as is true with most of nature (that I know of anyway), everything wants to find equillibrium. So, the high energy wants to move to the low energy in an attempt to equalize the distribution of energy.

So, it's 60 degs. F. inside your home and you want it to be 70 degs. F. You cruise over to your thermostat and turn it up to 70 F. This sends a 24 volt AC signal to your air handler that turns your fan on and fires up whatever heat source you have. Now, there's a given amount of (cubic feet) of air inside your home along with a bunch of other things which will need to have heat added to them like furniture, countertops, walls, etc. The engineers have figured out how much energy it takes to raise (or lower) that amount of air in a reasonable amount of time. So, "X" amount of heat or BTU's (British Thermal Units) is added to "X" amount of air for "X" amount of time to raise its temperature (Delta T) 10 degs. F., from 60 degs. F. to 70 degs. F. Fairly simple for the most part, most of the conditioning of the air is simply heating and filtering it.

Anyone who's lived in a colder climate knows how dry the air inside can get when the heat is on for a while. Very low humidity levels associated with the heat being on and the typically dry, cold air outside, was just something you had to deal with, better buy lot's of chapstick! On the other hand, when it's warm or hot outside, the air can hold lots of moisture and if we're not careful, when we try to cool it down, we can greatly increase the airs relative humidity. Doing this can have many deleterious effects such as respiratory problems and mold. I think it's safe to assume that most people would not like having the inside of their home feel like a cold, damp, cave. So the engineers had to figure out how to cool the air and take the water (humidity) out of it, and then get rid of that water.

This part of HVAC gets a bit more complicated. Most people feel comfortable with a relative humidity between 40% and 60%. So we want to cool the air and maintain this relative humidity (RH) range. There's a challenge though, we can lower or raise the temperature of the air a certain amount and not really change the dewpoint. If we want to change the dewpoint, we have to remove the water in the air. Mr. Carrier realized this in 1906 when he discovered that constant dewpoint depression provided, close to constant relative humidity. This discovery would later become the law of constant dewpoint depression.

So how the do we actually remove the water from the air? As most of us have seen with a cold drink on a hot, humid day, water that is in the air surrounding the drink condenses on the surface of the drink. The air immediately around the drink is cooled by the drink (heat moves from hot to cold). It eventually gets cooled to a point where its relative humidity (RH) reaches 100%. As the air gets cooled further, it can no longer hold the water that's in it, so it moves out of the air and condenses on the surface of the drink. If we wanted to measure the temperature of the air surrounding the drink we would find it's at its dewpoint.

So, to remove water from the air, we need to cool a surface, which in turn cools the air surrounding it to its dewpoint or below to allow the water to come out of the air and accumulate on that surface. If we angle that surface down, we can let gravity collect the water so we can then drain it through a pipe outside of the house. This is a very generic description of an evaporator coil or heat exchanger that is found inside of an air handler. This "coil" is a series of many small tubes, typically made of aluminum or copper, filled with evaporating refrigerant, that zig zag back and forth, interconnected with fins.

The fins are there to increase the total surface area that the air has contact with. Generally speaking, we need the temperature of this "coil" to be around 20 to 26 degrees cooler than the room temperature to remove or control the water content or humidity of the air. By doing this, we actually remove the water (Latent Heat) from the inside air and send it outside, which is also what we do with the Sensible Heat (the heat that you feel or sense). So, what an A/C system actually does is move heat (Latent and Sensible) from inside your home, to outside your home.

> ***Note:*** *Most molds of concern will flourish when the water content of surfaces is in the 70% to 100% range.*

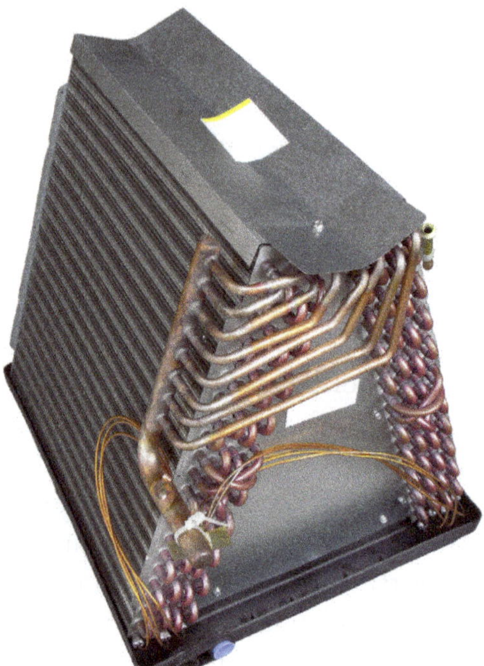

"A" Frame evaporator coil with drain pan.

How do the engineers take the "heat" from inside, and move it outside? Let's remember how heat or energy, wants to move, from high energy to low energy, or hot to cold. That said, the engineers make the coils energy or temperature much lower than the air inside the house. They then blow the higher energy or temperature air from inside the house across the cold, low energy coil. Energy or heat wants to travel from the air into the coil. So, the way I like to think about it is, in essence, we're really heating up the coil with the warm air. The reason I think about it this way is because when a system is low on refrigerant, the coil will tend to freeze up, which to most people, including me at the beginning of my journey, was counter intuitive. If refrigerant is the medium that cools the coil to cool the air, how can less refrigerant make the coil colder? The less refrigerant there is, the sooner it evaporates inside of the coil. The process of evaporation absorbs a lot of heat. If there's not enough heat available in the air to keep the coil from freezing, it will. You'll understand more as we go on.

Engineers know that when a substance experiences a state change, like changing from a liquid to a gas (evaporation), a lot of energy is transferred. If we take water for example, it only takes around 100 BTU's of energy to change the temperature of one pound of water at 33 degs. F. to 132 degs. F. It takes even less energy, 48 BTU's to raise the temperature of one pound of steam from 212 degs. F. to 312 degs. F. Basically, it takes one BTU to raise (or lower if you're removing energy) one pound of water 1 deg. F. It's linear until the water gets close to the boiling point. It then however, takes a whopping 970 additional BTU's to change one pound of water to steam at 212 degs. F. That's an enormous amount of extra energy required to make the water change states! This phenomenon is called Latent Heat of Vaporization.

This is great if you're a fireman trying to remove a ton of heat from a fire by causing the water from the fire hose to turn to steam when it contacts the burning material. It's not so great however, if you're trying to compress a refrigerant gas into a liquid so it may then evaporate to cool the air in your house. You see, it takes the same amount of energy to change a liquid to a gas (vaporization) as it does a gas to a liquid (Latent Heat of Condensation). The compressor in your A/C unit must use the same amount of energy (electricity that you pay for) to compress the refrigerant gas into a liquid as the amount of heat energy absorbed (heat pulled out of the air) by the refrigerant vaporizing in the coil. Of course there are always losses in effecieny across any system, so in actuality, you end up putting in more energy than you can take out. Sorry folks, no free lunches, natures law!

Say we lived on another planet that was really hot and we wanted to "cool" our homes down to 212 degs. F. (remember hot or cold is relative), instead of using refrigerant we could just boil off water to absorb excess heat. If you're using your noggin, you realize that water would not be water in this super hot environment, it would be a gas. As such, we would still have to compress it and cool it into a liquid so it could be boiled off. The air in our homes would have to be substantially hotter than 212 degs. F. for this to work which doesn't sound to comfy, but you get my point. So we need a refrigerant that will change its phase or state and boil or vaporize at a fairly low temperature. These substances are of course found as gases under normal conditions. When we compress these gases, at some pressure and temperature point, they change state into liquids. When they condense from gas to liquid they give off a tremendous amount of heat. As stated before, an identical amount of energy is released in this process as was needed in the evaporation process.

> ***Note:*** *This is one way thunderstorms maintain their intensity. As moist air is lifted and cooled, water vapor eventually condenses, which then causes huge amounts of latent heat energy to be released, feeding the storm.*

So we have this gas, say it's R-410A, that will boil off at a low temperature, around -55 degs. F. We've compressed this gas and pumped it into the condensor which further removes heat from the gas by using a fan to blow cool air across the condenser coil and turning the gas into a liquid. In this process, a bunch of heat has been removed from the original gas and blown outside to be absorbed by the outside air. It is now liquid and ready to absorb a bunch of heat and turn back into a gas.

This liquid, now cooler and still under considerable pressure, around 400 psi, is pumped through copper pipe up towards the coil in the air handler. Just prior to entering the coil the refrigerant is "metered" allowing the correct amount of liquid, at the correct rate, to enter the tubes of the coil. As this liquid refrigerant gets about half way through the coil it has absorbed a given amount of heat and finally reaches its saturation temperature and begins to boil or evaporate. It does this because there is much less pressure inside the tubes of the coil, which is what's keeping it in liquid form on the other side of the metering device, and there's a bunch of relatively hot air heating up the coil.

Typical "Mini-Spilt" air handler having the filter installed. Mini-Splits have the advantage of not having any duct work that the conditioned air has to travel through, thus avoiding leaks and temperature loss or gain. They also, however, have the disadvantage of not having any ductwork as they are really only good at conditioning one room depending on layout. This can affect how rooms like the kitchen and bathroom "feel".

> ***Note:*** *We typically look for a Delta T (difference in temperature) of 15 degs. F. to 20 degs. F. between the return air (purple arrow) entering the air handler and the conditioned air (blue arrow) leaving the air handler.*

As we've learned, it takes a lot of energy (heat) to boil something completely and in our case, this heat comes from the air inside our house. This heat is moving from the relatively hot air to the relatively cold refrigerant inside of the coil. By the time the refrigerant has passed through the entire coil it has fully evaporated (if everything is working correctly). If everything is in good working order, the refrigerant has absorbed a bunch of heat from the air and is now at a much lower pressure, around 110 psi. on the "suction" side of the metering device. This gas is then "sucked" back into the compressor in your outside condensing unit to start the process all over again.

The temperature of the compressed refrigerant as it enters the condensing coil is around 140 degs. F. As the refrigerant gets about halfway through the condenser coil it has cooled down to its saturation temperature at that pressure and begins to turn into a liquid. The further cooling of the liquid refrigerant below its saturation temperature by the condenser coil and fan is refered to as subcooling. The heat absorbed by the gas gets removed by the condenser heat exchanger or coil. The condenser fan pulls relatively cool, outside air across the coils of the condenser, energy moves from hot to cold and thus heat from inside the home is moved outside of the home. This is basically the same set of events that happen inside the evaporator only in reverse. As you can see, relatively speaking, even 95 deg. F. outside air is much cooler than the 140 deg. F. refrigerant. Imagine the difference between a hot 95 degree day in the summer versus a cold 40 degree autumn day.

> ***Note:*** *Compressing a gas takes quite a bit of energy and at one time being part owner of a business that used compressed air in its daily operations, I can tell you that our electric bills were outrageous. In an effort to become more efficient, read-take home more money, I wanted to know how much energy (money) those compressors were using versus how much work we were getting out of the tools that used the compressed air. When we bought the shop it was already set up for compressed air use so we just rolled with it because frankly, we didn't have the money to change it even if we wanted to. So my research led me to discover that around seven horsepower of electricity is required to produce every one horsepower worth of compressed air! Good Lord! Needless to say, as soon as we acuired the money, we switched every tool we could over to electric! Also remember that any time you change one form of energy to another you lose some in the process.*

Typical wall mounted Mini-Split condensing unit.

Typical pad mounted split system condensing unit. Notice the metal hurricane straps at each corner which are secured to the pad itself. This is code in Florida.

A traditional condensing unit and a newer mini-split condensing unit (black arrow).

Two pad mounted condensing units. Refrigerant lines (black arrows), Mounting pads (yellow arrows), Power to both units run through gray conduit (red arrow).

SYSTEM CONTROLS

Now that you have a basic understanding of how the system works, let's talk about what controls the system. The thermostat inside your home takes a dry bulb temperature (the sensible temperature) and then, based on what you want it to do, basically completes certain low voltage (24V) altenating current circuits. The cable used to connect the thermostat to the air handler and outside condensing unit is called communication cable. In simpler, "straight cool" systems (systems that only use compression of refrigerant to cool), the cable may only have five small gauge solid copper wires in it. A red 24V A/C wire that gets its power from the 24V AC transformer that is inside the air handler. A black or blue "common" wire which is used as a return path back to the 24V transformer. A yellow wire that is usually used to trigger the relay or contactor that turns the compressor on inside the condensing unit. A green wire that turns the blower fan on inside of the air handler and finally a white wire that is used to turn on a relay that powers electrical resistance heating strips inside the air handler.

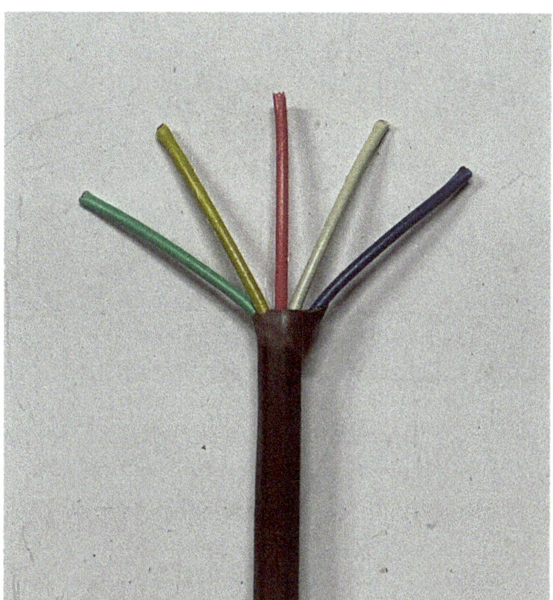

Solid, 18 gauge, 5 wire communication cable.

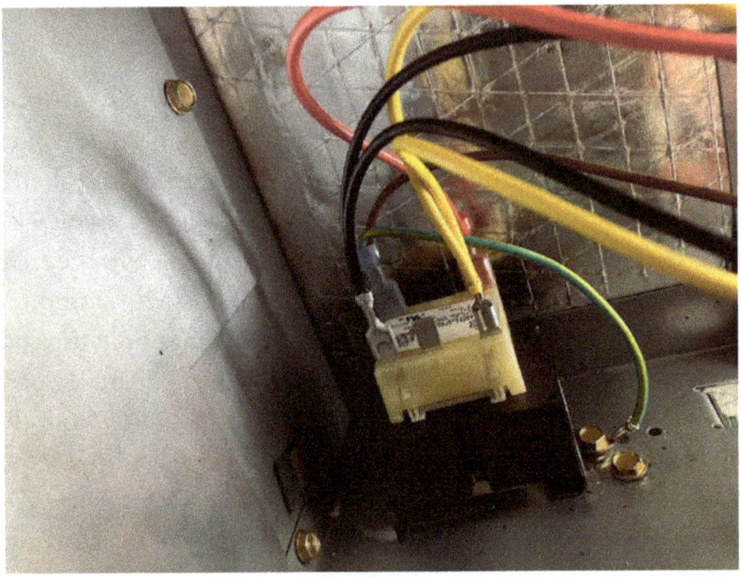

24V transformer inside of the air handler.

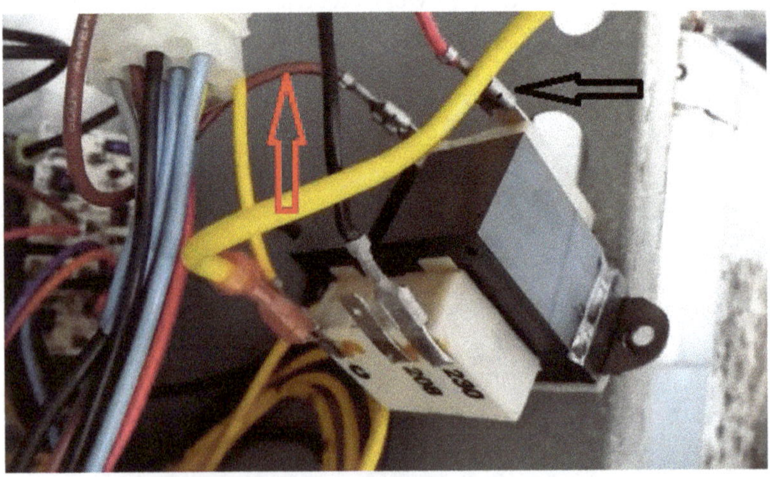

Close up of 230 volt to 24 volt transformer inside of an air handler. Red 24V AC feed wire that goes to the thermostat (black arrow), and Brown 24V AC common wire that returns from the thermostat (red arrow).

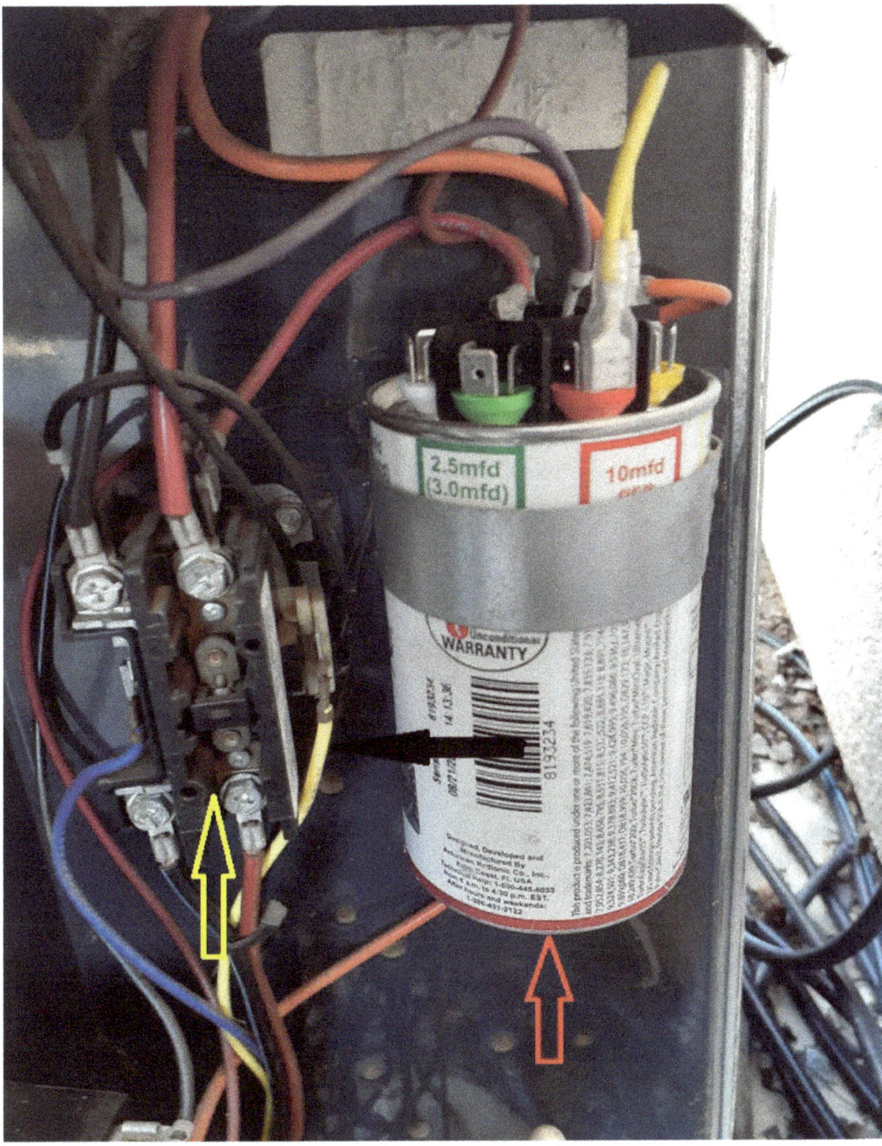

Contactor (yellow arrow), Capacitor (red arrow), Yellow trigger wire from thermostat (black arrow).

Typical air handler blower fan usually controlled by the green communication wire.

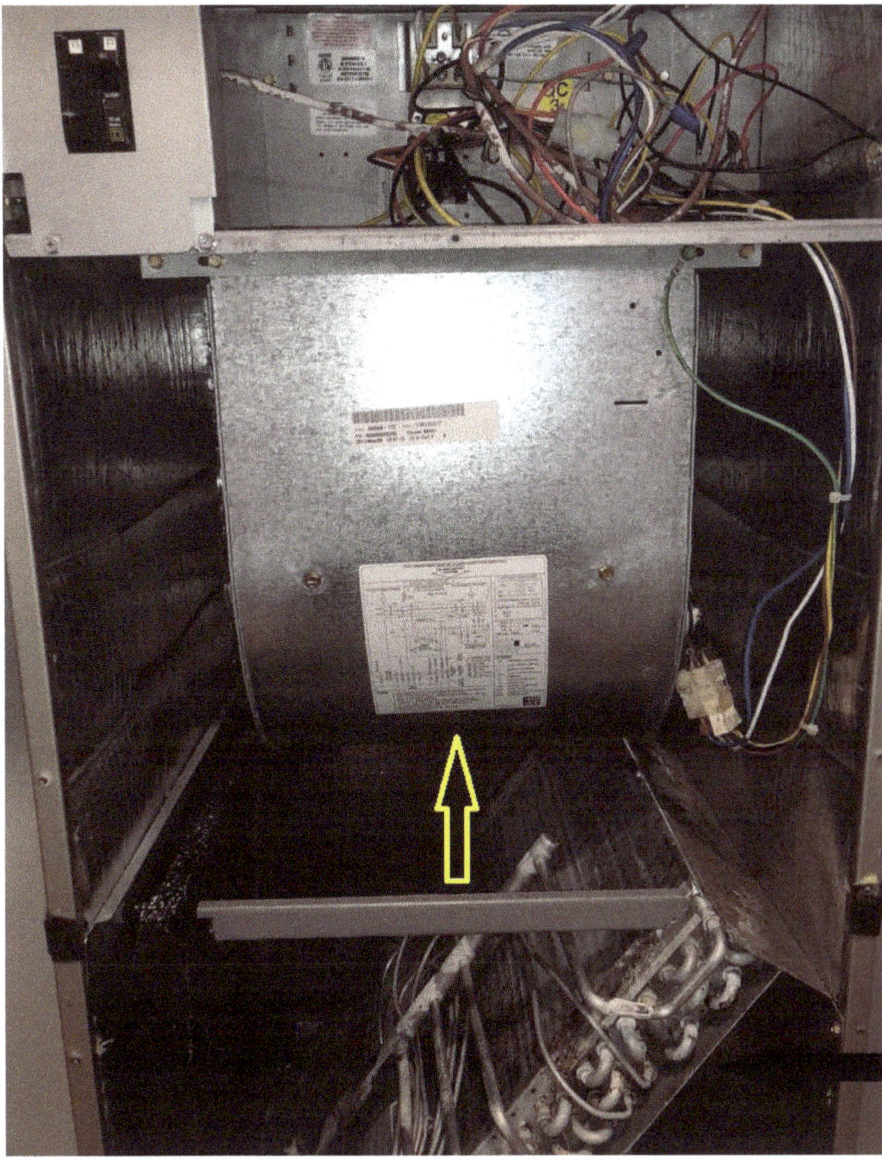

Blower fan assembly in place (yellow arrow), Evaporator coil in place (black arrow).

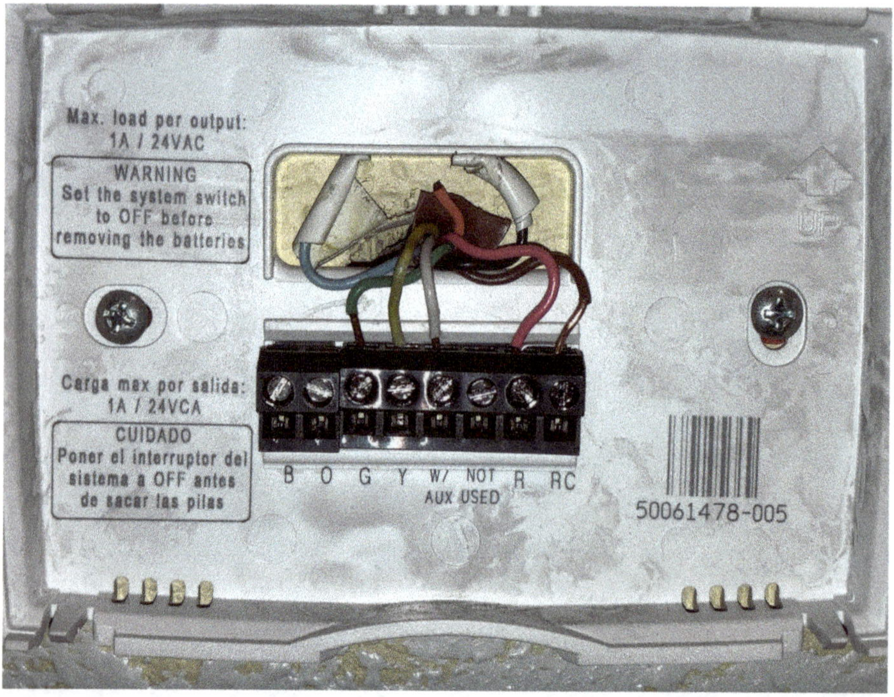

Thermostat base plate for straight cool with heat strips. Red is 24V power, Black is 24V common or return, Yellow to the compressor and condensing fan, Green to the air handler blower fan, White to heat strips.

Thermostat base plate for air conditiong with heat pump. Red, Blue, Yellow, and Green are the same as a straight cool system. Orange goes to the reversing valve, White and Black are auxillary heat strips.

> ***Note:*** *With heat pump systems it usually takes some time to generate heat using the compressor so instead of having the blower fan blowing cold air through the vents, a call for heat turns on the elecrtical resistance heat strips right away, along with the fan, the reversing valve and the compressor. Once the compressor is putting out enough heat, the heat strips turn off. The heat strips also act as emergency heat in case the heat pump doesn't work.*

More complex systems that use the heat from compression to heat the house will have more wires in the cable. These extra wires, typically an orange wire and a blue wire, are used to move a thing called a reversing valve and a the white and black wires will be used for second stage or emergency heat. More on this system in a bit.

So, the thermostat has 24V AC coming through the red wire in the communication cable from a 240V AC to 24V AC transformer located in the air handler and a blue or black "common" wire coming from the other side of the transformer. If we have a non-heat pump, straight cool system, the thermostat reads 80 degs. F., and we set it to 72 degs. F. and switch the button to cool, the thermostat takes 24V AC from the red wire and sends it to the yellow and green wires, which run to relays inside the air handler to turn on the blower fan and then out to the condensing unit to turn on the condensor fan and compressor.

> ***Note:*** *Relays use low amperage to move a high amperage switch into position and hold it there, in our case, 24V AC – less than a few amps to switch on the compressor and condensor fan that uses 240V AC and around 14 amps.*

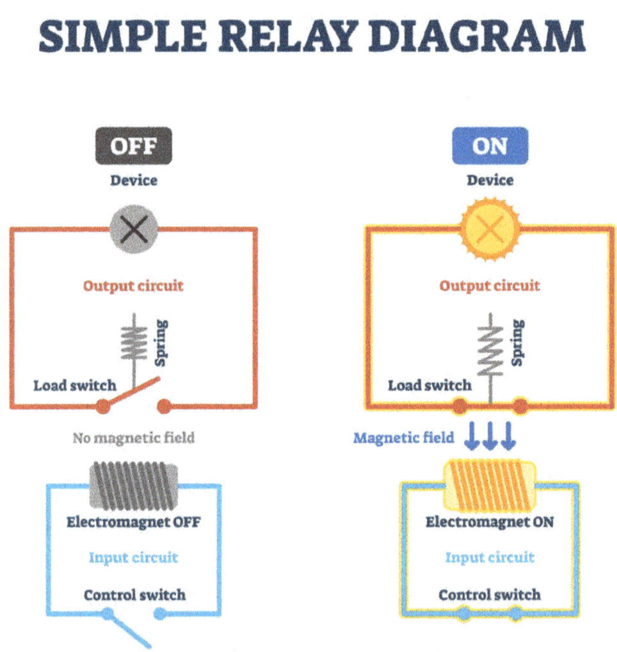

The relay on the left is at rest. When low amperage is sent through the electromagnetic coil on the bottom right, this magnet pulls the load switch closed completing the high amperage circuit.

The system is now on and cooling down the air inside your home. Usually when the temperature reading of the thermostat drops to one to two degrees below the set point (in some thermostats this is adjustable), in our case, 72 degs. F., the thermostat will then break the circuits or "communications" from the 24V AC to the yellow and green wires causing the system to turn off. Most thermostats will turn the blower fan on for a few seconds before turning on the compressor and will leave the blower fan on for a few seconds after it turns off the compressor. If your testing something on your system make sure to wait three to thirty seconds before assuming something isn't working.

If we wanted to heat up the air inside our home, we would set the thermostat higher than its current reading and switch the button to heat. The thermostat, in this case, would then complete the 24V AC circuit for the green wire which would turn on the blower fan first and then the white wire that turns on the heat strip relays. On a side note, if you live in a warm part of the country and the heat doesn't get used much, dust can build up on the coils. The first day or two after a cold snap, your tenant decides they're tired of being cold and they switch on the heat. You get a call saying there's a burning smell coming out of all of the vents! Don't panic, it's probably the dust burning off of the heat strips, if you have heat strips. This is not official advise saying you should totally dismiss a tenant telling you there is something burning. In my opinion, given these circumstances, I'd ask the tenant if they see any smoke and if they don't, have them wait about 15 minutes to see if the smell goes away, which it usually does.

HEAT PUMP SYSTEMS

In heat pump systems, the idea is, it takes less electricity to compress a gas, like when the system is in cool mode, than it does to run the heat strips which by resistance (meaning it's hard for the electricity to flow through it) causes a lot of heat. If we remember our refrigeration cycle, we take heat from the house and move it outside. In the case of a heat pump system, the engineers have simply reversed the flow of the cycle. In other words, it takes the refrigerant that has just been compressed and is hot, and sends it to the evaporater coil inside the air handler that is now playing the part of the condensor coil. The blower fan, blows the cool air from the inside of the house across the evaporater coil, heat rapidly moves from the compressed refrigerant gas to the relatively cold air, reducing the temperature of the refrigerant causing it to condense and give off even more heat. This liquid refrigerant now makes its way to the condesner coil which is now acting as the evaporater coil, and begins to boil off, changing from liquid to gas and while doing so, absorbing a lot of heat from the outside air. With a lower refrigerant pressure, the engineers can achieve a lower saturation temperature, thereby obtaining a substantial temperature difference between the condensor coil and the outside air, allowing what heat there is available in the air, let's say 32 degs. F., to be transferred into the refrigerant in the coil at say, 10 degs. F. So, as long as we can make the refrigerant colder than the outside air, which is a freezing 32 degs. F., we can pull heat out of it. Those engineers are genius!

That's super cool Jake, but how do they "reverse" the cycle? Well, with a reversing valve of course! I have to be honest, when I first heard of this part of the heat pump system, I thought it would be a bit more complex than it is. It's basically a "U" shaped piece of plastic that slides from spot "A" to spot "B", redirecting the flow of refrigerant, but hey, simpler is better.

A reversing valve before it's installed.

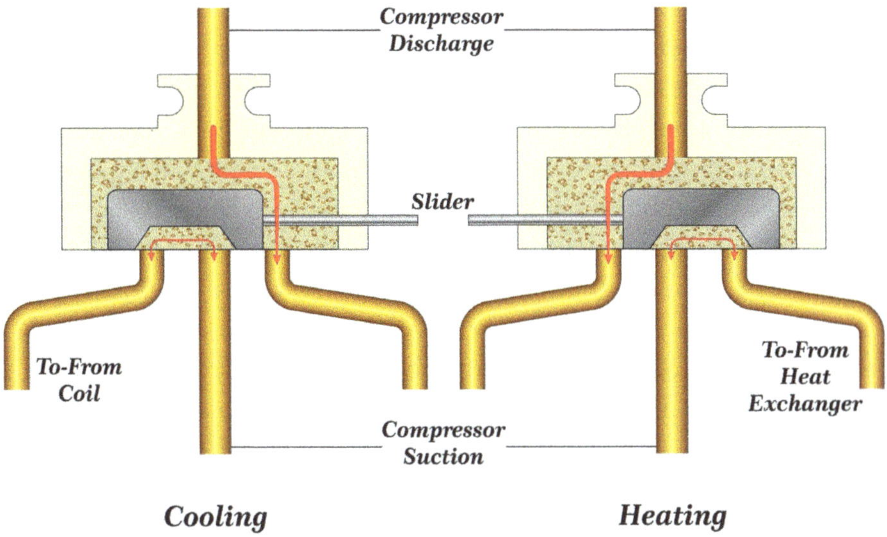

A pretty good diagram of how a reversing valve works. You can see the grey/black "U" shaped plastic tunnel that is moved by a small amount of refrigerant pressure that is controlled by a solenoid.

COMMON PROBLEMS

Now that we have a basic understanding of how the system works, let's look at some common problems that you may encounter.

1. System on and running in cool but not cooling.

How much volume and pressure of air is coming out of the vents? If there is little volume and pressure coming out of the vents, go straight to the air filter. Obviously if the air filter is clogged (basically your tenants disregarded your lease and haven't changed the filter in six months and it looks like a prehistoric dog that's been petrified at the bottom of an ancient lake and now wonder why the A/C won't work.) it will greatly reduce the amount of air that can flow through it. Hopefully it's just a dirty air filter. Now, if the air filter is super dirty like mentioned above and the system has been running for a while, you may have another problem.

Remember that under normal conditions, the engineers assumed a given amount of warm air would be transfering its heat into the refrigerant in the evaporater coil. If we don't transfer enough heat into the evaporating refrigerant, that refrigerant gets too cold, like freezing. There is still some amount of warm, moisture laden air flowing over the coil and the great difference in temperature between the coil and the air is causing water to condense on the coil. Well, the coil is now freezing and the water that condenses quickly freezes. This cycle continues as the system runs until the evaporater coil is one big block of ice and no air flows through it. Some air will probably make its way around the frozen coil and through the ducts and vents, but it will be miniscule.

Depending on how your system is set up, you may be able to remove the dirty filter and stick your head where the filter goes and using a flashlight, confirm the coil is frozen. If you have to take the lower panel of the air handler off to view the coil, BE VERY CAREFUL, there is high voltage, high amperage, electricity in the air handler, control power via the main breaker AND the disconnect box BEFORE removing the panel. MAKE 100% SURE THERE IS NO POWER TO THE SYSTEM!!

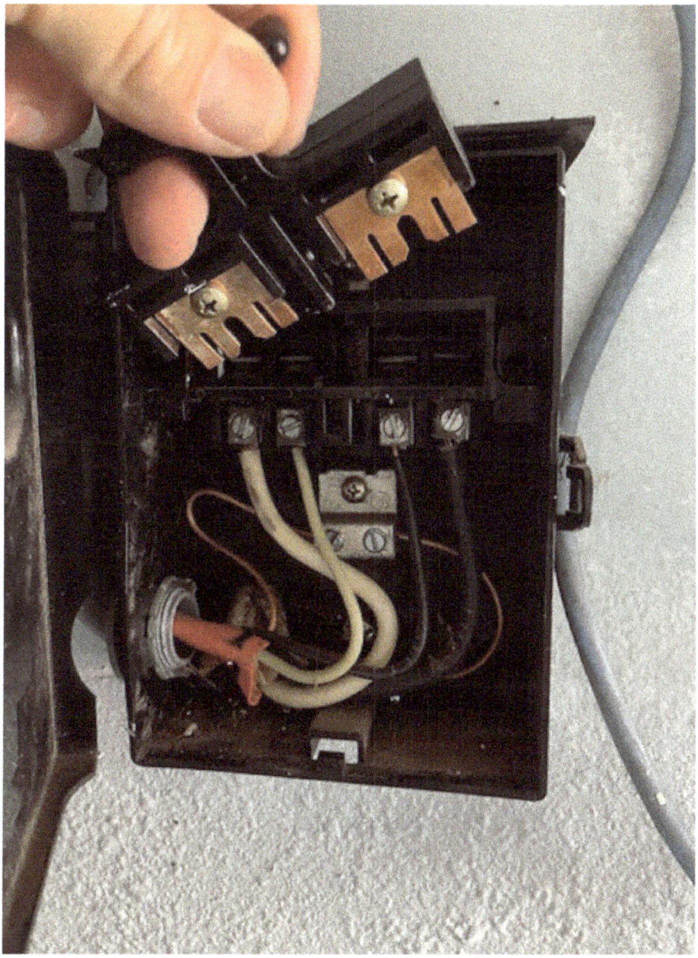

Typical "pull to disconnect" disconnect box.

An evaporator coil in the process of freezing. This is typically due to a very dirty air filter. Remember that the system is designed to ABSORB a certain amount of heat from the air that passes over it. If you restrict the amount of heat it can absorb, it will freeze. The other reason this happens is due to low refrigerant. Yes, I said low refrigerant. As a note, I'm not sure what the air filter is doing on top of the evaporator coil.

If you are ever unsure of the safety of anything you're thinking about doing, call a professional! So you've confirmed that you have a frozen evaporater coil. Take the system out of cool mode and manually turn the blower fan on.

Turn the system off and turn the fan to "on".

This will warm the coil and blow warm air over the ice to help melt it. As of now you have a simple problem that's become a bit more messy. That frozen block of ice is going to melt and only some of that water is going to make its way through the drain. The rest of it is going to drip down underneath the coil onto whatever is under it. This may be the fiberous ducting or the floor, either way I would place something under there to help absorb or catch as much water as you can. If you have a heat pump system you can remove the air filter, place whatever you can to catch the water, and put the system into heat which will rapidly melt the ice.

> ***Note:*** *Evaporater icing may also occur if the system is low on refrigerant. I know this sounds counterintuitive but remember, the engineers designed it so that a given amount of refrigerant boils off in the evaporater for a given amount of warm air. If there's not enough liquid refrigerant in the coil, more than what is supposed to boils off and if we remember, a great amount of energy (heat) gets transferred when a state change occurs. Too much refrigerant boiling off makes the evaporater too cold causing it to freeze the water that condenses on it. This will occur until the refrigerant level in the system gets too low to absorb enough heat to cause the coil to freeze, it will then just not cool so well or at all.*

2. System in cool, no cooling, not running, no airflow.

Check to see if the thermostat has power. It could be battery powered and the batteries are dead or there is a bunch of corrosion on the contacts. If all apears normal with the thermostat head to the main breaker panel and make sure none of the A/C related breakers have tripped. If all is normal there, head outside to the main disconnect box near the outside condensing unit and make sure the disconnect pull is oriented in the correct position.

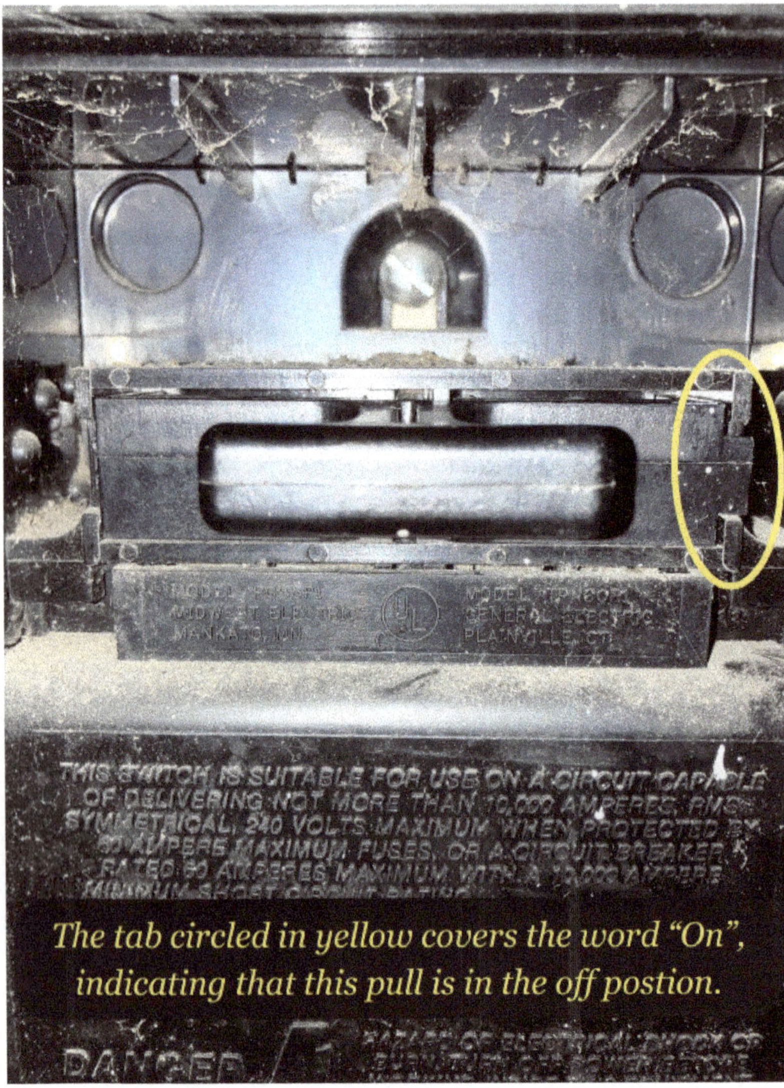

The tab circled in yellow covers the word "On", indicating that this pull is in the off postion.

This "pull", as seen in the picture above, will often have an "on" and "off" label on it. The pull itself has blades that interact with receivers in the disconnect box which allows current to flow. These blades on the "pull" are offset so that one may pull it out, disconnecting power but then flip it upside down and replace it so that the powered receivers are no longer exposed.

The "pull" in the disconnect pictured above is in the "off" position and so the blades are in a protective plastic pocket that sits above the receivers. To turn power on, remove the pull (Remember there is 240 Volts of angry electricity right there so BE CAREFUL or call a professional!), rotate it 180 degrees so the blades are now towards the ground and the "on" sticker is right side up. Align and quickly and firmly insert the disconnect "pull". You should now have power.

FLOAT SWITCHES

So we've confirmed we have power to the system yet it is not running. Typically, the smoking gun is the float switch. This switch is in the condensate drain line and is wired between the signal wire from the thermostat and the blower fan and compressor. If activated, the float switch will interupt 24V AC power going to the aforementioned and the system will not run. The switch itself is usually located in a vertical, white, PVC pipe of about 1 ¼" in diameter and about 3" tall. It is usually located very close to where the condensate drian line exits the air handler. The switch itself will usually have two black wires coming out of it as seen in the pictures below.

The switch sits inside the vertical housing and can be removed by simply pulling it out of this housing. The switch will have a skinny post that protrudes below it and has a black doughnut or tire shaped float around it. This float will move up and down on the shaft in response to the water level inside of the housing. If the switch is at the bottom of the post, the circuit is complete and the system will run normally. If for whatever reason, the float moves up on the post, the circuit will be interrupted and the system will turn off. If you pull the switch out and the system immediately turns on, your problem is either, the float switch got stuck in the up position or your drain line is not functioning properly allowing water to back up into the switch.

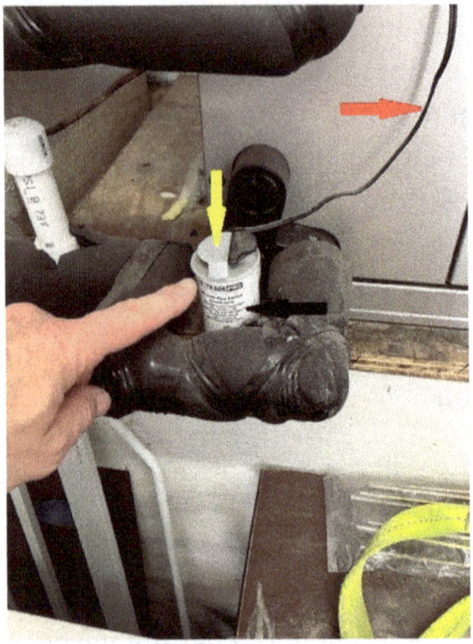

Typical float switch. Float switch housing (black arrow), Float switch inserted into housing (yellow arrow), wires from float switch (red arrow) to complete or interupt circuit.

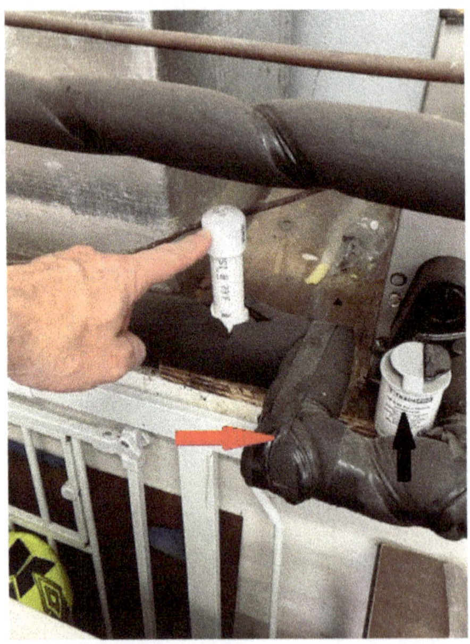

Float switch and housing (black arrow), Condensate drain line (red arrow).

Depending on your systems arrangement, you may have multiple float or water safety switches as in this condensate drain pain safety switch (black arrow) in an attic where the air handler is positioned horizontally.

A close up of the switch itself removed from the housing. The black tire or doughnut is the float. If it stays down like it's positioned in this picture, the circuit remains complete. If water, or anything else causes the float to move up on the the shaft it will break the circuit turning off the system. The switch itself simply pulls out of the housing.

The float switch is usually placed slightly above the drain line so that it activates before water can overflow the condensate drain pan inside of the air handler. If you have a problem in your drain line and your system does not have this switch and or it's not functioning properly, your system will continue to run and pour water out onto whatever is beneath the air handler. Don't underestimate the amount of water that the A/C system can pull out of the air, especially over a few days. It can be significant and you may not notice as it builds up behind the walls, eventually leaking out under a baseboard. The water damage to floors, especially wooden ones can be substantial. The drain line should be checked regulary for water flow and vacuumed out twice a year depending on use. White vinegar or a commercially available anti microbial should be added to the drian line during maintenance.

CONDENSATE DRAIN LINE

So, you've pulled the float switch and the system has immediately turned back on. You look inside the float switch housing and its almost full of water. Put the float switch back in the housing which should shut the system off. Go to the thermostat and turn the system off. Now you need to get some sort of wet/dry vacuum and go outside to where the condensate drain line exits the house, typically a white PVC pipe that is near the outside condensing unit.

Typical PVC condensate drain line where it exits the house (yellow arrow) and where it ultimately drains (black arrow).

Mmmmm yummy! This is the snot that will build up in your drain line causing a stoppage.

PVC condensate drain line with exterior "P" trap (black arrow) painted to match color of the house.

PVC condensate drain line with interior "P" trap.

Note: *It's probably a good idea to have the condensate drain line terminate or empty at least 24" away from the structures foundation. I believe new code is 18" away from the foundation.*

Vacuuming out the condensate drain line on warm day.

Mmmm, drain snot!

So we've vacuumed the condensate drain line and sucked out a bunch of water and snot. The vacuum is still running and the vacuum line is stable and not pulsating any more and there is a steady hum of the motor. At this point you've probably gotten everything you're going to get, out of the drain line. Shut down the vacuum and remove the hose from the drain line. Go inside and check to see that there is no water in the drain line or float switch housing.

Find a big pitcher and fill it with water. Head over to the air handler and take the cap off of the fill port on the condesate drain line (see below).

Pour a large quantity of water through the drain line, being careful not to fill it too fast so water backflows into the drain pan in the air handler possibly over flowing. If you have an assistant have them go outside and confirm that water is free flowing out of the condensate drain line. A common rookie mistake, ask me how I know, is to either not refill the drain line at all or not refill it enough. It wouldn't seem possible, but the blower fan in the air handler will pull enough air from outside, through the drain line when the system is in operation, that it will not let water or enough water drain out of the line.

This will cause water to back up into the float switch turning the system off. This is the purpose of having a "P" trap in the drain line that is completely full of water. This slug of water prevents outside air from being sucked through the drain line into the air handler cabinet preventing proper drainage.

Needless to say, you'll think you've fixed the problem and when you're about thirty minutes away with a smile on your face, you'll get a phone call from your tenant saying the air conditioner has stopped working again. You'll show up feeling like a donkey and repeat the whole process over again until you figure it out!

VOLT - OHM METERS VOM

No heat or no cooling. The thermostat is working but that's it.

We're going to quickly run through the basics mentioned before, clean air filter, empty float switch housing, all breakers and disconnects proper. We're going to have to go a little more in depth on this one which means you're going to have to have some equipment and learn some things. First you're going to need a Volt/Ohm meter that measures AC and DC and preferably has an amp ring. This is a good tool to have and know how to use for just about everything electrical on your car and in your home.

Here is a simpler version of a Volt/Ohm Meter (VOM).

Here is a simpler VOM with Alternating Current selected to test this 220 volt outlet in Europe.

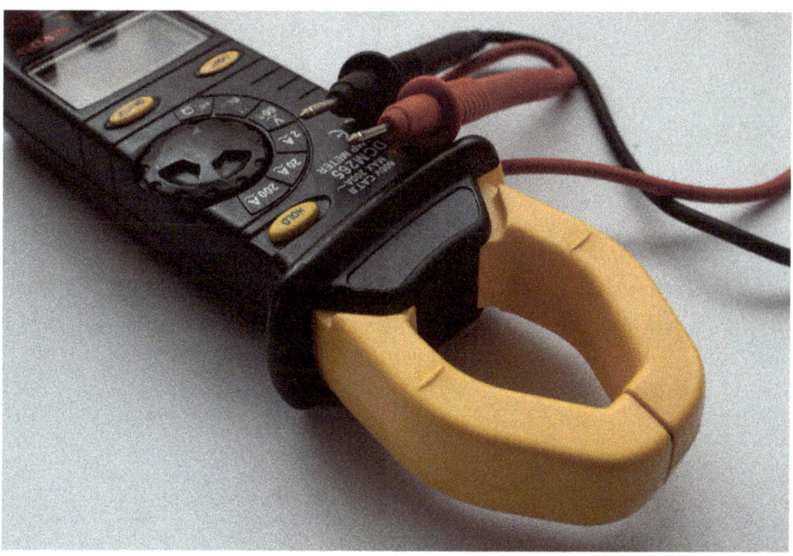

A more complex VOM that has an Amperage Ring and the ability to measure temperature with another probe.

CAPACITORS

Before you undertake this mission I want to reiterate, you're dealing with HIGH VOLTAGE electricity, BE CAREFUL – THERE'S USUALLY NO SECOND CHANCES WITH ELECTRICITY and if you're not comfortable, CALL A PROFESSIONAL! That said, I want to revisit the capacitor that was illustrated earlier in this chapter. Capacitors build up and store electricity. They can then release this stored up electricity – INTO YOUR BODY! Some capacitors are designed to bleed off their built up charge when not in use and some aren't. ALWAYS ASSUME THE CAPACITOR IS CHARGED! If you happen to complete the circuit across the terminals, you're going to regret it!

Barrel style capacitor. Operating voltage (black arrow), Microfarad range-UF or uF (red arrow) also known as capacitance, and the dangerous end of the capacitor – the terminals (yellow arrows), don't touch these with your skin or anything that conducts electricity.

450V AC, all metal, barrel style capacitor with 50uF or microfarads of capacitance, designed to be used at 50/60 Hz with the terminals on top.

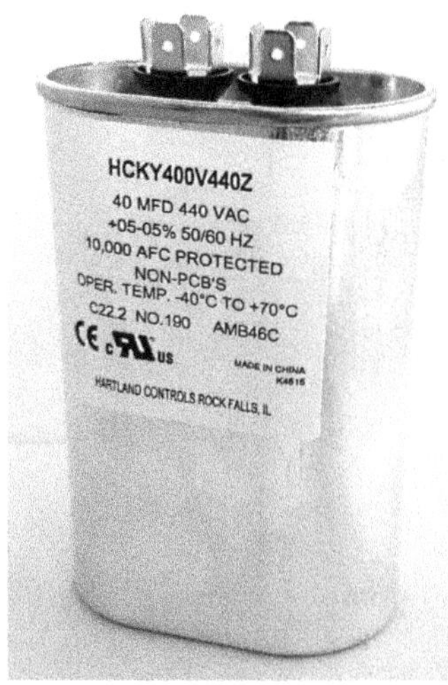

Oblong, metal case, 440V AC, 50/60 Hertz, 40 MFD microfarads (same as UF or uF), capacitor.

I've just given you a few visual examples of capacitors. Go slow and be very careful of where you're sticking your hand or the end of that metal tool. Capacitors can come in many different shapes and sizes. Basically, if there's an electric motor, somewhere near it or in it, is a capacitor.

TRANSFORMERS

Also as noted in the pictures before, there is a 240V to 24V transformer. The terminal ends of this transformer are not protected from wandering fingers or tools! This entire book is for informational purposes only and is not meant to be an exhaustive, all encompassing, list of how to's and things to be careful of. If you don't know what you're doing or how to safely do it, then don't! Call a professional!

Stay away from the terminals! (black arrows)

Now that we've gotten that out of the way, we're going to carefully remove the front cover of the thermostat, exposing the low voltage (24V AC) wires. Take your VOM and set it to alternating current and probe the red wire in the thermostat base plate with one probe of the VOM and probe the blue or black (could be any color wire) common wire. Do you get a reading of 24 volts? If not, first make sure you're probing the correct wires, then head over to the air handler. Carefully remove the upper panel of the air handler.

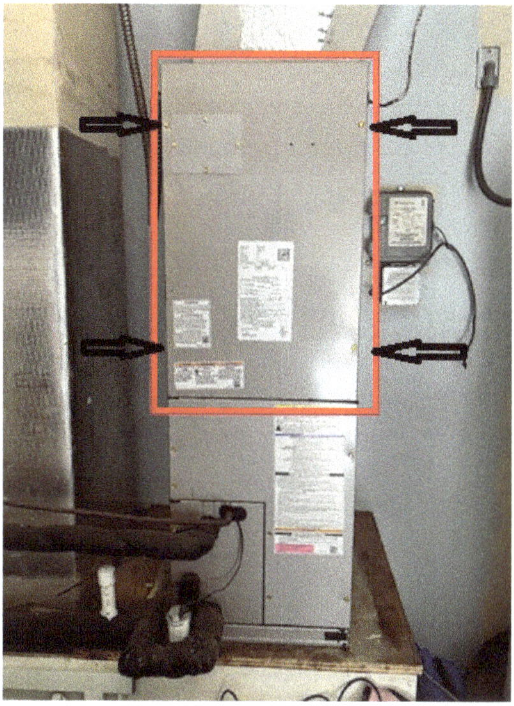

Upper panel outlined in red, remove screws (black arrows).

Behind that upper panel you'll see something like this. Check to make sure fuse is not blown (burgundy arrow), Probe 24V red wire terminal (black arrow) and Brown "common" wire terminal (yellow arrow).

Now that you have the upper panel removed you should see something like the picture above. Check to make sure the transformer fuse isn't blown then check to see if the transformer is putting out 24V AC. If it's not and the fuse is good, you probably have a bad transformer that will need replacing. If it is putting out 24V AC, you most likely have a communication wire that's has gone bad.

BAD COMMUNICATION WIRE

I know it sounds crazy that a wire that just sits there can just "go bad", but they do. Luckily for us, most of the time anyway, A/C guys will use six or eight wire communication cable and will just wrap the unused wires around the cable at both ends. You can remove the suspect wire(s) and replace them with any of these extra wires, just make sure you connect the correct wire on both ends of the cable. For example, you find that the transformer is good but there's not 24V coming through the red wire in the thermostat base plate. You have an extra purple wire in the communication cable. You disconnect the red wire, move it away, and hook up the purple wire at the terminal where the red wire was. You then go into the air handler and carefully remove the red wire from the 24V side of the transformer and replace it with the purple wire. Go back inside and test to see if you have 24V between the new purple wire and the common terminal. If you do, congrats, you solved your problem fairly easily. Use this plan or concept with any of the communication wires in the cable. Unfortunately, if your cable doesn't have any extra wires available you'll have to pull a new cable between the thermostat and the air handler.

This is a good example of extra, unused wires that are wrapped around the cable (black arrow) in the air handler cabinet. You should find the same on the cable at the thermostat.

Now let's say you have a good transformer and 24V AC at your thermostat but your system still won't cool. Put the thermostat face back on and set it to cool with fan on auto. Now head to your condensing unit outside. Where the main power cable, usually inside of some kind of conduit, enters the condensing unit will be a removable panel. AGAIN, THERE'S ANGRY HIGH VOLTAGE ELECTRICITY INSIDE THIS PANEL, BE CAREFUL OR CALL A PROFESSIONAL!

Main power conduit (black arrow), condensate drain line (green arrow), communication cable (red arrow), liquid line filter (blue arrow), removable panel (yellow arrow).

Typically what you'll see behind the panel. Angry Capacitor (black arrow), Main compressor and condensor fan relay (yellow arrow), Angry 240 volts waiting to shock you (orange arrows), Green arrows show where the low voltage 24V signal

and common wires hook onto the relay to trigger the relay. Manual relay activation button (white arrow), pushing this in will complete the relays high voltage circuit turning on the compressor and fan if it's working properly (AGAIN, THERE ARE MANY EXPOSED HIGH VOLTAGE AREAS VERY CLOSE TO THIS BUTTON – BE CAREFUL OR CALL A PROFESSIONAL!!!!!).

Now, EXTREMELY CAREFULLY, use something that DOES NOT CONDUCT ELECTRICITY and press the manual button. Does everything turn on? If it does, either your relay is bad or it's not getting the 24V to trigger it from the thermostat. Pull the disconnect to remove 240V power from the main relay and carefully probe the two low voltage terminals on the relay to see if you're getting 24V. If not, you may have a bad wire. If this is the case, do the same thing, if you can, as you did with the bad thermostat wire in the prior example. Pick an unused wire and wire one end into the relay and the other into the terminal where the yellow wire is in the thermostat. Check for 24 volts across the two low voltage terminals. Do you have it? If not, change the other wire (the common) if you can and test again. If you have 24 volts across the low voltage terminals and the relay still doesn't work, the relay is bad and must be replaced.

So you now have a basic understanding of how an HVAC system works and some common problems and trouble shooting methods. Use this information to your advantage to solve problems or keep an HVAC tech honest. Just remember, although I've given you some basic knowledge, an HVAC system is one of the most complex systems in a home and has dangerously high voltage electricity in it. ***That said, don't get cocky and kill yourself!! If you're ever unsure of what you're doing or how to safely do it, CALL A PROFESSIONAL!!!***

CHAPTER 25

CLOSING COMMENTS

My only goal for this book was to provide some real life experience and guidance to the average wage earner who is trying to get into the real estate game. The talk around the water cooler is filled with anecdotal horror stories of a friend who knew somebody, who had an uncle somewhere, who lost his first born child to the ravages of being a landlord. I wanted to arm you with both technical information and real life, unexaggerated, ups and downs so you could either move more confidently towards your real estate goals or decide that it's not for you. Every effort was made to be as accurate as possible with technical information and my recollection of events. That said, the only thing I would consider myself an expert in is breathing, I pretty much have that down no matter what the circumstance.

At the time of the writing of this book I own and manage six rental units and a SFR that I live in. I've held over a dozen mortgages, built and sold 7 new construction projects and turned $16,800 in credit card debt and dumb decisions, into $1.7 million in cash and equity within 14 years, all while working a full time job and taking care of a family of four. There have been ***PLENTY*** of people who've eclipsed my success for any number of reasons and the aforementioned was not meant to be braggadocious, rather to illustrate the result of my journey thus far. I've read plenty of books by other more financially successful real estate investors that offered good information, but to me, lacked detail. I took the time to write this book to fill in that gap. I truly hope that it provides you ongoing value! I hope this book will give you ideas and concepts to ponder so you can one day, do it better! I hope to one day read about you and your success, and learn from it! That said, there's only one thing left to do……***HOW BAD DO YOU WANT IT?!?!***

GOOD LUCK AND GOD BLESS!

AUTHOR BIO

My family and I moved to Central Florida in 1983 to escape the winters of the northeast. After graduating high school I went to work in the hospitality business for about 10 years before transitioning into public service for the next 20 years. As rewarding as public service may be, it doesn't really pay the bills all that well. I knew that I was going to need a reliable source of income outside of my day job. The go-to had always been the stock market, but we all know what happened in 2008! I got to witness first hand as senior co-workers getting ready to retire watched their investment accounts drop by 50%. The look on their faces as they realized that they would have to work another 10+ years is something I will always remember. In 2010 when the world was running away from real estate, I purchased my first Multifamily investment property. Since then I've held over a dozen mortgages, built and sold multiple new construction homes, and managed several Multifamily rental properties, including a horse farm!

www.ingramcontent.com/pod-product-compliance
Ingram Content Group UK Ltd.
Pitfield, Milton Keynes, MK11 3LW, UK
UKHW061439160126
10151UKWH00021B/308

9 781965 340387